EUROPE IN THE 16th CENTURY

Europe in the Sixteenth Century

DAVID MALAND M.A.

High Master, Manchester Grammar School

SECOND EDITION

Macmillan Education

First published 1973
Reprinted 1975, 1978, 1980, 1981
Second edition 1982

Published by
MACMILLAN EDUCATION LTD
Houndmills Basingstoke Hampshire RG21 2XS
and London
Associated companies throughout the world

British Library Cataloguing in Publication Data
Maland, David
  Europe in the sixteenth century – 2nd ed.
  1. Europe – History – 1492–1648
  I. Title
  940.2'32   D228
  ISBN 0-333-32712-8

Printed in Hong Kong

Contents

IX   FRANCE 1515 – 98

X   THE HABSBURGS IN EUROPE 1555 – 1600

XI   ART, MUSIC AND THE SCIENCES

List of Plates

Acknowledgements

The author and publishers wish to thank the following for permission to reproduce the photographs in this book:

The French Government Tourist Office: Plate 11;
The Mansell Collection: Plates 1, 2, 3, 4, 5, 7, 8, 9, 10, 12, 13, 14, 15, 16;
The Radio Times Hulton Picture Library: Plate 6.

List of Maps

List of Graphs

Genealogical Tables

I

The Economic Foundations
of the Sixteenth Century

Introduction

EUROPE did not begin to recover from the effects of the Black
Death (1347) until the middle of the fifteenth century, although
both the full extent of the disaster and the speed of recovery are
difficult to assess. Statistical evidence is hard to come by and the
little that is available needs careful interpretation. Only the
wealthier cities made a census of their population, and generalisa-
tions about the rest of Europe can only be supported from a variety
of sources which include parish registers, tax assessments, returns
of able-bodied men for military service and the published guesses of
contemporaries. If all these are taken together, however, they
demonstrate that the Black Death of 1347, its subsequent and
equally severe outbreaks, and its coincidence with a prolonged
period of tempestuous weather, crop failure and cattle disease,
reduced Europe's population by one-fifth, perhaps by one-quarter.

In other centuries when large numbers died from famine or
disease a succession of good harvests usually put the matter
right, but there was no such swift recovery from the Black Death.
The peasants who survived it found that the scarcity of their
labour attracted better terms of payment and land tenure, so that
they could at last afford to eat meat instead of living almost
exclusively off cereals. Since meat production demands more
land than arable farming, the population, despite its reduced
numbers, continued to require nearly as much land as before, and
to maintain this new balance between mouths to feed and land
available, the peasantry took care not to jeopardise its new-found
prosperity by raising large families. The only effective means of
birth control available in the fifteenth century was to marry late
in life. 44 per cent of the men in a Zurich census were listed as

bachelors; prostitution increased and there are many references to young men marrying much older women in order to reduce the risk of having many children. As a result the European population remained significantly below the level of 1347 until midway through the fifteenth century.

The next fifty years, however, witnessed an increase in numbers which is not easily explained. There was no advance in medicine to account for it nor any improvement in public health: sanitation in fact became decidedly worse after 1450 as cities became more crowded, so that the urban population was at greater risk than in the past. Nor was the Black Death over. Universally it never struck again with such pandemic force, but locally it recurred with great frequency and with no less virulence . . . 'It is remarkable that the Plague should never wholly cease', recorded the Naumburg Chronicle, 'but that it should appear every year here and there, making its way from one place to another, from one country to another.' Alternatively, the population increase has been attributed to the creation of a more peaceful continent with the ending of the Hundred Years' War between France and England, the peace of Lodi in Italy and the peace of Torun (Thorn) between Poland and the Teutonic Knights – but warfare proved to be no less sporadic, no less virulent than the Plague. Austria could not escape it, Burgundy was in conflict with her neighbours and civil war broke out in England. Moreover, the explanation cannot lie here since Europe's population increased at an even greater rate in the following century which was considerably more bloody in its international relations.

The increase in numbers would be easily explained if it were possible to demonstrate that more food was being produced, but this cannot be done. Herring and cod were being harvested from the northern seas in greater quantity (see page 17), but life in the last analysis depended on the traditional and unchanging techniques of arable farming. Throughout most of Europe stretched the great open fields, bastions of a primitive economy, which determined the time-honoured progression of the manorial calendar, preventing the adoption of new crop rotations and compelling adherence to traditional methods of cultivation. Teams of oxen scratched the surface of the earth with wooden ploughs as they had done for centuries and, as always, cereals were the staple crop – especially rye, oats and millet which yielded more per acre than wheat. But cereals rapidly exhausted the soil and it was necessary to leave land fallow one year in three in the north, one year in two in the south, and even two years in three in regions of particular infertility. In any given year, therefore, two-fifths of Europe's arable land was unproductive. Moreover, from 1450 to 1520 there was no escape from the threat of crop failure, and major subsistence crises took place in England, France, Germany, Bohemia and the Netherlands in 1481–2, in England, France and Germany in 1501–2 and everywhere, save France, in the 1520s.

Why, then, did the population increase? It seems more than probable, though not certain, that after three or four generations the peasantry was beginning to forget the advantage it had derived by keeping its numbers steady; they were perhaps encouraged by the growth of the towns, where the high death rate in over-crowded, insanitary lodgings required the perpetual recruitment of labour from the countryside, so that larger peasant families might hope to find employment away from the land for their extra children. The expansion of town life was important in other respects. Councils were beginning to store grain against emergencies, and a commercial middle-class, equipped with capital and armed with a system of market intelligence, began to finance an international trade in cereals. In many years there was a disposable surplus of corn in eastern Germany, in Poland and in Estonia, which could profitably be conveyed to western Europe – and the merchants of the Hanseatic League and the Netherlands were quick to exploit the fact. In areas accessible to shipping, therefore, the chances of a timely relief from starvation were significantly increased by the development of international trade.

Not only did this assist the growth of population; it was also to have a disrupting influence on the traditional pattern of social and agrarian life which had been evolved originally to meet the immediate needs of the landowners and their peasants. The existence of a local urban market would encourage the production of a surplus, but such markets were few and far between. The medieval manorial economy was, therefore, a subsistence economy. The landlord offered land and protection, the peasant his labour, and the exchange of services was regarded as both reciprocal and personal. After the Black Death had reduced the population by at least one-fifth, relationships became less personal, more contractual, and the value of the peasant's labour might even be expressed in terms of cash. The development of a more highly-organised trade in foodstuffs took the process a stage further. It was, of course, a development limited to coastal areas and rivers, and particularly to the grain-producing regions of the south-eastern Baltic, but whenever the improvement of commercial techniques made it possible for one district to supply another from a distance, the first to profit by it were the landowners. Their standard of living was materially improved when the export of a surplus of rye allowed them to import luxury goods not made in their locality. Direct barter over such distances was out of the question and so these landowners became more accustomed to cash transactions, and even encouraged their peasants to commute their labour services for rents – unaware, of course, that any decline in the purchasing power of money would diminish the value of these.

By 1520 the development of international trade routes and markets had gone some way to break down the medieval patchwork of separate self-regarding subsistence economies based on recipro-cal and personal relationships. In its place there was beginning to emerge a more interrelated economy where cash values were assigned more frequently to services and to goods and where information about prices in one region could stimulate, even determine, production in another. A dearth of corn in Brittany could now result in the production of a surplus in Poland. Nor was this interrelationship confined to foodstuffs since the demand for wool in the Netherlands had already begun to encourage a marked shift in England from arable to pastoral farming. The greater use of money, the expansion of trade and the ever-growing economic interdependence of one region upon another were to be factors of great importance in the sixteenth century. They afforded greater opportunities for profit; they also created greater tensions, even crises, in the traditional framework of society. Yet, for all that, Europe remained, even in the sixteenth century, an agricultural not a commercial community, and despite the tremendous efforts of a few to distribute grain, wool, olive oil and spices along the European coastline from Danzig to Ragusa, the bulk of commerce was confined to local markets.

This is understandable. Long-distance trade was hampered by an abiding hatred of foreigners, interrupted by marauders both by land and by sea, and restricted everywhere by the limited means of transport and communication. Roads, indicating rather a right of way than a prepared surface, were poor, and heavy transport had remained unchanged since the invention of nailed horse-shoes and rigid shoulder collars in the eleventh century. Mule trains were effective but expensive. By water the transport of bulk was easier, but there was no way to circumvent the currents, the fish weirs and the riparian tolls demanded by those whose land adjoined the rivers; on the open sea there were the vagaries of the elements to contend with and most ships were confined to local coastal work. Nevertheless, by 1520 there were a number of established commercial centres linked to local industries which operated trade routes across the entire continent. Exceptional though they were, the importance of these trade routes in the development of sixteenth-century Europe requires their more detailed study.

The Mediterranean

One area of exceptional activity was the Mediterranean. Alongside the innumerable variety of short-haul coastal trades, there existed the long-distance routes which spanned rival cultures, races and religions in the attempt to maintain food supplies throughout the region. Some great cities were well placed to draw upon their immediate neighbourhood – Cairo and Alexandria were fed from the Nile valley, Milan from the Lombard plain and Marseilles from Provence and the Rhône valley – but others had come to depend upon a highly-developed system of market intelligence which enabled them to import supplies over greater distances. Extraordinary reserves of capital were needed to finance such voyages and also to withstand the risks of delay or destruction; it took eleven days to sail from Tunis to Livorno, two months from Cartagena to Alexandria, but these were fair weather schedules and Mediterranean storms could prove as dangerous to fifteenth-century craft as to the ships of St Paul.

Grain was the staple commodity of long-haul trade, involving the transport across the Mediterranean of over 50,000 tons of wheat, barley and millet every year. The Catalans had formerly played an important role in this but by 1500 the trade had been monopolised by the merchants of Genoa, Venice and Ragusa. Sicily and the neighbouring province of Apulia in Naples were

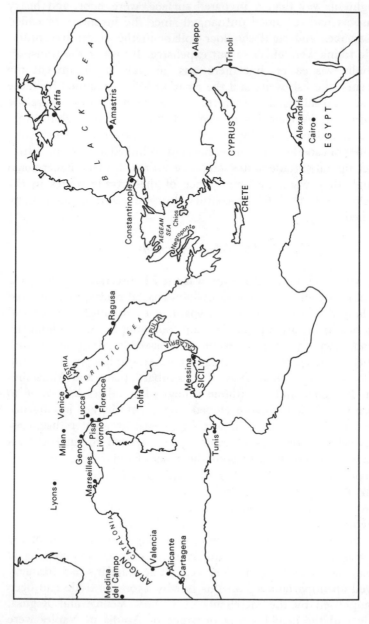

Centres of trade and industry in the Mediterranean region

the principal centres of grain production in the western Mediterranean and nearly 10,000 tons a year were exported from Messina – most of it to Aragon which ruled the island, or to Genoa, Aragon's ally. It was an expensive trade. Export licences could cost up to half the value of the cargo and the merchants had to meet heavy insurance charges in addition to the costs of transport. Consequently, grain which was priced at 10 reales the *fanega* in Sicily was sold at Alicante in Spain at over 22 reales. Despite this the demand for grain in the western Mediterranean outstripped the resources of Messina, and an even more expensive trade had been established with the Levant ports, the Aegean Islands and with Egypt. By 1520 this trade was increasingly subject to interference by the expanding Osmanli empire (see page 99).

Olive oil, wine and cheese were produced throughout the Mediterranean region and were traded locally in great quantity, but they were also carried across a complex network of long-haul routes to supplement local deficiencies elsewhere or to satisfy the preferences of areas capable of paying for them. Southern Spain and southern Italy were the principal areas of oil production, but north Italian merchants bought it in bulk in order to re-export it elsewhere in exchange for other produce. Luxury wines, especially the sweet heavy wines of Cyprus and Crete, were sold all round the Mediterranean, and sugar from these islands, supplemented by supplies from south-eastern Spain, was in great demand. There was also an important trade in salt. It could be produced wherever hot sun and the lack of tidal variation made it an easy matter to evaporate sea water, but there were specialist centres of production at Istria and in Sicily, whose exports were handled by the Venetians. Similarly, though fishing was a universal occupation in the Mediterranean, the dried fish and salted fish produced along the Messina Straits and the Provençal coast were highly valued in other regions.

The most profitable function of Mediterranean trade was the supply of spices to enliven the jaded palates of the rich who, for most of the year, could eat only dried or salted meats. Early in the Middle Ages caravans from the East had brought their loads of pepper, ginger, cloves, cinnamon, nutmeg and mace across the great Mongolian empire to the shores of the Black Sea, where both Genoa and Venice had established colonies to receive not only the spices but also the perfumes, the carpets and the dyes which

Europe lacked. When the Mongols lost control of their empire in 1340, a new route was found from China and the spice islands (Indonesia) to India where Arab traders brought the cargoes to Ormuz or Aden and shipped them overland to Aleppo or Alexandria. Most of the produce was then handled by the Venetian traders who imported something like 3,500,000 pounds of spices into Europe every year at great profit to themselves.

By the sixteenth century the spice trade was once again in difficulties. The Osmanli Turks were expanding across the Middle East. In 1516 they took Aleppo and two years later Egypt was theirs. Their campaigns temporarily disrupted the overland route from Ormuz and Aden, but thereafter the Turks were anxious to renew it so that they could levy heavier duties on the goods passing through their land. This alone did not trouble the Venetians, who could simply pass on the higher charges to their customers. Their main concern was that their seaborn empire in the eastern Mediterranean made them the first targets of Osmanli expansion into Europe, and that in the likely event of warfare their trade would be denied them by the enemy. More serious, however, was the threat to their monopoly by the Portuguese, who had discovered a sea route direct to India. (See pages 23 – 30.) As a result, Portuguese pepper was on sale in the international market at Antwerp early in the sixteenth century and at the Spanish fairs at Medina del Campo. Worse followed when the Portuguese attacked the Arab traders at Ormuz and Aden so that the overland supplies on which Venetian wealth was based began to dwindle. In 1509 there was not enough to justify the expense of sending galleys, and in later years the Venetians were compelled to purchase Portuguese pepper secretly at Medina del Campo in order to maintain deliveries to their own traditional customers. Fortunately for Venice the Portuguese abandoned their warfare with the Arabs in 1520 and the overland trade was given a new, if precarious, lease of life.

A third function of Mediterranean trade was to supply raw materials to the textile industries of north Italy. It was by no means the only centre of production in the Mediterranean but the skill of its craftsmen was so famous that the demand for its goods could only be met by importing raw materials in great quantity. The chief of these was wool and, as with the grain trade, the shipments were controlled by merchants from Genoa, Venice and Ragusa.

The best quality was purchased from England but supplies were cut towards the end of the fifteenth century when England began to make her own cloth for the markets of the Netherlands. The Italians, therefore, turned to Spain, only to find that Spanish wool was also being sent to the Netherlands and it was necessary to buy the inferior produce of North Africa and the Balkans. To cleanse the wool and to assist the processes of dyeing, alum was also in great demand. At first it was imported by the Genoese from Asia Minor until a local supply was discovered in 1462 at Tolfa near Civitavecchia. As this lay in the Papal States the popes derived a rich profit from the workings of the *Societas Aluminum* – as did the Medici of Florence who became the principal shareholders in the company. By 1520 there were 8,000 miners employed there, producing nearly enough alum to meet the needs of the Italian textile industry.

Other raw materials urgently required in north Italy were raw silk and leather hides. Florence in particular was famous for its leather goods – clothing, harness and furniture – though Spain ran a close second. Fortunately for the Italians, the Spaniards had enough hides at home to satisfy their needs so that the long-haul trade in hides from North Africa fell almost exclusively into Italian hands. Silk production was more or less general throughout the Mediterranean region, especially among the Moslem races who had also established it in Spain, but north Italy could provide effective competition at Lucca whose reputation dated back to the thirteenth century. Its silk-throwing mills anticipated the technical advances of the eighteenth century and were jealously guarded from the eyes of competitors. Operated by undershoot water-wheels, they required only a few men to oversee several hundred spindles and the product was as fine as that of any rivals. To keep the mills supplied there was an important trade in raw silk which passed across the Mediterranean from the main production centres of Valencia in Spain, Tripoli in Syria and Calabria in south Italy to Messina in Sicily, where it was finally shipped north to Lucca.

The economic strength of north Italy made it paramount in the Mediterranean region. Industrially it faced competition from Spain, commercially from the Dalmatian port of Ragusa, but Venice alone was a match for both. Since the days of the fourth Crusade in 1204 Venice had exploited the weakness of the Byzantine empire to win control of coastal bases in the Adriatic and to advance its colonies across the Aegean into the Black Sea. The rise of the Osmanli Turks destroyed its hold on Negroponte in 1470, but by way of compensation in 1479 it occupied Cyprus athwart the main sea route from Constantinople to Cairo. The spice trade supplied the major profits of this commercial empire and the means by which to trade with the rest of Europe, but Venetians were involved in all the other long-haul trades, and had made their city with its population of 100,000 an industrial centre famous for its textiles, glass and shipbuilding. Their agents and ambassadors supplied them with unrivalled market intelligence, their book-keepers developed sophisticated techniques of double-entry book-keeping and their financiers were expert in the handling of bills of exchange and other instruments of credit. Although Venetians were worried by the Osmanli advance and the Portuguese discoveries, they had the resources to cope with or adapt to problems of this kind. The greatest single danger which threatened them sprang from their ill-advised, and economically unnecessary, attempt to expand their political power on the Italian mainland so that by 1500 they were exposed to the emnity of their immediate neighbours (see page 112).

Among these was Milan, a city of 100,000 people engaged in textile production and expert in metallurgy, especially the manu-facture of armour. Its bankers too had won an international reputation for their wealth and skill so that throughout Europe Lombard had become a synonym for banker. Milan lay advanta-geously at the centre of a rich farming region famous for its rice, and of trade routes which ran northwards across the Alps to France and South Germany, southwards through an easy pass in the Appenines to Genoa. Genoa had formerly been the equal of Venice. Its Black Sea colonies of Amastris, near Trebizond, and the Crimean base of Kaffa had marketed the produce of the overland spice trade until the collapse of the Mongol empire had destroyed their value. Subsequently, they were engulfed in the fifteenth century by the advance of the Osmanli Turks, who also drove the Genoese from all their Aegean bases save Chios. Nonetheless, its banking skill and its share in the long-haul trade made Genoa the second commercial city of the Mediterranean.

Florence was yet another Italian city to enjoy a European reputation. Its wealth was founded on textile manufacture and leatherwork and it had ventured into commerce by the acquisition of the port of Pisa. On the whole, however, Florentines were chary of the risks involved in dealing in commodities at a distance and preferred to employ others to act on their behalf. They themselves dealt in money, and the complexity of their operations is indicated by a contemporary account of the art of borrowing money in Florence to sell at a profit on the exchange at Lyons – a process remarkable for the number of stages involved in the transaction.

If thou hast money in Florence and wilt have exchange in Lyons because thou mayest have profit from the exchange back again, so give to me who need money 64 scudi in Florence, if that be the exchange rate: against this I promise to have a mark of gold paid in Lyons to Tommaso Sertini. I give thee a bill on Salviati, thou sendest him to Tommaso so that he may cash it or deal with the re-exchange. The letter wherein thou dost this is called the Advice or *Spaccio*. Tommaso carries out thy orders. He pays thy mark of gold in Lyons to Piero and receives from him a bill on Federigo in Florence in accordance with which he has to pay thee 65½ scudi in so many days. Tomasso sends thee this re-exchange and when it matures thou hast made 1½ scudi. Herein, however, thou hast to run the risk of three failures, mine, Tommaso's and Piero's. Thou, therefore, must look with Argus eyes at the firm to whom thou shouldst give the bill, him to whom thou remittest it and him by whom this second man should have the re-exchange drawn.

Among the great industrial-financial families of Florence such as the Pazzi, the Strozzi, and the Frescobaldi, the most important in the fifteenth century was that of the Medici. The family's history epitomised the economic development of the city; its earliest fortunes were established in woollen cloth, it then engaged in commodity dealing and finally took up banking. Cosimo de Medici, who died in 1464, was the most prosperous of the family and his bank the largest of the day. His role had been to set up not one single family firm but a group of interrelated though legally separate partnerships in which he or his relatives held a controlling interest. He himself was senior partner in eleven such partnerships which allowed him to direct a co-ordinating policy while leaving administrative details to subordinates. His son, Piero, devoted too much time to politics and his grandson, Lorenzo, to politics and art: each, therefore, allowed his subordinate managers too free a hand and the family fortunes declined. The most disastrous step was taken in 1471. Despite the proven wisdom of Cosimo's refusal to provide loans to monarchs, Lorenzo's manager at Bruges agreed to lend heavily to Charles the Rash of Burgundy. In the event the Bruges House collapsed in 1478. Subsequently, Lorenzo by his political conflict with Sixtus IV forfeited his family's fruitful connection with the papal bankers, and by the time of their expulsion from Florence in 1494, the Medici were reduced to misappropriating public funds in order to honour their commitments elsewhere.

South Germany

The cities of south Germany were much smaller than those of north Italy, their population ranging from 10,000 to 20,000, but their wealth was considerable, and, like the Italians, was based on a judicious combination of international trade and local industry. Though many routes crossed the Alps from Italy, the major long-haul land route bringing spices and Italian manufactures from Venice lay through the Brenner Pass and Innsbruck to the three great cities of Munich, Augsburg and Nuremberg. There the goods were despatched to Regensburg, Prague, Krakow and Vienna in the east, to Ulm and the Rhineland in the west, and northwards to the Baltic and the Netherlands. The Venetians were perpetually concerned to maintain free access for their goods across the Alps, but they wisely left control of the route to the self-interest of the Germans. This was no loss since the Germans maintained their headquarters in Venice at the *Fondaco dei Tedeschi*, where they acquired not only goods for sale but the benefits of Venetian market intelligence, book-keeping and finance.

The capital required to withstand the risks involved in long-haul trade was supplied initially from the local textile industries. South Germany produced a good quality of linen and a blend of linen and cotton known as fustian. There was also a long tradition of metalwork and mining, but the extraction of ores had had to be confined to shallow deposits which were soon exhausted. In the fifteenth century, however, new techniques were invented which were later described in great detail by Agricola (Georg Bauer) in his *De Re Metallica* published in 1556. These completely altered the character of the mining industry. With improved methods for supporting the shaft walls, mines could go deeper, the ores were hauled up by windlasses and for very heavy loads the Germans developed the use of geared wheels and the horse whim. Deeper mining created a new problem of drainage. On hillside mines adits could be bored to the surface below the entrance to the pit; elsewhere it was discovered how to operate a system of rag and chain pumps. Balls of rag were fixed at intervals to a moving chain worked by horses and as each rag entered the barrel of the pump it acted as a piston to force the water up. Agricola describes how these were often worked in series at depths of 500 feet or more; in one case at Chemnitz in the Carpathians the depth was 660 feet and ninety-six horses were needed to work the pumps.

As a result, copper production began to boom in Bohemia, South Germany and the Tyrol, and with the discovery of calamine in Carinthia and the Tyrol its fusion with copper produced brass. Moreover, the copper ores were found to contain considerable quantities of silver. Since ancient times men had known that when argentiferous copper ores are heated with lead the molten copper and lead remain separate while the silver transfers itself to the lead. The next stage is to mix this alloy in a cupel, a porous clay crucible, which is exposed to blasts of air. The lead is thus oxidised and removed, leaving a small button of silver in the cupel. What was novel in the fifteenth century was the scale of production. Not only were the ores mined in greater quantities, but far more powerful means were devised to process them. Water-powered trip hammers crushed the ores, blast furnaces were constructed to melt them down and enormous bellows, also water powered, produced the blasts of air to oxidise the alloys of lead and silver.

The capital required to install this massive equipment could be found only in the south German cities whose merchants had been enriched by textile production and transcontinental trade. For them the mining and metallurgical industries represented an attractive investment. European demand for silver, copper and brass was so great that enormous profits could be anticipated for those who could control not only their production but also the means of distributing them across the continent. Consequently, the merchants of Nuremberg, Augsburg and Munich systematically bought up the regalian rights from landowners incapable of exploiting their own mines, and began to export their products along the routes in which they had formerly been the middlemen. In the latter half of the fifteenth century they set up branches in Italy, France, Spain and the Netherlands to market their produce, using the profits of their trade to set up banking houses and to speculate on the European exchanges. So successful were they that by 1520 the Houses of Welser, Paumgartner, Meuting and Hochstetter had begun to rival in international importance the long established firms of north Italy. None, however, could outstrip the Fuggers of Augsburg whose history over three generations epitomised the main features of south German expansion in this period.

The Fuggers had not been the first in the field. Hans Fugger was a linen weaver who came to Augsburg about 1380, attracted by the opportunity to supplement the profits of his craft by dealing in his own merchandise. His sons advanced the business further by importing raw cotton from Venice for the local manufacture of fustian, and then began to handle consignments of silks and other luxury textiles. Before long they were dealing in spices too, and because of the Fuggers' interest in the overland trade from Venice the youngest grandson Jacob, born in 1457, was apprenticed to the *Fondaco dei Tedeschi*. So successfully did he learn to imitate the commercial and financial skills of the Venetians that by 1480 he was recognised as the head of the family business, exercising a personal control over all its activities until his death in 1525. It was Jacob who transferred the family's attention to the mining industry. He acquired a major share of the Tyrolean silver and copper mines by providing loans for Duke Sigismund, and expanded his operations across south Germany and into Hungary by the same means when the duke's heir, Maximilian, became Holy Roman Emperor in 1497. Where the Fuggers could not establish sole control of production Jacob made cartels with his rivals to keep the prices high, as when he split the German copper market with the Hochstetters. Instead of competing on both the southern route to Italy and on the northern route via Danzig and Stettin to the Netherlands, the firms agreed to monopolise one each. Jacob Fugger astutely settled for the northern trade and his influence grew rapidly in Antwerp.

He continued to advance loans to princes but no longer primarily to secure regalian rights. Despite the unfortunate example of the Medici, members of his house became bankers to emperors and popes alike. The Medici collapse in fact gave him his first entrée into papal banking. Thereafter he handled the transfer of papal revenues from Germany to Rome, and even assisted in the collection of funds from the sale of indulgences throughout the Empire (see page 86). As for the emperor, when Charles V was elected in 1519, Jacob Fugger committed himself irrevocably to his cause by making available to him a loan of 543,000 gold florins. So, in three generations, the Fuggers had advanced from textile production, by way of overland trade and mining, to become the greatest banking house in Europe, and when Jacob died in 1525 the firm's capital was estimated to be worth two million gold florins.

The Baltic and the Netherlands

The long-haul northern trades had been dominated since the fourteenth century by the Hanse, a league of nearly eighty cities scattered along the Baltic and the North Atlantic coasts. The network of its commerce stretched from the Bay of Bourgneuf and the North Sea to the Baltic and the White Sea, and through its factors in Bruges it made contact with the Italian and south German traders. The member cities were divided in four circles, centred on Danzig, Brunswick, Cologne and Lübeck. Of these Lübeck was the overall headquarters since by its geographical location on the short overland route to Hamburg it linked the Baltic coastal trades with the commerce of the North Sea and the Netherlands. Although the league began to lose coherence in the fifteenth century as member cities began to exploit the short-term advantages of trading independently, it could still act decisively and effectively. When England, for example, began to sell her wool in the Baltic in exchange for naval stores and furs, the Hanse intervened dramatically in the Wars of the Roses by mobilising the fleet which brought Edward IV back to the throne in 1471. In return it was granted the exclusive right to handle England's exports to the Baltic from its London base, the Steelyard, and for fifty years no English king dared to challenge its privileges. Even as late as 1521, it was Hanseatic seapower which brought success to Gustavus Vasa in his bid for the Swedish throne.

England and Sweden might be vulnerable to the Hanse but not the Netherlands. As sand began to silt up the River Zwyn and thus destroy the pre-eminence of Bruges, sailors from Holland

Centres of trade and industry in Central and Northern Europe

and Zeeland by-passed the overland route from Hamburg to Lübeck by pioneering the sea route through the Danish Sound. When the Danes began to tax this route in the 1490s their registers revealed the predominance of Dutch shipping in their waters. Unlike the merchants of the southern Netherlands, whose industrial hinterland and well-established fairs allowed them to wait for trade to come to them, those of Holland and Zeeland had already begun to sail out in search of cargoes wherever they could be found. Initially they ventured into the Baltic to hire themselves as carriers to Hanseatic contractors, but by 1500 they had become something of an independent force, rivalling the tonnage of the Hanseatic fleet.

As in the Mediterranean, the provision of food supplies was the staple of Baltic trade. Most of it was done by short-haul traders, buying and selling along the coast according to the state of local harvests, but there was a major long-haul route in grain from Danzig across the Baltic, reaching out on occasion down the Atlantic coast to Portugal and Spain. This was because east Germany and Poland lie in a different weather area to the rest of Europe so that grain is often produced there when harvests elsewhere are ruined. Encouraged by the Hanseatic merchants who could offer an efficient means of collection and delivery, the Polish landowners therefore set about the systematic production of a surplus for export. The Dutch, however, were also eager to deal in Polish grain and though Danzig was a major Hanseatic base its merchants were not prepared to keep their stocks lying on the wharves if Hanseatic ships were not immediately available. Despite all the ordinances of Lübeck the Dutch began to make such free use of Danzig that they nicknamed it their 'bread basket'.

A major interest of the Hanseatic League was the distribution of fish. When cod came inshore from the ocean bottom to spawn off the Lofoten Islands in northern Norway, they were fished with hook and line, gutted and dried into a leathery product known as stock fish. Because it was virtually imperishable it was an ideal commodity for long-haul trade and the Hanse exported it from Bergen, not only to northern Europe but sometimes as far south as Italy. Cabot's discovery of the Newfoundland codbanks in 1497 represented a potential danger to the Hanseatic monopoly not fully realised by 1520. A more immediate threat was the Dutch challenge to the herring fisheries. Herring had been fished off the coast of Skane in Sweden since the sixth century and barrelled in salt for distribution. The Hanse monopolised the trade because they alone could supply the fisheries with the quantities of salt they needed. Initially this came from Lüneburg in north Germany, but so great was the demand that over 2,400 tons a year had to be imported at a distance from the salt pans of the Bay of Bourgneuf. In return for these supplies the Hanse distributed up to 13,000 tons of salted herring every year.

This was too valuable a trade for the Dutch to ignore. Not only did they go fishing in the North Sea but, recognising that the herring live in shoals near the surface in order to feed upon the plankton, they invented a drift net fifty to sixty fathoms long which they towed at night when the luminous surface shoals were easily detectable. They also developed better methods of salting the fish and by 1520 they produced a new type of boat, the *buizen* or *busses*, which revolutionised the industry. Unlike the open boats used hitherto, the *buizen* were decked vessels of up to one hundred tons carrying coopers and salters so that the catch could be processed at sea and exported immediately the fleets returned to port. By their successes in this field the Dutch established the foundations of their wealth and commercial power in the sixteenth century.

Baltic trade was not confined to grain and fish. The forest regions supplied amber, furs, wax, potash and the indispensable naval stores of pitch, hemp and timber. Pines and firs from Norway, oak and firs from Poland and the eastern seaboard were required in great quantity by the shipbuilding centres of Portugal, Spain and the Netherlands, while England, though her oak supplies were sufficient for her needs, depended on the Baltic trade for her masts of pine and fir. The difficulty of transportation was so great that barely five per cent.of the delivered price related to the cost of timber on the stump. Once the timber had been felled the suppliers exploited the hard frosts of winter to drag it, sometimes on sledges, down to the rivers from whence it was floated to the ports. Large ships were needed for such a bulky cargo, but the presence of sandbanks in many Baltic harbours prevented the entry of ships over 400 tons. To secure a maximum load, therefore, the decks were loaded as well as the holds, thereby increasing top-hamper so that it was dangerous to sail except in good weather.

Moreover, most of the ships had to return in ballast since one cargo of any other produce would pay for several of timber.

Wool and cloth provided useful return cargoes, though the bulk of the trade in wool and cloth was carried on along the North Atlantic coast. England which had once been an important supplier of wool through the Merchants of the Staple at Calais had switched over to cloth production by 1500, selling a small amount of heavy hard=wearing material to the Hanse and great quantities of unfinished cloth for the industry of Flanders. Flanders and northern France comprised the major European textile centre where many towns had given their names to their distinctive products – Ypres to its distinctive diaper pattern, Arras to its hanging curtains, Cambrai to cambric, Lille to lisle thread and Valenciennes to valence. It was also the centre of a major commercial organisation which brought its raw materials from England and Spain and exported its products up river by barge into central and southern Germany or shipped them along the Atlantic coast and into the Baltic. After 1450 the arrival of the Merchant Adventurers, bringing unfinished cloth from England instead of wool, disconcerted the old-established centres of production which were too restricted by their own guild regulations to adapt freely to changed circumstances. In their place the merchants of Antwerp made their own city the centre of what was called the 'new draperies'. They bought up English cloth and put it out for finishing by domestic labour in the region where the craft guilds could neither interfere with the new techniques nor protect the workers from exploitation.

Entrepreneurial action of this kind required a great deal of capital, but Antwerp was already growing rich from its position at the centre of a big industrial region linked by waterways. Barges laden with the iron ores and metalwork of Namur, the coal and munitions of Liège came down the Sambre, along the Meuse (Maas) and finally up the Scheldt to Antwerp; while down the Scheldt and its own tributaries other barges carried rich textiles from Valenciennes and Tournai, tapestries from Brussels and Oudenarde and coal from Mons. All this, along with Antwerp's bell foundries and armament production, had made the city an important entrepôt for manufactured goods. In addition, Italians with spices and oriental luxuries, north Germans with Baltic naval stores, south Germans with fustian, copper and silver, Spaniards with wool and wine, and Merchant Adventurers bringing unfinished cloth, sailed regularly into Walcheren Roads where their cargoes were transferred to smaller ships to reach Antwerp by the Scheldt. Finally there was the old continental route from the Rhineland. Formerly it ran from Cologne to Bruges but in the fifteenth century the caravans of pack animals turned north-east after crossing the Meuse and took the road to Antwerp through a region where provisions were cheap and the way was clear of tolls. Most of these shipments by river, sea or land were timed to arrive for the great Brabant fairs held in Antwerp and in nearby Bergen-op-Zoom. The Easter Fair at Bergen preceded the Pentecost Fair at Antwerp, and St Baro's Fair in August at Antwerp was followed by the winter fair at Bergen. For twenty-two weeks in every year, therefore, Antwerp was the centre of international trade.

The rise of Antwerp was not due solely to the happy coincidence of industry and waterways. Politics too had played an important role in its development although initially to its disadvantage. Its early attempt in 1338 to become a centre for English trade in the Netherlands had been stifled by the count of Flanders who preferred to favour Bruges, but in the fifteenth century the tables were eventually turned. The Burgundian dukes who acquired the separate local lordships of the Netherlands (see pages 93–9) were jealous of the exclusive privileges enjoyed by the older Flemish towns and were anxious to encourage a rival. Moreover, during the confused events of the 1480s, when Maximilian of Habsburg fought the French and his own subjects in the Netherlands to establish his right to succeed his Burgundian father-in-law, Antwerp remained loyal to him and in 1488 was duly rewarded when Maximilian ordered all foreign traders to move there from Bruges. The Germans obeyed immediately since they dared not antagonise the emperor's son. The Welsers, the Hochstetters and Meutings transferred their business to Antwerp, the Fuggers made it the major copper market in Europe and Habsburg influence at Rome ensured that it became the Northern Staple for the sale of papal alum. The other nations were not disposed to contest the change. Bruges was already in decline. Its long established textile industry could not compete with the 'new draperies' and its commerce was depleted as the River Zwyn became silted up. Moreover, like most other towns, it insisted that all foreign trade be handled through local firms. Antwerp alone, despite much local opposition, allowed the foreigner full liberty to trade on his own.

The transfer of foreign merchants from Bruges to Antwerp resulted in an unforeseen advantage for the city. Since 1460 the Portuguese had maintained a factor in Bruges, not only to market the produce of their early voyages along the African coast, but also to purchase cloth, silver, copper and metal goods from the German traders for resale to the Africans (see page 29). In order to keep in touch with the Germans the factor finally followed them to Antwerp in 1499, the very year in which the Portuguese discovered their route to India. In 1503 the Portuguese formally declared Antwerp to be their principal pepper market and within a year a thousand tons of spices had been distributed there. The flow of commerce attracted the flow of capital and the Antwerp branches of the great banking houses of Italy and south Germany began to play a vital role in European finance. The Antwerp Bourse, opened in 1484, became the home of international commission agents, brokers, dealers in bills of exchange and speculators who gambled on the rates of exchange and the movement of commodity prices. There was also speculation in government loans which were first raised on the Bourse in 1511 for short-term operations and subsequently the rates of interest rose and fell erratically, varying from 11 to 31 per cent per annum.

With its prosperity securely based on the triple foundations of industry, trade and finance, the great age of Antwerp was about to dawn. Symbolically perhaps its ruler, Charles of Burgundy, inherited in 1516 the thrones of Aragon and Castile. Antwerp, therefore, became the commercial capital of the Spanish Empire and very shortly afterwards the market for American silver.

The Portuguese Discoveries

For all their dramatic novelty the oceanic discoveries of the fifteenth century must be seen in the context of a long period of preparation and development. Almost all the geographical knowledge on which the great explorers depended had been available since the thirteenth century when Europe, by its contact with Arab civilisation, had recovered the ancient works of Ptolemy and Strabo. Their ignorance of America apart, their estimates of the shape and size of the world were to prove most valuable and the so-called *Catalan Atlas* of 1375 contained an accurate description of the shape of India long before the Portuguese first sailed there. Means of navigation had also been well established since the thirteenth century; the compass had made it possible to measure the direction of a ship's progress and the cross-staff to measure the angle of a star's elevation and thus to establish a ship's latitude. The fifteenth-century quadrant was simply a more sophisticated version of the cross-staff, and no one had yet devised an instrument to establish longitude. It was known that the difference between the longitude of two places could be expressed as a difference in time, allowing 15 degrees for each hour, but there was no means of measuring the time except by hour glasses. These, however, were easily broken in a storm and easily forgotten too, so that the chronological record became progressively less accurate. By using the *Ephemerides*, the star tables of Regio-montanus of Nuremberg, it was sometimes possible to calculate longitude when certain stars and planets were shown to be in conjunction at a certain hour, but throughout the period of the great discoveries the hallmark of the great navigator was his ability to determine his position by intelligent guesswork.

In the later Middle Ages something of a revolution had taken place in the design of shipping so that the rig of the fifteenth-century caravels and carracks, though remaining familiar to seamen until as late as the Napoleonic Wars, would have seemed strange to the crews of a twelfth-century cog. The cog, a short stubby 'roundship' with a single mast carrying a square sail, was virtually unnavigable until the introduction from the East of the Latin or lateen sail – a triangular fore and aft sail by which it was possible to bear into the wind. Ships were, therefore, enlarged to take both types of sail until by the time of the great discoveries they carried square sails on the fore and main masts, a sprit sail on the bow sprit and a lateen sail on the mizzen mast. Ships had to be lengthened in order to carry the extra masts and consequently became more seaworthy, though the length of a fifteenth-century carrack was rarely more than three times its width. Columbus's *Santa Maria*, longer than his other vessels, was only 95 feet long by 25 feet wide.

A better understanding of navigation and the provision of more navigable ships were the prerequisites of oceanic exploration, but so difficult and costly a venture also required the resources of a government to develop and sustain it. Most countries were preoccupied with other matters. The Mediterranean and Baltic States were enmeshed in the commercial and political rivalries of their own regions, France and England were engaged in the Hundred Years' War and Castile was committed to driving the Moors from the peninsula. Portugal too was at war with the Moors but, unlike Castile, she had cleared her own territory by 1250 and had continued the war thereafter as a maritime campaign against the Moorish strongholds in Morocco, seizing Ceuta in 1415. This campaign never slackened in the fifteenth century, remaining the prime concern of Alfonso V (1438–81), and it was supplemented by a novel attempt to out-flank the Moors by exploring the West African coastline in the hope of establishing an alliance with the ancient Christian kingdom of Abyssinia. No one knew the precise location of the legendary land of Prester John but its existence had been demonstrated by embassies travelling overland to Europe.

The direction of the enterprise was undertaken by Dom Henriques, better known in England as Prince Henry the Navigator. His character was complex. A scholarly ascetic, inspired with crusading fervour to destroy the power of Islam, he was also passionately interested in the techniques of maritime exploration and shrewdly aware of the rich overland trades in gold and ivory which ran below the Sahara from Timbuktu to the Guinea Coast. He even dreamed of finding a sea route to the spice markets of India. Appointed governor of the Algarve his court at Sagres, in sight of the Atlantic waves breaking on Cape St Vincent, became a centre for seamen navigators and academic cartographers. They pooled their skills and information and nerved themselves to break the two psychological barriers which stood in their way. No one as yet had voluntarily sailed out of sight of land; no one as yet had rounded Cape Bojador, traditionally regarded as the limit of the navigable ocean. Urged on by Dom Henriques, who also financed their voyages, they broke these barriers exploring the West African coast as far south as Guinea and discovering the uninhabited islands of Madeira and the Azores. It was there that the Portuguese introduced not only sugar cane from Cyprus and the Malvoisie grape from Crete, but also the slaves to till the land.

Portugal was already a slave-owning country and though the slave trade had been monopolised by Moslems, Christians were not reluctant to compete with them. Moreover, since all the inhabitants of West Africa were assumed to be Moslems, it was regarded as a Christian duty to capture and enslave them. As the Portuguese pressed southward a papal bull of 1454 encouraged them 'to attack, subject and reduce to perpetual slavery the Saracens, pagans and other enemies of Christ southward from Cape Bojador . . . , including all the coast of Guinea'.

When Dom Henriques died in 1460 the pace of exploration slackened. Alfonso preferred to fight the Moors on land in accordance with the time-honoured traditions of knightly combat and, though his seizure of the Moroccan seaports safeguarded his sea captains from harassment by interlopers, little was done to extend the area of discovery. One licence only was granted, to Fernão Gomes to explore a hundred leagues of coastline every year in search of trade. As a result Gomes pioneered the route from Sierra Leone to Nigeria and the Cameroons, but in 1471, the year in which he reached the equator, his licence was revoked. It was not until the accession of John II (1481–1495), that a more vigorous direction was given to the task of exploration. A commercial base protected by a fortress was established in 1482 at Mina (Elmina) on the Bight of Benin, where the Portuguese sold leather, textiles, weapons, wine and wheat in return for ivory and slaves, and for gold brought overland from the Sudan. Encouraged by the profits to be won and by the king's own enthusiasm, the Portuguese pressed on beyond the equator. They reached the Congo in 1483 and four years later Cape Cross in south-west Africa.

By now, however, they were disheartened by the discovery that the African coast seemed to run interminably southwards away both from the spice markets and from the domains of Prester John. In 1487, therefore, John II decided to send an expedition overland to Abyssinia. Pedro da Covilha travelled first to Alexandria and Aden and then to India, returning to Cairo in 1489 to meet two Jews whom John had sent to seek him out. Through them he passed on the alluring prospect of the wealthy emporia he had seen in Calicut and Goa and also affirmed that there was an easy sea route from East Africa to India. Subsequently he reached Abyssinia. Welcomed as an honoured guest he was also refused permission to depart, and was seen there by a Portuguese ambassador in 1526 apparently prosperous and reconciled to his lot.

By a rare coincidence, when Covilha left for Abyssinia in 1487 three ships sailed from Lisbon under Bartolomeu Dias with the declared intent to 'serve God and his Majesty, to give light to those in darkness, and to grow rich as all men desire to do'. Blown by storms around the Southern Cape they made their landfall at Bahia dos Voiqueiros and discovered to their delight that the coastline at last ran northwards. But Dias could not exploit the opportunity. With few supplies and a restive crew he was forced to return home – his disappointment softened by John II's enthusiastic welcome and his decision to name the stormy cape the Cape of Good Hope. Preparations were in hand for a new expedition when news arrived that the Spaniards had discovered the West Indies. Since everyone assumed that Columbus was correct in his belief that these were the Spice Islands, the Portuguese were bitterly disappointed. It seemed that the fruits of exploration, undertaken single-handed for nearly a hundred years, were to be denied them at the eleventh hour. John II hastily prepared a fleet to sail across the Atlantic to challenge the Spaniards for possession of the Indies, but warfare was averted in 1494 by the Treaty of Tordesillas. In order to be free of Portuguese interference the Spaniards agreed to allocate to Portugal all discoveries made east of a line to be drawn 370 leagues west of the Cape Verde Islands. Though this deprived the Portuguese of access to the West Indies, and represents their realisation that they dared not challenge Spain for possession, the drawing of the line suggests that Portugal had secret intelligence from some unknown sea captain of a land mass in the area of Brazil. Certainly the Portuguese had ventured further and further into the south Atlantic to avoid the fever-ridden coasts of West Africa, and their subsequent voyages were to give substance to the conjecture.

When Manuel I (1495 – 1521) succeeded John II he decided to renew the search for an eastern route to India. Vasco da Gama in the São Gabriel, his brother Paulo in the São Rafael, a third ship and a supply vessel – in all a complement of 170 men – set sail from Lisbon in July 1497. They began with a long tack to the south-west as other Portuguese had done before them, coming within 600 miles of South America. Then, turning eastwards to the Cape, they made landfall having sailed for three months out of sight of land. The journey of 4,500 miles tooks its toll, and scurvy,

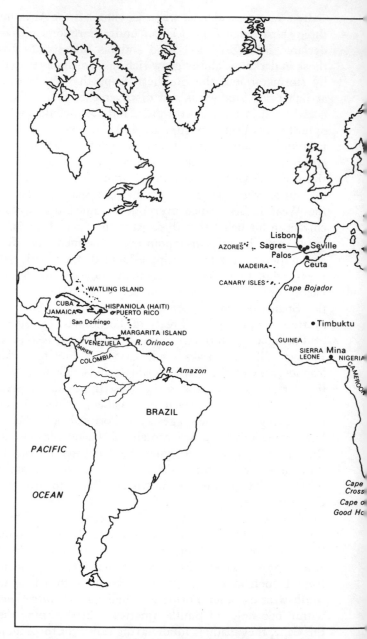

The extent of Portuguese and Spanish discoveries by 1520

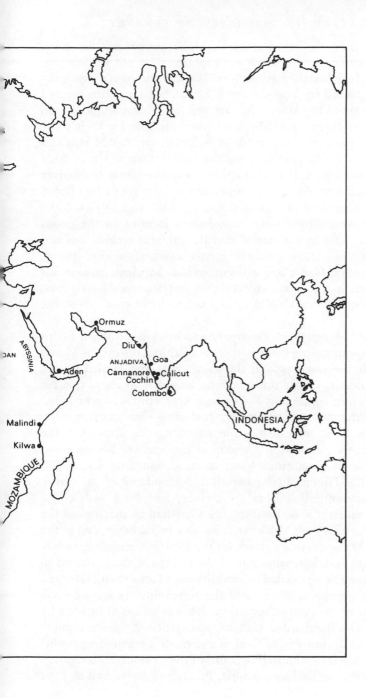

ABYSSINIA

DAN

Ormuz

Diu

ANJADIVA Goa

Cannanore Calicut

Cochin

Colombo

Aden

Malindi

INDONESIA

Kilwa

MOZAMBIQUE

caused by deficiency of vitamin C, broke out among the crew. This was an illness with which sea captains were not yet familiar, but by landing over Christmas – in Natal – the men's condition rapidly improved on a diet of fresh food. Da Gama then pressed on northwards. In March he arrived at Mozambique to an unfriendly reception from the local Arabs, jealous for their trade with India, but their local rivals at Malindi entertained him and supplied him with a pilot to cross the Indian Ocean. On 17 May he sailed into Calicut. It was something of an anticlimax to discover that the local samarin was unimpressed by the goods he offered for trade. The cloth, honey and sugar which had attracted the natives of West Africa were regarded as inferior to the goods supplied to India by the Arabs, and the samarin seemed inclined to support the Arabs in their cabals against the Europeans. Nonetheless, da Gama left without serious incident, and on his return home in 1499 was able to demonstrate conclusively that the Treaty of Tordesillas had turned out to be of great advantage to Portugal.

A further advantage of the treaty was established when Pedro Alvarez Cabral, sailing from Lisbon with thirteen ships in March 1500, made the usual tack to the south-west and landed on the shores of Brazil. Under the treaty he was able to claim this for Portugal before continuing his voyage. One ship was sent home to report the news, five others, including one captained by Bartolomeu Dias, were lost while rounding the Cape, but the remaining seven arrived at Calicut in September. Religion and commerce were to advance hand in hand, since da Gama had imagined the Hindus to be heretical descendants of an earlier Christian community. Cabral, therefore, had been ordered to exhort the samarin to do his duty as a Christian by driving out the Arab traders who were Moslems. The ploy failed badly, and in the event the Arabs staged an attack on the Portuguese, killing nearly fifty of them and destroying one of their ships. Cabral escaped to Cochin, where he succeeded in establishing a factory, and returned home with enough spices aboard the remaining six ships to pay for the cost of the entire expedition. He was followed in 1502 by da Gama who bombarded Calicut, strengthened the Portuguese alliance with the samarin of Cochin and made a resounding profit.

Manuel now styled himself as 'Lord of the Conquest, Navigation and Commerce of Ethiopia, Arabia, Persia and India' and in 1505 he appointed Dom Francisco del Almeida to be his viceroy in the East. In order to safeguard the route Almeida established fortresses at Kilwa in East Africa, at. Anjadiva off the coast of India, at Cochin and at Cannanore. In. addition, he patrolled the Red Sea to intercept Arab trade and his subordinate Albuqerque seized the Arab base of Ormuz in 1507. With Egyptian aid the Arabs retaliated by challenging a Portuguese fleet off the island of Diu in 1509, but were themselves destroyed by Almeida. Historically this battle was of great significance for its demonstration of the superiority of European sails and artillery over the galleys and grappling irons which had dominated naval warfare for 2,000 years. It also underlined the critical importance of seapower in the development of Portugal's commercial empire. 'Let it be known' reported Almeida 'that if you are strong in ships the commerce of the Indies is yours', but Albuqerque who succeeded him in 1509 was astute enough to realise that seapower might be ineffectual without the support of well-chosen shore bases. He had an excellent eye for a strategical site. Ormuz had already fallen to him, he coveted Aden and Diu in vain, but he did succeed in taking Goa and Colombo.

Imperious, irritable and aggressive though he was, Albuqerque was yet careful to restrict the role of his shore bases to the protection of shipping. He did not regard them as imperial bridgeheads from which to launch the conquest of the hinterland; 'My will and determination is, as long as I am governor of India, neither to fight nor to hazard men on land except in those parts wherein I must build a fortress.' The fortress once established, Portuguese interference in local affairs was kept to a minimum and everything was done by marriage, conversion and employment to assimilate the local population peaceably into the life of the garrison and the factory. Meanwhile, protected by the efforts of Almeida and Albuqerque, the royal Lisbon fleet left Lisbon every March, arriving in Goa in September. The return fleet departed in December if its route lay along the East African coast, in January if it sailed direct for the Cape, to reach Lisbon in the following autumn. On arrival the precious cargoes were shipped directly to Antwerp in order to secure the best price for them and to purchase the return cargoes, especially the copper and silverware manufactured in south Germany. In addition, the Portuguese continued the work of exploration in the East, pioneering the first

European route to the Spice Islands of Indonesia and reaching beyond as far as China and Japan. This new commercial network, referred to as the 'country trade', served a dual purpose. It facilitated the collection of spices in readiness for the arrival of the annual fleet in Goa and, by exporting Indian cottons to Indonesia in return for spices, helped to finance their purchase. Potentially it was even more profitable than the trade from Goa to Antwerp.

The daring innovation of the Portuguese achievement is undeniable yet it should not be exaggerated. Their ships and seamanship were founded upon a century of development and their method of organisation was derived almost entirely from the long-established practice of Genoa and Venice. These states had created commercial empires founded upon shore bases and colonies won from the Byzantine empire. They had settled mere handfuls of their citizens, introduced new crops and guaranteed their cultivation by importing slaves; they had excluded rivals and controlled both the organisation of shipping and the direction of policy from the metropolis. The development of Madeira and the Azores, the preference for bases rather than for territorial conquests and the licensing of the annual fleets revealed how closely the Portuguese modelled themselves on the Genoese and the Venetians. Few individuals began their career in the East as private adventurers: the majority were clergy, civil servants, soldiers or seamen, more or less under the authority of governmental agencies. The viceroy in Goa represented the king. Hereditary captaincies were granted in Madeira and the Azores and the economic and political development of the empire was controlled by royal councils; the *Casa de Ceuta*, the *Casa de Guinea*, the *Casa de Mina* and the *Casa dos Indias*. The real novelty lay in the immense distances to be covered from Guinea to Indonesia since the scale of the enterprise had been dramatically enlarged. Indeed, by 1520, it became a question whether or not an empire of such vast extent could be retained successfully within the structure of a bureaucratic machine established in Lisbon and backed by a population of just over one million people.

The Spanish Discoveries

Da Gama sailed for three whole months across the South Atlantic before he made his landfall at the Cape and subsequently gained access to the rich markets of the Orient. Columbus, on the other hand, discovered a relatively barren island after only six weeks at sea, but the terrifying novelty of his voyage to the west and the vast unknown areas which were subsequently opened up for colonisation caught the imagination of Europe and made him by far the most famous explorer of the fifteenth century.

Born in Genoa in 1451, Columbus had been shipwrecked off Lisbon in 1476 and settled there with his brother Bartolome who was a map maker. Soon he became well-read in the theories of the ancient Greek authorities on the size and shape of the world. From these he argued not that the world was round, since this was accepted by all educated men, but that the shortest route from Europe to the Spice Islands lay across the Atlantic Ocean. Portugal, however, had its own experts in this field who soon discovered several errors in his reasoning. In the first place, they noted that Columbus had tried to strengthen his case by deliberately under-estimating the size of the world. From all the various estimates ever made about the length of the degree, he had clearly selected the shortest one and, instead of following the accepted authority of Eratosthenes who had estimated the circumference of the Earth to be 25,000 miles, he had relied on Strabo's estimate of 18,000 miles. Moreover, it appeared that Columbus had exaggerated the eastward extent of Asia, assisted in part by the tales of Marco Polo who had miscalculated the length of his overland journey to the East. Consequently, when Columbus formally presented his proposals to the Portuguese government in 1485, they were rejected on the very reasonable grounds that they totally misrepresented the length of the western route to Asia and that the eastern route therefore remained the most promising one to pursue. When news arrived that Dias had rounded the Cape the matter was regarded as settled.

Self-confident and ambitious for fame, Columbus refused to abandon his belief. With neither wealth nor status to recommend him, he forced himself into the presence of several rulers to petition their support, but no European state was yet prepared to enter the field against Portugal. In 1492, however, the centuries-old struggle between Castile and the Moors was triumphantly resolved when Isabella's army entered Granada. In the mood of national and religious euphoria which succeeded this signal victory over Islam, the queen agreed to provide Columbus with the ships he needed and invested him as admiral, 'with all the dignities and privileges hereto pertaining in such territories as he should discover'. As with Portugal, so with Spain the work of exploration was to represent an intriguing blend of religious zeal, greed and ruthless curiosity.

Columbus had need of all these qualities to carry him across the Atlantic. The three ships in his command were nothing more than coastal traders; the largest, the *Santa Maria*, was only 95 feet in length, and none of them was even equipped with lateen sails. The crew was even more inadequate. Volunteers were reluctant to man the ship and in order to make good his complement of one hundred men Columbus had to pressgang criminals from the gaols. The makeshift flotilla left Palos on 3 August 1492, reaching the Canaries by the end of the month. There the discoverers embarked upon unknown waters, but by a singular stroke of luck their course coincided with the north-east trade winds which carried them within six weeks to Watling Island in the Bahamas. From there Columbus sailed to northern Cuba which he took to be a promontory of the Asian mainland. When the *Santa Maria* broke up under the strain he left a section of the crew at Navidad in Hispaniola (Haiti) and returned home with the remaining ships. Again he was remarkably fortunate. His ships sailed so far to the north that they ran into the winter westerlies which brought them safely to the Azores and thence to Spain.

Disconcerted though he was by the native savages who had greeted him and even more by his failure to find evidence of spices, Columbus was convinced that he had discovered a route to the Indies. His enthusiasm was shared by Ferdinand and Isabella who, within five months, assembled a fleet of seventeen ships to carry men, animals, tools and seeds to colonise Hispaniola. They landed safely in November 1493 and as no trace remained of the men who had been left at Navidad, Columbus selected a different site, naming it Isabella. His difficulties now began. An excellent cartographer, he proved a poor colonial governor and neither the site nor the men were suitable for colonial settlement. Isabella lay on an unhealthy and unprotected shore, the settlers were intractable and dreamed of finding gold and adventure in preference to the toil of agriculture. Those most difficult to control were sent to explore the interior, while Columbus sailed off to find the Indian mainland. Disconsolate at finding nothing more exciting than Jamaica he returned to find the settlers stricken by fever and the peaceful natives harassed to the brink of war.

Leaving his brother Bartolome in command, he sailed for Spain to answer criticisms of his conduct, but Ferdinand and Isabella stood by him and sent him back with more colonists. This time he was heartened to discover the Orinoco estuary – evidence of a great land mass which he took to be India – and then turned north for Hispaniola where Bartolome had removed the colony to a better site known later as San Domingo. The colonists, however, remained at odds with each other, with the natives and with Columbus, and in 1499 he was superseded and sent home in irons. He was immediately released and restored to his title by Ferdinand and Isabella but was no longer entrusted with authority. In his place they sent out a proven disciplinarian named Bobadilla. A pattern was thus established which was to be repeated many times as the Spanish Empire expanded across the West Indian islands and into the American mainland. The problems of colonial government could not be left to discoverers and adventurers, and the Spanish Crown which granted supreme authority to individual commanders in the initial stages of exploration withdrew them once a colony was established. Moreover, the Crown was determined to forestall any traces of bastard feudalism in its overseas empire, preferring to introduce Castilian institutions staffed by men experienced in administration and amenable to direction from Madrid.

From the time of the first, specifically colonial, expedition of 1493 the principal director of the enterprise was Juan Rodrigues de Fonseca, archdeacon of Seville, who was chairman of a standing committee to advise the Council of Castile on colonial affairs. By 1509 this committee was being referred to as the Council of the Indies though its formal institution under that title did not occur until 1524. Its representative in the colonies was the *Real Audiencia*, a well-established instrument of Castilian administration composed of a president and four *auditores* whose authority extended comprehensively over matters administrative and judicial. The first *audiencia* sat in Hispaniola in 1511, the prototype of many others as the empire expanded. Economic affairs were also a matter for government direction and in 1503 the Atlantic trade was made a royal monopoly granted to the city of Seville. As the principal Castilian port it was already experienced in handling shipments to the Canary Islands; and as the centre of an Andalusian trade in pottery, tools, wine, oil and grain, it was well placed to supply the very products which the colonists required. To control the Atlantic trade the Crown appointed the *Real Audiencia y Casa de Contratación*. Unlike the *Consulado*, a representative body of merchants and producers established after 1520, this was an institution of the Crown similar to any other *audiencia* but with a very specialist role combining the functions of a court of justice and a board of trade. It regulated shipments, licensed shipping, determined the departure dates of convoys, resolved all disputes and founded a school of hydrography. Despite the charges of inefficiency and delay which are levelled against most sixteenth-century institutions this one achieved remarkable success in establishing colonial trade on a firm footing.

In addition to regulating trade through Seville the Government was anxious to develop food production in Hispaniola so that it in turn could supply future expeditions of discovery and colonisation. This was a matter in which Castilians had acquired considerable experience from the days of the Reconquista. When land was recovered from the Moors it had been assigned along with its Morisco labour force to Castilian settlers who had been made responsible for developing agriculture and cattle ranching. This device known as the *encomienda* was easily adapted to the New World where groups of Indian villages were 'commended' to a Spanish settler. He would protect them and instruct them in Christianity; in return they paid him tribute and worked at his direction. The natives who lived outside the *encomiendas* were also obliged to work for the Spaniard under a system known as the *repartimiento*: this was operated by the magistrates who shared out the workers among the other settlers and determined their rates of pay. Both institutions smacked of slavery and Isabella, unlike her Portuguese counterpart, was horrified to learn of them. But the governor sent a blunt report to indicate that without forced labour the colony would collapse and the practice was officially recognised in 1503.

This, however, was not the end of the affair. The Spanish Church, which devoutly believed in its pastoral duty to protect its members, whatever their race, established three new dioceses to serve the empire overseas. In 1511 a Dominican priest named Montesinos preached a powerful Christmas sermon in Santo

Domingo on the abuse of Indian labour and was immediately sent home by his Order, not to silence him but rather to enable him to plead his case at court. As a result the laws of Burgos, promulgated in 1512, declared that Indians were to be free men, that their conversion was to be achieved by peaceful means and that though they were to be put to work for the colonists the demands on their labour were to be restricted. Despite their good intentions the laws remained too vague to be effectively enforced, and another priest, Bartolome de las Casas, who had formerly been granted an *encomienda* in Hispaniola, became a passionate champion of the natives' rights and continued to denounce the *encomienda* system as despotic and unjust.

Humanitarian appeals had no effect on settlers who had risked everything to cross the ocean, and whose prosperity depended on forced labour to till the fields of yams, cassava and sugar cane, to man the score of sugar mills, to herd the pigs and cattle and to pan the golden nuggets from Hispaniola's streams. The problem was resolved by the gentle Tainos themselves. Unused to heavy labour and disheartened by the brutal treatment they endured, they lost the will to live. Their ultimate extinction within a few years could not be averted. In great alarm the settlers raided neighbouring islands for slaves and purchased negroes from the Portuguese bases in West Africa. Others decided to move on to other islands. Cattle ranching had been started in Jamaica by 1507, and Diego Velasquez established a settlement in Cuba in 1511 which proved successful in producing tobacco and sugar as well as panning gold. An expedition to Puerto Rico, however, failed to overcome the tenacious resistence of the local Caribs.

Meanwhile, the search for a labour force, reinforced by the powerful urge to discover a passage to the Spice Islands, had already drawn the Spaniards in increasing numbers to the American mainland. In this enterprise three of Columbus's original companions played a prominent part. Pinzon explored the north Brazilian coast as far as the Amazon delta in 1499; Hojedo discovered the pearl fisheries on Margarita off the coast of Venezuela – so called because the sight of wooden huts built on piles driven into the water reminded him of Venice – and de las Casas surveyed the Gulf of Darien. A settlement was founded on Margarita which lasted for twenty-five years until both pearls and natives had been exhausted. More important was the decision of the Spanish government in 1509 to despatch 2,000 settlers to the mainland. On arrival half were to follow Diego de Nicuesa to Darien while Hojedo led the others to the north-eastern coast of Colombia. In the event the expedition came near to disaster. Hojedo gave up the attempt after 900 men or more had died from disease and wounds, and, in the dangerous period of uncertainty which followed, the lead was taken by Vasco Nuñez de Balboa who may properly be termed the first of the *conquistadores*. Courageous, able, endowed with extraordinary reserves of energy and wholly ruthless, he sent home the royal officials and abandoned Nicuesa in an open boat. He then advanced on Darien where, by alternate demonstrations of conciliation and intimidation, he persuaded the local Indians to supply the colonists with food and gold. It was a remarkable and successful achievement but his methods had antagonised King Ferdinand. In 1513 he was replaced as governor of Darien by de Avila and, unable to accommodate himself to another's command, was eventually executed for conspiracy.

Before his death, however, Balboa had discovered the Pacific Ocean. At one blow the dreams of wealth engendered by Columbus were destroyed and the American mainland, instead of being the triumphant goal of the Spanish endeavour, was revealed as yet another obstacle in the all important race with Portugal to reach the Spice Islands. Further colonisation seemed profitless and the Spanish Government directed its attention instead to finding a sea route to the Pacific. In 1519, unaware that the Portuguese had already discovered Indonesia, Magellan began his voyage of circumnavigation.

The Cultural and Spiritual Foundations
of the Sixteenth Century

The Urban Environment of the Italian Renaissance

THE history of the Renaissance is not the history of arts nor of sciences nor of literature nor even of nations. It is the history of the attainment of self-conscious freedom by the human spirit manifested in the European races. It is no mere political mutation, no new fashion of art, no restoration of classical standards of taste. The arts and inventions, the knowledge and the books which suddenly became vital at the time of the Renaissance had long lain neglected on the shores of the Dead Sea which we call the Middle Ages. It was not their discovery which caused the Renaissance but it was the intellectual energy, the spontaneous outburst of intelligence which enabled mankind at that moment to make use of them.

This famous and stimulating analysis of the Renaissance by the Victorian historian J. A. Symonds presented nearly as many problems as it solved. It pre-supposed a false view of the Middle Ages and over-estimated the abruptness of the break with the past, but for all that, it established that what mattered was neither the scholarship nor the art but a fundamentally novel attitude to life in general.

This novel attitude resulted from the particular environment, peculiar to north and central Italy, where as a result of great industrial and commercial expansion (see pages 8–12) urban life had become the socially accepted norm. Chaucer's 'Merchant's Tale' referred to Lombardy as the 'Land of Towns' and as early as the thirteenth century Salimbene of Parma had seized upon the predominance of urban life as the one factor which distinguished Italy from the rest of Europe. What is more the local gentry, the feudal knightly class, had been increasingly drawn into town life on equal terms with leading commercial and industrial families, so that whereas the gentry north of the Alps lived separately on their estates, in Lombardy and Tuscany they made their town house the centre of their social life. It was in this integrated society of merchants, industrialists and landed gentry therefore that the feudal and ecclesiastical elements which had been so powerful in formulating the standards of Europe in the Middle Ages were now superseded by the urban and secular forces which emerged in the Italian city-states.

Sometimes it happened that a princely family or a family aspiring to princely status won control of a town as did the Sforza in Milan, the Este in Ferrara, the Gonzaga in Mantua and the Montefeltre in Urbino. Even so the new despots were men of the same cut as their fellows and the specifically urban character of their courts was scarcely altered. Although an 'aristocratic' preference for noble pursuits and an enthusiasm for chivalry might seem to indicate a revival of the social norms which were current throughout the rest of Europe, it was little more than a social game, a contrived phantasy which only superficially resembled the culture of, say, the Burgundian court. Indeed *Il Cortegiano*, the most influential book produced by the 'courtly society' of the Montefeltre of Urbino, revealed an image of the ideal gentlemen far removed from the conventional picture of the medieval knight (see page 48).

It mattered less that individual despots might control the destinies of individual cities from time to time than that the whole area should be free of an overall ruler. The popes and emperors had formerly played a commanding role in Italian affairs, prompting the factions of the Guelfs and the Ghibellines which had had grievous repercussions on the political stability of many cities, but by the fifteenth century they had become too remote and too ineffectual to impose their rule upon the country as a whole. Nor was there any local family or city state capable of dominating the others. The Visconti dukes of Milan, had come near to doing so at the start of the fifteenth century, but their progress had been halted and reversed by the stubborn resistance of Florence, and the Peace of Lodi (1454) had left the whole of north and central Italy independent of any single politic authority. (See page 109.) The degree of autonomy thus enjoyed by the Italian city states was as important a factor in the development of the Renaissance as the urban environment which initially gave it birth. Because there was no controlling Italian dynasty, no universal censor, no central court to dictate cultural standards and to discourage nonconformity, the Italian states were free to go their different ways, stimulated by an intense civic pride which prompted them to compete with each other in cultural as well as political rivalry. The result was a remarkable diversity of cultural achievement and intellectual independence unequalled in the rest of Europe, characterised by the reappraisal of classical literature, the provision of a new source of patronage and the encouragement of an exciting new attitude to life by which Italians were tempted to believe they could achieve perfection in all things.

After 1530, however, when Spain had established her control over most of the peninsula, the originality of artists and writers was stifled within the rigid framework of a variety of courts which subjected themselves to Spanish power, conformed to Spanish standards of etiquette and good taste and obeyed the dictates of the Roman Inquisition whose authority was in the last analysis enforced by Spanish troops. Formality, conformity and orthodoxy triumphed over freedom of expression, and the artists and writers, no longer free citizens, became the subjects of princes who owed their thrones to Spanish might. It was not coincidental therefore that the true nature of the Italian Renaissance should have been extinguished in the sixteenth century except in Venice, the one city state to preserve its political independence of Spain (see page 393).

The Italian Renaissance, therefore, sprang from the uniquely urban environment of north and central Italy, an environment in which urban values predominated and in which no single ruler was able to control the variety of intellectual and cultural experiments or monopolise the services of artists and scholars. It is always possible to dispute the sources of any movement, and with so complex a phenomenon as the Renaissance, the attentions of historians have been variously directed to finding its roots in the painting of Giotto, the poetry of Petrarch, the teaching of St Francis or even as far back as in the foundation of the Italian communes in the tenth century. At no time before the defeat of the Visconti, however, could the general characteristics of the Renaissance be said to be predominant, nor did they survive the triumph of Charles V in 1530. In short, the Italian Renaissance was the product of a century of civic autonomy.

The Studia Humanitatis and Renaissance Optimism

Medieval man had been permanently in touch with classical literature since the days of Charlemagne. Scholars throughout the Middle Ages had ransacked their libraries and monastic cells for manuscripts of classical authors, and when the Crusades had opened their eyes to the Hellenistic legacy acquired by the Arabic world, they had visited the Islamic universities of Asia Minor and of Moorish Spain in order to translate from Arabic the classical authorities whose works had been lost to Europe during the Dark Ages. At first sight their enthusiasm for the past, as reflected for example in the *Philobiblion* of Richard of Bury, tutor to Edward III of England, seemed to be as intense as any to be evinced in Renaissance Florence, but in reality it was altogether different in character. Medieval interest was confined to those classical authorities whose practical knowledge superseded their own and the universities readily absorbed the bulk of Ptolemaic astronomy, Galenic medicine, Roman law and above all the physics and the logical method of Aristotle whom they honoured as the Great Doctor.

It was an entirely practical operation confined to the assimilation of useful information which might be absorbed without damaging the existing intellectual framework based on Christian philosophy. The premise was a sound one; the Christian faith was treasured as a means to salvation and as the only guarantor of order in medieval society. To abandon it or put it into jeopardy would have seemed suicidal, and the scholars, all of whom were churchmen, selected from the legacy of a pagan world only those things which might serve their practical needs without contaminating their culture. Consequently, it was permissible and useful to study the science of the ancients but not to be influenced by their poetry or philosophy, to read the natural history of Pliny but to eschew the poetry of Ovid. Indeed as one authority declaimed 'Indecenter enim eadem ore Christus praedicatur et Ovidius recitatur', (It is unseemly for the same mouth to preach Christ and recite Ovid) – which was perhaps a sensible rule if only to preserve the peace of mind of celibate scholars from the sensual and pagan world of the *Ars Amatoria*.

What distinguished the fifteenth-century Italians from their European contemporaries therefore was not their discovery of antiquity, but their enthusiasm for the entire body of classical literature and for the moral, social and aesthetic standards it contained. This in turn sprang directly from their novel state of political and cultural independence, since they now lived in a society which no longer shared the social values of a world dominated by feudal and ecclesiastical standards. They were perplexed to find that the heroes of their own environment – the merchants who made their fortunes in trade, served with distinction on municipal councils and achieved the highest civic honours – were disregarded in the literature of western Europe which acclaimed instead the ideals of saintly piety or knightly courage. The merchant, if he were mentioned, was written off as a shameless rogue or consigned to damnation as a usurer and a cheat.

Consequently, the Italian citizen came to adopt a scale of values which the medieval world as yet refused to acknowledge. Repudiating the feudal and ecclesiastical culture of contemporary Europe, he turned instead to the city state of antiquity, not because its ruins still stood around him, but because, like Coluccio Salutati, he found a relevant parallel in the history of republican Rome to the successful resistance of Florence against the Visconti, and because in the writings of Cicero he found a mirror in which he might discern his own reflection. Palmieri accordingly took his cue from Cicero – 'He who passes his life in solitude and is neither experienced nor skilled in important matters in public offices and in the business of the community will never become just and courageous' – and the very title of his book, *Della Vita Civile*, represented a proud and defiant assertion of the values of an autonomous urban society.

The prospect of this rediscovered world in which the leading citizens were awarded the highest honours for the pursuit of civic virtues intoxicated the imagination of the Italian merchants and bankers who found themselves much closer in spirit to the Roman *equites* than to their contemporaries in Europe, but the process did not stop there. As readers of Cicero's *Ad Atticum* they soon came to realise the debt the Romans owed to Greece, and in their enthusiasm resolved to rediscover this legacy for themselves. So great was this enthusiasm that the practical reasons which had initially prompted so great an interest in classical antiquity were soon forgotten as the Italians became absorbed in the past for its own sake. No longer concerned to find historical parallels with the present, nor even to seek their own identity in the world of republican Rome, they began to imagine that the classical world was one superior in all respects to their own. No single incident reveals this better than Burkhardt's famous story of Julia's tomb.

A report arose, that on April 18, 1485, the corpse of a young Roman lady of the classical period – wonderfully beautiful and in perfect preservation – had been discovered. Some Lombard masons digging out an ancient tomb on an estate of the convent of Santa Maria Nuova, on the Appian Way, beyond the tomb of Caecilia Metella, were said to have found a marble sarcophagus with the inscription, 'Julia, daughter of Claudius'. On this basis the following story was built. The Lombards disappeared with the jewels and treasure which were found with the corpse in the sarcophagus. The body had been coated with an antiseptic essence, and was as fresh and flexible as that of a girl of fifteen the hour after death. It was said that she still kept the colours of life, with eyes and mouth half open. She was taken to the palace of the 'Conservatori' on the Capitol; and then a pilgrimage to see her began. Among the crowd were many who came to paint her; 'for she was more beautiful than can be said or written, and, were it said or written, it would not be believed by those who had not seen her'. The touching point in the story is not the fact itself, but the firm belief that an ancient body, which was now thought to be at last really before men's eyes, must of necessity be far more beautiful than anything of modern date.

(Burkhardt, *The Civilisation of the Renaissance in Italy*)

Despite the intensity of their feeling for the past glory of Greece and Rome, and their almost desperate desire to identify themselves with its culture, the Italian merchants were scarcely equipped to venture into so specialised a field of study without substantial aid. This was provided by a new type of classical scholar, the humanist, whose role it was to make available the corpus of classical literature in a form intelligible to his patrons. The first task of the humanist was to recover the classical manuscripts which the medieval scholars had overlooked or ignored as irrelevant to their purpose. These they pursued with the single-mindedness of treasure seekers and their patrons went to great lengths to finance them. Vespasiano da Bisticci, a bookseller and biographer, recorded the sacrifices of one Nicolao Nicoli, who sold his farms in order to build up his collection of books and whose discovery of Cicero's *De Oratore* was typical of many other finds. 'The book', wrote Vespasiano 'was found in a chest in a very old church; this chest had not been opened for a long time and they found the book, a very ancient example, while searching for evidence containing certain ancient rights'.

In addition to collecting manuscripts the humanists made copies of them for other patrons, edited them and developed techniques of textual criticism in order to establish their authenticity. Private collections began to expand at a remarkable rate alongside the more famous libraries of Venice, Florence and the Vatican, and by and large the process of recovering the texts of ancient Rome was complete by the mid-fifteenth century. The introduction from Germany of the printing press after 1460 was therefore more important for Greek than for Latin studies, since there were few Greek manuscripts in circulation and even fewer scholars capable of editing and copying them. The first Greek scholars in Italy were in fact imported from Greece and Byzantium. In 1438 a council had met at Ferrara to discuss relations between the Latin and the Greek churches and several delegates including the Cardinal Bessarion were persuaded to remain behind. Their pupils in turn went to Byzantium to complete their studies and collected manuscripts in great number until the city fell to the Osmanli Turks in 1453. The next task was to establish the apparatus of Greek scholarship, the first Lexicon appearing in 1478, and the first Grammar in 1497. Without the printing press, however, knowledge of Greek literature would have been confined to a small coterie, but through the Aldine Press of Aldo Manuzio in Venice it was made available for all Italians by the early sixteenth century.

The *Studia Humanitatis* from which the humanists derived their name – a name still preserved in the university chairs of humanities and especially in the Oxford *Schola Literae Humaniores* – represented a comprehensive discipline which included grammar, rhetoric, history, poetry and moral philosophy, based upon the study of the relevant classical texts. The humanists themselves differed as widely in the quality of their classical scholarship as in the interests which absorbed them. Some were nothing more than blinkered pedants, preoccupied with the linguistic minutiae of the text and apparently oblivious to its content. Others were so obsessed by the content that they could bring nothing of their own to their studies which consequently became derivative, parasitic and ultimately sterile. A third group conceived so great an admiration for the literary style of Cicero that they refused to acknowledge the worth of any other style but his, nor of any other language but the Latin of his day. Such men condemned Petrarch for writing his sonnets in Italian, and if they had had their way they might have strangled in its infancy the vigorous vernacular to which Dante and Bocaccio had given literary form. Fortunately the Ciceronians were unable to combat the civic patriotism of those who took pride in the development of their own language, and the works of Leonardo Bruni, Alberti and Palmieri paved the way for the brilliant achievements of Lorenzo de Medici, Guicciardini and Machiavelli who made Italian as important a language as Latin for the expression, respectively, of lyric poetry, history and political thought.

Some humanists were especially employed in public life because of their skill in rhetoric, a literary form much valued in classical times as a means of training for political life. Many were therefore employed as secretaries to the princes and city states, drawing up their public documents in flawless Latin and writing speeches in which the policies of the day were given a noble ancestry by skilful allusions to classical antiquity. Florentine resistance to the Visconti dukes was strengthened by the propaganda of the city's humanists who drew upon the struggles of republican Rome to find encouragement for their fellow citizens. 'Other peoples', declared Leonardo Bruni, 'were founded by fugitives or exiles or peasants or obscure strangers. But your founder is the Roman people, conqueror and lord of all the world . . . and so by right of inheritance the lordship of the whole world belongs to you too, Florentines. And it follows that all the wars waged by the Florentine people are just wars.' The logic was doubtful but as propaganda the oration was singularly effective.

Among the varied categories of humanists there was a small group of exceptional genius who could study the past with interest and affection without forgetting the needs of their own age, and whose concern was not limited to finding classical precedents for their own situation. Such men were humanists in the sense that the twentieth century understands the word. Men of profound scholarship, they admired the arts, delighted in poetry and tested their intellects against the philosophers of the past. Above all they affirmed the dignity of man and believed in the power of education to enhance that dignity. Outstanding among them were three great figures of the Italian Renaissance: Politian, Ficino and Pico della Mirandola.

Angelo Poliziano (Politian) lived from 1454 – 94 at the centre of the Florentine Renaissance. At the age of 16 he had translated the first four books of the *Iliad* into Latin and ten years later was appointed Professor of Greek and Roman Literature at Florence. As a classical scholar his speciality lay in philology, a specialist field in which he nonetheless aroused great interest by the fluency of his own writing, in particular through his *Miscellanies*. He could successfully compete with the Ciceronians in the composition of Latin prose and verse, but he condemned them for subordinating their personalities to the principle of imitation and he joined with Lorenzo de Medici to write lyric verse of great charm in the vernacular. His greatest contribution to Renaissance thought was made in the inner circle of scholars, among whom were Lorenzo and Marcilio Ficino, which derived its inspiration from the work of Plato. Whereas Aristotle was identified, unfairly, with the arid scholasticism of the medieval university (see page 80), Plato by contrast was held to combine the virtues of stylistic elegance with a mystical insight into the nature of beauty, truth and God. He taught that what we see is merely an imperfect reproduction of invisible models (universal forms) which exist eternally in the mind of God; that there is no truth or beauty as such in the world but only a pale reflection of the supreme beauty and the supreme truth which are in God. The dignity of man according to Politian lay in his ability to understand these universal forms through the power of reason, though he emphasised that the vision of truth could only be imperfectly realised. The final consummation was achieved after death when the soul, released from the material prison-house of the body and of the world, fled to its spiritual liberation in the presence of God.

This potent mysticism which had formerly inspired the early Fathers of the Church was given special emphasis in Florence not only by Politian but also by Marcilio Ficino (1433 – 99). His Latin translation, *Corpus Platonicum*, was one of the greatest achievements of Renaissance scholarship. But of equal importance was his concern to establish Italian humanism securely within a Christian philosophy by such profound works as his *Theologia*

Platonica and *De Religione Christiana*. From the *Symposium* of Plato he derived the belief that love is a desire for beauty and that all beauty is but a reflection of the beauty of God, who is thereby the object of all human love. So important was Ficino's teaching that Cosimo de Medici gave him a villa near Careggi where Politian and the young Lorenzo joined him to elaborate his thesis.

Another prominent member of this Platonic Academy was Giovanni Pico, count of Mirandola (1463–94). As a philologist and editor of classical texts he displayed an astonishing range of erudition but, like the others, it was merely the groundwork on which to base his own philosophy. His great oration on *The Dignity of Man* embodied his view that man was rather more than a link between the material and spiritual worlds: indeed he was master of his fate. In a remarkable blend of Platonic philosophy and Old Testament imagery, he invented a creation myth of his own whereby God addresses his creature Adam:

The nature of all other beings is limited and constrained within the bounds of laws prescribed by Us. Thou, constrained by no limits, in accordance with thy own free will, in whose hand We have placed thee, shalt ordain for thyself the limits of thy nature . . . thou shalt have the power to degenerate into the lower forms of life, which are brutish. Thou shalt have the power, out of thy soul's judgement, to be reborn into the higher forms which are divine.

For some Italians Pico's writings smacked of heresy, indeed of paganism, and Savonarola roundly attacked the humanists collectively for perverting Christian thought. 'Go to Rome and all over Christendom; in the houses of great prelates and great scholars they think only of poetry and the art of rhetoric. Go and see though; you will find them with humanists' books in their hands, trying to find out about the cure of souls from Virgil and Horace and Cicero.' In fact the Renaissance humanists did less damage to the church than the Renaissance popes whose preoccupation with secular affairs blinded them to their spiritual responsibilities; very few humanists were intellectually hostile to religion and the Neo-Platonist school did much to rescue Christian thought from the dead hand of medieval scholasticism. Nonetheless, the revival of a belief in the dignity of man conflicted forcibly with medieval preoccupations with the fall of man and his subsequent expulsion from paradise. The optimistic self-confidence of the Renaissance sprang in part from a profound and self-conscious awareness of being different, not only from contemporary Europe but also from the Europe of the past thousand years. Although the Middle Ages as a chronological term was not invented until after 1600, the Italians of the fifteenth century were convinced that they had emerged from a period of cultural impoverishment. The artists and poets assumed that aesthetic standards had deteriorated since the fall of Rome and Lorenzo Valla, one of the humanists, affirmed that 'not only has no one spoken Latin correctly for many centuries but no one has even understood it properly when reading it'. Italians in general began to believe that the civilisation of the ancients had been ignored and that its revival was the work of their own day. 'This is the age of gold' declared Marcilio Ficino,' which has brought back to life the almost extinguished liberal disciplines of poetry, eloquence, painting, architecture, sculpture, music and singing to the Orphic lyre.'

These attitudes were directly stimulated by the urban environment of the Italian Renaissance. Participation in commercial and civic life not only put a premium on involvement in this world – as opposed to the medieval idea of withdrawal into an ascetic life of penance and self-denial – but also encouraged men to believe that by their own efforts they could achieve success in whatever they set out to do. Political and commercial setbacks or the onslaught of the plague might temporarily destroy this mood of confidence, and the religious hysteria aroused by Savonarola or the guilt-ridden fears revealed in the letters of the Merchant of Prato, Francesco Datini, (see Iris Origo, the *Merchant of Prato*) were by no means untypical. Nonetheless the rules of compound interest inspired the belief that wealth had no limits, and there was increasing evidence to substantiate the view of Pius II that 'in our change-loving Italy where nothing stands firm and where no ancient dynasty exists, a servant can easily become a king'. The result of so many success stories was to destroy the barriers to ambition and the voyages of discovery coincided with and confirmed this new spirit in society.

One of the first Italians to demonstrate a degree of self-confidence which medieval man would have regarded as both blasphemous and overweening was Leon Battista Alberti who proclaimed that

'Man can do all things if he will' – and himself very nearly did so. He excelled as an artist and architect (see page 54), was proficient in many other disciplines and a contemporary, perhaps autobiographical, account revealed that 'he was able to handle with skill weapons, horses and musical instruments; and he was also an enthusiastic student of arts and letters and of particularly unusual and difficult things. By study and meditation he made himself master of everything for which he might be praised.' Through Alberti the Renaissance discovered the ideal of *l'uomo universale*, the many-sided man, not perfect in one thing but in all.

The most famous exposition of this theme was by Baldassare Castiglione, a Mantuan of noble birth who had served in many courts before settling at Urbino in the cultivated society of the Montefeltre. It was in this setting that he placed his book *Il Cortegiano*, a symposium on the virtues of the ideal courtier. Athletic and military qualities were taken for granted and the courtier was required to be well-mannered and well-read – the latter by Renaissance standards of course: 'I would have him more than passably learned in letters, at least in those studies which we call humanities. Let him be conversant not only with the Latin language but with the Greek as well, because of the abundance and variety of things that are so divinely written therein. Let him be versed in the poets as well as in the orators and historians . . . ' This paragon of scholarship and warfare was also to be expert in political wisdom to inform his prince's council chamber, and in music, dancing and painting to delight his court. Above all he was to possess the nonchalance and grace to carry the day in everything without revealing the effort. So talented that no prince could ever have been worthy of his service, the courtier enshrined the Renaissance image of *l'uomo universale*, and the ideal entranced not only Italy but the rest of Europe since the book became the most widely-read study of manners and behaviour in the sixteenth century.

Patrons and Patronage in Renaissance Italy

Lorenzo Valla when comparing the splendour of his own day with the barbarism of the recent past confessed that he did not know: 'why those arts which most closely approached the liberal ones – painting, sculpture, modelling, architecture – have been so long and so greatly in decline, and have almost (together with literature) died out altogether; nor why they have revived in this age and so many good artists and writers appeared and flourished'. The principal reason for the revival was because the towns provided an entirely new source of patrons for the arts. Commissions in the past had been made by corporate bodies, above all by the church, and this practice continued throughout the Renaissance, but to this patronage was added that of individual bankers, merchant princes and *condottiere* captains.

At first the individual patrons were reluctant to advertise their benefactions too publicly. Cosimo de Medici in 1419 preferred to act in concert with others, doing his social duty as a prominent citizen by embellishing his city with a careful eye to the political gains to be derived from patronage of every kind, but equally careful not to make enemies by overdoing it. Others with guilty fears about the consequences of a lifetime spent in making money gave generously to commission altar pieces, private chapels and even churches in the hope of saving their immortal souls. But gradually the desire to win social esteem and to achieve a kind of immortality by becoming identified with the creation of a work of art began to be more freely recognised. Cosimo himself admitted it; 'I know my fellow citizens. In fifty years' time they will only remember me by the few poor buildings I leave them.' Another Florentine, Giovanni Rucellai, built several palaces and churches because, 'they do honour to God, to Florence and to my own memory' – and he emphasised the final motive by having his name emblazoned across the architrave of his Church of Santa Maria Novella.

For similar reasons the daily life of the despot Borso d'Este was commemorated in a series of frescos at Ferrara and the Gonzaga dynasty of Mantua was given immortality by the artist Mantegna. The men who provided patronage in this way had wasted little time in gaining wealth or power and they were not prepared to wait indefinitely for posterity to accord them the social honour they desired so intensely. Sometimes too they sought respectability and fame in this way in order to cover up their tracks and distract attention from their lowly origins. As a result the artists and sculptors who had formerly served the church or a feudal prince were offered employment on a much larger scale within the Italian cities.

In the fifteenth century a work of art was regarded as the creation of the donor rather than of the artist himself. Vespasiano who described the buildings commissioned by Cosimo, referred to them as Cosimo's buildings without reference to the architects, and artists generally were employed as tradesmen to carry out the precise instructions of their patron. Although the urban environment provided a rich field of employment for the artists, their freedom of action, their creative role was extremely limited by modern standards. When Perugino, for example, was commissioned to d‹ an allegory of the *Battle of Love and Chastity* for Isabella d'Este, the painting was programmed in great detail and with astonishing erudition by her humanist adviser Paride da Ceresara. Perugino himself was bound by contract to observe every detail of his instructions and was forbidden to introduce anything of his own invention. Similarly, when Cosimo's son Piero commissioned Matteo de'Pasti in 1441 to illustrate a series of triumphs derived from Petrarch's verses he received the following letter from the artist:

Now please send me the instructions for the other triumph so that I can go ahead . . . I have got the instructions for the triumph of fame but I do not know if you want the sitting woman in a simple dress or in a cloak as I would like her to be. The rest I know; there are to be four elephants pulling her chariot, but please tell me if you want only young men and ladies in her train or also famous old men.

If de'Pasti's letter smacked of a grocer's list, it accurately reflected his status in contemporary society as a tradesman. Cosimo de Medici is supposed to have said that artists were men of genius, not to be treated as packhorses, but until the end of the fifteenth century the liberal arts were confined to literature while sculpture and painting were regarded as mechanical skills. With rare exceptions artists were recruited from the lower middle classes and served their apprenticeship like any weaver or carpenter in the workshop or *bottega* of a master painter from whom they learnt the whole business of picture making. Their training was technical and practical rather than aesthetic or theoretical and was confined to grinding colours, preparing canvases or wall surfaces, sketching in the outlines and occasionally painting portions of the masters' pictures. The only indication of any social status was the superiority of painters, who belonged to the guild

of apothecaries, over the sculptors, who were ranked with brick-
layers and stonemasons.

The first to challenge this traditional view was appropriately
perhaps Leon Battista Alberti, *l'uomo universale*. As a painter
and architect he was affronted by the exclusion of his skills from
the liberal arts, but as an established man of letters he was well
placed to champion his cause in influential circles and his *Trattato
della Pittura* demonstrated that painters required a special
understanding of history and mathematics which differentiated
them from mere craftsmen. Considerable though his influence was,
Alberti failed to alter public opinion significantly and the case
had to be re-stated with even greater vigour at the start of the
sixteenth century by Leonardo da Vinci who demanded that
painting should rank as the equal of poetry. 'If you call it
mechanical because it is by manual work, that the hands represent
what the imagination creates, your writers are setting down with
the pen by manual work what originates in the mind.' In the
struggle for recognition of painters Leonardo was prepared to
sell short the sculptors since 'Sculpture shows with little labour
what in painting appears a miraculous thing to do.' Yet it was the
sculptor Michelangelo in combination with Lorenzo de Medici
who did more than anyone to win respect for the dignity of the
artist.

Lorenzo was the first patron to advance beyond the role of
customer by demonstrating a concern for the artist himself.
In his gardens at San Marco he created an informal academy in
which discussion about the nature of beauty supplemented the
development of practical skills and where men of letters met
artists on equal terms. Michelangelo, who spent a brief period at
San Marco, was ultimately to establish himself as an artist of
such unique genius that he could claim the right to express this
genius on his own terms not on his patrons'. He walked out on
Pope Julius II, for example, when displeased by his comments,
and the Warrior Pope was compelled to approach the city of
Florence to intervene with Michelangelo on his behalf.

By the end of the Italian Renaissance the artists had won
their battle for recognition as the peers of scholars and poets,
and the shift in opinion is reflected by an incident from Benvenuto
Cellini's *Autobiography*. A competent sculptor and a brilliant
silversmith, Cellini was also a superb raconteur and if he took

liberties with the truth his story nonetheless revealed his own exalted views of the status of the artist. In 1545 he finished a statue of Perseus for Duke Cosimo of Florence and stormed out of the duke's presence when his demand for 10,000 crowns was questioned by his patron:

The following day, when I came to the court to pay my respects, his Excellency beckoned to me and when I approached said angrily, 'Cities and great palaces are built with tens of thousands of ducats.' I immediately replied that his Excellency would find any number of men who knew how to build cities and palaces, but as for making statues like my Perseus, I doubted whether he would find a single one in the whole world.

Renaissance Art in Italy

The most significant group of early fifteenth-century artists and architects was to be found in Florence and included four men of outstanding ability; Filippo Brunelleschi (1377–1446), Tomaso di Giovanni, known as Masaccio (1401–28), Donato di Niccolo de Bardi, known as Donatello (1386–1466) and Leon Battista Alberti. The first of these was trained as a goldsmith, worked as a sculptor but established his true claim to fame as an architect. In 1419 he created a colonnade of delicate semi-circular arches along the ground floor of the Foundling Hospital in Florence; each arch was balanced on the floor above by a small rectangular window under a shallow pediment, and the long, low line of the building was set off by a flight of steps across the entire façade (see plate 1).

The motifs were clearly derived from classical Rome. The humanists had recovered Vitruvius's treatise on Roman architecture which provided Renaissance architects with an abundant repertory of classical forms and designs, and Brunelleschi had visited Rome to measure the dimensions of the many ruins which still survived in the fifteenth century. He was influenced moreover by the Tuscan Romanesque vaulting of the eleventh century, which he mistakenly assumed to be a direct survival of Roman style. What was remarkable however was not the derivation of the forms, although this in itself indicated a rejection of Gothic architecture, but Brunelleschi's original treatment of them. The arches of the colonnade, for example, apart from their delicate, almost insubstantial lines, are so devised that the height of the columns is used as a yardstick to determine their distance from each other and from the wall. The total effect of the building is to establish a mood of balance, order and serenity which acknowledges its classical inspiration without being slavishly imitative.

Brunelleschi's brilliance in imparting a sense of ordered coherence to his buildings was also demonstrated in his designs for several Florentine churches. At San Lorenzo for example he established an entirely novel pattern of mathematical relationships between the sections of the church. The area of the nave is four times the square at the crossing, the transepts themselves and the choir repeat the dimensions of the central square, while the aisles and side chapels are one-quarter of its area. Similarly, at Santo Spirito the proportions were extended upwards to determine height as well as area. The height of the nave is twice its breadth, the ground floor and the clerestory are of equal height and the aisles have square bays, each one half as wide as it is high. The precise relationships may escape the observer but the emotional impact is immediate. Unlike the Gothic builders, who tried to impress man with his insignificant status and lead him in humility towards the altar, Brunelleschi established a calmer, more rational mood of dignity and stability. Within his logical compositions, man himself becomes the measure of his surroundings.

Excited as he was by mathematical relationships, Brunelleschi applied this interest to painting, where he discovered the formula by which to determine how objects appear to diminish in size as they recede into the background. His studies in perspective were of vital importance in the development of Renaissance art. A century before him Giotto in the Arena Chapel at Padua had taken the first steps in painting from symbolism back to naturalism. In so doing he had retained the iconographical conventions of his day, but had altered the traditional techniques of presentation in order to give more life to the incidents he portrayed by revealing them in the round – 'Wherefore', as Boccaccio commented, 'the human sense of sight was often deceived by his works and took for real what was only painted'. Giotto's work, however, had been wholly intuitive and though many had tried to follow his example none could do so with success until Brunelleschi had formulated for them the rules of perspective.

The first great artist to exploit these rules was Masaccio. Tragically he died in his twenty-eighth year but in his brief lifetime he made tremendous advances on the work of Giotto. His study *The Holy Trinity, the Virgin, St John and Donors* in the Church of Santa Maria Novella was not only constructed according to Brunelleschi's formula but also owed much to his influence as an architect, since the figures are arranged as though in a chapel whose style resembles those designed by Brunelleschi. In all his work Masaccio achieved an effect of simplicity and grandeur. The figures of his rendering of *The Tribute Money* (see plate 2) are so solidly alive, their poses so natural and their gesture so dramatic that the sixteenth-century artist Vasari could say of his work 'The things made before his time may be termed merely paintings; by comparison his creatures are real, living and natural.' Moreover, like one of Brunelleschi's churches the whole picture is so carefully composed that any modification of it would destroy its logical coherence.

The sculptor Donatello had accompanied Brunelleschi on his visit to Rome and his studies of antique bronzes and statues were reflected in his subsequent work. He was also influenced by the new formula for determining perspective and demonstrated, both in a marble relief of *St George and the Dragon* and a gilt bronze relief of *The Feast of Herod* that, like Masaccio, he could create naturalistic figures in a dramatic scene. Donatello's reputation, however, was established by his free-standing statues whose realism and vigour astounded his contemporaries. *St George* stands firmly in his niche on the wall of Orsanmichele in Florence, exuding a calm defiance to all comers; the *Condottiere Gattemalata* in Padua conveys all the ruthless determination of the mercenary and established a new genre of equestrian statues; most moving of all, the bronze of David as a young stripling, relaxed in his moment of triumph, revived for the first time since antiquity the use of the nude figure in sculpture (see plate 4).

The achievements of these three Florentines was commemorated and analysed by Alberti who dedicated to them his *Tratatto della Pittura*. In this he affirmed the value of Brunelleschi's discovery of perspective in the creation of a more naturalistic composition; he shared with Donatello the joy of the ancients in the beauty of the body and encouraged the study of anatomy; he stressed the importance of arranging figures in dramatic groups and tried to rationalise the special nature of Masaccio's success in constructing his pictures by concluding that beauty was a matter of proportion – 'The harmony and concord of all the parts achieved in such a way that nothing could be added or taken away or altered except for the worse'. Alberti himself was no mere theorist but an excellent architect who delighted in the application of classical forms. For Sigismondo Malatesta of Rimini he designed a church of which the façade was daringly derived from a Roman triumphal arch, embellished with Corinthian columns, pilaster strips, semi-circular arches, round medallions and a triangular pediment. Since he failed to complete it no proper judgement may be made but the total effect of the medley of antique forms is distracting. Later, however, he used the same device of a triumphal arch with great success and sophistication in the impressive west front of San Andrea at Mantua.

It was in the field of domestic architecture that Alberti's power of invention was most successful since there were no surviving Roman houses on which to model the town house he designed for Giovanni Rucellai of Florence (see plate 3). Alberti's decision to apply a scheme of pilasters and rounded windows to an ordinary three-storey building, designed as a cube, was to influence secular architecture in Europe for many generations. The relation of the parts to the whole, the articulation of the three storeys, the use of the three classical orders, Doric, Ionic and Corinthian, the lines of pilasters which separate yet link together the windows, and the crowning cornice all combine to create not only a satisfying pattern but also a sensation of ordered stability and harmony in keeping with Alberti's own definition of beauty.

The problems of form and composition and the relationship between beauty and mathematical proportion were the special interest of Piero della Francesca (1416–97) who worked principally in Umbria but who also spent four years in Florence under the influence of Masaccio and Alberti. 'Painting', he wrote, 'is nothing else but a demonstration of planes and solids, made smaller or greater according to the distance at which they are seen.' A cold definition perhaps, but it reflected his own concentration on the study of regular solids and perspective which led him to produce books on both these subjects and finally to abandon painting altogether to devote his time to mathematics. His pictures, as one would expect, are logically constructed, the perspective impeccable and the figures solid and well-proportioned. But though there was deliberate dramatic contrivance in the composition, there is little to appeal immediately to the emotions. Even the use of colour is usually restrained so that nothing sensuous may distract attention from the emphasis on form. Nonetheless, there is an emotional intensity about his work which, with his feeling for pure form, explains why, of all the early Renaissance painters, Francesca is the most admired of today.

Sandro Botticelli (1444 – 1510), whose paintings are full of flowing lines and graceful rhythms, seems almost out of place among the artists who were preoccupied with anatomy, perspective and form. In *The Birth of Venus*, for example, he was so determined to establish the impression of an infinitely tender and delicate being that he turned his back on the solid observation of Piero and Masaccio and gave his goddess an unnaturally long neck, but so entrancing is the flowing line that the distortion is lost on the observer. Since his work appeared to have much in common with the late Gothic tradition in northern Europe, and as Botticelli himself fell later under the spell of the puritan Savonarola, it would be tempting to regard him as a medieval figure in a Renaissance environment. Yet he trained in the *bottega* of a Florentine artist and his most famous paintings, *Primavera* and *The Birth of Venus* (see plate 5), were done for the Medici. Languorous and charming as they are they nonetheless embody a wealth of Neoplatonic allegory and mysticism which owes far more to Marsilio Ficino than to medieval legend, and their execution identifies Botticelli firmly as a Renaissance artist. In later life, however, he lost the self-confident optimism of the days of the Neoplatonic Academy and concentrated instead on religious studies which have an emotional intensity more in keeping with the art of Germany and the Netherlands.

Meanwhile, at Padua and subsequently at Mantua, Andrea Mantegna (1431 – 1501) had established himself as the most direct successor to Masaccio. His figures are in the heroic mood, impressive in their naturalism, statuesque in their poses. In all Mantegna's work the scene is composed as though for a stage setting, and as a true Renaissance artist he made a careful study of ancient armour and architecture in order to give greater realism to his scenes from biblical and Roman history – not least for his Paduan frescos of the *Legend of St James*. During his time in

Padua he married the sister of Giovanni Bellini (1430–1516) and greatly influenced his work by teaching him the techniques of perspective and dramatic realism which informed the composition of his own pictures. Later, however, Bellini moved to Venice where his style became less majestic and austere and where, in the luminous light of the Adriatic, he discovered the fascination of colour. Unlike Mantegna and the Florentines who emphasised the importance of *disegno*, the drawing of the line, to which the addition of colour was subordinate, Bellini learnt to use colour itself as the primary means of establishing the form of an object. In his later work there is greater warmth than any yet displayed in Italy. A golden light informs the canvases and, underlying all, a hint of the poetic imagination, the lyricism, which, with its devotion to colour, was to characterise the Venetian School of Giorgione and Titian (see page 400).

Towards the end of the fifteenth century Italian art seemed to have reached a high plateau of achievement on which scores, indeed hundreds, of artists demonstrated a degree of competence which in any other age would have marked them out for the admiration of contemporaries and the attention of historians. The problems which had plagued the followers of Giotto had been solved, sophisticated techniques of space composition were the property of every *bottega* and with Piero della Francesca, Mantegna and Bellini the story could well have reached its conclusion, to be renewed in different circumstances in, say, France or the Netherlands. Instead, the fresh originality of Italian art was given a new and even greater lease of life by the unheralded appearance of three men of extraordinary genius – Leonardo da Vinci (1452–1519), Michelangelo Buonarotti (1475–1564) and Raphael Santi (1483–1520) – whose work may be regarded as the high summer of the Italian Renaissance.

Leonardo was a genius of great complexity. His notebooks reveal him as an expert in geology, botany and anatomy, hydraulics and even aeronautics; and in his letter of self-recommendation to Lodovico Sforza it was only after the recital of his abilities as an architect and engineer, as a designer of fortifications and an inventor of new weapons, that he finally referred to his skill in painting. With so many gifts he has been acclaimed as the epitome of *l'uomo universale*, but there was a uniqueness about him which made him independent of his age and he shared little of the urban, classically-inspired humanism of such a man as Alberti. Inspired by both a scientific curiosity and a mystical romanticism he was driven to experiment unceasingly in order to fulfil the host of creative ideas which teemed in his imagination. He did, however, develop Alberti's views on the superior status of the artist over the craftsman (see page 51). When he painted the fresco of *The Last Supper* in Milan, the Prior of San Marco complained that he would spend a whole day before his work without once reaching for his brush. In part this may have been a deliberate demonstration of the artist's refusal to work to the same schedule as an interior decorator, but even more it reflected the Renaissance desire to achieve perfection. In Leonardo's case the intellectual energy which prompted him to fill his notebooks with so many alternative solutions to the problem in hand, created such a tension between the conception and the execution of the work that, rather than compromise the image of perfection in his mind's eye, he left the work too often unfinished.

Leonardo learned the crafts of making colours and casting metals in the *bottega* of Verrochio, one of the more important Florentine artists of the late fifteenth century, but his manner of painting was intuitive and idiosyncratic and altogether superior to his masters. The figure of the second angel in Verrochio's *Baptism of Christ* is clearly by his hand, and stands out so sharply against the competent mediocrity of the rest of the painting that the legend of Verrochio's jealous expulsion of him from the *bottega* may well be true. He found no difficulty in securing independent commissions and by 1483 was working in Milan for Lodovico Sforza. In the *Virgin of the Rocks* he developed a technique of composition begun in an unfinished *Adoration of the Kings* by which the central group is given prominence by arranging it in the form of a pyramid. In the *Adoration* the other worshippers are thrust into the background; in the *Virgin of the Rocks* (see plate 7) there are no other figures and the pyramidal group is set within a deliberately evocative romantic landscape. In Milan too, Leonardo painted his *Last Supper* but returned to Florence after the French invasion of 1499 and the removal of his patron. By now the chief features of his style had been evolved and revealed him to be not only novel but also different in character from his contemporaries. He shunned the clarity of line, 'the enamelled daylight of the Quattrocento' (Lord Clark) and introduced a note of mystery into his work by softening the sharp outlines, blurring them as he put it, so that light and shade should blend, 'without lines or borders in the manner of smoke'.

In addition to inventing this *sfumato* quality Leonardo made great play with light and shade – *chiaroscuro* – and achieved a wholly idiosyncratic effect by which light rarely falls directly on the face or hands of his principal figures but rather in some miraculous way seems to glow from them. Finally in the Mona Lisa, which not only demonstrates the pyramidal principle of construction and the mysterious effect of *sfumato* and *chiaroscuro* to perfection, he invented the technique of what he called aerial perspective in painting in the blue mountains of the background. This was a discovery as important as Brunelleschi's.

You know that in an atmosphere of uniform density the most distant things seen through it, such as the mountains, in consequence of the great quantity of atmosphere which is between your eye and them, will appear blue, almost of the same colour as the atmosphere when the sun is in the east. Therefore you should paint the nearest building in its natural colour, and that which is more distant make less defined and bluer; and one which you wish should seem as far away again make of double the depth of blue, and one you desire should seem five times as far away make five times as blue.

Michelangelo Buonarotti considered himself to be a sculptor first and foremost, although his genius also found expression in poetry, architecture and painting. In the event no medium proved adequate enough to express the frightening intensity of his feelings, that *terribilità* which contemporaries both admired and feared and which revealed him to be a man apart from the confident humanism of the high Renaissance. Ultimately he passed through a spiritual crisis of disturbing gloom to become a man of deep religious faith, and it is symbolic that his career, begun in Florence in the circle of Lorenzo de Medici, should have ended in Rome at the height of the Counter-reformation (see page 391).

The story of his life to 1520 can only indicate the first stages of his development. His initial success as a sculptor in Medician Florence was influenced by the current taste for nude studies in the classical style and by Bertoldo di Giovanni, curator of the Medician collection of sculptures, who taught him the technique of *contrapposto* by which the hips remain frontal while the upper torso twists to one side to convey a sense of vigour and intensity of effort. In his *Battle of the Centaurs* Michelangelo demonstrated his skill in handling a tightly-knit mass of struggling nude figures, his *Pietà* found a perfect solution to the technical problem of placing a fully-grown man's body across a woman's lap, and the triumphal pose of his *David* represented the ideal to which all fifteenth-century sculptors had been working. The fall of the Medici and the rise of Savanarola unsettled him in Florence and in 1502 he was invited to Rome by Julius II. The Warrior Pope in a mood of self-aggrandisement commissioned him to devise a tomb whose splendour would perpetuate his fame for ever, and Michelangelo, fascinated by the challenge of the task, went out to Carrara to select the giant blocks of marble which he needed. There he stayed for over six months, gazing intently at the rough slabs, his mind full of the images which he felt were lying latent within them, awaiting realisation by his hands. As he expressed it in one of his sonnets, 'The best artist has not one idea that a piece of marble, still unworked, does not contain within itself; and that potential form is realised only by the hand that obeys the judgement.'

Michelangelo returned at length to Rome to find that Julius II was excited by a different task altogether, the construction of a new St Peter's in which his tomb might be enshrined. In high dudgeon at this change of plan, and suspecting unfairly that it had been engineered by jealous rivals in order to reduce his influence with the pope, he left for Florence. Julius immediately pursued him with a commission to paint the ceiling of the Sistine Chapel in the Vatican. Michelangelo protested angrily that he was a sculptor, not a painter, but the magnitude of the task so impressed him that he finally agreed to undertake it provided he was allowed to do it in his own way. Although it was customary to employ philosophers and theologians to compile the programmes for commissions of this kind, Julius agreed to his terms and Michelangelo set out to illustrate the Book of Genesis, along with figures of the Old Testament prophets who had foretold the coming of the Messiah, and of Sybils who by legend had heralded His coming to the pagan world.

He planned to divide the enormous barrel vault of the Sistine Chapel into panels for each scene by painting in a series of cornices to look like genuine architectural features of the roof, with figures of nude athletes sitting at each intersection and the prophets and Sybils disposed along the edges of the vaults. It was also necessary to work out a most elaborate system of perspective so that the individual studies and scenes from the Book of Genesis should carry conviction when seen from the chapel floor. Finally when the intellectual problems had been resolved in detail there remained the physical effort of executing them on the 600 square yards of the ceiling, and from 1508 to 1512 Michelangelo worked in great discomfort, lying on his back at the top of the lofty scaffolding.

In his treatment of the characters as heroic nude figures Michelangelo revealed his sculptor's interest in the human form. He also reflected the influence of the Villa Medici where he had come to believe that man in his ideal form, naked as his creator had made him, was the only subject worthy of the artist. Indeed, in choosing to illustrate the Book of Genesis he was primarily concerned to reveal the special dignity of man as a creature of God, created in His own image. He confided his intention to Francesco de Hollanda. 'The kind of painting that I so highly celebrate and praise consists only in the imitation of any creature whatsoever that immortal God created with His great care and wisdom . . . and consequently the most noble and excellent among works of art will be that in which has been copied the most noble of beings, the one who was created with the greatest refinement and science.' As a result the greatest of all his scenes is the *Creation of Adam* in which the idealised nude hero receives the gift of life from the outstretched hand of God (see plate 6).

While Michelangelo was working on the ceiling of the Sistine Chapel Raphael was summoned to Rome to decorate the other chambers of the Vatican. With neither the intellect of Leonardo nor the emotional power of Michelangelo his genius was of the rare type which appropriates and adapts the techniques of others without a trace of plagiarism; whatever is borrowed is transmuted and the final work surpasses all that has gone before. He began in Umbria as a pupil of Il Perugino, one of the finest artists of the last decades of the fifteenth century, and moved to Florence in 1504 where he was influenced by the work accomplished by Leonardo and Michelangelo. In particular he made himself a master of the pyramidal design as the most accomplished painter of Madonnas. The perfect balance of his *Madonna del Granduca* (see plate 8), the poise, the modelling of the features and the clothes, reveal that he had found a triumphant solution in this genre to the problems with which his predecessors had wrestled.

In 1508 he was invited by Julius II to decorate a suite of rooms, the *Stanze*, designed for use as papal offices. It was Raphael's first attempt at large scale work of this kind but so well did he meet the challenge that the *Stanze* frescos represent the most consistently successful collection of High Renaissance art. The several rooms commemorated examples of divine intervention in the history of the Church, the establishment of the Church, the history of Constantine and the miracles performed by the popes. The most famous room, the *Stanza de la Segnatura* illustrated the theme of human intellect inspired by God; poetry is represented by *Parnassus*, theology by the *Disputa* – the disputation concerning the blessed sacrament – and philosophy by the *School of Athens* where Plato and Aristotle hold court. Raphael was passionately interested in historical detail, an interest indicated by his appointment as surveyor of Roman antiquities, and the iconography of his frescos revealed a profound intellectual understanding of the past. More remarkable still was the total mastery of composition he displayed in executing them. The wall surfaces presented many problems with windows and doors cutting into them at irregular intervals, but so successful is the planning of the individual scenes that it is these which appear to determine the placing of the windows and doors. A sense of harmony, order and serenity permeates each separate composition; the groups are so well balanced, the relation between the details and the whole so superbly organised, embodying the most exacting requirements of Alberti's definition of beauty, that the frescos stand for all time as the finest embodiment of Renaissance art.

For all the calmness of his own personality and the apparently effortless brilliance of his art, Raphael was in fact grossly overworked. In addition to his painting in the Vatican, he was appointed architect of St Peter's and accepted a host of private commissions which could never have been completed without a well-organised workshop of assistants and pupils. Amid the turmoil of his business he yet maintained the quality of his art, as evidenced in the *Galatea*, a brilliant study of pagan beauty, and the *Sistine Madonna*, the finest and most profoundly spiritual of all his Madonnas. In looking at such works as these it seems as though the age of endeavour has given way to one of achievement; the mood of order and serenity which informed Raphael's paintings, and the technical devices by which they were achieved represented a triumphant solution to the problems of the previous century of painting. His successors could only escape from the sterile imitation of his achievement by creating for themselves new problems to be solved. Raphael himself began to fret for some new challenge and in his final years, from 1517 to his death in 1520, he discovered one in the altarpiece of the *Transfiguration*. A harsh light illuminates dramatically the contrast between the celestial radiance into which the figure of Christ is received and the murky discord of the human throng below, whose animated movements and strident gestures strike a new note of nervous tension in Renaissance art. In this last work of Raphael it is clear that the high summer of the Italian Renaissance was at its end. (See page 391).

Northern Humanism

The French historian Michelet remarked that the discovery of Italy was of more immediate importance in the fifteenth and sixteenth centuries than the discovery of America – and since the development of an independent urban environment in Italy had had no parallel in the rest of Europe the notion of discovery is a valid one. Contacts between the two cultures had of course been maintained by the considerable traffic of merchants, diplomats and armies across the Alps, and the German invention of the printing press enabled the results of Italian scholarship to be known outside the peninsula, but so different was the environment of northern Europe from that of Italy that there was little initial enthusiasm for the products of the Italian Renaissance. An urban culture had little appeal for a society dominated by the landed nobility and monarchs who clung to the cultural forms associated with their own environment. There were several urban areas, especially in south Germany and the Netherlands, whose wealth and economic importance had grown considerably through the expansion of international trade in the fifteenth century, but they remained subordinate to the authority of a Burgundian duke, a German prince or a Habsburg emperor. Not even Antwerp or Augsburg enjoyed the autonomy of Florence or Venice and within the cities of northern Europe there was no self-confident assertion of civic pride, no repudiation of feudal and ecclesiastical standards and no self-conscious awareness of a national past rooted in the splendours of the ancient Roman Empire. Culture was dominated by the universities which were almost exclusively clerical in character, and the Schoolmen, preoccupied with the bitter conflict between the Thomists – adherents of St Thomas Aquinas – and the Nominalists, were not disposed to allocate university funds to any but the traditional disciplines.

With such formidable obstacles to the acceptance of Italian ideas, their reception in northern Europe came about almost paradoxically through the medium of royal patronage. The emergence of Italian courts in the late fifteenth century, the princely splendour of the Gonzagas in Mantua, the international importance of the Sforzas in Milan, the semi-royal style enjoyed by the Medici in Florence and the patronage exercised by the popes imparted to the Italian Renaissance the appearance of a courtly culture which made it acceptable, even desirable, in the eyes of northern rulers. Not surprisingly it was the courtly ideal of Castiglione's *Il Cortegiano* which most readily captured the imagination of the north. Moreover, as the early Italian humanists had found employment in public service as diplomats and publicists, so in northern Europe the courts began to employ secretaries with some skill in Latin and a flair for rhetoric, and both Henry VII and Louis XII commissioned Italians to write their national histories. Nonetheless, a society with its own strongly-entrenched traditions of art and learning was both cautious and critical in its reception of what Italy had to offer. Like the tropical and American plants imported by the discoverers, the products of the Italian environment were not likely to flourish freely north of the Alps. Some never took root at all; others were modified. Much interest was aroused by Italian humanism, for example, but the New Learning, as it was termed in northern Europe, developed a special character of its own. Its pagan associations were stripped away and the skills of Italian scholarship were appropriated to reinforce the religious attitudes and to further the study of the Bible.

Despite the close connections, both commercial and political, which bound Spain to Italy, the opposition of the powerful University of Salamanca was enough to confine humanist studies to a mere coterie of scholars until, in Cardinal Cisneros, (Ximenes)

(1437–1517), archbishop of Toledo and Primate of Spain, the cause of humanism found an unexpected and formidable champion. In 1508 he founded his own University at Alcala in order to challenge the exclusive Thomism of Salamanca and encouraged linguistic studies for a special purpose of his own. Greek, for example, was valued as the language not of Plato and Euripides but of the New Testament and of many of the Early Fathers; oriental languages too were studied in order to throw light on problems of biblical commentary, and Cisneros planned to produce an edition of the Bible in the languages in which it had first been written. Classical study was thus made respectable. Even the University of Salamanca grudgingly admitted Antonio de Nebrija, a famous grammarian and lexicographer who formulated rules for the pronunciation of classical Greek – but expelled him in 1512 when he presumed to employ his scholarship in editing the Vulgate. Cisneros rescued him and appointed him to the team of scholars which in 1520, three years after Cisneros' death, finally published the Complutensian Polyglot Bible.

A bitter feud between Thomists and Nominalists in the University of Paris distracted attention from the New Learning so that when Guillaume Budé (1468–1544), the first French humanist of any distinction, wished to learn Greek, the only teacher he could find was a peripatetic Greek whose incompetence had denied him employment in Italy. Budé was as wholly absorbed in classical studies as any Italian and became an expert on the monetary system of ancient Rome. This, of course, did nothing to recommend the pursuit of humanism to the University of Paris and more valuable in this respect was the example of Lefèvre d'Etaples. Moreover, Lefèvre also enjoyed the patronage of Margaret of Valois, sister of Francis I and cousin of Louis XII. In 1493 he returned from Florence with his mind full of the ideas of Politian and Pico della Mirandola, but he remained essentially a humanist theologian rather than a classical scholar and as such was able to carry greater weight in Paris. He was devoted to the study of Aristotle, the key figure of medieval university teaching, and re-edited his work in order to restore the original text and to rescue it from the accumulated mass of medieval commentaries. He then began to treat the New Testament in similar fashion, publishing a new translation of the Epistles in 1512, along with a revolutionary type of commentary which dispensed with the traditional apparatus of scholastic interpretation. His later work, especially his translation of the Gospels, was compromised by the Reformation since his commentary on such controversial issues as the doctrine of justification by faith was condemned by the University of Paris, and despite his influential patron he had to take refuge in Switzerland (see page 320).

In England a little Greek was being taught before 1500 at Cambridge and in the newly-established *Schola Literae Humaniores* at Oxford but, as in Spain, powerful patronage was required to establish it beyond question. This was supplied by the Lady Margaret, mother of Henry VII. At the request of John Fisher, bishop of Rochester and an enthusiast for the New Learning, she founded two Cambridge colleges, Christ's and St John's, where Latin, Greek and Hebrew were to be taught for the sake of better biblical scholarship. Richard Fox, bishop of Winchester, tried to redress the balance at Oxford in 1517 by founding Corpus Christi College for the same purpose. Outside the university world John Colet played an important role in establishing classical studies; he could scarcely be termed a humanist since he was an ascetic in the medieval tradition, but he adopted humanist techniques of scholarship in order to study more closely the Epistles of St Paul and demonstrated a humanist enthusiasm for education by founding St Paul's School in London to produce learned Christians. Its first High Master, William Lilly, a well-known grammarian and Greek scholar, ensured that learned Christians were capable of reading Greek. In England too was Colet's friend, Sir Thomas More, a man of many parts, who seemed to embody much of the Italian idea of *l'uomo universale* – a politician, lawyer, administrator, courtier, scholar and writer whose *Utopia* was written with wit and a close eye for the details of political and social life. In his readiness to die on a matter of conscience, however, he showed himself to be much more a man of the northern Renaissance than a member of the court of the Montefeltri.

In Germany the reception of humanism proceeded in a similar fashion, the only novelty being the career of Johann Reuchlin, (1455–1522). Reuchlin studied the classics in Italy but was introduced into the mysteries of the Hebrew *Cabbala* by Pico della Mirandola. On his return to Germany he began the study of Hebrew and in 1506 produced the first Hebrew grammar to be compiled by a Christian – a classic example of the New Learning being applied to the sources of Christian belief. Unhappily for Reuchlin a converted Jew named Pfefferkorn demonstrated his enthusiasm for his new faith by securing an imperial mandate, supported by the Dominican Order in Cologne, to seize and burn all Hebrew books. The Emperor Maximilian had not personally approved the order and rescinded it in Reuchlin's favour, but the Dominicans were not to be frustrated so easily. They brought heresy charges against Reuchlin in the Faculty of Theology at Cologne in 1513 and it was not until the case had been taken to Rome that he was finally acquitted in 1519. The bitterness of the dispute reflected the animosity of traditional Schoolmen for the new learning and provoked another German humanist, Ulrich von Hutten, to publish a savage satire on the obscurantism of scholastics. In his *Epistolae Obscurorum Virorum* he poured scorn on their commentaries about commentaries and parodied their intellectual controversies; in an imaginary disputation, for example, he demonstrated by scholastic logic that no man could be a member of more than one university since, if a university is a body and a body has many members, it would be impossible for a member to have several bodies.

A particular type of Christian humanism was developed in the Netherlands by the Brethren of the Common Life. They represented what was termed the *Devotio Moderna*, a movement which reacted against the formalism and theological subtlety of scholasticism by emphasising the importance of spiritual communion with God. Although the roots of their movement sprang from the mysticism of St Thomas à Kempis (see page 81), the New Learning from Italy provided the Brethren with the very tools they needed to produce a version of the scriptures free from scholastic accretion. Their school at Deventer was founded in the middle of the fifteenth century by Rudolf Agricola, a musician and poet who had studied for many years in Italy and Germany. Among his pupils was Alexander Hegius who eventually became headmaster, and whose proficiency at Greek and Latin was so great that Deventer, by 1500, had become the most advanced centre of classical scholarship in northern Europe.

It was this environment which produced Desiderius Erasmus (1460–1536), the most outstanding figure of northern humanism. He was the illegitimate son of a Dutch priest who sent him to school at Deventer but when both his parents died of the plague Erasmus reluctantly agreed to enter the Augustinian community at Steyn. Nonetheless, the classical grounding he had had at Deventer stood him in good stead and provided a means of escape from the monastic life he loathed; the bishop of Cambrai heard of his ability, appointed him as his Latin Secretary and sent him to the College de Montaigu in Paris to continue his studies. The college was by no means a centre of the New Learning and Erasmus found the course old-fashioned and uninteresting, but he used his time well to read widely in Latin literature and soon won renown for a prodigious memory and a polished Latin style. In 1499 he became tutor to Lord Mountjoy and visited England, where he met Fisher, Colet and More whose brand of Christian humanism impressed him greatly. In the same year he published his *Adagia*, a collection of over 2,000 proverbs culled from Greek and Latin literature, which was much in demand among those who sought to boast a smattering of classical education. It was even more highly valued by others for his lively and satirical comments on contemporary society, and Erasmus's gift for a well-turned phrase won him an immediate reputation throughout northern Europe.

For all his enthusiasm for classical studies, Erasmus was not essentially a literary connoisseur. He had little taste for poetry, classical literature he admired for its moral wisdom rather than its style and his study of classical languages was undertaken primarily to prepare him for the revision of the scriptures. In this he demonstrated the influence of Deventer and, in a manner inconceivable to an Italian humanist, he translated the *Hecuba* of Euripides merely to prepare himself for his study of the Greek version of the New Testament. He challenged the exclusive right of theologians to read and interpret the scriptures since he believed that Christ's teaching was intelligible to all, provided that it was divorced from the glosses, the commentaries and the errors which had been accumulated over the centuries. Philology was, therefore, a better tool than dialectic to reveal the true word of God, and his object was to make this word available to the public at large:

I wish that all might read the Gospel and the Epistles of Paul. I wish that they might be translated into all tongues of all people so that not only the Scots and the Irish but also the Turk and the Saracen might read and understand. I wish the countryman might sing them at his plough, the weaver chant them at his loom, the traveller beguile with them the weariness of his journey.

By his readable style and his sharp eye for the religious abuses of his day, Erasmus advanced the ideals of evangelical simplicity and personal piety established by the Brethren of the Common Life. In 1503 he wrote the *Enchiridion Militis Christiani* (The Handbook of the Christian Knight) – a northern counterweight to Castiglione's *Il Cortegiano* – which emphasised the primacy of faith above reason but mocked the errors of blind credulity. 'Honourest thou the bones of Paul hid in the shrine, and honourest thou a piece of his carcase shining through a glass, and regardest thou not the whole mind of Paul shining through his epistles.' Six years later he returned to the attack with even greater invective in the *Encomium Moriae* (The Praise of Folly). Folly applauds her most devoted followers who are characterised as fossilized monks, nincompoop Schoolmen and Warrior Popes, and the inadequacy of the episcopate is savagely revealed: 'They are satraps, caring nothing for religion, its blessings and its ceremonies and holding it cowardly and shameful for a bishop to die otherwise than in battle. Their clergy valiantly follow their example and fight like warriors for their tithes.' Similarly, in an anonymous attack on Julius II, his *Julius Exclusus* in 1513 imagined the Warrior Pope's discomfiture at being denied admission to the gates of Heaven.

In 1519 Erasmus published the *Colloquia* which crowned his international reputation, outstripping even the *Adagia* in popularity. Designed as an elementary reader it comprised a series of imaginary dialogues in conversational Latin, but in its compilation he demonstrated to perfection the impeccable scholarship, the linguistic flair and the lively satire which helped to assure the survival of humanism in northern Europe. Because of his authority and prestige classical literature was admired and enjoyed by an increasing number of scholars and the cultural monopoly of the Schoolmen was shattered. Moreover, by devoting the techniques of classical scholarship to the service of the Church, Erasmus in company with men like Reuchlin, Lefèvre and Cisneros revealed the special quality of northern humanism which, for all its debt to Italy, pursued its own unique and independent course.

Erasmus's final years were to be embittered by the crisis of the Reformation. His earlier writings had done much to expose the inadequacies and abuses of contemporary church life and unwittingly he supplied the Lutheran reformers after 1520 with a rich fund of ammunition to support their cause. Like the majority of northern humanists, however, Erasmus remained loyal to Rome and the charge of the Schoolmen that he had prepared the way for the Reformation was inaccurate (see page 249).

Art and Music in Northern Europe

Northern Europe in the fifteenth century showed little enthusiasm for Italian art. The northern humanists, and Erasmus in particular, were remarkably indifferent to art in general, and the guilds of artists and masons were as conservative as the Schoolmen – with the significant difference that because of their own flourishing tradition they had no need to fear comparison with Italy.

It was scarcely suprising, for example, that the Palazzo Rucellai should have been ignored north of the Alps, when the full splendour of the Gothic style was being revealed in the exuberant tracery of the flamboyant Palais de Justice at Rouen or in the purity of the perpendicular line of King's College Chapel. The visitors to Italy who commented on the new development in architecture had little understanding of its principles, and were more likely to be impressed by the untypical, heavily ornate Certosa of Padua than by the simple classical proportions of the Foundling Hospital in Florence. The reception of Italian architecture before 1520 was, therefore, confined to the adornment of public buildings with sundry classical ornaments – as at Tours where the upper sections of the cathedral towers are bedecked with balustrades, columns and rounded arches. Even the Italian wars and the presence of a Florentine architect, Giuliano da san Gallo, in Paris had little immediate effect on French style. The two most important buildings begun in 1515, Chenonceaux and the new wing at Blois, were essentially medieval constructions with Italian trimmings; only at Chambord, begun in 1519, was any attempt made to plan the building as an organic whole, and even there the roof line is nothing but a delightfully Gothic fantasy (see plate 11).

In painting as in architecture the north enjoyed a flourishing tradition of its own, centred principally in the Netherlands where the Books of Hours decorated for the dukes of Burgundy in the fourteenth century had established a taste for naturalist observation by their delicately observed scenes of daily life. Where the Italians tended to idealise what they saw, seeking to convey the essence of what natural objects should be in their purest forms, the Netherlanders concentrated on the accurate portrayal of what they could see at a particular moment of time, holding as it were a mirror to the world around them. They lacked the anatomical studies and the rules of perspective by which the Italians constructed their pictures from scientific principles; instead they took delight in rendering the texture of things, especially flowers, fabrics and precious stones, by meticulous attention to the observation of every detail. This is apparent, for example, in the landscape studies which formed the background of the altarpiece at Ghent completed in 1432 by Jan van Eyck, court painter to Philip the Good, and the outstanding artist of the Netherlands in the early fifteenth century. His preference for oil in place of tempera not only gave his pictures greater depth and brilliance than contemporary Italian works, but also allowed him to work more slowly – patiently building up his composition detail by detail until he had achieved a faithful copy of the subject matter.

A similar mastery of naturalist observation is found in the paintings of his contemporary, Roger van der Weyden, 1400–64, who was however more intensely emotional in his treatment of religious subjects. When he visited Rome it was as a pilgrim, not as an artist, and his style bore few traces of Italian influence. There was in fact a significant difference between the choice of religious subjects favoured in Italy and in the north. By and large the Italians tended to concentrate on the power of God as the omnipotent creator and on His intervention in history at the Incarnation; the north was more preoccupied with the condition of fallen man, his judgement and his redemption by the Crucifixion. Moreover, in their treatment of these themes the northern artists demonstrated a degree of emotional fervour which sometimes verged on hysteria. The uninhibited fantasy of Hieronymus Bosch of Brabant (1482–1516) gave tangible expression to the most morbid and tormented fears of medieval man. A similar tension was evident in the work of his German contemporary, Matthias Grünewald whose altarpiece at Isenheim (see plate 9) is among the most disturbing and yet most moving examples of northern art. There is nothing of the Italian preoccupation with the discovery of the laws of beauty and proportion: Grünewald is concerned only to preach and he does so by the brilliant transposition from one mood to another. The outer wings of the altarpiece when closed contained a Crucifixion. The intensity of the tragedy and the physical agony are conveyed with brutal realism, and the greenish tinge of decomposing flesh is reflected in the predominant green tone of the bleak and sombre landscape which lies in the background. When the wings are open, however, there appear panels of the Annunciation, the Incarnation and the Resurrection which, by their brilliant colour, and in contrast to the Crucifixion panels, convey a sense of the artist's own ecstatic vision.

In the later fifteenth century the reputation enjoyed by Italy attracted many northern artists to work there for a period, but they were so strongly imbued with the traditions of their own environment that most of them did little more than acquire a few Italian mannerisms without assimilating the purposes which informed them. Jean Fouquet (1420–80) was one of the few Frenchmen to visit Rome and to be influenced by Italian techniques. In, for example, his painting of *Stephen Chevalier and St Stephen* he abandoned the northern convention that the saint should be made much larger than the donor who worships him, and both the figures were modelled very much in the style of Piero della Francesca. Nonetheless, the obvious interest which Fouquet took in the texture and surface of objects – the fur, the fabric and the precious stones of Chevalier's dress in particular – indicates a much closer link with the school of Van Eyck than with Italy. A more receptive visitor to Italy was the Netherlander Jan Gossaert called Mabuse (1478–1535). His paintings of the *Danae* and of *Neptune and Amphitrite*, both by their subject matter and their composition, revealed an obvious debt to Italian masters; more surprisingly his *St Luke painting the Virgin* achieves a sense of balance and a serenity of mood quite out of character with the religious art of his own environment.

In Albrecht Dürer (1471–1528) northern Europe produced its greatest genius and moreover the only artist before 1520 to demonstrate a genuine understanding of Italian art. He was first apprenticed to Michael Wolgemut in Nuremberg where he learned not only to paint but also to make woodcuts for the printing press; later he moved for a while to Cologne to work with a family of copper engravers. The art of line engraving demanded an exacting and objective form of accuracy which accorded well with the northern tradition of realist observation, and in the engraver's burin Dürer found a tool which allowed him a much greater command of detail than was possible with the chisel. Woodcuts and engravings alike, however, both fascinated him because they could be produced more swiftly than conventional paintings. This was of considerable importance to Dürer whose inventive brain poured out an endless flood of new ideas which required immediate execution. Moreover, since prints were cheaper to produce than paintings, Dürer was less dependent on a patron to finance his work and could etch or carve whatever most attracted him – whether it was *The Men's Bath House*, a study of grasses, or the illustrations of the *Apocalypse* which he published as a collection of woodcuts in 1498.

He visited North Italy soon after his apprenticeship had been completed in 1494 and again in 1504. He admired what he saw, not least the relative freedom enjoyed by the Italian artists: 'Here I am a lord' he reported 'at home a parasite' – though coming from a master of a Nuremberg Guild this was something of an exaggeration. More than any other northern artist he assimilated Italian techniques and grafted them on to the tradition of realist observation in which he had been trained. His quick mind soon grasped, for example, the principles of perspective and in his *Nativity* (see plate 10), engraved in 1504, he handled the composition of the scene as self-confidently as any Italian. What eluded him to some extent was the representation of the human body. He filled his sketchbooks with anatomical studies until he realised that the Italians were less concerned to make an accurate copy of the human form than to create an idealised representation of human beauty. This he found to be an almost impossible task. He studied Italian theories of proportion and experimented with the human form, distorting the limbs by lengthening or shortening them, until in his engraving of *Adam and Eve* he came very close to the Italian style.

There was, however, a more basic obstacle in his path. Whereas Alberti or Leonardo took it for granted that an ideal form of beauty could be created by the artist, Dürer reflected something of his northern, more medieval, background by maintaining that man was an imperfect creature and that absolute beauty was the work of God alone. Indeed, like most other German artists, he saw the world through the eyes of a religious visionary. The subject matter and the treatment of his *Melancholia* or his *Knight, Death and The Devil* indicated that he was still possessed by the spirit of the medieval world, and his series of woodcuts to illustrate the revelation of St John depicted the horrors of doomsday with an intensity far removed from the urbane and humanist mood of Italy.

The influence of Italian art on northern Europe was very limited before 1520 but few would have challenged the primacy of Italian artists even if they did not always rush to imitate them. In music, however, the situation was reversed, for it was in the cathedral schools of the Netherlands that Europe learned its music. Dufay, the leading composer of his time, began his training at Cambrai and as a member of the choir accompanied its bishop to the Council of Constance. His talents were so admired by the Italians that after the Council he was persuaded to spend some time in the households of the Malatesta of Rimini and the Bentivogli of Bologna before serving for a while in the papal choir. Finally he returned to Cambrai to teach, and enhanced his European reputation by his compositions in the Netherlands tradition of polyphony, a graceful and intricate style in which the several voices follow their own melodic path in apparent independence of each other. Dufay's most famous pupil was Okeghem, who was lured away to Paris to become Maître de la Chapelle to Charles VII and Louis XI. He developed a new style in music, counterpointing the separate lines of polyphony so that the attraction of the melodic line was strengthened by the creation of harmonic chords.

The art of counterpoint was as exciting aesthetically and as intellectually exacting for northern musicians as the rules of perspective were for Italian artists, and it is significant that in the sixteenth century an Italian writer should have compared Okeghem with Donatello for having 'rediscovered' music as the other had 'rediscovered' sculpture. Josquin des Près who was Okeghem's pupil in the art of counterpoint developed an even more sophisticated technique. Having triumphantly solved the technical problems of counterpoint he went on to give greater stress to the principal melodic line so that in its composition he could make the music express more accurately the sentiment and mood of the words. As a result his services were in demand both in Paris and at Rome, where he was compared with Michelangelo since each was held to be without an equal in his art.

The emotional expressiveness of Josquin's work required the services of highly-trained choirs and afforded the virtuoso performer a greater opportunity to demonstrate his skill. Indeed it is difficult to say whether it was the greater complexity of music which led to the rise of professional performers or vice-versa; in any case musical performance became more expensive to maintain. In the Netherlands the church choirs could draw upon the wealth of towns like Ypres, Bruges and Ghent and the Burgundian court was the principal agent of patronage. Philip the Good and Charles the Rash were especially fond of music; they sang and composed themselves, employed the finest composers and took their musicians with them everywhere. So too did their descendant Charles V whose Flemish choir was the finest in Europe by 1520. As a result professional music which had been used almost solely for the service of the church, was considerably secularised, not merely by the device of using secular themes for religious motets and masses, which was in any case a tradition of long standing, but by the greater development of music as a field for secular enjoyment. In the sixteenth century, however, the church in the Netherlands lost much of its wealth and the great age of its music began to come to an end even in the lifetime of Charles V. The attractions of other European courts proved to be too great and though Netherlanders continued to be the finest composers in Europe their talents were generally employed outside the Netherlands.

The Eve of the Reformation

Although it was generally agreed by many thoughtful clergy and laymen that the church in the fifteenth century was in need of reform, this in itself was not a novel situation nor did it presage the Protestant Reformation. Ecclesiastical abuses and clerical inadequacy had always existed in one form or another without invalidating doctrine or provoking a schism; when the spiritual condition of the church had been debased in the past, reforming groups had emerged to supply a remedy – as in the eleventh century when a great period of reform was initiated by Pope Gregory VII. The particular problem in 1500 was that although the need for reform was urgent the papacy did nothing to provide the perceptive leadership which the situation demanded. In fact by its own example it made matters worse.

After the collapse of the conciliar movement the popes appeared to spend little time on matters spiritual or theological. They publicly acknowledged their mistresses; the advancement of illegitimate children and nephews to serve their personal ambitions made nepotism respectable; and their preoccupation with political and cultural affairs obliged them to raise money by any means available. Simony, the sale of ecclesiastical offices, had become one of the corner stones of papal finance (see page 147) and, as Savonarola complained, the financial exploitation of papal services perverted not only the function of the papacy but encouraged the widespread development of pluralism, immorality and inattention to spiritual duty among the clergy as a whole.

The scandal begins in Rome and runs through the whole clergy; they are worse than Turks and Moors. In Rome you will find that they have one and all obtained their benefices by simony. They buy preferments and bestow them on their children or brothers who take possession of them by violence and all sorts of sinful means. Their greed is insatiable, they do all things for gold. They only ring their bells for coin and candles; only attend vespers and choir and office when something is to be got by it. They sell their benefices, sell their sacraments and traffic in masses.

The 'scandal in Rome' was allowed to run unchecked through much of Europe because of the failure of the bishops to exercise their pastoral role of guidance and instruction within their diocese. Many of them held their sees because of family influence, sometimes being appointed before they were of an age to fulfil their duties; some purchased preferment without heed to the responsibilities it entailed; others, whose education and administrative ability attracted the attention of their governments, were rewarded for services in the secular administration with offices in the church. Jean of Lorraine became bishop of Metz at the age of three and subsequently held in plurality three archbishoprics, six bishoprics and nine abbeys; Albrecht of Brandenburg purchased the office of archbishop-elector of Mainz along with two other bishoprics;

Cardinal Wolsey held several bishoprics and abbeys, none of which he had time to visit, and Ferdinand of Aragon provided appointments in the Aragonese church for many of his illegitimate sons. As a result, diocesan leadership was too often incapacitated by secular considerations and the parish clergy was left to go its own way. In such a situation piety and good instruction were outweighed by ignorance and inefficiency to the detriment of the spiritual life of the church.

A special feature of the fifteenth century was the decline of the monasteries. Their function had been to act as spiritual power-houses where the monks, by their life of discipline and of self-denial, had served the community by their prayers, and so well respected was their role that the community had willingly rewarded them with benefactions of land and money. By 1500 society no longer afforded them the gratitude and the veneration they had once enjoyed. Instead there were complaints that the regimen of life established by their founders was no longer adhered to, that their wealth had sapped their austerity, that their tradition of scholarship had fallen into decay and that the provision of charity had taken second place to the exercise of their financial rights as landlords. So suspicious were the burghers of many German towns, for example, that they left their charitable bequests to be administered by lay corporations rather than by the monasteries. Within the monasteries there had always been those for whom a strict adherence to the rule of chastity had proved too great a task, but the stories of irregularity in monastic life began to grow in number in the fifteenth century. Popular feeling was expressed in Germany by Sebastian Brandt's lampoon *The Ship of Fools* and in England by Simon Fish's *The Supplication of the Beggars*; both reflected the opinion of many that the monks should be allowed to marry in order that they might leave other men's wives alone. Despite individual examples of reform by Cisneros in Castile, or by the Brethren of the Common Life in the Netherlands, the monasteries were held in such low regard that a general antipathy to monks for their ignorance, immorality and greed became the central theme of a growing mood of anti-clericalism.

More serious than the inadequacy of the clergy, and essentially a consequence of it, was the emergence among the laity of a dangerously mechanistic attitude motivated by fear. The church had always encouraged a measure of devotion to the Virgin, to

St Anne, her mother, and to the saints in general, along with the practice of pilgrimage to famous shrines and the veneration of relics, but in the later Middle Ages this got out of hand. Men became morbidly obsessed by fear of the plague, fear of marauders and above all fear of the pains of Hell. Because God was conceived to be a terrible judge whom no man dared approach directly, particular attention was paid to means of appeasing His vengeance, either by appeals to the Virgin and others who might intercede with Him or by the performance of placatory rights. This explains the expansion of the cult of the Virgin, the greater popularity of pilgrimages – although these often degenerated into riotous outings – and the superstitious belief in the efficacy of relics. Whereas a thriving and responsible priesthood might have reversed this trend within a generation, clerical ignorance and greed exacerbated it beyond measure. At all levels of the ecclesiastical hierarchy the fund-raising potentialities of relics, pardons and masses for the dead were rigorously exploited along with the fears which prompted so unhealthy an interest in mechanical devices to assuage the wrath of God.

The trend was epitomised by the sale of indulgences which represented an unfortunate by-product of the penitential system of the medieval church. The process of confession when it was adjudged by the priest to be motivated by a genuine penitence was followed by the gift of absolution and the imposition of a penance. The performance of the penance was intended to benefit the penitent who clearly derived psychological advantage from it, but the church by whose authority the penance was awarded could remit when occasion demanded. In 1095, for example, the crusaders were granted full remission of all the penalties which they would otherwise have had to perform, and by 1343 the theory of remission was given full expression in the bull *Unigenitus*. According to this, Christ's sacrifice was held to have been so great that it represented a treasury of superfluous merit to be dispensed by the pope to those who were penitent.

Now this treasure is not hidden in a napkin but entrusted to be healthfully dispensed – through blessed Peter, bearer of Heaven's keys, and his successors as vicars on earth – to the faithful for fitting and reasonable courses, now for total, now for partial remission of punishment due for temporal sins ... and to be applied in mercy to them that are truly penitent and have confessed.

When in the fifteenth century the church began to discover the profits to be derived from the sale of indulgences, the essential point that indulgences remitted the penalty not the guilt was conveniently overlooked. They were hawked about as letters of credit on God Himself, and their sphere of influence was even extended to souls in purgatory so that their time of ordeal might be reduced. Columbus, for example, affirmed the value of discovering gold because 'gold constitutes treasure, and he who possesses it has all he needs in the world and also the means of rescuing souls from purgatory and restoring them to the enjoyment of paradise'; and Leo X reinforced the popular misconception by claiming 'I will close the gates of Hell against you and open for you the doors of Paradise'. The scholars might privately explain the theory of indulgences in limited and cautious terms but the ordinary man had heard a very different story from someone like the Dominican Tetzel who sold indulgences in the market places throughout Germany to the accompaniment of pipe and drum like any itinerant pedlar of quack nostrums. 'It is incredible' wrote a contemporary, 'what this ignorant and impudent friar gave out. He said that if they contributed readily and bought grace and indulgence all the hills of St Annaburg would become pure massive silver, that so soon as the coin rang in the chest the soul for whom the money was paid would go straightaway to Heaven.'

In short the Christian church was passing through a dangerous phase in which the hearing of sermons, the saying of prayers and attendance at mass were ceasing to be aids and incentives to holy living but, rather, a series of contrivances to enable man to sin and then to escape the penalty. The score was cleared not by repentance but by the superstitious participation in a rite or by the payment for a mass, a candle or an indulgence. Unfortunately, this was by no means the full extent of the spiritual crisis which beset Christianity at the end of the fifteenth century. The philosophical infrastructure of the church, as expressed by the great Schoolmen of the thirteenth century, had been thrown into confusion. St Thomas Aquinas, by an intellectual *tour de force*, had achieved a reconciliation between the revealed truth of the Bible and the demonstrable rational truth of Aristotelian science. Scholasticism, therefore, had represented an intellectually satisfying synthesis of faith and reason. Subsequently, however, two English Franciscans, Duns Scotus and William of Occam, had exposed a series of logical flaws in Thomist reasoning. Their own followers, the Nominalists, claimed that neither the existence of God nor the orthodox doctrine of the Trinity – nor indeed the doctrine of transubstantiation which sought to give a philosophical foundation to the vital experience of Christ in the Eucharist – were capable of demonstration by rational argument. This did not breed agnosticism but the conviction that these doctrines were derived solely from God's own revelation of Himself. Reason and faith were again divorced and the validity of the scholastic achievement was undermined.

The majority of Schoolmen tried to pretend that nothing had happened and scholasticism survived as a habit of thought rather than a process of thinking. The terminology of Thomist philosophy was perpetuated, but without its informing spirit it led to the type of arid dialectic caricatured by Erasmus. 'They have their syllogisms, their majors and minors, inferences, corollaries, suppositions; and, for a fifth act of the play, they tell some absurd story and interpret it allegorically, tropologically, anagogically and make it up into a chimera more extravagant than poet ever invented.' It was evident by 1500 that the Schoolmen had nothing new to offer save glosses on glosses, commentaries on commentaries and exhaustive debates on how many angels could stand on the end of a pin or on the fate of excommunicated fish. Those who found this unedifying had two courses open to them. Some like Erasmus adopted the New Learning, others turned to the mystics; in each case they were impelled to seek something more directly relevant to human religious experience.

Significantly many of the northern humanists were laymen who resented not only the clerical monopoly of university posts but also the inadequacy of the clergy as a whole. With wit and invective they exposed the abuses of the day in the vain hope that those whom they mocked might amend their ways. Moreover, by their biblical scholarship and new translations, the northern humanists threw new light upon the scriptures. Erasmus had hoped that by releasing the original texts from the accumulated commentaries of the Schoolmen the word of God might appear in all its simplicity and thereby put an end to religious controversy. In fact the new translations prompted the formulation of new controversies. The readers discovered, as one of them put it, 'little about the pope but much about Christ' and there were interesting conclusions to be drawn by those who noticed that the Greek word *ecclesia* was better translated as congregation than as church. The penitential system too was subjected to closer examination by those who went behind the ponderous, legalistic Latin of the Vulgate's *facere poenitentiam* (to do penance), to discover the more spiritual emphasis of the Greek *metanoien* (to change one's whole attitude).

Whereas such matters attracted the attention of a small group of influential and vocal scholars, the reaction from scholasticism to mysticism affected thousands of people. Mysticism which believes in the spiritual apprehension of truths which are beyond the comprehension of the intellect is an integral feature of all the major religions. There had always been Christian mystics even though the church was naturally suspicious of those who insisted on approaching God directly, rather than through the sacraments and what might be termed official ecclesiastical channels. As a movement which had little sympathy for rational speculation about religious truth, it had made but little headway during the heyday of the scholastics. It came into its own, however, when men began to turn away in dissatisfaction from the arid dialectic of the fourteenth-century Schoolmen. For these people there was great comfort to be found in the words, for example, of St Thomas à Kempis:

Of what use is it to discourse learnedly on the Trinity if you lack humility and therefore displease the Trinity. Lofty words do not make a man just or holy; but a good life makes him dear to God. I would far rather feel contrition than be able to define it. If you knew the whole Bible by heart and all the teachings of the philosophers how would this help you without the grace and love of God?

St Thomas, born into the world of Deventer in 1380, was by no means anti-intellectual, but he attacked those who maintained that the intellect alone was self-sufficient. 'Many have lost their devotion by attempting to pry into matters too high for them. It is faith and a holy life that are required of you, not a lofty intellect or knowledge of the profound mysteries of God.' Reason, therefore, had to be humbled before faith. 'For God wills that we become perfectly obedient to Himself and that we transcend mere reason on the wings of a burning love for Him.' This was the essence of the mystic experience – the consuming love which so absorbs the soul that it is brought into a direct personal and spiritual communion with God, or as the Franciscan, St Bonaventure, expressed it, 'The reaching out of the soul to God through the yearning of love'. There were dangers in this path as in any other and the calm stability of St Thomas à Kempis was not always found among the more emotional Franciscan Friars who succeeded St Bonaventure. Emphasising the importance of the 'inner light' by which the soul perceives God, they began to reject all other authority including that of the church. The church retaliated with persecution, not merely to defend its position but also out of concern that too naïve a confidence in the working of the Holy Spirit induced in certain mystics a degenerate interpretation of their human fantasies and desires as the voice of God. When St Catherine of Siena claimed that by annihilation of herself in spiritual communion with Christ, her heart had been transformed or rather recreated as the heart of Christ, her evident saintliness saved her; but when an ordinary woman, Marguerite Parete, claimed that her soul had been annihilated in God, she was burned by the Sorbonne in Paris.

What cut across this trend was the influence of the German Dominicans who did not abandon the intellectual structure of scholasticism but who undertook the spiritual guidance of the Rhineland nunneries. For their new charges the terminology of the Schoolmen raised more problems than it solved and so the Dominicans were led to explain theology in increasingly mystical terms – as Goethe remarked much later, mysticism was 'the scholastic of the heart, the dialectic of the feelings'. Others went out to the laity at large, among them Meister Eckhart, who found it impossible to expound the theology of the schools in the vernacular and so began to preach in more mystic terms about the nature of God – employing the paradoxes so characteristic of mystic exposition. 'God's simple nature is formless of form, unchanging of change, beingless of being, thingless of thing and, therefore, it spreads forth into all things in this changing world and all finite beings find their last end in Him.' The importance of his teaching was considerable and his German congregations began to respond with great enthusiasm to his insistence that in all men there was some spark of the divine being which longs to return to Him.

Any attempt to expound theology in more simple language invites the danger of misrepresentation and Eckhart was accused of pantheism for his view of the unity of 'all finite things in the divine nature'. Unlike the Franciscans, however, who seemed to concentrate solely on the nature of their mystic experience, Eckhart roundly affirmed that from this experience must issue practical piety: 'God's purpose and contemplation is fruitfulness in works.' His followers, Heinrich Suso and Johann Tauler, continued his work. Through their written work they did a great deal to foster a revival of German writing, but their translation of scholastic concepts into the vernacular, despite the orthodoxy of their intent, encouraged novelty of thought, and because of the importance attached to the operation of the individual soul, individual thought was also impelled into action. A sacramental faith administered by a priesthood was thereby threatened by a personal faith relying on an inner light in direct communion with God. The danger of heresy and misunderstanding especially among the mass of ordinary people was, therefore, very great, but the effect of the Dominicans' teaching in the Rhineland had a widespread and salutary effect by encouraging a greater degree of personal piety expressed in the performance of charitable works and the practice of family prayers.

Within the broad framework of medieval Christianity there were, therefore, many conflicting strands. There was evidence on the one hand of ecclesiastical indiscipline which in turn reflected the secularisation of the papacy: in addition, as popular attitudes to religion became more superstitious and more mechanistic, the philosophical foundations of the faith were being discredited. On the other hand there were ecclesiastical reformers, Christian humanists, mystic preachers and men of a simple piety who sought, by criticism or by example, to improve the spiritual condition of the Christian church. Not all these various strands directly touched upon the experience of Martin Luther, but it was into this complex environment that he was born and an understanding of it helps to explain not only the explosive doctrines he evolved, but also the reaction of his contemporaries to it.

Martin Luther's Spiritual Crisis

The religious condition of Europe in 1500 was such that a reform movement of some kind seemed likely, but the fact that the

Reformation occurred and the manner of its development were due primarily to the personality and the spiritual experience of the German monk Martin Luther, and secondly to the particular circumstances within the Holy Roman Empire which afforded him the opportunity to challenge the authority of Rome and of the Emperor Charles V without being immediately silenced for his heresy.

Luther was born in 1483, the son of a Saxon miner who had made his way in the world to rent his own smelting furnaces at Mansfeld and who had acquired sufficient wealth and social ambition to provide his son with an excellent education. Luther attended the university of Erfurt, at that time a centre of Nominalist teaching, and then, as his father had intended, graduated in its school of law. In 1505 however he astounded his father by refusing to take up a legal career and withdrew to a monastery of the Augustinian Eremites, an order of monks which had reformed itself of the abuses then current in monasticism. He tried to mollify his father's disappointment by explaining that he was constrained 'by the terror and agony of sudden death'. Such a fear was wholly in keeping with the morbidity of contemporary religion and it gives some substance to the legend that as a young student, terrified out of his wits when caught in an unusually severe thunderstorm, Luther had pledged himself to St Anne that if he survived the storm he would enter a monastery. From the Order's point of view he was an excellent novice. Ordained in 1507, he was seconded to the new university of Wittenberg for a time and then sent to Rome in 1511, in part as a pilgrim, in part to conduct some business for the Order at the Vatican. On his return he received his doctorate at Wittenberg and was appointed priest of the Castle Church and professor of biblical theology. For the next five years he established a reputation for lucidity and scholarship which delighted the university's founder and patron, the Elector Frederick the Wise of Saxony, and drew many students to his lectures.

Behind this façade of the apparently successful scholar monk was a life of intense spiritual agony. Luther's dilemma can be simply stated. He believed that God required him to keep His law in all its points; he also believed that this was beyond his ability and that therefore he was damned. Nothing in his ordered life could give him comfort. Neither the discipline of the monastery nor the rigorous mortification of the flesh could assuage the over-powering sense of guilt which beset him. 'I was a good monk' he wrote in later life 'and I kept the rule of my Order so strictly that I may say that if ever a monk got to Heaven by his monkery, it was I . . . if I had kept on any longer I should have killed myself with vigils, prayers, reading and other works.' His training in philosophy and his biblical scholarship conspired to convince him that God was a just and terrible judge, and although the Nominalists at Erfurt had taught that God would not deny grace to any man who voluntarily declared his love for Him, Luther's over-scrupulous conscience made him question the validity of his own life. 'However irreproachable my life as a monk I felt myself in the presence of God to be a sinner with a most unquiet conscience nor would I believe Him to be pleased with my satisfaction. I did not love, rather I hated this just God who punished sinners.'

The spiritual despair which he experienced began to affect his health, bringing about acute nervous tension and severe constipation. Naturally enough he became increasingly introverted, obsessed with his own spiritual and physical condition and Staupitz, his sympathetic vicar-general, tried to distract him from his self-concern by sending him to Wittenberg and to Rome. He also prescribed a course of reading in the German mystics to break down Luther's fear of God but although Luther was deeply influenced by their teaching he dared not surrender his soul in love to a God whose justice terrified him. Between 1513 and 1515 however, when Luther was preparing a course of lectures on the Psalms, he was particularly struck by the point that in Psalm 22 the God of Majesty is revealed also as the God of Compassion. At the same time moreover he was working on the Greek text of the Epistles and found that the righteousness of God, *justitia dei*, had two different senses in Greek: in the classical Greek of Xenophon *dikaiosune* referred to judgement and by extension to condemnation: in the Greek of the New Testament and the Septuagint, where the authors had first been steeped in Hebrew, it meant to make matters right. As a result God's grace could be interpreted as a liberating force, redeeming rather than condemning, and with this in mind Luther discovered a new meaning in the text 'the just shall live by faith'. Though God's laws might be beyond man's fulfilment, He has nonetheless promised to those who believe in Him the grace to be redeemed through the merits of his own son Jesus Christ.

Night and day I pondered until I saw the connection between the justice of God and the statement that 'the just shall live by His faith', then I grasped that the justice of God is that righteousness by which through grace and sheer mercy God justifies us through faith. Whereupon I felt myself to be reborn and to have gone through open doors into Paradise. The Holy Scripture took on a new meaning and whereas before 'the justice of God' had filled me with hate, now it became to me inexpressibly sweet in greater love. This passage of Paul became to me a gate to Heaven.

It also became the theme of his lectures at Wittenberg and its most direct exposition was in his commentary on the Epistle to the Galatians in 1519.

If justification was by faith alone then there was nothing to be said for the mechanistic aids which men relied upon to avert God's wrath or to win his favour, since works alone, whatever their intrinsic value, could not achieve salvation: above all the validity of indulgences was challenged. Privately and with characteristic directness Luther had criticised his own patron, the elector of Saxony, who enjoyed the privilege on All Saints' Day of selling indulgences to the pilgrims who came to the Castle Church at Wittenberg to see his collection of over 1,700 relics. Very shortly however, Luther was given the opportunity to raise the matter in a more public manner. Albrecht of Brandenberg, the archbishop elector of Mainz, had recently bought his preferment, along with a licence to retain two other dioceses as well, for the sum of 30,000 florins which he had borrowed from the Fuggers. The pope not only countenanced his double offence of simony and pluralism but obligingly gave him leave to redeem the debt by a special sale of indulgences – ostensibly for the rebuilding of St Peter's at Rome. The sales were entrusted to John Tetzel whose manner of deceiving simple people with false promises had already aroused a great deal of concern and it was against him that Luther was to appear in the public eye.

Tetzel was denied access to Saxon territory, not out of respect for Luther but because the elector did not welcome rival salesmen just before All Saints' Day. Some of Luther's parishioners however crossed the frontier nearby to buy his 'papal letters' only to discover that when they presented them to Luther in the confessional he refused to remit their penances. More to the point he then prepared ninety-five theses on the subject and posted them to the door of the Castle Church. This was a common enough way of exposing a subject for academic debate and might have gone unremarked had not Luther deliberately chosen the very eve of All Saints' when the city was crowded with pilgrims to purchase the Wittenberg indulgences. A local printer with a nose for a good story gave the theses a more newsworthy appearance by translating them from Latin into German and publishing them throughout the empire.

As a result of the printing press therefore all Germany was made aware of Luther's views. His main contention was that any man who was truly penitent was already assured of God's pardon and needed no mechanical aids to salvation. There was also an autobiographical touch in his insistence that an awareness of being damned is a necessary preliminary to salvation.

In this disturbance salvation begins. When a man believes himself to be utterly lost light breaks; peace comes and the word of Christ through faith. He who does not have this is lost even though he be absolved a million times by the pope and he who does have it may not wish to be released from purgatory for true contrition seeks penalty.

Theology apart, there was much to entertain the German reader. It was one thing for Luther to restore the doctrine of indulgences to its earliest and its most simple form – that the church had authority to remit its own penalties; it was quite another to deliver home truths about the greed of the Roman curia. When Luther argued that the Church's authority did not extend to purgatory, he could not resist the jibe that if the pope believed that he exercised jurisdiction there, he ought to empty the place out of charity instead of demanding payment for his services. Moreover, though it is impossible to guess what Luther might have written had he known the full story behind Tetzel's commission, he was scornful enough about the avowed objectives of rebuilding St Peter's:

. . . the revenues of all of Christendom are being sucked into this insatiable Basilica . . . Before long all the churches, palaces, walls and bridges of Rome will be built out of our money. First of all we should rear living temples, next local churches and only last St Peter's which is not necessary for us. We Germans cannot attend St Peter's.

'Luther has committed two sins' wrote Erasmus. 'He has touched the pope's crown and the monks' bellies', and it did not take long for the injured parties to demand satisfaction. In 1518 Luther was summoned to answer for his views in Rome. At this dangerous crisis of his life he was saved by his friendship with Spalatin, the librarian and chaplain to the elector of Saxony, and by Frederick the Wise himself. Frederick did not applaud Luther's views on the sale of indulgences but he was intensely proud of his new university at Wittenberg and of the young professor who had added to its reputation. Consequently at Spalatin's tactful prompting he declared that Luther must be examined in Germany and this was therefore done at Augsburg by the Cardinal Cajetan. Cajetan was a man of exemplary life, a scholar of considerable reputation and a stern critic of the abuses within the church. As general of the Dominicans (to whose Order Tetzel belonged) and as papal legate he had no option however but to demand from Luther a retraction of his theses. Luther regarded the meeting as a sham, made a few telling points about the bull *Unigenitus* (see page 78) and left Augsburg in high dudgeon, bitterly complaining that Cajetan was 'as unsuited to understand the matter as an ass to play the harp'. Despite Cajetan's report and Rome's indignant demands, Frederick still stood by Luther, and the death of Maximilian in January 1519 ensured that in view of the elector's importance in the forthcoming election nothing might be attempted against his protégé.

Meanwhile John Eck, a formidable scholar from Ingolstadt, had published an attack on Luther's theses which was initially taken up by one of Luther's colleagues, Andreas Carlstadt, an older, self-important man who demanded his share of the lime-light. In 1519 Carlstadt and Eck met in a public disputation at Leipzig, but when it became patently obvious that Carlstadt was no match for Eck, Luther was permitted to take over his own defence. Eck's strategy was well conceived. He confronted Luther with the absolute nature of papal authority and compelled him to admit the similarity of his views with those of Huss, the Bohemian heretic of the previous century. This may have won the debate for Eck but it only served to drive Luther away from Rome. Challenged with an authority which he could not respect he decided to repudiate it: he claimed that infallibility lay not in the papacy, an institution of human origin, but solely in God's own words, the

Scriptures: 'If the pope acts contrary to Scripture we are bound to stand by the Scriptures . . . you may rest assured that I am right in suspecting the court of Rome of being governed by the real anti-Christ of whom St Paul spoke.' Within a few months, Luther's doctrines were condemned in the bull *Exsurge Domine* and early in 1521 he himself was excommunicated.

Before the excommunication was published Luther had produced three pamphlets of great importance. In the first, *An appeal to the Christian nobility of the German nation*, theology played second fiddle to nationalist pride, and a plea was made for a national church independent of papal exactions and corruption. 'Rome is the greatest thief and robber that has ever appeared on earth or ever will. Poor Germans that we are, we have been deceived. We were born to be masters and we have been compelled to bow the head beneath the yoke of our tyrants. It is time the glorious Teutonic people should cease to be the puppet of the Roman pontiff.' Abuse of this nature belonged to the well-established tradition of the investiture dispute of the Middle Ages: it was made relevant to 1520 by Luther's skill in giving a specific and articulate form to grievances which had been accumulating for generations. Quite different in tone was his pamphlet on the *Liberty of a Christian Man* in which he worked out the religious and ethical implications of his doctrine of justification by faith. Since faith alone secures salvation, works were of no particular importance, but he was anxious to establish that the Christian did not therefore become lazy or licentious: 'Good works do not make a good man but a good man does good works.' Christian liberty therefore was the joyful expression of a loving obedience to God made manifest through the service of one's neighbours.

The most revolutionary of his pamphlets was the powerful theological treatise on *The Babylonish Captivity of the Church*, which was so radical in its condemnation of the entire sacramental system of the church that Luther wrote in Latin deliberately to limit its readership to those with the education to understand it. In brief, Luther questioned the validity of five of the seven sacraments. Marriage and confession, for example, the one a valuable institution, the other a useful exercise, could not be regarded as sacraments because they had not been directly instituted by Christ himself: nor for that matter had penance and extreme unction. Ordination too he rejected on the grounds that all Christians were priests and it was simply a matter of selecting some of them for the performance of particular functions within the church. As a result the only valid sacraments left were baptism and the Eucharist.

He also had novel things to say about the Eucharist. He insisted that the priests should no longer reserve the chalice to their own use since Christ had summoned laity and clergy to drink of the one cup, and he rejected the doctrine of transubstantiation which had been formulated by the scholastics on the basis of Aristotelian science and philosophy. By this theory the substance of bread and wine, though preserving their accidental forms of bread and wine, were changed (transubstantiated) into the substance of the body and blood of Christ. Luther rejected this as he rejected much of Aquinas' philosophy. In order to explain the Real Presence in terms which admitted its mystery but repudiated any hint of magic, Luther made use of a metaphor proposed by Wyclif and Huss, that Christ co-existed in the elements as fire co-exists within a bar of red hot iron. This theory of consubstantiation moreover allowed Luther to play down the mediatory role of the priest at the Eucharist, since it accorded with his desire to abolish a separately ordained priesthood.

Taken together and stripped of their anti-clerical and xeno-phobic sentiments, the three pamphlets embodied what were to become the essential tenets of Lutheranism. The keystone of it all was the doctrine of justification by faith alone which rendered good works meaningless unless inspired by faith, and which totally invalidated such things as pilgrimages, indulgences and masses for the dead. Nor was there anything to be gained by the worship of relics or the adoration of saints – not even of the Virgin – since man did not need intermediaries between himself and God. Faith in Christ made every Christian his own priest, creating thereby what Luther called the priesthood of all believers. There was therefore no need for a separately ordained clergy: ministers would have to be appointed to direct the services and assist their congregations but they were to enjoy no special privileges pertaining to their Order. As a result the laity were to receive the chalice at the Eucharist while the clergy were free to marry and to live ordinary lives. Neither the pope nor a general council could override the exclusive authority of the Scriptures, and the interpretation of the Scriptures was to be a private matter in which each individual was to be guided only by the 'inner light' of the Holy Spirit within him. As a result of this strict reliance on scriptural authority alone, Luther reduced the Sacraments to two, baptism and the Eucharist, although he admitted that penance might be regarded as a partial sacrament since Christ had urged penitence on His followers. The Real Presence in the Eucharist was guaranteed for Luther by Christ's statement 'this is my body', but he replaced the theory of transubstantiation by his own of consubstantiation. Finally, because Luther could not readily accept that so miserable a creature as man should play any part at all in his own salvation, he believed that faith could never be achieved by man's own desire but was bestowed upon him through the operation of divine grace. Since this left the initiative with God rather than man, Luther was therefore compelled to deny free will.

When Luther was summoned to appear before the diet at Worms in 1521 he knew that there was no going back on his beliefs. Before he set out to face whatever Charles V and the princes might decree, he wrote with characteristic pugnacity and determination:

unless I am convinced by the testimony of Scripture or by evident reasoning – for I trust neither in popes nor in councils alone since it is obvious that they have often erred and contradicted themselves – unless I am convinced by Scripture which I have mentioned and unless my conscience is made captive by God's word, I cannot and will not recant, since it is hard, unprofitable and dangerous to act against one's conscience.

3

International Conflict 1450-1520

France and Burgundy

THE Hundred Years' War between France and England ended in 1453. During its protracted course the English had at one time occupied south-western France, at another the northern provinces, but in the final outcome the revival of French power – traditionally associated with the inspiration of Jeanne d'Arc – deprived them of all their territories save Calais. There was, however, a third party to the conflict, the Duchy of Burgundy, whose intervention first on the English, then on the French side, had been a significant factor in the course of the war.

When the last of the Capetian dukes of Burgundy (Bourgogne) died without heirs in 1361, the duchy reverted to King John II of France. He was, however, in no position to enjoy this feudal windfall since the circumstances of the Hundred Years' War required him to honour his parole to Edward III of England and return to London as a prisoner. Consequently, in order that the duchy be properly governed, he assigned it as an apanage, that is with virtually independent sovereignty, to his first son Philip the Bold (Philippe le Hardi). The dangers inherent in such an arrangement were not immediately made obvious to the French crown. Philip regarded himself as a loyal feudatory of France and his marriage to Marguerite of Flanders in 1369, designed to recover territory in the Netherlands belonging to the previous line of Burgundian dukes, was also undertaken to deny the English access to this area. As a result of this and of subsequent family alliances, Philip became the ruler of Flanders and Artois and also of Franche Comté, the so-called Free County of Burgundy which adjoined his duchy. This policy of dynastic expansion was taken further by his son, John the Fearless (Jean sans

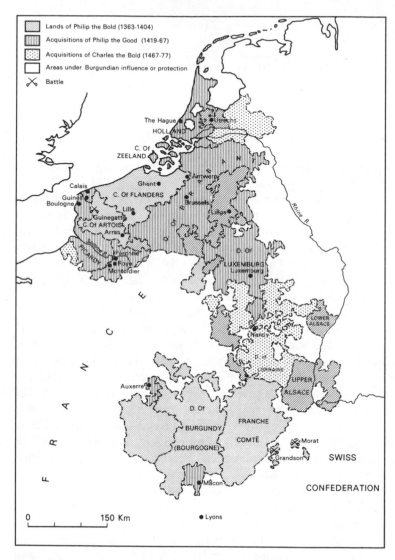

The legend of the map reads:

- Lands of Philip the Bold (1363-1404)
- Acquisitions of Philip the Good (1419-67)
- Acquisitions of Charles the Bold (1467-77)
- Areas under Burgundian influence or protection
- ✗ Battle

Map labels:

The Hague
HOLLAND
Utrecht
C. Of ZEELAND
Calais
Ghent
Antwerp
Guines
Boulogne
C. Of FLANDERS
Lille
Brussels
Liège
Guinegatte
C. Of ARTOIS
Arras
Péronne
D. Of LUXEMBURG
Luxemburg
PICARDY
Roye
Montdidier
Rhine R.
LOWER ALSACE
Nancy
LORRAINE
UPPER ALSACE
Auxerre
D. Of BURGUNDY (BOURGOGNE)
FRANCHE COMTÉ
Morat
Grandson
SWISS CONFEDERATION
Mâcon
F R A N C E
0   150 Km
● Lyons

The Burgundian lands in the fifteenth century

Peur) who secured control of other provinces in the Netherlands.

It was understandable that John the Fearless should wish to establish a physical link between his two groups of territories by trying to gain possession of Luxemburg. This, however, was contested by his cousin, the Duke of Orleans. When Orleans was murdered at John's instigation, a civil war broke out in France between the adherents of the rival dukes. For this reason John refused to join the French king at the battle of Agincourt, though he was not yet prepared to side with Henry V of England who had judiciously offered to assist his effort to extend his authority in the Netherlands. In 1419, when John met the dauphin Charles at the Bridge of Montereau to negotiate a settlement, he was murdered, and his son Philip the Good (Philippe le Bon), despite his strong attachment to the French cause, had no option but to side with England. This alliance, of considerable importance at this stage of the Hundred Years' War, lasted until 1435, by which time the ambitions of Philip the Good in Holland and Zeeland had brought him into conflict with the duke of Gloucester who coveted these same provinces. Accordingly he negotiated a new settlement with the dauphin, now Charles VII. In order to secure his active support in the war and to expiate the murder of his father, Charles VII assigned to him the counties of Mâcon and Auxerre, adjacent to Burgundy, the county of Boulogne and the area of the Somme towns, extending from the river to the frontier of Flanders and constituting the greater part of Picardy. Seven years later Philip occupied Luxemburg and established members of his family in the bishoprics of Liège and Utrecht.

Three generations of dynastic matchmaking supplemented by the fruits of diplomacy and war had thus created not so much a state but a miscellaneous combination of duchies, counties, prince-bishoprics, and city-states, which individually owed allegiance to the dukes of Burgundy. What was lacking was an administrative framework to institutionalise the personal authority of the dukes and to create a sense of unity, although some useful steps had already been taken towards this end. Ducal power was exercised in the Netherlands by *Chambres des comptes* in Brussels, Lille and The Hague, and the individual assemblies or estates of the separate provinces had been persuaded to send representatives to a common States-General. From this of course the French provinces were excluded, these being administered by the Dijon

Chambre des comptes. The dukes themselves deliberately contrived to transcend the cultural and political barriers which divided their subjects by the elaborate manner of their public life. Indeed, the ritual ceremonial of their court, the ostentatious display of their dress, the exaggerated chivalry of their Order of the Golden Fleece and the brilliance of the artists and musicians whom they employed, won them an international reputation envied by other rulers. A royal reputation, however, was no substitute for a royal title, and it was Philip's son, Charles the Rash (Charles le Téméraire) who openly undertook to fulfil the family's ambition to create a monarchy running the full length of the Rhine. The plan was startling but by no means impracticable nor rash. Only in the execution of it did Charles finally deserve his nickname.

Charles recognised that Burgundy's success depended on the weakness of the French monarchy. His father, however, had agreed in 1463 to sell back the Somme towns to France. Angered by this Charles pursued an independent policy and brought together all the enemies of Louis XI in one formidable coalition, the League of Public Weal. Its most important members were the dukes of Brittany, Bourbon, Anjou, Orleans and Berry who wanted something of the independence enjoyed by Burgundy and had private scores to settle with the king. Anjou's action was of particular importance because in the event of dying childless he had promised the succession to Provence to Charles the Rash, a promise which opened up the prospects of a truly middle kingdom from the North Sea to the Mediterranean. Louis XI survived the danger by handing back to Burgundy the Somme towns and ceding in addition the minor counties of Guines, Péronne, Montdidier and Roye. His other enemies were rendered powerless within twelve months by his skilfully turning them against each other (see page 128). In matters of intrigue Louis regarded himself as far superior to Charles – 'a man' he said 'of little worth and little sense'. He began to question Charles's exercise of sovereign rights reminding him of his obligations to the crown of France, offered aid to a rebellion which opportunely broke out in Liège and, over-confident in his ability to better Charles in any personal encounter, paid him a surprise visit at Péronne in 1466. Unwittingly, however, he had entered a hornet's nest. Charles was so infuriated by Louis' offer to the Liègeois that he immediately took him prisoner, compelled him to renounce his sovereign rights and humiliated him beyond measure by taking him to Liège to witness the savage punishments inflicted on the very rebels whom he had promised to support.

The second part of Charles's strategy was to seize what territory he could to link up his scattered possessions more effectively and to force the emperor into granting him a royal title. In 1469 he took Alsace from Sigismund of Austria as reparation for an unpaid loan, in 1473 he overran Guelders and in the same year he met the emperor Frederick III at Trier (Trèves). Frederick, though embarrassed by other problems, refused to bow to Charles's threats and saved the day in an effective if undignified manner by escaping in secret from the city. Louis XI meanwhile had recovered his poise and in 1474 he engineered an alliance among the states most threatened by Burgundian expansion including Austria, Lorraine, the cities of the upper Rhineland and the Confederation of the Swiss Cantons. This was a master stroke of diplomacy, not only because it left France uncommitted to direct action on her own part, but also because the Swiss Confederation had had to be weaned away from its traditional hostility to Sigismund of Austria.

Charles counter-attacked with brilliant effect. A treaty with Edward IV of England, signed in London in 1474, brought back into the field the most powerful enemy of France and raised again the spectre of the Hundred Years' War. But Charles mistook the thought for the deed. By some unaccountable aberration he went off to give support to the archbishop of Cologne in a petty dispute with the emperor and when Edward disembarked at Calais he found no trace of the reinforcements promised from Burgundy. Edward refused to fight alone, while Louis XI had no other desire than to hasten the English withdrawal. The two kings met at Picquigny in 1475 where the offer of a generous pension to the English king induced a swift conclusion to the war. This left Charles without his only ally but, staking everything on a show of force, he overran Lorraine and moved up the Rhine to challenge the Swiss Confederation. At Grandson near Lake Neuchâtel in 1476 and again at Morat, his heavy cavalry was defeated by the steadfastness of the Swiss infantry. Louis XI, whose troops had been standing by at Lyons in case of a Burgundian victory, urged the Swiss to pursue their advance, and sent money to Lorraine so that René might recover his Duchy. This he did successfully in 1477 and when Charles's army challenged his at Nancy, Charles was killed.

Charles's death without a son put paid to the Burgundian dream of a Rhineland kingdom. The duchy of Burgundy reverted immediately by feudal law to Louis XI leaving the provinces of Franche Comté and the Netherlands to Charles's widow, Margaret of York. Her ability to retain them was another matter, and Louis might well have won the entire inheritance for France had he but demonstrated his usual diplomatic skill. Margaret summoned a States-General only to discover that its members were unwilling to raise troops on her behalf, expressing the hope that the matter might be resolved by marrying Charles's surviving daughter, Mary, to a French prince. Instead of waiting upon their deliberations Louis ordered the invasion of Franche Comté, Artois, Boulogne and Flanders and thereby shocked the Netherlands into resistance. The States-General immediately declared war and Mary was married in haste to Maximilian of Habsburg, son of the emperor, Frederick III. Maximilian won the only important battle of the war at Guinegatte in 1479 but Louis struck damaging blows to the economy of the Netherlands by destroying crops, thereby depleting the grain staple at Ghent, and by interfering with the herring fisheries. Mary gave birth to two children, Philip in 1478 and Margaret in 1480, but she died in a riding accident in 1482. At this the Netherlands Estates decided to abandon their support for Maximilian, for whom they entertained no personal loyalty, while safeguarding to some extent the interests of his children. A settlement was made at Arras in 1482. Louis agreed that Philip was to rule the Netherlands, although the county of Flanders was declared to be within the jurisdiction of France, while Margaret was to marry the dauphin Charles when they came of age, her dowry to consist of Franche Comté and Artois which were handed over immediately.

Maximilian refused to be excluded from the settlement. In a bid to exploit the economic rivalry between Brabant and Flanders he appeared at the Antwerp fairs in the autumn of 1483 to proclaim the dismissal of the ministers who governed in Philip's name. This led to a protracted civil war until the problem was suddenly resolved by Charles VIII of France. For reasons of his own (see pages 129–30) he married Anne of Brittany in 1488. The Netherlands Estates declared their anger at this repudiation of the settlement of Arras. Franche Comté and Artois rebelled against French rule and popular opinion swung round to Maximilian, the only person in the past decade to have shown himself uncompromisingly hostile to France. Charles was already enthralled by the prospect of greater glory to be won in Italy and did not wish to be distracted by a long campaign against the Netherlands. In the hope of gaining Naples and a greater military reputation, he abandoned Franche Comté and Artois and restored Margaret to her father by the peace of Senlis.

Europe and Islam 1453 – 1520

There was nothing new about the Moslem threat to Europe. William of Malmesbury had written in the twelfth century, 'This little portion of the world which is ours is pressed upon by warlike Turks and Saracens; for three hundred years they have held Spain and the Balearic Islands and they live in hope of devouring the rest.' Since then most of the Iberian peninsula had been recovered and the initiative had passed from the Moslem powers of North Africa and Egypt to the Osmanli Turks. These followers of Osman were only one among the many Ghazi tribes of Asia Minor whose fierce devotion to Islam was expressed in a life of simple piety combined with nomadic warfare against the outposts of the old Greek Empire of Constantinople (Byzantium). Originally they operated in the service of the Seljuk Turks of Anatolia until Osman had established for himself in 1307 an independent province in Bithynia. From there his successors were able to take over the rest of the Seljuk Empire.

In 1354 they struck out in a new direction and invaded Europe. In a remarkable series of campaigns they occupied Rumelia and overran the eastern mainland from the Gulf of Corinth to the River Danube. Constantinople alone remained as an isolated Christian enclave between the Rumelian and Anatolian provinces of the Osmanli Empire, but plans for its reduction were hastily abandoned when a Mongol horde invaded Asia Minor from the east, destroyed a Turkish army at Angora in 1402 and ravaged most of Anatolia. Secure, however, in their Rumelian provinces the Turks were able to withstand this threat, and from their temporary capital at Adrianople they mobilised their forces to recover most of Anatolia. By 1451, therefore, under the leadership of a new and gifted sultan, Mehmed II, the Turks were ready to renew their challenge to Constantinople.

Constantinople was the proud capital of a Christian empire which had survived a thousand years of conflict with barbarian hordes and Moslem armies. Paradoxically its most successful enemies had been the Christian powers of western Europe who resented the independence of the Greek Orthodox Church and whose unsuccessful Crusaders against Islam had vented their frustration on the city in 1204 by putting it to the sword. Constantinople never recovered its former power and in 1453, isolated by the Osmanli armies and denied assistance by European powers preoccupied by their own affairs, its capture was assured. Thereafter it was rebuilt by Mehmed and restored to importance as the economic and political centre of the Turkish Empire.

Restless for further victories, the Turks began to push out their frontiers at every point. Trebizond, the last remaining Greek outpost on the Black Sea coast of Anatolia, was taken in 1461, the desert region of Karaman in south-eastern Anatolia was overrun in 1464, and over in the east the Turcoman tribes of Azerbaijan were defeated though not rendered harmless in 1473. The Genoese lost their Black Sea colonies of Amastris (1461) and Kaffa (1475), and from Kaffa the advance continued against the Krim Tatars of the Crimea. From Rumelia the rate of expansion was equally dramatic. The Turks took Mistra, Athens and the Morea between 1458 and 1460, Serbia in 1459, Bosnia in 1464 and Albania in 1479. As a result the entire Balkan peninsula south of a line formed by the Danube and Sava rivers was in Osmanli hands. Yet this was not the end of their expansion. From the moment of their capture of Constantinople the sight of dockyards prompted them to build from scratch a fleet of galleys to patrol the Black Sea and to drive the Genoese and Venetians from their colonies in the Aegean. The Italians were totally unprepared for such a move and consistently underestimated the new found naval strength of the Turks. Lesbos was seized from Genoa in 1462, Negroponte from Venice in 1470 and when the conquest of Albania provided the Turks with a naval base at Scutari, their galleys began to raid the Adriatic.

The energy, the ruthlessness and the power of the Osmanli Turks was only equalled by their restlessness for further victories – a direct consequence of their descent from the Ghazi tribes of the thirteenth century – but it was necessary to have a leader who could direct them to the best advantage. Mehmed II had been such a leader. Throughout his reign the rate of expansion had been extraordinarily rapid: under his son Bayezid (1481–1512) the Empire stagnated. Bayezid was probably as aggressive by nature as any other Osmanli sultan, but he faced a particular problem of his own which limited his freedom of action and ultimately seems to have sapped his resolution. On his accession, his brother Jem had escaped from court to challenge him for the throne and fought against him in the borderlands of Karaman before taking refuge in Egypt. Fearful of assassins in his brother's pay, Jem fled in 1482 to the Knights of St John in Rhodes who sent him as a prisoner to France and subsequently to Rome. While Jem remained alive in European hands Bayezid dared not engage his forces in a major war for fear that once his attention was engaged in one half of his empire, his brother might land in the other half to raise rebellion. Consequently, although he paid a pension to the pope to ensure that Jem was not released from captivity, he dared not move against Europe until Jem's death in 1495. Thereafter he pursued a successful campaign against Venice for control of the islands off the Dalmatian Coast and invaded Moldavia to establish the local *voivode*, Stephen, as his vassal in 1504.

Compared with Mehmed's wide ranging campaign, Bayezid's achievement seemed insignificant and his army leaders murmured their dissatisfaction. Moreover, there was need of a strong show of force on the eastern frontier, not only against the Mamluk rulers of Syria and Egypt, but also after 1503 against the new Shah Ismael of Persia. Ismael was a member of the Shia, a combination of Moslem sects whose leaders traced their descent not to the prophet but to his son-in-law. On his accession Ismael began to persecute the more orthodox sect of Sunnites who represented the majority of his subjects. This concerned the Osmanlis intimately. Not only were they Sunnites themselves but they were already disturbed by the presence of Shiite sects among their subject population in Anatolia. When these broke out in an abortive rebellion in 1511 Bayezid's sons decided to replace their father in order to pursue a more aggressive policy. The most aggressive of them, Selim, naturally won the support of the army, and after he had killed his brothers in a short civil war he deposed Bayezid who died shortly afterwards.

Selim was a born soldier, aptly named the Grim. He immediately marched through Anatolia, killing or imprisoning more than

40,000 Shiites before advancing further east against Shah Ismael in 1514. His troops had to make their way through the difficult terrain of Armenia and it was an exhausted army which met the Persians at Tchaldiran. The Persians greatly outnumbered the Osmanlis, but they lacked artillery and their infantry was no match for the janissaries (see below). Although their cavalry broke through on the left wing they failed to unsettle the janissaries and finally fell victim to their firearms. Selim could not exploit the opportunity to march south into Persia itself as winter was approaching; but before withdrawing he annexed Tabriz in Azerbaijan, Kurdistan and the northern regions of Mesopotamia. For the rest of his reign the Turks were safe from Persia.

In his next campaign Selim struck out against the Mamluk rulers of Syria and Egypt. They had formerly enjoyed great power in the Middle East but they were no longer capable of meeting the Osmanlis in battle. They gambled everything on a show of force north of Aleppo but Selim was not deterred. In 1516 he destroyed their army at Marj Dabik. Before the battle the Mamluks had lodged their supplies and their state treasury in Aleppo but when news arrived of their defeat, the citizens closed the gates against them and offered their city to the Turks. Selim advanced swiftly and took Damascus checking his army only on the edge of the desert south of Gaza. Further progress seemed unwise. As his conquest of Syria had served its purpose by safeguarding the eastern frontier of the empire, a desert campaign so far from home, with the additional hazard that his troops would be harassed by Arab tribesmen, might jeopardise all he had gained. Selim, however, was like Mehmed II; his ruthlessness in seeking territories to conquer made him determined to deal with the Mamluks once and for all, and in 1517 he launched a new campaign across the desert. Despite the difficulties experienced by his troops he succeeded in reaching Egypt, capturing Cairo and executing the last of the Mamluk sultans.

Selim's campaigns had made the Osmanli Turks the major power in the Middle East. Syria was absorbed completely within the Empire, Egypt was made a tributary state ruled by an Osmanli pasha, and by succeeding the Mamluks as protectors of the holy cities of Medina and Mecca the Osmanli sultans achieved a position of great honour and prestige throughout Islam. Economically, too, Egypt was a valuable asset. Its corn, rice and dates were badly needed to supply the empire, and the Venetians were compelled to pay a rich tribute in order to have access to the overland routes which brought the spices from the Red Sea and the Persian Gulf. One difficulty remained to be resolved. Osmanli navigation between Constantinople and Alexandria was harrassed by the European base at Rhodes where the Knights of St John plundered the shipping lanes along the southern Anatolian coast. Selim ordered a fleet to be equipped in Constantinople in order to land his troops on Rhodes but in 1520 at the very outset of the campaign he died. The Knights of St John were granted a few months' respite until his successor, Suleyman, carried out his plans in 1523.

The territorial extent of the Osmanli Empire in 1520 is frequently underestimated by western Europeans who are usually unfamiliar with the region. From the Bosnian frontier as the crow flies, Trebizond lies more than 1,300 miles to the east; a similar journey to the west would take the traveller into Northern Ireland. The rapidity of the conquest, is more easily apprehended, but neither map nor date list can provide an explanation of the astonishing ease with which the Turks acquired so vast an area in so short a time.

One obvious advantage enjoyed by the Turks was the failure of their enemies to unite against them. This was true of the petty Balkan states whose jealousies and long-standing feuds prevented them from coming to each other's aid; it was equally true of the major European powers. When Constantinople was threatened in 1453, one of the few men to try to rally European support for the city was Aeneas Sylvius Piccolomini, then bishop of Siena: 'Mohammed is among us; the sabre of the Turks waves over our heads; the Black Sea is shut to our ships; the foe possess Wallachia whence they will pass into Hungary – and Germany. And we meanwhile live in strife and enmity among ourselves.' The Burgundian court responded with an emotional scene at the so-called Banquet of Vows when all those present vowed to go on crusade – but nothing practical was done. Other states allowed the fall of Constantinople to pass with nothing more than conventional expressions of regret. This was partly due to the general lack of sympathy for the Greek Orthodox Church, an attitude reciprocated by the Greeks who refused to submit to Rome in order to secure western aid.

The truth was that crusading zeal had more or less evaporated.

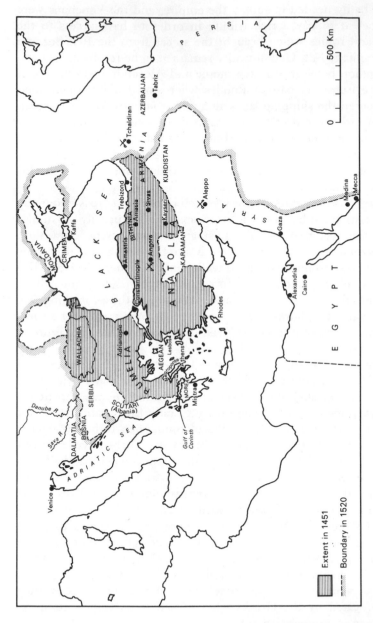

The Empire of the Osmanli Turks

Extent in 1451
Boundary in 1520

Pope Nicholas V responded to the bishop of Siena's appeal by ordering the imposition of a tithe to pay for a crusade, but the money, passed into his own treasury without further comment; Venice preferred to pay the Osmanli tolls than join a crusade which might disrupt her trade with Aleppo and Alexandria, and by 1507 there were representatives of over 60 Florentine firms busily engaged in seeking markets in Constantinople. The Italian Wars preoccupied the attention of other powers and after 1520 the Most Christian Kings of France, as they were styled, were ready to advance their interests against Charles V by allying with the Osmanli Turks. The address of Henry VIII to the Venetian ambassador in 1517 reflected not only the unwillingness of Europeans to fight the Turks, but also a compelling reason why they should not do so: 'Domine Orator. You are sage and of your prudence may comprehend that no general expedition against the Turks will ever be effected so long as such treachery prevails among the Christian princes that their sole thought is to destroy one another.'

The Osmanli Turks, however, did not grow powerful merely because their enemies proved incapable of united action against them. The underlying cause of their success was that they retained their original character as nomadic warriors, *sipahis*, restless herdsmen of the waste who lived only for fighting and for plunder. Inured to the vagaries of climate, these hordes of cavalry fought with equal ferocity among the mountains, on the plains or in the desert. Their taste for rice and their use of camels as supply animals made it easy for them to operate at great distances from home, as the Venetian Busbecq commented in the sixteenth century: 'Rice keeps well and provides a wholesome food, a little of which suffices to feed a large number. Camels can carry very heavy burdens, endure hunger and thirst and require very little attention.' The land they conquered was divided into fiefs, the smallest unit, the *timar*, being large enough to support one *sipahi* and his servants. Regional groups of *timars* were known as *sanjaks* and all the *sipahis* of the *sanjak* fought together under their *sanjakbeg*. These in turn assembled under the principal feudatories of the sultan, the *beglerbegs*, the lords of lords. In time of war the Beglerbeg of Anatolia could summon 50,000 *sipahis* to his banner, and his colleague in Rumelia, 80,000. In addition to these were the personal *sipahis* of the sultan, 15,000 in all who held no fiefs but served for pay and for the honour of being his household cavalry.

The Osmanli empire resembled a military machine geared to perpetual expansion, unable to adjust itself to conditions of peace. The *sipahis*, land-hungry freebooters though they were, rarely settled down to the life of landed proprietors, and in the early days of the empire it was unusual for a son to inherit his father's land. The fief in fact was generally regarded as a mere resting place between campaigns. Throughout their empire, therefore, the Osmanlis never assimilated with the local population: they constituted an army of occupation, exploiting the skills and services of their subjects. In order to produce a force of infantry, the janissaries, they conscripted approximately one-fifth of all the Christian boys in their empire at intervals of about five years. To ensure both their success as soldiers and their loyalty to the sultan, the boys were given a remarkable education. The first step was to divorce them entirely from the subject races by converting them to Islam. A forced conversion would have been disastrous since once they were armed they might have turned against their masters, but there was little need for coercion. The quality of Christian education which these children had received at the hands of simple peasants was less than adequate to survive a thorough course of education in the doctrines of Islam. Moreover, the Dervish order of the Bektashi, which exercised considerable influence both at court and among the janissaries, tended to teach a mystical faith in which all organised religions, whether Christian or Islamic, were transcended in a personal communion with God. The janissaries never wavered in their new faith and became the steadfast supporters of the sultan.

By 1520 the janissaries constituted a force of 12,000 highly trained infantry whose disciplined manoeuvres in the centre of the battlefield provided an invaluable element of stability amidst the impetuous charges of the *sipahis*. Moreover, they became proficient in the use of firearms and artillery which made them the equal of any European force, and superior to any other in the Middle East. Their high morale and professional skill was strengthened by the exceptional rigour of their life. Marriage was forbidden them as was the pursuit of any other occupation, but in return they were held in high esteem and were rewarded with good pay and many opportunities for promotion in the sultan's service. Their only weakness was a tendency to put their love of warfare above their loyalty to an inactive sultan like Bayezid. On such occasions they acted like the Praetorian Guard, and exercised their power to initiate a palace revolution in order to promote the succession of a more warlike ruler.

In addition to their military services the janissaries provided a useful body from which to recruit men of other skills which the Osmanlis lacked. Technicians, engineers and architects were drawn from their ranks and the most intelligent were selected for employment in the administration of the empire. In this way some became the chief advisers of the sultan. Ibrahim, born of Greek Christian parents, was conscripted into the janissaries, became Beglerbeg of Rumelia and finally, in 1523, Grand Vezir to the Sultan Suleyman. Indeed, of nearly fifty grand vezirs of the fifteenth and sixteenth centuries only five were of direct Osmanli descent, which prompted the description of the council of vezirs as a slave market. The Venetian, Marcantonio Barbaro, who observed the empire closely, wrote that 'it is a fact truly worthy of much consideration that the riches, the forces and the government, and in short the whole state of the Osmanli empire, is founded upon and placed in the hands of persons all born in the faith of Christ who by different methods are made slaves and transferred into the Moslem sect.' To add substance to this point it should be remembered that the sultans themselves were frequently of mixed descent since their harems were filled with women from their subject races.

One factor that has often been underestimated in the West was the tolerable nature of Osmanli rule. From time to time the Turks were capable of great cruelty, especially when they suspected rebellion, but in general their government proved remarkably acceptable to their subjects. Within a brutal framework their efficient administration guaranteed internal peace and security, Constantinople was restored to more than its former greatness as a commercial city, and trade conducted by the subject races began to revive throughout the Balkans and the Middle East. Moreover the conquest of the Balkans put an end to the severities of seigneurial rule. The new fief holders demanded taxes but not forced labour. Their principal concern was to maintain themselves between campaigns, and consequently 'they had no cause to make exorbitant demands on tenants for the upkeep of lordly establishments such as those of their predecessors, and some contemporary evidence shows them on the best of terms with the small proprietors on their lands' (D. M. Vaughan). Peasant agriculture enjoyed greater security with less interference from the fief holders than ever in the past, and the population had little cause to envy the serfs of Hungary and Poland. Even the *devshirme*, the regular levy of young boys for the janissaries, though it could never be regarded as a blessing, was frequently accepted as a means of advancement for the sons of peasants who had little enough of their own to offer to their children.

In short, the relative prosperity and tranquillity enjoyed by the Balkan peoples was more instrumental in securing their obedience to the new regime than the fear of bloody reprisal should they rebel. What ultimately induced this acquiescent mood was the degree of toleration afforded to Christianity. Islam was a crusading religion and the Osmanlis were its devoted adherents, yet except on odd occasions they rarely persecuted the Christians among their own subject races. The Greek Orthodox Church was protected and its patriarchs continued to enjoy a privileged position in Constantinople. Mehmed in particular was skilful in exploiting the Greek Christian's hostility to Rome and for men like Gennadios, the first patriarch to be appointed after 1453, the 'turban of Mehmed' was indeed to be preferred to 'the pope's tiara'.

Acceptance of the sultan's yoke did not compel the Balkan Christians to renounce their faith, nor did it expose them to a tidal wave of barbarism. The environment of the Osmanli Empire with its predominantly military character was not conducive to the pursuit of culture and refinement, but if the soldiers in the field were brutal and uncivilised, their rulers showed themselves to be men of learning, sympathetic to the arts. Their Islamic tradition had made them heirs to the culture of Arabia and Persia; their conquest of Anatolia had introduced them not only to the building techniques and art forms of the Seljuk Turks, but also to the speculative scholarship for which the universities of Sivas, Amasia and Kayseri had been renowned since the thirteenth century; their prolonged contact with the Greek empire of Constantinople had resulted in their acquisition of the corpus of Greek science and philosophy. Mehmed himself read Greek, possessed his own library and intervened in the sack of Constantinople to rescue what he could of manuscripts and works of art. He was the patron of the Greek humanist Critoboulos and of Italians too. Bayezid's elder son, Kirkud, and Suleyman the Magnificent, were also men of learning who enjoyed the company of scholars and the work of artists. Even Selim the Grim erected among others the splendid mosque in Damascus which still bears his name and his architect Sinan has been acclaimed 'as one of the great architects of the world; a mysterious personage, a janissary and military engineer by training, no one knows of what nation, Greek or Albanian or Armenian, who built more than a hundred mosques all over Turkey between his fiftieth and ninetieth year, and who, in his capacity as a figure of the Renaissance, had correspondence with the painter Titian' (Sacheverell Sitwell).

The fall of Constantinople must not, therefore, be compared too closely with the fall of Rome a thousand years before. Its loss was a severe blow for Christendom – and one for which Christendom must share responsibility – but it cannot be interpreted as a triumph of barbarism over civilisation. The Osmanli Turks for all their brutal preoccupation with warfare were representatives of a culture which could claim its own distinction. Alongside the German woodcuts which understandably portrayed the Turks as evil monsters must be set Bellini's sensitive and thoughtful study of Mehmed II.

The Italian Wars 1454 – 1519

If the expansion of the Osmanli Empire aroused little more than conventional expressions of alarm among the rulers of western Europe, each and every shift in the kaleidoscopic pattern of Italian politics was followed with intense concern. Italy had been torn apart for several hundred years by economic rivalries, civic feuds and personal vendettas which offered countless opportunities for speculative intervention by foreigners. The major conflict of the later Middle Ages had involved the papacy and the empire, but other princes too had come to regard certain regions of the peninsula as their own particular spheres of interest. The dangers of the situation were finally recognised when in 1454 the rulers of Florence, Naples and Milan decided to settle their differences at the Peace of Lodi. Too weak to dominate their neighbours, too powerful to be dominated in turn, this coalition of former enemies was able to frustrate the designs of foreigners by establishing an uneasy equilibrium in the affairs of Italy. For nearly forty years the peninsula was more or less at peace, but as a new generation of rulers came to power the unresolved antagonisms between the states were once again submitted to the arbitrament of war.

Of the five major powers in Italy, the kingdom of Naples was quite different from the others, being neither mercantile nor urban in character but dependent upon agriculture and sheep farming. Its king, Ferrante, descended from the bastard line of the royal family of Aragon, was manifestly insecure. His kingdom was claimed as a fief by the papacy, his Adriatic ports were threatened by the extension of Venetian power, Apulia was raided by the Osmanlis, and Ferdinand of Aragon, whose empire extended across the Mediterranean to include the island of Sicily, awaited the opportunity to restore his family to the Neapolitan throne. In addition, the claim of the dukes of Anjou who had briefly governed Naples in the fourteenth century had been inherited by Charles VIII of France who was eager to make himself a name by intervening in Italy. Nor could Ferrante depend upon his own subjects for support. Both he and his aggressive son Alfonso were universally unpopular and though they had survived a rebellion in 1485, the conspirators led by the prince of San Severino had fled to the court of Charles VIII in the hope of returning at the head of a French army. Everything depended upon maintaining the alliance with Florence and Milan but this too had become increasingly insecure. Ferrante had married his daughter, Isabella, to Gian Galeazzo Sforza, the young duke of Milan, but the duke's eclipse by his uncle Lodovico (see below) had infuriated Isabella and embittered relations between the two states.

The popes who plotted to enforce their feudal rights in Naples were themselves in danger of losing control within their own territories. The papal states which lay across the centre of Italy were notorious for lawlessness. Every town had its local leaders who defied the pope's authority, and Rome itself, with its proud republican tradition, was generally avoided by the popes who feared for their safety among its crowded streets. It is not surprising that in the face of such a problem the popes should have allowed their political ambitions to engulf their pastoral role as the spiritual leaders of the Church. Sixtus IV (1471–84) used measures similar to those of any secular prince to establish his control, raising armies to destroy opposition and appointing relatives to govern for him in the place of local families. His ruthless policies made him remarkably successful in asserting his authority but, unlike any other prince, he could not ensure the survival of his government by establishing a dynasty. His *nipoti*, the relatives whom he appointed, were immediately replaced by the *nipoti* of his successors. The confusion was made worse because the general practice of electing elderly men to the papacy meant that each new administration had only a short time in which to establish itself. In 1492, however, with the election of Rodrigo Borgia as Alexander VI, the papal states came under a man of great experience in public business who had spent many years in the administration of papal departments. He intended, with the military support of his illegitimate son Cesare, to make his rule effective throughout the papal states and to play an influential part in the politics of Italy.

North-west of the papal states lay the wealthy city of Florence which exercised control over most of Tuscany and had recently acquired the port of Pisa. For centuries it had been a battle-ground for civic factions until Cosimo de Medici succeeded in establishing his personal authority behind a front of popular support. His skill in packing the assemblies and committees with men whose interests lay in furthering his rule, and his adroit exploitation of the benefits which Florence derived from his government, allowed him to direct the city's policies without antagonising the general public by too great a display of personal authority. Lorenzo, his grandson, was much less astute both in the conduct of the family firm (see page 12) and in the open demonstration of his power. He cut a princely figure among the fiercely republican citizens of Florence and made his household an international centre for artists, scholars and poets. His public style and his assumption of authority as though by right of succession made him many enemies and his lavish patronage was criticised when taxes had to be collected. On both counts he was publicly assailed by Savonarola, a Florentine monk who combined republican zeal with a puritan attitude to the arts. His hellfire sermons denounced the fashions current among Lorenzo's artists as irreligious and obscene, his polemical tracts called for a return to democratic government, and both were singularly effective in mobilising public opinion against the Medici. Lorenzo was skilful enough to ride the storm until his death in 1492, but his son, Piero, was an inadequate successor. Arrogant in demanding public recognition of his right to rule but palpably unfitted for the task, he merely added force to the revolutionary factions which were stirring in the city.

If Florence well deserved its reputation for domestic tumult, its rival, Venice, was justly proud of its long tradition of well-ordered government. A group of leading families, listed in the so-called 'Golden Book', had won a monopoly of political power and from their number were elected the doge and the council of ten. Under this oligarchy Venice had prospered for more than a century. Her rulers were too skilful in the art of government to fail to distribute the material benefits of their rule among the population as a whole; her citizens were too mindful of the advantages enjoyed by their state to prejudice them by agitating for a different constitution. Personal taxation was low since the republic's chief source of revenue was derived from the customs duties levied on the massive flow of goods which passed through the lagoons. Armed with this wealth the Venetians built the finest arsenal in Europe, providing the armaments and galleys by which their trade was made secure, and sent ambassadors in their scores to defend their interests across Europe and to supply a regular fund of reliable market intelligence (see page 124). So surely founded was Venetian pre-eminence in the commerce of the Mediterranean and of Europe, that neither the Portuguese discoveries nor the conquests of the Osmanli Turks could do more than temporarily unsettle it. More serious was the hostility of the republic's Italian neighbours. In an ill-judged departure from the pursuit of trade, the Venetians had established themselves on the mainland and advanced their frontier westwards along the valley of the Po. By this means they not only forfeited the strategic advantage that they had formerly enjoyed of insularity among the lagoons, but committed themselves to the defence of a region without natural boundaries or defences against the armies of the three powers most jealous of their expansion – the emperor to the north, the pope to the south and the duke of Milan to the west.

Milan was a thriving commercial centre in the heart of Lombardy which in the fourteenth century had come very near to being the capital of northern Italy. Led by the Visconti family, its empire had extended across the Apennines into Tuscany until the stubborn opposition of the citizens of Florence had finally turned the tide against Milan. When the last Visconti died in 1447, Milan was taken over by Francesco Sforza, a mercenary captain, or *condottiere*, of great repute whom the Visconti had commissioned to defend the city. When no one proved capable of unseating him, the other rulers, anxious to arrive at a general settlement at Lodi, agreed to recognise his right to govern Lombardy. His rule imposed a heavy burden on the city since he dared not govern without a large and costly army, but the maintenance of peace promoted the expansion of trade and the Milanese became reconciled both to the usurper and to his heavy taxes. Indeed the construction of the Duomo in Milan, the Certosa in Pavia and several other public buildings throughout Lombardy bore witness to the duchy's prosperity and to the readiness of its inhabitants to enjoy the fruits of peace.

Francesco Sforza died in 1480 leaving his son, Gian Galeazzo, in the care of his brother Lodovico, known as Il Moro. It proved to be a classic case of the wicked uncle appropriating the rights of his nephew, although in all fairness it was clear that Gian Galeazzo was a sickly child unlikely to make a success of government. Lodovico by contrast began with great éclat. His court, inspired by his talented wife Beatrice d'Este, provided a rich source of patronage for artists and scholars, and Lodovico proved to be a sound administrator. There was, however, a weakness in his character. Behind the rich and capable façade of his government he went in fear of rebellion and of the rivalry of other states and, able politician though he was, he never dared to trust in the outcome of his own policies. He was justifiably suspicious of Venetian ambitions in the Po valley; he feared the duke of Orleans who had married the last Visconti princess; he was uneasy about the emperor's claim to be the feudal suzerain of Milan; but none of these immediate neighbours caused him as much anxiety as the distant king of Naples.

The marriage of Isabella and Gian Galeazzo, intended to preserve the alliance between Naples and Milan, proved to be its undoing. Isabella refused to acquiesce in Lodovico's assumption of power, nor could she submit to take second place at court to Beatrice d'Este. Her complaints became more violent . . . 'If you will not help us' she wrote to Ferrante, 'I would rather die by my own hand than bear this tyrannous yoke and suffer in a strange

country under the eyes of a rival'. Ferrante's threats of war could
not be taken lightly. His fleet was capable of blockading Genoa
while his army, passing through the territory of his ally Florence,
would find an easy route across the Apennines into Lombardy.
The death of Lorenzo de Medici in 1492 removed the one man
who could hope to hold the balance between the two powers, and
when his son Piero declared himself in favour of Naples, Lodovico
had to act swiftly. His brother, Cardinal Ascanio Sforza,
persuaded Alexander VI to ally with Milan, the offer of Bianca
Sforza as a richly-dowered wife for the emperor Maximilian
secured the promise of his support, but Lodovico dared not rest
his defence on diplomacy alone. Instead he determined on a pre-
emptive strike against Ferrante by calling upon Charles VIII
of France to pursue his claim to Naples with the aid of Milanese
troops.

Charles needed no encouragement from Lodovico. The rich
works of art, the wealthy cities and the historic milieu of Renaissance Italy afforded him the prospect of spoils far richer, and
opportunities for glory more compelling, than any offered in the
borderlands of Burgundy and Flanders. His army was well
equipped with light artillery, his heavy cavalry was the best in
Europe (see page 122) and he could count upon the services not
only of Milan but also of the many Italian exiles including the
Neapolitan rebels of 1485 who had found refuge at his court.
Charles was full of visionary plans. His claim to Naples, though
inadequate, had captured his imagination and he planned to make
the pope his prisoner so that the papal claim to suzerainty over
the Neapolitan kingdom might be silenced. He also spoke with
great enthusiasm of leading a crusade from Neapolitan ports,
and if his pious intention caused little anxiety in Constantinople,
it nonetheless alarmed the Venetians who feared that it would
disrupt their commerce in the eastern Mediterranean.

Charles was so eager to lead his people like some new Moses
into their promised land that he overlooked the need to safeguard
national interests nearer home. By marrying Anne of Brittany he
had forfeited his legal right to Artois and Franche Comté, but it
ran quite contrary to his father's policies to restore them without
a struggle to Maximilian at the Peace of Senlis, 1493 (see
page 98). Moreover, though it cost little to purchase English
neutrality at Etaples in 1492 by renewing to Henry VII the pensions

granted at Picquigny to Edward IV, it was foolhardy to imagine that the cession of the Pyrenean counties of Roussillon and Cerdagne to Aragon by the Treaty of Barcelona 1494 would distract Ferdinand from his own ambitions in Naples. It was equally foolish, of course, for the Italians themselves to fail to recognise what was now happening. Foreigners had frequently intervened in Italy in the past to secure an immediate local advantage but rarely to sustain a long campaign. The French invasion of 1494 was a different matter altogether. Charles was the ruler of a powerful and well-organised kingdom equipped with all the resources necessary to prosecute a major war. Aragon too could not fail to follow suit in order to protect her interests in Sicily and Naples, and between the forces of these two major powers the Italian states were soon to lose control over their own destinies.

This was immediately made clear by the campaign of 1494–5. Ferrante's plan to seize Genoa and to hold the Apennines alongside Piero de Medici was frustrated by the vigour of the French advance from Lombardy. The duke of Orleans occupied Genoa before the Neapolitan fleet arrived, while the main force burst into Tuscany brushing aside all resistance with brutal efficiency. To save the Florentines from the consequences of their alliance with Ferrante, Savonarola led a popular rising against Piero and welcomed Charles VIII into the city as the protector of its new constitution. Ferrante's army withdrew in haste to Naples but the onset of an abnormally mild autumn allowed the French to follow in close pursuit. By Christmas, Charles was in Rome where Alexander VI was obliged to recognise not only his title to Naples but also to surrender to him the Osmanli prince, Jem in preparation for the crusade against Bayezid. Ferrante died a few weeks later as the French invaded his kingdom. His son Alfonso was so universally detested that no one would fight in his defence, and by February 1495 Charles was king of Naples.

Ferdinand of Aragon together with the emperor Maximilian and the citizens of Venice had observed the French campaign with growing dismay and within a month of Charles's entry into Naples they had formed the League of Venice to drive him out. They found a ready ally in Alexander VI, eager to escape the indignity of being Charles's private chaplain, and an unexpected one in Lodovico Sforza. Gian Galeazzo's death in 1494 had made the Neapolitan campaign unhappily irrelevant as far as Lodovico was concerned, and his fears were now engaged by the duke of Orleans who was not only the commander of the French rearguard in Lombardy but also the descendant of the last Visconti princess.

News of the League's formation took Charles VIII by surprise but, scornful of its military power, he stayed in Naples until he had refilled his treasury from the taxes levied every spring on the vast flocks of migrant sheep. He then moved north into the Apennines and at Fornova met the army of the League. The battle was inconclusive as neither army was defeated but Francesco Gonzaga of Mantua, who commanded the Italians, claimed a victory on the strength of capturing the French baggage train – and commissioned Mantegna (see page 56) to paint for him a *Madonna della Vittoria*. He was no doubt justified since Charles decided that he could do no more without reinforcements and set off for France. Lodovico, who had dreaded his arrival in Lombardy, hastily changed sides in order to assure Charles, in company with the duke of Orleans, a swift and safe passage across the Alps. The garrison left by Charles in Naples did not survive for long. The demands made upon the population by the French and by the exiles who had returned in their company provoked a revival of loyalty to the royal family, and when Alfonso renounced his claim in favour of his popular son, Ferrantino, a national rising took place. This gave Ferdinand of Aragon his first opportunity to intervene directly in the kingdom by sending his finest soldier, Gonzalo de Cordoba, who defeated the French at the Battle of Atella in 1496. Ferrantino was killed in the battle but for the time being the Spaniards were prepared to put his uncle, Federigo, on the throne. The news of the battle deterred Charles from making an immediate return to Italy, and two years later he died.

For all its drama the French campaign appeared to have altered very little in the political structure of Italy. The states and their ruling families were the same as before except in Florence where Savonarola's democratic republic had been established with French aid. New constitutions, however, could not eliminate traditional habits of faction and Savonarola's popularity was short-lived. His pietistic zeal, his insistence that his programme was the will of God had been happily accepted when his sermons were directed against the Medici; when he turned upon his fellow-

Labels on map: CARINTHIA, Novara, Milan, LOMBARDY, Pavia, Lodi, Marignano, Mantua, Venice, Agnadello, Trieste, Fiume, Fornova, Po R., Genoa, Bologna, Ravenna, TUSCANY, Pisa, Florence, FLORENCE, PAPAL, SIENA, STATES, ABRUZZI, Rome, Cerignola, TERRA DI LAVORO, Naples, Atella, APULIA, CALABRIA, SICILY

Papal States
Venice
Florence
Milan
Naples

Italy at the end of the fifteenth century

citizens they handed him over to the pope's commissioners and had him burned in 1498. His constitution survived him until 1513.

What Italians failed to recognise in 1498 was that although they had largely survived the war unscathed, the French and Spaniards had whetted their appetites for Italian territory and had every opportunity to satisfy them in the future. Federigo ruled in Naples by the consent of Ferdinand of Aragon and Lodovico Sforza was not to rule much longer in Milan once Louis, duke of Orleans, had succeeded Charles as Louis XII of France. Within twelve months of his accession he had crossed the Alps and made himself master of Lombardy. Lodovico had contributed to his own defeat by spending his money on his court instead of on his army, and no Italian state was prepared to help him after his treachery to the League of Venice. His own commanders, angry at the promotion of a favourite, deserted to Louis and the people, hoping to be spared the heavy taxes of the Sforzas, made no resistance to the French army. In 1500 the pendulum of popularity swung away from the French as it had done in Naples in 1496 and a revolution brought Lodovico back to power. But Lombardy, unlike Naples, was not far distant from the French king's reserves and within a few months Louis' army was arrayed against Lodovico's at Novara. The outcome was determined by the Swiss infantry who had been recruited by both sides. Those on the French side, however, represented the Common League of Swiss cantons and, after remonstrating with their fellow countrymen in Lodovico's army, they persuaded them to lay down their arms. Consequently, in 1500 Louis occupied Milan for the second time and Lodovico was sent to France as a prisoner.

No sooner had he settled in Milan than Louis XII revived the French claim to Naples by coming to a secret agreement with Ferdinand of Aragon in the Treaty of Granada (1500). The pope's traditional interest in Naples was recognised by inviting him to endorse the treaty and in return Cesare Borgia was assured of French assistance in establishing his father's authority throughout the papal states. Under the treaty, Louis was to be king of Naples and rule the Abruzzi and Terra di Lavoro and Ferdinand was to be grand duke and occupy the southern provinces of Apulia and Calabria. The central area was deliberately left to be resolved by the fortunes of war. Federigo himself was given no warning of the attack. Indeed when Gonzalo de Cordoba crossed over from Sicily he thought the Spaniards had come to strengthen his defence against the French. So angry was he at the deception that in 1502, when the struggle was clearly over, he preferred to surrender to Louis rather than to Ferdinand. He too was sent off to France but, unlike Lodovico, as a free man to be compensated with the duchy of Anjou. As soon as he left, the allies fell out over the disposal of the central territories. Cordoba's victories at Cerignola and on the Garigliano river settled the matter in Spain's favour and by 1503 the kingdom of Naples was entirely under Ferdinand of Aragon's control.

After 1503 Louis, Ferdinand and Maximilian were in conflict

over issues outside Italy but in 1508 they agreed to settle their differences at Cambrai in order to unite their forces against the republic of Venice – a far cry from the Peace of Lodi when the Italians had met in similar fashion to keep the foreigners at bay. Louis inherited from the Sforza dukes the traditional frontier disputes with Venice in the Po valley, Maximilian claimed the restoration of Trieste and Fiume to his duchy of Carinthia and Ferdinand wanted to recover the Apulian ports which Venice had occupied by stealth during Charles VIII's short reign in Naples. Even the new pope, Julius II, (1503–13) who had roundly declared against the embroilment of foreigners in Italy with the dramatic cry *Fuori i barbari* (Keep the barbarians out), was prepared to ally with them in order to settle the papacy's longstanding differences with Venice over territory and jurisdiction. The attack was launched by Louis XII whose army won a major victory at Agnadello in 1509. As a result, the Venetians withdrew their forces from the mainland in order to defend the lagoons – a desperate manoeuvre which in the event proved to be an involuntary master-stroke since none of the allies was yet ready to follow up the victory. A curious peace descended on the mainland towns as they waited for one side or the other to claim jurisdiction over them. As the months passed by, the allies became fractious with each other and by 1510 Julius was at war with Louis over a variety of issues, including the French king's calculated insult in calling a general council at Pisa to discuss papal authority.

By mobilising the accumulated discontents of the past months, Julius reversed the diplomatic situation in 1511 by forming a Holy League in which Venice, Spain, the Empire, the Swiss Cantons and subsequently England were arrayed against France. While warfare broke out in northern France and along the Pyrenees, a French army led by Gaston de Foix conducted a successful campaign through the papal states, but in winning a great victory at Ravenna in 1512 Gaston de Foix was killed. Without his leadership the French were unable to hold their ground in Italy. Lodovico's son, Massimiliano Sforza, was restored to Milan by the Swiss in 1513 and France's solitary ally, the republic of Florence, was compelled to accept the rule of the Medici. In the same year a Medici was elected to the papacy as Leo X. Success, however, brought its own problems for the Holy League. Massimiliano was as much at odds with Venice as any of his predecessors had been, and Venice and the papacy had again drifted into war.

The diplomatic quadrille of the past five years was finally completed when France and Venice became partners against the rest and Louis invaded Lombardy in November 1513. As in 1500 he was met at Novara by Swiss infantry in the service of a Sforza, but this time it was Louis who was defeated. When he died just over a year later he was succeeded by Francis I, a vigorous and vain young man, who wanted to cut a successful figure on the battlefields of Europe and who wasted no time in invading Italy in 1515. The Swiss were still there to block the French advance, but by marching through one of the less-frequented passes, Francis turned their flank and forced them back to Milan. The issue was resolved at Marignano in a battle of memorable intensity. Neither the Swiss infantry nor the French cavalry could gain the upper hand, and for two whole days they struggled against each other until the arrival of a Venetian force settled the matter in favour of France.

Marignano settled the fate of Italy for the next five years. Francis regained Milan, Massimiliano was sent to France with a royal pension and by the Treaty of Noyon with Ferdinand's successor Charles, France and Spain agreed to guarantee each other's right to Lombardy and Naples respectively. Venice, as France's ally at Marignano, was restored to the frontiers she had held in 1494. Leo X secured French recognition of his family's right to rule Florence but in return was obliged to relinquish Parma to Milan and to publish the Concordat of Bologna which confirmed the authority of French kings to make their own appointments within the French Church. The Swiss, unwilling to risk their reputation in a second fight with France, ceded their bases in Lombardy and by the perpetual peace of Fribourg pledged their services to France in all future wars. With the collapse of the last vestiges of the Holy League Maximilian was left isolated. Without money or allies he attempted a single-handed invasion of Milan in 1516, failed dismally, and was compelled to add his signature to the Treaty of Noyon.

Warfare and Diplomacy

In most respects the armies of the period 1450–1520 resembled those of earlier centuries. The pike, the lance and the sword remained in general use and continued thus for many years to come. The long-bow on the other hand had had its day except in England where its solid virtues – a range of 250 yards and a firing rate of six shafts a minute – were still widely extolled. The continental archers preferred the cross-bow. It took one minute to load and fire, and its range was only 150–200 yards, but its square-ended armour-tearing bolt was of greater value than the arrow in bringing down heavy cavalry. Even more effective was the arquebus with its heavy bullet. A new development was the matchlock. Since there was no need to apply the match to the touch hole, the soldier could now concentrate on aiming it and his accuracy was assisted by a barrel rest stuck in the ground. This, of course, made it a difficult weapon to handle and its main use was in the defence of fortified positions, but by 1512 it was being used in the field, protected from a sudden cavalry charge by a shield of pikemen.

The use of artillery for siege work was already well-established, but Europeans no longer competed with each other to produce guns of ever greater dimensions. Unlike the Turks who continued to cast huge cannon on the site of their siege works, they preferred to develop portability and accuracy of aim. Cast iron was likely to fracture and wrought-iron bars, welded in crude iron tubes bound by iron hoops, were difficult to manoeuvre. Bronze was more expensive, but it could be accurately cast by bellfounders, an art in which the Germans and the Flemings were the most proficient.

Light artillery had been first developed by the Burgundians and the French quickly followed suit. Guicciardini, the Florentine historian, reported the alarm of the Italians in 1494 when they came up against guns which were, 'lighter and all cast in bronze . . . drawn by horses with such dexterity that they could keep up with the marching speed of the army . . . and could be used as usefully in the field as in battering walls'. Guicciardini overstated the case. There were still many problems to be overcome in using artillery effectively, not least that of supplying ammunition in bulk for guns with as many as seventeen different calibres, but it was the French artillery which drove the Spaniards out of their defensive position at Ravenna and took its toll of the Swiss infantry at Marignano. Nor was there any doubt that artillery had altered the character of siege warfare. The lofty curtain walls, secure against scaling ladders, were too thin to withstand bombardment. As a result the angle bastion was developed in 1496 by the Knights of St John at the Boulevard of Auvergne on the island of Rhodes. The angle bastion was a solid construction which projected from the curtain wall at an angle to the field so that the adjacent walls could be covered by flanking fire. It was too expensive to be adopted universally. Verona had reconstructed its defence works by 1520, but the cost was so great that throughout the sixteenth century it was only the cities of major strategic importance which rebuilt their walls in this way.

Four or five hundred heavily armed men-at-arms charging forward on powerful horses represented a formidable force which was capable of halting a column of pike. This had been the case for so long that the cavalry was disinclined to adapt itself to changing circumstances and its professional pride was reinforced by the class barrier which separated it from the infantry. When the Chevalier Bayard, admired throughout Europe for his courage and his chivalrous spirit, was invited to dismount outside the walls of Padua in 1509, in order to storm the breach, he refused to do so on the grounds that he could not fight alongside foot soldiers, 'of whom one is a shoemaker, another a farrier, another a baker, and suchlike mechanics who hold not their honour as do we gentlemen'. It was the 'mechanics' who were winning the day as the Swiss had demonstrated to the Burgundians at Grandson and Morat. They formed up in massive squares of about 6,000 pike men, 85 of them standing shoulder to shoulder on a 100-yard front with 70 ranks behind them. Not only could they brush aside a cavalry charge but advance at the trot to drive opposing infantries from the field. Everything, however, depended on drill and discipline and on the selection of open country for their battle-ground. In rough country they tended to fall into disorder, arrayed against firearms and artillery they presented too bulky a target and above all their very solidity militated against manoeuvrability. Gonzalo de Cordoba, therefore, re-arranged his Spanish infantry to fight in rather smaller groups accompanied by troops carrying firearms, a practice followed by other countries.

The problem of providing well-trained troops in great numbers was met differently by each military power. Charles VII of France had issued an ordinance in 1448 to establish in every parish a *franc archer* whose services were rewarded by exempting him from taxation, but the system failed on military and administrative grounds. After their defeat by Maximilian at Guinegatte in 1479, the French abandoned their infantry altogether and hired foreign troops instead – after 1516 these were invariably Swiss. Their cavalry was recruited in three ways. The least satisfactory was the feudal summons, the *ban* and *arrière-ban*, which produced horsemen in great numbers but with little training. The *gendarmerie* were more professional, serving for short periods interspersed with long leaves on their own estates. Best of all were the household cavalry who served the king full-time. Spain had fewer cavalry than France and relied instead on the urban militia who volunteered to serve abroad in Italy where they soon established their superiority even over the Swiss. In Italy the reputation of the *condottieri* has suffered from the criticisms of their own countrymen who were appalled by the apparently effortless success of the French army in 1494. While it is true that they formed private companies, hiring themselves out each season to one state or another, they were skilled in their craft and the legend of their treachery has been exaggerated. The problem at the time of the French wars was not the existence of the *condottieri*, but the fact that there were not enough for them to be arrayed against the invader. Worse still, of course, was the inability of the individual Italian states to combine their forces together against the national armies of France and Spain.

It is misleading, however, to describe any army at the end of the fifteenth century as being national in character, or even predominantly professional. The nucleus of French men-at-arms who rode behind Charles VIII, or of Spanish infantry who served under Gonzalo de Cordoba, was invariably swamped by bands of ill-trained troops of many nationalities seeking employment, adventure and loot. These in turn were accompanied by a horde of camp-followers. In 1495, for example, the French army which had been badly mauled at Fornova returned to France with more than 10,000 camp-followers swarming in its train. Their function was supplying essential services, provisioning the troops, tending the wounded and helping to construct fortifications, but their presence made for disorder and presented commanders with intractable problems of organisation and control.

A necessary adjunct to warfare was the provision of detailed intelligence about an enemy or an ally and for this the traditional type of formal embassy was useless. The Italians were the first to realise this. So finely balanced were the rival factions in many cities where a marriage contract, a family dispute or a bankruptcy could cause an immediate shift in foreign policy, that it became necessary for other cities to be informed of such events by someone who could gauge their significance. Spies were employed, of course, and governments often made use of their own subjects who travelled abroad on private business, but such agents had to operate under cover and could not negotiate efficiently with other governments. To maintain a working alliance and to sustain a regular flow of information, there was no substitute for the permanent accredited agent – the resident ambassador.

The device proved so successful within the Italian peninsula that the Italians began to appoint resident ambassadors to other European courts. The Visconti of Milan were the first to do so in order to maintain their close alliance with the emperor Sigismund, but by the Peace of Lodi all the major cities were represented in this way across the whole of Europe. A form of diplomatic reporting was evolved and courier services were developed so that information could be received both regularly and frequently. The Venetians excelled at this. Despatches arrived every fortnight, sometimes every week, and a returning ambassador was required to present the fruits of his observations in a major speech before the senate. Consequently, these *Relazioni degli Ambasciatori Veneti* have since become a regular quarry of information to be mined by historians researching into the conditions of other states in the fifteenth century. The European monarchies were slow to follow suit. Spain maintained a resident ambassador in England from 1495 and Louis XII was represented at Rome, Venice, Madrid and Vienna, but, outside Italy, diplomacy still remained a hit or miss affair to be conducted by spies or by an occasional formal embassy.

One man much experienced in the diplomacy and warfare of the early sixteenth century was Niccolo Machiavelli who wrote extensively on both subjects. He was a man of many parts, playwright, poet and historian, but his principal interest lay in politics and he wanted above all else to be employed at the centre of affairs. For many years he was a civil servant in the government of Florence and served on several embassies, though never as a permanent ambassador. Diplomacy fascinated him and he was painstakingly thorough in the presentation of his reports. The kind of material he looked for was indicated in a letter to a young friend going on embassy to the court of Charles V. He advised him to report his arrival, then his interview with Charles and subsequently to enquire around the court for information about the emperor. Was he of independent mind or influenced by others – and, if so, by whom? Was he popular? Did he prefer Spain to the Nether- lands? Having exhausted the subject of Charles he was then to examine the other members of the court in similar fashion. It was hardly surprising that when Machiavelli himself went on an embassy to Julius II he should have sent home forty-nine des- patches in fifty days.

His other great interest was in warfare, though his views on the subject were those of an amateur layman. In his view the weakness of Italy was caused by the recruitment of mercenaries. If they were triumphant he said they were only too likely to dominate the state for whom they fought; if they were incompetent then all was lost. In 1503 he laid plans before the government of Florence to set up a militia force of citizens and three years later was appointed secretary to the committee responsible for administering it – the *Nove dell'Ordinanze e Milizia*. The enterprise foundered on the reluctance of the citizens to take up arms for any length of time, and in 1512 in its first major engagement, the militia was routed and the Medici restored to Florence by the Holy League. Machiavelli was exiled, a bitter punishment for one who yearned to live in the public eye. He sought consolation by writing up his theories in *The Art of War*, 1521, supporting his case with a wealth of historical detail about the bravery of ancient Rome to com- pensate for the miserable showing made by his fellow citizens.

His other works, the *Discorsi* and *Il Principe*, also written in exile, were prompted by his anxiety to secure employment once again, even under the Medici, by demonstrating his skilful analysis of affairs. They also revealed an interesting combination of idealism and disenchanted cynicism. Unlike his fellow Florentine historian, Guicciardini, who pessimistically believed that the Italians had fallen prey to their own weakness, stupidity and corruption, Machiavelli diagnosed their failure as a failure of leadership. *Il Principe*, therefore, represented an attempt to marshal all the means by which a man with the necessary qualities of shrewdness and energy might seize power in Italy and mobilise its citizens to drive away the foreigner. Behind the positive intention, however, the cynical detachment of the disappointed politician gave the book its unique character. Its pungent aphorisms were widely quoted and made its author famous for a philosophy of statecraft in which fraud and deceit were regarded as legitimate devices to employ against the big battalions. 'Were men good' he wrote 'this doctrine should not be taught, but because they are wicked and not likely to keep faith with you, you are not obliged to any such strictness with them.' The tone throughout was wholly secular, the only criterion being the success of the state. 'The sagacious politician will always respect religion even if he hath no belief in it, since there have been frequent proofs that through inculcating it, even by craft, much valour has been raised for the defence of the country.'

Despite his attempt to strip away the hypocritical pretensions of contemporary life by an honest and objective analysis of men's actions Machiavelli revealed the jaundiced and one-sided views of the embittered exile. In his *Art of War* he had much of value to say in criticism of the mercenaries, but he failed to admit that they could also be men of professional skill and proven loyalty. Similarly, in *Il Principe* he reflected sadly on the policies of Ferdinand of Aragon who 'never talks of anything but peace and good faith, yet had he ever observed either he would several times have lost his credit and his estates' – ignoring the fact that Ferdinand, though ruthless, was also a man who could be both faithful and peace-loving on occasion. In short, he failed to grasp the complexity of human nature. He looked upon war and diplomacy as sciences whose rules once mastered and applied would result in the successful manipulation of political power. The fate of his own militia, the defeat of Florence and his own sad banishment from public life demonstrated how wrong he was.

4

The Western Monarchies by 1520

Royal Authority in France to 1515

THROUGHOUT the course of the Hundred Years' War, the Valois kings had been so preoccupied, first with the problem of survival and later with the organisation of victory over England, that they had willingly reduced their burden of administration and jurisdiction by allowing members of their own family and certain trusted nobles to undertake the government of their own private territories. The regions of greatest independence were the apanages of Burgundy, Bourbon, Orleans and Anjou, which were granted with virtually sovereign powers to junior members of the royal family. But among the more conventional fiefs too, the noble houses of Brittany, Armagnac, Albret and Foix had become accustomed to administer their territories with little reference to the king. Consequently, by the time the English had been defeated, Louis XI inherited from Charles VII not so much a kingdom as a confederation of self-regarding princedoms.

At first sight Louis XI (1461–83) was scarcely the man to cope with the problem. Intensely jealous though he was of his royal prerogative, he excited general ridicule by the exaggerated home-spun costumes he affected and by his neurotic pretence to be on one occasion a leper, on another the illegitimate son of Charles VII. He was a man of strange moods; suspicious to the point of insanity, superstitious to the extent that he could never again wear clothes in which he had once received bad news, and impelled by a curious restlessness to be always on the move. This same restlessness, however, resulted in a tireless application to matters of government, and in executing his decisions he revealed himself to be ruthless, crafty and cruel. Complex though his character might be and difficult the circumstances of his reign,

Louis derived strength from two special features of the French monarchy as it had developed by 1461. The Salic Law by which no female descendants of the royal family could transmit a title to the throne safeguarded his position by reducing the number of potential claimants. Civil war might be a constant feature of French history, but from 987–1794 no king was ever deposed nor did anyone succeed to the throne in defiance of the Salic Law. In addition, during the crises of the Hundred Years' War, the royal prerogative to raise taxes, imprison offenders and confiscate property without reference to any other authority had been accepted in law, and all that was needed was a king sufficiently determined to enforce his rights.

Louis faced his first major crisis in 1465. The League of Public Weal stage-managed by his powerful enemy and nominal vassal, Charles, duke of Burgundy, brought together his other enemies of England and Aragon in combination with the principal fief holders of the French crown. These included Charles, duke of Berry, the envious brother of the king, René, duke of Anjou and Charles, duke of Orleans who complained that their families' claims to Naples and Milan respectively were not more actively supported by the king, John, duke of Bourbon, who resented the fact that royal officials still exercised authority within his apanages, and Francis, duke of Brittany, who accepted no such limitations to his private jurisdiction and who conducted his own foreign policy, but was yet jealous of the greater independence enjoyed by Burgundy.

For the next ten years or so Louis was in great danger. He suffered many defeats and humiliations, mainly at the hands of Charles of Burgundy, but his enemies at home failed to exploit their advantage by acting effectively in concert against him. On the rare occasions when he was able to seize the initiative, Louis wisely mobilized whatever allies he could find abroad to embarrass his most dangerous opponent Charles of Burgundy, who sought to establish a separate kingdom along the Rhine. Finally, Charles over-reached himself, forfeiting the invaluable aid of England whose king made peace with Louis, and was killed by the Swiss at the Battle of Nancy in 1477 (see page 97). His duchy immediately reverted to the Crown and of his other territories Louis occupied Picardy, Artois and Franche Comté.

Meanwhile conspiracies formed and reformed at home but

were no more successful in the long run than the League of Public Weal. Louis' capacity for intrigue, his ruthless isolation of an enemy, his ability to buy off opposition by short-term concession and, above all, his unassailable right to the throne stood him in good stead. Moreover, the timely deaths of his brother, of Charles of Orleans and of the powerful counts of Armagnac and Foix strengthened his hand by removing some of his most powerful opponents. Francis of Brittany was sufficiently overawed by Louis' success to abandon his claim to conduct an independent foreign policy; John of Bourbon was compelled to relinquish Beaujolais to his brother Pierre de Beaujeu, the one man on whom Louis relied and to whom he had married his daughter Anne; Louis, the new duke of Orleans, was obliged on his accession to marry the king's other daughter, Jeanne, not as a mark of favour but because she was deformed and incapable of child-bearing, – thus the duke could never hope for heirs and his apanage would ultimately revert to the crown. Finally, by the death of René of Anjou in 1480 and of his nephew in 1481, the entire apanage of Anjou, including the duchies of Anjou and Bar with the counties of Maine and Provence, reverted to Louis XI.

Louis' achievement must be accounted a triumph for the French monarchy, but it would be misleading to regard it as the outcome of a deliberate preconceived plan. Louis XI wanted to be more powerful and he became so, but the result was not automatically related to the desire. For most of his reign he lived from hand to mouth, his policies were expedients and his success owed much to the stupidity of many of his opponents and the fortunate death of others. His own death very nearly jeopardised all that had been gained. His final months were spent at Plessis-du-Parc, his body paralysed, his mind insanely active in imagining conspiracies against him, so that the castle was rigged about with booby traps and the only noble admitted to his presence by his guards was Pierre of Beaujeu. Beaujeu and Anne his wife deserved the trust placed in them. When Louis died they saved the frail and backward Charles VIII from the ambitious plans of Louis of Orleans who wanted to divorce his wife and marry Anne, the heiress to Francis of Brittany. The Beaujeus stood firm and the civil war which Louis and Francis waged against the Crown was unsuccessful: 'La Guerre Folle', as it was called, ended in 1488 with the betrothal of Charles himself to Anne of Brittany. Thereafter the kingdom was relatively undisturbed. There were no crop failures, no widespread epidemics and Charles's enthusiasm for the Italian war won the support of his more aggressive nobles, who directed their energies against the Italians instead of against the Crown.

When Charles died in 1498 the throne passed by Salic law to Louis of Orleans. As Louis XII, he divorced Jeanne and married the widowed Anne of Brittany. What had formerly been the dangerous ambition of a disgruntled over-mighty subject now served the interests of the French monarchy. In order to mollify Pierre of Beaujeu, however, Louis recreated for him the apanage of Bourbon – an expedient which revealed that the road to national unification was not as clearly signposted in the fifteenth century as has often been assumed. Moreover, for one dangerous moment in 1501 the daughter of the Beaujeus was suggested as a bride for the future Charles V, with Brittany and Burgundy as her dowry. Fortunately for France the proposal failed and when Louis died in 1515 his cousin, Francis I, inherited a united monarchy. To ensure its continuance he married Claude, the daughter of Louis and Anne of Brittany, and the day of independent duchies and apanages was over.

The task of bringing together the different provinces under the direct jurisdiction of the kings of France was only one aspect of French history in the later fifteenth century. Within these provinces royal jurisdiction had to be made effective, but it would be anachronistic to suppose that the monarchs of the period pursued this aim with any coherence or consistency. Rather, within an inherited situation they provided practical and piecemeal solutions to the problems which faced them. One major problem was the existence of a powerful and highly-privileged estate of nobles. The greatest of them remained virtually autonomous within their territories. Many possessed strong castles from which to defy each other or the king, and all of them exercised judicial and administrative authority in their own seigneurial courts. In practice nothing could be done to alter this. Royal authority could extend to punish individual nobles for treason or for exceeding their privileges, but the privileges of the class were inviolable. It was ludicrous, for example, that the wealthiest class, exacting feudal dues and services from its own tenants, should be exempt from royal taxes, but the Valois kings conceded that it was safer to tax the poorest who paid little but could not protest, than to challenge the rich whose powers of opposition were singularly effective. The only gains to be made were in the field of jurisdiction where, in a piecemeal fashion, the agents of the crown claimed cognisance of the more important cases by issuing special writs to summon them before the royal courts.

Another problem was presented by the rich and privileged position of the Church. It enjoyed the possession of vast estates, its courts administered a separate jurisdiction from the king's, it was exempt from taxation and its power of excommunication equipped it with a powerful defensive weapon. It also appointed its own abbots and bishops, a practice confirmed by the Pragmatic Sanction of Bourges in 1438. This independence had been developed in the first place to prevent papal interference in French affairs, but it also deprived the kings of France of any patronage or influence within their Church. Louis XI had, therefore, tended to ignore the Pragmatic Sanction and to reassert the pope's authority – provided he acted on Louis' recommendations – to appoint the senior clergy. The Church protested strongly at this infringement of its 'Gallican Liberties' and the dispute was not resolved until Francis I secured the Concordat of Bologna in 1516 (see page 120), which gave to him alone the authority to make appointments. What appeared at first sight to be a victory over the papacy was in fact a triumph of the monarchy over its own clergy, and this power to appoint nearly one hundred bishops and archbishops and over five hundred abbots became an effective lever in royal hands to secure clerical obedience to royal policies. In the same period, ecclesiastical jurisdiction was eroded in part by the practice, already established in the seigneurial courts, of summoning important cases before the royal judges.

The towns of France were frequently in conflict with their neighbouring nobility and clergy, especially over matters of jurisdiction, and therefore depended to a large extent upon royal support. Nonetheless, the charters which they had received from the crown made them virtually self-governing in matters of day-to-day administration, and their citizens had purchased exemption from the royal taxes. Louis XI acquired a reputation for being ruthless with the liberties of the towns, in particular by organising the sale of municipal offices, but isolated acts of interference had little impact upon urban independence as a whole, and those who bought their offices from the crown were more concerned to defend their own interests than to promote the king's. No significant step was taken by the crown until Francis I appointed *contrôleurs des deniers communs* in 1515, whose task it was to supervise municipal finances and thus to interpose a measure of royal direction.

The agents of royal government had, therefore, to operate within a society hedged about by privilege and enjoying a considerable measure of self-government. These agents themselves constituted a highly-privileged body. All *officiers*, from the great councillors of state, to whom the kings granted noble status, down to the most insignificant provincial clerks, were exempt from taxation and enjoyed a remarkable degree of security and independence thanks to the tradition of purchasing their offices. Consequently, it was difficult to remove them for incompetence, while the problem of communication in a kingdom the size of France made it almost impossible to call them to account. They worked with energy and enlightened self-interest to promote the king's jurisdiction at the expense of seigneurial, ecclesiastical and municipal courts, because in this way their own authority too was inflated and with it the profits to be derived from their work, since no one signed a writ or passed judgement without the receipt of a payment known variously as a *pourboire* or *pot de vin*. Moreover, though they remained loyal to the king on the whole, they frequently identified themselves with the promotion of local interests or the advancement of their own families.

The royal agents derived their authority from the curia regis, the medieval court of the king attended by his principal feudatories and his chief officers of state. Over the years it had been pruned and refined by removing those whom the king did not wish to be privy to his business, and by hiving off specialist functions to separate councils or committees which developed a corporate life of their own (see below). This left the royal council, variously known as the *Conseil du Roi*, the *Conseil d'Etat*, or the *Conseil Privé*, as the effective centre of royal government, responsible for framing edicts, administering their application and adjudicating in matters arising from them. Justice and administration were, therefore, inseparable, but specialist functions of the judicature, such as the issuing of judgements and the determination of penalties, were delegated to a subordinate off-shoot of the council known as the

Parlement. This met regularly in Paris in order to maintain continuity of action and to be permanently accessible to plaintiffs while the kings moved about their realm or waged war against the English. During the fifteenth century it came to be recognised as the *Parlement* of Paris because of its location there and to distinguish it from other bodies set up to deal with similar business at Toulouse (1443), Grenoble (1456), Bordeaux (1467) and Dijon (1476). Others were appointed later at Aix, Rouen and Rennes and several other provincial capitals.

It was customary for the Paris *Parlement* to register all royal edicts before they became effective. Its opposition to certain edicts of Louis XI had brought it into conflict with the king who threatened to remove its business to the jurisdiction of other committees of the council, but under Charles VIII its right of registration was formally recognised. The dispute demonstrated how royal agencies could develop a corporate identity in opposition to the royal council. It was not, however, a constitutional conflict but rather an indication of the jealous determination of royal servants to fulfil a function which they had come to believe was their special prerogative. The Paris *Parlement* was in no way analagous to the English parliament for which the nearest equivalent was the *Etats Généraux* or States-General. Throughout the Middle Ages, French kings had summoned a variety of baronial gatherings to advertise a special situation or to publicise a need for support. In addition, several provinces, especially those more recently assimilated into the kingdom, still possessed their own elected assemblies of the three Estates: the nobility, the clergy and the townsmen. These two quite different types of assembly were combined after a fashion by Louis XI, but the first full and formal meeting of the States-General on a truly national scale did not take place until 1484. It rarely met thereafter. The fact that the nobility opposed royal policy in 1484 lent colour to the view that Charles VIII and his successors regarded it as something of a constitutional restraint to be avoided as much as possible. On the contrary, Charles's intention had been to use the authority of the States-General as a national assembly to override the privileges and particularist attitudes of the provinces, but he failed because its members preferred to act as delegates rather than as representatives with full powers.

In addition to the *Parlement* of Paris there were three other offshoots of the royal council which were collectively described as sovereign courts; the *Chambre des comptes*, the *Grand Conseil* and the *Cour des aides*. The *Grand Conseil* dealt with legal business, the other two with finance. None of these courts could do more than outline general policies and deal with a few individual cases of particular importance. For general administration the country was divided into bailiwicks (*baillis*), known in some areas as seneschalcies (*sénéchaux*). Here, in conjunction with the provincial *parlements* royal *officiers* transmitted the edicts of the councils, held their own courts, applied the laws and dealt with cases summoned before them from the seigneurial and ecclesiastical courts. Compared with the extensive and thorough-going administration which was later to be developed in France, this small bureaucracy was extremely limited both in its scope and in its effect, but its function was vital to the evolution of royal power for it drew the kingdom together in obedience to the king's law.

The legal and administrative framework by which royal policy might be transmitted from the council down to the villagers of France was thus established, but its significance must not be exaggerated. The patchwork of interlocking and frequently conflicting jurisdictions of the nobles, the clergy and the towns was not abolished but merely modified in part by the development of a royal bureaucracy. An examination of only one aspect of its work, the administration of taxation, reveals the complexity of the situation. First of all there were the *finances ordinaires*, the patri-monial rights of the Valois kings, which accounted for about one-fifth of their revenue in the fifteenth century. These were collected through the bailiwicks and transmitted to officials known as the *trésoriers de France*. In addition to these were the *finances extraordinaires*, the taxes which the kings could levy without reference to any assembly. The chief of these was the *taille personelle*, ostensibly a universal tax but one from which the nobility, the clergy, the *officiers* and a large number of townsmen were exempt. In the Midi and the south-west however there was the *taille réelle*, a tax not on persons but on land, and since this was levied on all land officially classified as *roturier*, whether its owner was privileged or not, it was potentially more valuable to the crown.

The agents responsible for the collection of the *taille*, both *personelle* and *réelle*, were the *élus*, a name which indicated that they had been elected to the task by the provincial Estates in the days long past when every province had had its own assembly. By the fifteenth century they were crown nominees and their areas of responsibility, known as *élections*, corresponded more or less to the diocesan boundaries. The total to be raised was prescribed by the royal council and apportioned among the four *généralités* of Languedoil, Languedoc, Normandy and Outre-Seine-et-Yonne. Each *généralité* in turn determined the amount to be raised by each *élection*, basing its decision upon the reports of thc *élus*, so that some consideration would be given to local conditions such as a good harvest or an epidemic of the plague. Within the *élection* each town and village was informed of the amount to be raised, and this part of the operation was conducted by elected *asséers* who knew the wealth or poverty of their neighbours. Other elected agents supervised the collection. Disputes, and there were many, were referred to the courts of the *élus* for arbitration and a final appeal could be made to the *Cour des aides*.

The system was complicated by the fact that some provision had to be made for the provinces such as Picardy, Burgundy, Dauphiné, Provence, Brittany and Guyenne, which were acquired in the course of the fifteenth century and which were known as *pays d'états* because they retained their own Estates and had neither *élus* nor *élections*. In these provinces the Estates apportioned and collected the *taille* according to the local traditions of tax collection. All in all, therefore, the wealthiest paid nothing, the structure of assessment and collection was by no means universal, and it must be regarded as something of an achievement that by 1500 the crown had nonetheless derived an annual income from the *taille* of between four and five million livres.

Among the other *finances extraordinaires* were the *aides* and the *gabelle*. The *aides* were originally a series of purchase taxes of about five per cent of the value of all goods sold in the markets. Later they were restricted to the sale of fish, meat, wood and wine. Their collection was administered by private individuals known as *partisans* or *traitants* who paid the king a sum more or less equivalent to the value of the taxes and made what profit they could by collecting them themselves. The collection of the *gabelle*, a tax on salt, involved a third and quite separate hierarchy of officials. Moreover, the incidence of the tax varied from one region to another. Flanders, Artois and Brittany were wholly exempt. In Languedoc, Provence and Dauphiné, where salt was produced in great quantities, the tax was low. In the rest of France, the *pays de grande gabelle*, the tax was hated above all others, partly because the official salesmen adulterated the salt in order to make a profit for themselves, and partly because the collectors were empowered to enter houses indiscriminately to search for illicit supplies of untaxed salt.

Just as the kings had unified their kingdom more by a series of expedients assisted by good luck than by the consistent application of a logical principle, so their administration developed in piece-meal fashion. Its character was complicated by the survival of institutions from an earlier age; its efficiency was impaired by the great privileges enjoyed by separate individuals, classes and regions; its operation was conducted by men who frequently served their own interests rather than the king's, and its financial system was weakened by the exemption of all who could best afford to pay taxes and by the complex and varied systems of collection. Nonetheless, it was the most advanced example of an organised and united kingdom that Europe had to offer by 1520.

The Kingdoms of Castile and Aragon to 1516

In 1450 the kingdoms of the Iberian peninsula went their separate ways. Granada was the remnant of the Moorish empire which had formerly governed most of Spain; Aragon was engaged in political and commercial rivalry with the Mediterranean states; Portugal was committed to the exploration of the West African coastline, and Castile, the most backward of the four, depended for its livelihood on the rearing of sheep. The first step to their ultimate unification under the rule of one man – Philip II (see page 343) – was unwittingly taken in October 1469 with the marriage of Ferdinand of Aragon to Isabella of Castile.

It was not an auspicious event. The marriage was declared unlawful by the pope on grounds of consanguinity, and neither party had much to offer in the way of future prospects. Ferdinand could hope to succeed his father, John II, as king of Aragon but the nature of his inheritance was threatened by French armies in the Pyrenees and by rebels in Catalonia. In Castile the situation was still worse. Henry IV was virtually insane, and the kingdom was dominated by the great noble families led by the Warrior

Spain in the reign of Ferdinand and Isabella

Archbishop of Toledo. Isabella's claim to the throne depended upon the general presumption that Juana, Henry's reputed daughter, was illegitimate, but Henry could not bring himself to admit that he had been made a cuckold and married Juana to Alfonso V of Portugal who was pledged to defend her right of succession. Isabella and Ferdinand were nonetheless well-fitted to challenge the difficulties which faced them. Isabella's was the more attractive personality of the two. Her private life was well-ordered and sustained by a genuine religious piety, and in public affairs she proved to be both capable and energetic. Above all she was gifted with an equable temperament which permitted her to endure both the political crises of her reign and her husband's numerous infidelities with apparently unruffled calm. Ferdinand lacked her stability and serenity, and there was a vicious, mean side to his nature, but he was expert in intrigue and diplomacy and no less capable than Isabella in political affairs. His very faults made him an admirable foil to his wife, and between them they successfully defended their marriage and secured control of their respective kingdoms.

The pope was persuaded to legitimise their marriage and

Ferdinand succeeded to Aragon on his father's death in 1474. Henry IV died in the same year and Alfonso invaded Castile to champion Juana's right to the throne. Isabella showed great energy and determination in rallying to her side the churchmen and many of the nobles, while Ferdinand successfully exploited his influence with the great Castilian families of Enriques and Mendoza to whom he was related. As a result the Portuguese were defeated at the battle of Toro in 1476, Juana was confined to a convent, and Isabella was crowned as queen of Castile. It was significant that Ferdinand was excluded from the coronation; both kingdoms remained wholly separate and everything was to depend on the co-operation of the two sovereigns to provide a common policy, though not a common administration for their kingdoms. On the face of it Ferdinand was condemned to a subordinate role. He had no formal rights in Castile but was required by the marriage settlement to reside there except when Isabella gave permission for him to visit Aragon. Once Isabella had been crowned, however, she deliberately identified Ferdinand with her government, even authorising him to administer justice in her name; Ferdinand with characteristic shrewdness recognised that the institutions of Castile allowed greater opportunity for the crown to exercise its authority, and that Castile was the more important partner in this alliance of kingdoms. Aragon was a third the size of Castile, its population numbered one million against Castile's seven million and, after many years of plague and civil war, its great days of commercial influence were being ended by Italian competition. Consequently it was in Castile that the future greatness of the Spanish monarchy was to be established.

The history of Castile had been the story of the *Reconquista*, of the long struggle to repel the Moors beginning with the liberation of central Spain in the eleventh century and continuing two centuries later with the recovery of Andalusia. As the frontier was advanced southwards towards Granada, vast estates were created, the *latifundios*, which were allocated to noble families who pledged themselves to undertake their defence in return for considerable powers of self-government. The autonomy thus created was aggravated by a long succession of ineffectual rulers who by the reign of Henry IV had very nearly forfeited their control. There were, for example, the great military Orders of

Santiago, Calatrava and Alcantara whose services against the Moors had been rewarded with estates whose combined annual revenue amounted to 145,000 ducats, and whose rights of jurisdiction extended over nearly one million vassals. As the pace of the crusade slackened off in the fifteenth century, these Orders represented a powerful element in the aristocratic feuds and civil wars which characterised Castilian politics, and Isabella was determined to regain control.

When the grand mastership of the Order of Santiago fell vacant in 1476, Isabella rode across Castile for three days in order to attend the election of a successor, and by her energy and determination secured the appointment for Ferdinand. Her royal authority, however, was not yet established beyond question, and Ferdinand shrewdly waived the honour in favour of a candidate selected by the order, thereby retaining a useful measure of goodwill. Later, as royal power became stronger, Ferdinand became grand master of the other Orders in 1487 and 1494, and when the grand mastership of the Order of Santiago was offered to him once again in 1499 he accepted it with becoming grace. These appointments not only denied to other nobles the opportunity to make themselves troublesome but enabled the Crown to enjoy the revenue of the Orders, jurisdiction over their vassals and patronage of more than 1,500 offices with which to reward their own servants.

Isabella treated her nobles firmly yet with restraint. She recovered the royal estates they had plundered in Henry IV's reign by guaranteeing their right to land acquired in earlier reigns, and while she allowed the leading families to monopolise the traditional offices of Castile, she limited their function to the performance of strictly prescribed duties. Her own royal prerogative, above all her right to be the final arbiter in matters both judicial and administrative, was strengthened by her practice of holding her own *audiencia* every Friday, and by creating subsidiary tribunals in the provinces to demonstrate the reality of her authority and its supremacy over the magnates' own jurisdiction. This was as far as Isabella was prepared to go. Provided the nobles accepted her sovereignty she was content to leave them in possession of their territories. The three hundred or so grandees of Castile, therefore, retained control of over half the land, and families like the Guzmans, dukes of Medina Sidonia, or the Mendozas, counts of Tendilla and Priego, were still capable of raising thousands of troops from their own estates. They nonetheless respected Isabella's ultimate authority, partly because it was exercised with restraint, and even more because the queen's active policies against Granada, in Italy and in the New World provided them with so many opportunities for excitement and profit in her service.

Isabella's reputation for a faith which was fervent to the point of mysticism, her determination to reform clerical abuses and her decision to renew the crusade against the Moors, allowed her to maintain a firm control over the church in Castile. She found a useful ally in Jimenes de Cisneros (Ximenes), a talented scholar (see page 65) and a formidable enemy of clerical corruption who became the archbishop of Toledo and was later appointed cardinal. Together they set about the reform of the clergy. So necessary was this task that the secular clergy, for example, had to be ordered in 1473 to celebrate mass at least four times a year, and there were over four hundred Andalusian friars who found the new reforms so unpalatable that they chose to embrace Islam and emigrate to North Africa, taking their wives and possessions with them. In her reforming zeal, and without any reference to Rome, Isabella was, therefore, able to insist on her right to nominate suitable candidates to all the major benefices in Castile and thus to control the church. The popes indeed gave her support. They allowed her to collect the *subsidio*, a tax on the clergy, and, in order to promote her crusade against Granada, the *cruzada*, a tax on the sale of indulgences. These continued to be sold and the tax collected by the queen long after Granada had fallen, thus providing her with a useful source of additional revenue.

One important consequence of the *Reconquista* had been the emergence of the towns as independent corporations, each with its own militia, the *hermandad* or brotherhood of archers, to defend itself against the Moors, and subsequently against local magnates and even against the crown. The anarchy of the fifteenth century, however, had proved so harmful to the commercial interests of the towns that in 1476 they agreed to unite their military forces in one *Santa Hermandad* under the command of Ferdinand's brother, Alfonso de Aragon. Isabella was thus provided with a strong army of two thousand men, supported when necessary by the local companies of urban archers who acted on her behalf to restore order in the provinces. The *Santa Hermandad* combined the functions of a military force with those of a judicial tribunal, and its *alcaldes*, or judges, were empowered to deal summarily with offenders – usually by death or mutilation. The severity of their jurisdiction supported by the military strength of the towns proved to be so successful that after 1494 the *Santa Hermandad* was disbanded and the urban *hermandad* assumed the more modest role of a local police force. Moreover, within the towns, urban independence was substantially eroded after 1480 when Isabella appointed royal agents to act alongside the *regidores* or mayors. The *regidor* preserved the outward pomp of his office but the *corregidor* ensured that civic policies were kept in line with those of the royal council.

Isabella's government was, therefore, recognised and indeed supported by most of her nobles, clergy and townsmen and their general acceptance of her authority was paralleled by the decline of their representative institution, the *Cortes*. In any case, the *Cortes* would have been ill-equipped to defy the crown. Its role was to petition rather than to legislate, it met only when summoned and its consent to new laws was not required unless these conflicted with existing legislation. Isabella consulted it on taxation, but was not dependent on its generosity since she derived a considerable income independently from her own estates, from the clergy and from the *alcabala* which claimed one-tenth of the value of all commercial transactions. Since the nobles and the clergy were exempt from taxes granted by the *Cortes*, they ceased to attend its sessions and it became an easily-managed assembly representing eighteen Castilian towns.

Isabella could thus develop and administer her policies independently of the *Cortes*, and the linch-pin of her government was the Council of Castile, with its sub-committees and subordinate councils to deal with special matters such as the *Santa Hermandad* or the military orders. Grandees were not allowed to attend the council as of right – although their service might be invited since Isabella was in no way antagonistic to them as a class – and the administration was staffed in the main by lesser nobles, the *hidalgos*. Many of them were trained in law (*letrados*), and their recruitment was a matter of particular concern to Isabella and Ferdinand who sought out likely candidates during their royal progresses. There was nothing very novel in all this but a special council was appointed to improve the administration of royal finance. Because of its efficiency, and even more because Isabella's reign was one of internal peace, the total of royal income rose from 800,000 maravedis in 1470 to 20 million by 1500 (34 maravedis = one silver real, and 375 = one gold ducat).

One institution of considerable importance was the *mesta*, a corporation of the migrant shepherds whose flocks were vital to Castile's economy. During the Middle Ages migrant sheep-farming had become more profitable than arable farming, not only because so much of the land was arid, but also because the danger of Moorish raids discouraged permanent settlement. Every April the flocks of sheep migrated from their winter pastures in Estremadura and La Mancha to travel by appointed routes, the *canadas*, to Leon and Asturias in the north, returning south again in September. The *mesta*, whose original function had been to supervise the sale of stray sheep, had become a powerful corporation with jurisdiction over all the pasture lands and *canadas*. Within its vast territories arable farming was forbidden even though there was a serious shortage of cereals in Castile, and on this issue the crown might well have tried to reduce the *mesta*'s power. Many of the pasture grounds, however, belonged to the military orders of which Ferdinand was grand master, and Isabella derived a useful income from the *servicio y montazgo*, a duty levied on the sheep as they passed along the *canadas*. Moreover, since a member of the royal council was always president of the *mesta*, its jurisdiction was essentially an extension of that of the crown.

In addition to controlling the flocks of sheep on which Castile's economy depended, Isabella's council also regulated the wool trade which passed to Northern Europe through the city of Burgos. When the city's business was dislocated by the expulsion of the Jews in 1492 (see below), the council introduced from Aragon the institution of a *consulado*, a kind of trade guild with judicial powers to implement its policies. When many merchants preferred to move on to Bilbao, the centre of the Vizcayan iron trade, a *consulado* was also established there in 1510. Unlike the *Casa de Contratación* in Seville which directed the trade with America, the *consulado* was not directly a government agency, but its introduction from Aragon was a mistake. It had already failed to save the Catalan ports from Italian competition, and its rigid corporate structure with its emphasis on protective policies was not well suited to what should have been an expansionist phase in the Castilian economy.

Among the other institutions through which Isabella exercised control, one of the most important was the Inquisition. It was established in 1478 to deal with the *conversos*, Jews converted to Christianity, whose orthodoxy was often in doubt. It acted independently of Rome, its *suprema* or governing body was run as a department of state subordinate only to the Council of Castile, and its powers were extensive. In 1480 it burned 2,000 heretics among the *conversos*, reconciled 20,000 to the Church, and forced 120,000 to take refuge in flight. The towns protested at the dislocation which this brought about in their business, but Isabella's devotion to orthodoxy was greater than her concern for the economy. As a logical extension of the programme the Jews themselves, hitherto exempt from the Inquisition's jurisdiction, were expelled in 1492, and 150,000 or more were lost to Castile.

Isabella's pursuit of orthodoxy was not confined within her own kingdom. To the south lay the Moslem kingdom of Granada where over half a million Moors survived from the race which had once dominated the Iberian peninsula. In 1481 Isabella renewed the crusade against them, but the campaign had to be fought in mountainous territory where cavalry could not operate and where the infantry was reduced to siege warfare against the Moorish towns. King Muley Hassan and his brother El Zagal (The Valiant) maintained an effective resistance which delayed the Castilian advance, and Isabella was driven to pawn her own jewels in order to keep her army in being. Gradually, however, the infantry under Gonzalo de Cordoba began to acquire the skills which later made it so effective in the Italian Wars, and the Moorish kingdom suffered from the defection of Muley Hassan's son Boabdil who allied for a time with the crusading army. Eventually, in 1492, the city of Granada surrendered, and the kingdom was incorporated into Castile – an occasion celebrated by Isabella's decision to support the expedition of Christopher Columbus. The Moors were allowed to retain their own religion and their language, their laws and their magistrates, since the conquering army was in no position to exact less generous terms, but the existence of a separate infidel population, nearly one-eighth that of Castile, could not be tolerated indefinitely. Cisneros over-ruled the arguments of those who counselled caution and determined to achieve his missionary endeavour by force. In 1502 he secured the royal assent to an edict expelling all those over the age of fourteen who refused baptism, and it was left to Isabella's successors to deal with the problem of a population whose allegiance to the crown was as suspect as its adhesion to Christianity.

In Aragon a different set of institutions and traditions made it difficult for Ferdinand to imitate the successes of Isabella in extending royal authority. Aragon, Catalonia and Valencia were separate kingdoms, each jealous of the others and within each one the privileges of the nobility, the clergy and the towns were rigorously maintained. In Aragon, for example, the *Cortes* was required by law to meet regularly, representatives of all the estates were required to attend, nothing could be done by way of legislation or taxation without its consent, and between sessions a standing committee, the *Diputación del Reyno*, kept a close eye on public administration and royal expenditure. Valencia, as a kingdom recovered from the Moors, was rather more amenable to royal direction; Catalonia, on the other hand, was more independent-minded than Aragon. The Aragonese oath of loyalty in fact embodied principles which were common to all three kingdoms and which demonstrated the extent of Ferdinand's problem – 'We who are as good as you, swear to you, who are no better than we, to accept you as our sovereign king and lord, provided that you observe our liberties and laws, but if not, not.' In Aragon these 'liberties and laws' were preserved and protected by a *justicia* who could not be removed from office by the king and whose independence of action made him altogether unique in fifteenth-century history.

Ferdinand did not try to remedy the situation. After many decades of civil war he was content to be acknowledged as the sovereign power within the constitution, and he dared not risk rebellion by overriding the privileges and traditions of his kingdoms. He introduced the Castilian Inquisition and encouraged closer relations between the two countries by promoting inter-marriage between the nobility and appointing a few Castilian bishops and civil servants to posts in Aragon, but he did not imitate the policies of Isabella in respect of the *Cortes* or the towns. In any case he would have gained very little by doing so. The extension of royal authority in other kingdoms was designed to expose the people more directly to the authority of the royal tax collectors, but the relative poverty of Aragon at the end of the fifteenth century saved it from this, especially as Ferdinand could more easily exploit the greater wealth of Castile. It was Castilian money, and Castilian infantry, which allowed him to intervene so successfully in the Italian wars (see page 118) and to establish a measure of control in North Africa by the conquest of Mers-el-Kebir, Oran, Tripoli and Algiers. If Aragon was saved by its poverty from the more authoritarian monarchy of Castile it was, however, denied the opportunity to restore its wealth by sharing in the expansion of the Castilian economy. Its merchants were denied access to the wool trade and the Castilian fairs. They were also excluded from America, although this was not just a matter of Castilian prejudice; not only were the Catalan ports badly placed to trade across the Atlantic but their merchants had no capital with which to finance colonial ventures; a privilege which in the event was reserved for their former rivals, the Genoese.

The fact that Spain consisted of a series of separate kingdoms made it liable to sudden disruption, as events proved when Isabella died in 1504. Ferdinand's greatest concern had been to transform the personal alliance between their kingdoms into a permanent union by securing the succession of one person to both thrones, but the death of his son Juan in 1497 had made the matter uncertain. Of Juan's sisters, Juana was married to Philip of Burgundy (see page 98), Catherine was betrothed to Arthur of England and subsequently to Henry VIII, and Isabella to Manuel of Portugal. It was on his daughter Isabella that Ferdinand's hopes had been pinned, since her child would have inherited all the Iberian kingdoms, but she had died in childbirth and her son with her. As a result, Queen Isabella had left Castile to Juana, a just decision but one which excluded Ferdinand temporarily from Castilian affairs. Juana, however, was subject to moody hysteria, her husband's notorious infidelity finally drove her to insanity and Philip of Burgundy, with the support of men like Cisneros, claimed the throne for himself. His death in 1506 and the public recognition of Juana's insanity opened the field once more for Ferdinand's intervention.

From 1507 Ferdinand governed Castile at the head of a council of regency, but it was almost too late for his purpose since he had married a niece of Louis XII in the meantime, and if she had produced a son then, the thrones of Aragon and Castile would of necessity have remained separate. When she died childless, Ferdinand was able to secure general assent to the nomination of Juana's son, Charles of Burgundy, to the kingdoms of Castile and Aragon. Consequently, when Ferdinand himself died in 1516 it was a young Burgundian prince, grandson of the emperor Maximilian as well as of Ferdinand and Isabella, who succeeded to a complex of separate thrones which gave him authority, not only in Spain, but also in America, North Africa, Italy and the Netherlands.

The Papacy, the Empire and the Habsburgs

In the idealised structure of Christendom invented by medieval man, the pope and the emperor represented two supreme but complementary authorities, the spiritual and the temporal, whose function was to act in harmony for the greater glory of God and for the well-being of His people. Events, however, had tarnished the image. Pope and emperor had fought bitterly against each other and neither had been able to challenge the rise of European monarchies which resented interference in their own affairs. As a result these two great international offices had dwindled in importance to become the localised prerogatives of an Italian prince and an Austrian duke.

At the end of the thirteenth century when an accommodation of sorts had been arranged between the papacy and the empire, Pope Boniface VIII had tried to reassert his universal authority in the bull *Unam Sanctem*, but his efforts only served to provoke fiercer opposition to his claims among the western monarchies. The inadequacy of papal power was then exposed by the imprisonment of the popes at Avignon in the fourteenth century, and its dignity was destroyed by the emergence of two rival popes in 1378 and of three after 1409. The disunity of Christendom was thereby demonstrated at a critical period when the Osmanli Turks were invading the Balkans and the Hussite heresy was gaining ground in Bohemia. So great was the danger that, despite their local conflicts, representatives of England, France, Italy, Germany and the Iberian peninsula met together in the Council of Constance to find a remedy. From the papal point of view the remedy proved to be as dangerous as the disease, since the council declared in

1415 that, as it derived its authority from Christ, the popes were subject to its jurisdiction.

As a result, the rival popes were compelled to abdicate their claims, and the election of a new pope, Martin V, restored a semblance of good order to the church, but neither Martin nor his immediate successors were allowed to forget their subordinate status. Their actions were questioned and frequently overruled by subsequent councils; one pope was even suspended from office, and the very function of the papacy was variously defined as a human and fallible institution or as one divinely appointed but nonetheless subject to correction by a general council. When the last of the councils dispersed in 1443 it was not surprising that the popes should subsequently adhere to the belief that nothing, not even widespread heresy, was more harmful to their interests than the summoning of a general council.

In consequence the popes began to make themselves as powerful as possible as the territorial rulers of the papal states and, by raising money in Rome itself, to diminish their financial dependance on the national churches which had supported the conciliar movement. This was done by charging fees for the registration of bulls, the issue of dispensations, the sale of indulgences and for all the business of the church which required the pope's signature. 'If we send envoys to ask aid of a sovereign we are laughed at', said Pius II in defence of this policy, 'If we impose tithes on the clergy they appeal to a future council. If we issue indulgences and encourage the contribution of money by spiritual gifts we are accused of avarice.' But no defence could conceal the fact that the spiritual function of the papacy was compromised by its preoccupation with fund-raising. Worse still, the corruption which attended these new fiscal devices was institutionalised and given permanence by the creation of a bureaucracy to administer them. The sale of offices within the new bureaucracy became so valuable a secondary source of income that eventually entire departments were created whose duties were either nominal or fictitious. In return for the purchase price of his office, the office-holder received the interest on his capital investment in the form of a salary for doing virtually nothing. As the rate of interest averaged eleven per cent, the demand for papal offices began to grow until by 1520 there existed nearly 2,000 appointments in the papal service which had no bureaucratic function but which represented an investment of 2½ million gold florins on which the annual return was as much as 300,000 gold florins.

Additional income was derived from the revenue of the papal states, but in order to make themselves masters of this turbulent region the popes had to immerse themselves in matters of administration, defence and foreign policy. By and large they were successful (see page 111) but the role of ruthless despot contrasted badly with the traditional function of the papacy as the spiritual head of Latin Christendom. Moreover, this development encouraged the independent mood of the national churches across Europe and justified them in regarding the papal curia not only as a centre of venality and corruption but also as an Italian institution inextricably enmeshed in local politics.

If the ecumenical character of the papacy had been impaired, so too had the international authority of the Holy Roman Emperor. No longer coterminous with the boundaries of Christendom, no longer holy, Roman or imperial, the empire had become almost exclusively a German institution, although Switzerland, north Italy and the Netherlands still remained nominally within its jurisdiction. Even in Germany itself the imperial concept seemed irrelevant in the midst of three hundred or more feudal, ecclesiastical and urban states which sought by different means to establish their individual autonomy. They had begun to do so during the long struggle between the emperors and the popes, and in 1356 the Golden Bull had enshrined the powers of the princes under a new Imperial Constitution. The emperor was to be elected by seven princes – the palatine of the Rhine, the margrave of Brandenburg, the duke of Saxony, the king of Bohemia and the archbishops of Mainz, Trier and Cologne – and the election was to be independent of any papal veto, although strictly speaking a new emperor was to be known as king of the Romans until he had been crowned by the pope. The constitutional assembly of the empire was the *Reichstag* or Diet which comprised the college of the seven electoral princes and the college of the other feudal and ecclesiastical princes. A third college was added in the fifteenth century in which the so-called free cities of the empire were represented. Instead of being a legislative assembly with authority to enforce its decisions, the Diet turned out to be nothing more than a convention of sovereign princes whose power to obstruct any decision they disliked

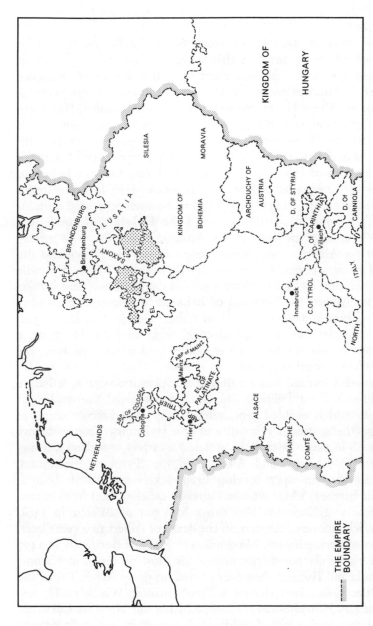

The Holy Roman Empire and the Habsburg lands

denied the emperor any opportunity to impose his policies upon Germany.

The emperor was saved from being totally ineffectual in German affairs by the fact that he might also be an important German prince in his own right, and the degree of influence exerted by him was proportionate to the extent of his own personal territories. Albert II, the energetic head of the House of Habsburg who became emperor in 1437, was master of a private empire which included the Tyrol and territory in Switzerland, Styria with Carniola and Carinthia, Upper Alsace, Upper and Lower Austria, the kingdom of Hungary and the united kingdoms of Bohemia, Moravia, Lusatia and Silesia. Frederick III, however, who succeeded him as emperor in 1439 had no such territorial foundation to support his authority since the Habsburg Empire was divided among the family. In Austria, Frederick was merely regent for Albert's posthumous son, Ladislas; in Alsace and the Tyrol he was regent for his cousin Sigismund; Styria, Carniola and Carinthia he had to share with his cantankerous and jealous brother, Albert; the kingdom of Bohemia, an elective monarchy, rejected him in favour of a local noble, George Podiebrad, and the Hungarian throne, also elective, went to John Hunyadi, a vigorous leader of the Magyar nobles and a national hero for his Balkan campaign against the Turks.

Frederick himself was a cultured if superstitious man, lethargic and ill-suited for political life, but he possessed the quality of tenacity which enabled him, after a long and difficult reign, to salvage the scattered remnants of the Habsburg Empire before his death in 1493. Initially he suffered a variety of setbacks, losing Austria to Ladislas and Alsace and the Tyrol to Sigismund. Ladislas died in 1457, leaving Frederick in control of Austria, but his brother Albert who had already expelled him from Styria, Carniola and Carinthia also drove him out of Austria in 1461. Frederick recovered Austria on the death of Albert two years later, and by marrying his son Maximilian to Mary of Burgundy in 1477 made his family potentially one of the most powerful in Europe. Bohemia and Hungary however eluded his grasp. When Podiebrad died the Bohemians elected a Polish prince, Wladislav II, and in Hungary Hunyadi was succeeded by his son Matthias Corvinus. The latter was a gifted soldier who overran not only part of Bohemia but also Austria and Styria in 1485 so that Frederick was compelled to wander throughout Germany as an emperor in exile from his own patrimony. It was at this nadir of his fortunes that Maximilian was temporarily expelled from the Netherlands (see page 98) and the Habsburg cause appeared to be doomed. The jigsaw of estates was reconstructed in 1490 when Frederick won control of the Tyrol from Sigismund, and Maximilian recovered Austria on the death of Matthias Corvinus. Wladislav of Bohemia had meanwhile been elected to the Hungarian throne, but he promised to help Maximilian secure the succession to both his kingdoms should he die without direct heirs.

If Maximilian was spared some of the problems which had confronted his father in holding together the German territories of the Habsburg family, he met with nothing but frustration in his plans to strengthen his authority within Germany as Holy Roman Emperor. He was a huge figure of a man with something of a military reputation from his successes in Austria and the Netherlands, a keen huntsman and athlete and something of a scholar and poet, but none of these qualities could overcome the resistance of the German princes whose concern it was to extend their own authority by restraining the emperors.

The struggle for power took place within the context of a genuine attempt to reform the institutions of the empire. In order to control the anarchy which prevailed between the German states and above all to put an end to the gangster knights who terrorised the neighbourhoods of their castles, Berthold, archbishop elector of Mainz, carried most of the princes with him in an effort to establish better government. Maximilian for his part was ready to meet all Berthold's proposals provided that, in return, he was given money with which to raise troops. Since it was clear that once he had troops behind him he might then repudiate his concessions, the endless round of discussions came to nothing. The Diet (*Reichstag*) met at Worms in 1495, for example, to set up a supreme court of justice for the empire, the *Reichskammergericht*, to approve a universal tax to be known as the imperial common penny, and to create a permanent executive council, the *Reichsrat*, of seventeen members without whose consent the emperor might not act. Maximilian refused his assent to the *Reichsrat* since he was permitted to nominate only one of its members, the attempt to raise an imperial tax foundered dismally and provoked the Swiss to declare their independence of the empire, and the *Reichskammergericht*, though appointed, was unable to operate effectively for lack of funds.

In 1500 Maximilian, who was desperately anxious to intervene in the Italian Wars, agreed to the formation of a different type of central council, the *Reichsregiment*, in which he was denied effective power, in return for a contribution from the clergy and the free cities to pay for an army of 30,000 men. In the event, the working of the *Reichsregiment* was frustrated by the efforts of Berthold to make Maximilian its servant and of Maximilian to be its master. It served only one useful purpose, as a council of regency during Maximilian's brief and unsuccessful incursions into Italy. One incident demonstrated what was to be a cardinal feature of German politics in the sixteenth century. By a sudden stroke of force in 1504, backed by a general approval of his policy, Maximilian carried out a decision of the *Reichskammergericht* to determine the disputed succession to Bavaria-Landshut. Encouraged by his success, Maximilian summoned the *Reichsregiment* to Cologne in 1505 in order to increase his powers within the empire. The princes who had approved his action in Bavaria immediately acted in concert against him and unanimously rejected his proposals. A pattern was thus established to be repeated on many future occasions. No sooner did an emperor achieve success by a show of force in one field, than the German princes combined to make his victory valueless.

For all his apparent gifts, and he was undeniably a more regal figure than his father, Maximilian was frustrated at every turn, not only as emperor but also as head of the House of Habsburg. He was, of course, spared the civil war between brothers and cousins which had characterised his father's reign, his titles to Austria, Styria and the Tyrol were not questioned, and within the Netherlands he ultimately established his control. Nonetheless, he was unable to consolidate his personal authority by establishing common institutions for his scattered territories. He did set up a central treasury at Innsbruck, but the creation of a central court of justice was universally opposed and Maximilian had to exercise his jurisdiction separately within each duchy, in accordance with its individual processes, traditions and laws. His most significant and successful achievement as head of the House of Habsburg was the promotion of dynastic alliances, not only with Castile (see page 146) but also with Bohemia and Hungary. Wladislav's close friendship with Maximilian, strengthened by the anxiety with which both regarded the Osmanli advance through the Balkans, resulted in a double marriage in 1516. Maximilian's grandchildren, Mary and Ferdinand, were married to Wladislav's children, Louis and Anna, despite the opposition of Jan Zapolya, a Transylvanian prince who resented German infiltration into Hungary and who had hoped to marry Anna himself. The consequences both of the marriage and of Zapolya's anger were to be made evident after 1520 when the circumstances attending the invasion by Suleyman the Magnificent led to the recovery of the Bohemian and Hungarian thrones by the House of Habsburg.

The outcome of the marriage between Philip and Juana of Castile was even more important for the Habsburg dynasty. Their elder son Charles, heir to the Burgundian territories of Franche Comté, Artois and the Netherlands, was selected by Ferdinand of Aragon to inherit the thrones of Aragon, Castile and Naples – to say nothing of the Spanish empire in the New World. To crown this edifice, Maximilian assigned to him the Habsburg empire in Germany and prepared the way for his election as Holy Roman Emperor. Charles's territorial powers, however, made him an object of suspicion to the German electors who knew full well that an emperor's authority was effective only in proportion to his own domains, and who therefore looked with some favour on the claims of Henry VIII of England and Francis I of France. Francis in fact came near to success. He had the declared support of the Rhineland electors of Trier, Mainz and the Palatinate and that of the elector of Brandenburg, but in the final analysis he talked too convincingly of restoring law and order, he was seriously disadvantaged in German eyes by papal support, and he lacked money. Maximilian before his death in 1519 had warned Charles that money would settle it one way or another and it was with the backing of the Fuggers and Welsers, their loans secured against the pasture lands of the Castilian *mesta*, that Charles won over the electors, who consoled themselves with the thought that as a busy Spanish king he might leave German affairs to the care of his younger brother Ferdinand.

5

The European Economy and Overseas Trade in the Sixteenth Century

Inflation and Population Growth

THE clearest evidence of a universal rise in food prices throughout the sixteenth century is provided in the records of the market sales of wheat. Naturally enough where wheat was produced for export, as in Poland, prices were low; in the Mediterranean region where wheat was imported they were high. In every region, however, the figures for the sales of wheat, averaged out over five-yearly periods, indicated a general and persistent rise (see

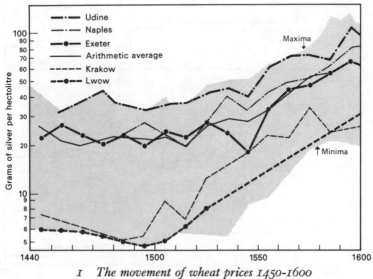

I   The movement of wheat prices 1450-1600

figure 1). In Valencia the price rose from forty grammes of silver, the hectolitre, to a peak of one hundred and forty grammes, in Lwow from five to thirty, and in Paris, a special case perhaps as an expanding capital city, from twenty to one hundred and twenty. Overall the price had risen nearly five-fold by the end of the sixteenth century and a similar trend is recorded in the sales of meat, beer, wine and other foodstuffs. Manufactured goods on the other hand rose by only half this rate.

The process of inflation was not remarked upon for many years. Some Europeans rarely handled coins at all; exchanging goods for goods in simple barter, or goods for services, they had little or no experience of measuring the value of a commodity against a coin. Others were so accustomed to seasonal and other fluctuations in the price of domestic and imported goods, that the persistence of an upward trend escaped them until about the middle of the century. By modern standards the annual rate of increase – approximately 1.7 per cent per annum but with variations from region to region – was negligible, but coming as it did after more than a century of stable prices it naturally provoked an outcry once the cumulative effect of the increases had been noticed.

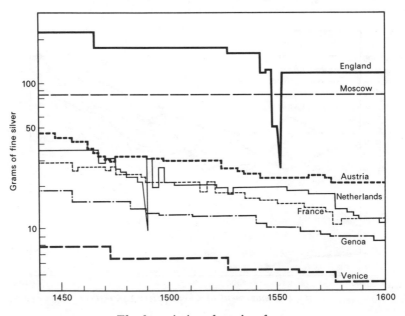

2   *The depreciation of monies of account*

Money lenders and bankers, monopolists, corn dealers, and landlords who raised rents, were identified as the architects of inflation and subjected to popular abuse. But these were merely scapegoats; they let inflation work to their advantage, or sought to minimise its disadvantages by raising their own prices, thereby contributing to its momentum, but they did not initiate the trend.

One solitary and perceptive observer, the Sieur de Malestroit, who worked in the French Mint, essayed the first coherent explanation of the rise in prices by pointing out that the rise in prices was apparent rather than real because of the universal depreciation of monies of account. Monies of account were as Malestroit commented, 'A mystery which few can understand', but the essence of their function within each state was to provide an accounting unit to measure and thereby to standardise the value of coins in circulation. It did not matter if a money of account was not itself a coin in current use: roubles no longer circulated in Muscovy nor maravedis in Spain, but it was by reference to them that the values of other Russian and Spanish coins were assessed. In France the livre tournois was in fact minted at Tours: it established the value of the denier and the sou so that twelve deniers equalled one sou and twenty sous one livre. Similarly, the German mark was valued at twenty schillings or two hundred and forty pfennigs, and the pound sterling had twenty shillings or two hundred and forty pence.

Monies of account fell in value during the sixteenth century (see figure 2) because coins were judged not as today by their nominal value, but by their bullion content. When the value of silver depreciated because greater supplies were made available in south-eastern Europe and in the New World, a silver coin was regarded as being less valuable by the traders who used it. Consequently, where they had asked, say, six silver shillings for a commodity, they subsequently demanded seven. A more important factor than the variation in the values of precious metals was the action of several governments which made a quick profit by reducing the content of gold or silver in their own coins. As a result, when the silver content of the English shilling fell from one hundred to forty grammes, between 1543 and 1546, the traders immediately demanded more shillings in return for the sale of their goods and prices doubled in the next few years. Malestroit had, therefore, isolated a useful and accurate explanation of the rise in prices. It was not, however, the only one since he could not explain why prices continued to rise in England after Elizabeth had stabilised the coinage, nor why prices should have risen at all in Spain where no interference with coinage took place before 1597.

Appropriately enough it was in Spain at the University of Salamanca that an alternative explanation was suggested by Martin de Azpilcueto Navarro, which was in effect what is now termed the Quantity Theory of Money. The point of the theory is that if more money is put into circulation while the amount of goods for sale remains constant then, all things being equal, the price of the goods will rise. As Navarro put it, 'In countries where there is great scarcity of money, all other saleable goods . . . are given for less money than where it is abundant' and 'we see by experience that in France where money is scarcer than in Spain, bread, wine, cloth and labour are worth much less.' Behind it all Navarro saw the effect of the imports of American bullion: 'In times when money was scarce saleable goods and labour were given for very much less than after the discovery of the Indies which flooded the country with gold and silver.' Quite independently and with no reference at all to American imports, Erik XIV of Sweden similarly attributed inflation in his own country to the over-production of coin from the Sala silver mines: 'Concerning the high prices which now more than aforetime prevail, the real cause is that His Majesty (his father Gustav) in the immediate past . . . has issued so much coin that the land is almost full of money which for that reason is come into contempt.'

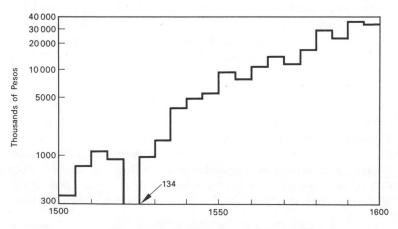

3   The value of bullion imports into Seville

The Quantity Theory of Money was advocated most strongly in France by Jean Bodin who employed it to discredit the theories of Malestroit. Bodin declared that as the rise in food prices was out of all proportion to the extent by which the monies of account had been depreciated, the basic explanation of the price rise could only be the influx of American bullion. The figures supplied by Hamilton of the imports of silver into Spain (see figure 3) would appear to lend weight to the theories of Navarro and Bodin, even allowing for the fact that some of this silver was re-exported to Asia, but they do not become significant until it is known how much gold and silver was already in circulation before the New World was discovered. This, of course, can only be guessed at, but the most recent estimate (see *Cambridge Economic History* volume IV) suggests that there were over 3,500 tons of gold and 37,400 tons of silver in Europe by 1500; over the next century and a half 181 tons of gold were added and 16,886 tons of silver. In other words, the bullion imports were significant but not as all-important as Bodin and Navarro believed. Moreover, they did not coincide very neatly with the rate of inflation in Spain. Prices rose by 2.8 per cent per annum between 1501 and 1562, during the period when bullion imports were getting under way, but by only 1.3 per cent per annum afterwards when the silver began to pour in. It is possible, of course, that after 1562 so much silver was re-exported to pay foreign bankers and to maintain Spanish armies in foreign countries that Spain began to suffer a shortage rather than a surplus of bullion, which reduced the rate of inflation. This would not have applied to Italy, however, where there is virtually no correlation between silver imports and the price rise. Prices remained stable to 1550, shot up by 5 per cent per annum until 1570 and then began to level off.

In recent times Luigi Einaudi has tried to apply the theories of Malestroit and Bodin in combination so far as France was concerned. He estimates that in the period 1515–54, 90.09 per cent of the price rise was caused by the devaluation of the livre tournois and 9.91 per cent by other factors, among which he includes the increased supply of bullion. In the later period the effect of devaluation is gradually outweighed by the other factors which were to account for 27.73 per cent of the price rise between 1555 and 1575 and for 64.53 per cent during the last decade of the sixteenth century. The other factors, however, need not relate too closely to the supply of bullion: it is recognised that if money circulates more quickly this is equivalent in its effect on prices to an increase in the total amount in circulation, and it is evident that this happened to an increasing extent in the sixteenth century because of the greater speed of transactions between the European centres of trade and banking. To this may also be added the effect of the expansion of credit facilities which released more money for the purchase of goods and thereby contributed to inflation. No doubt all these explanations are valid to a certain extent, but they fail to account for one significant feature of the European price rise. If the European economy was being affected by monetary inflation, which is what all these theories propose, then the price of all commodities should have risen with a certain degree of uniformity. In fact it was only the agricultural products of food, drink, wool and fuel which increased sharply in price, while manufactured goods lagged behind. This suggests that the most critical factor affecting the price rise was an increase in the population which created a corresponding increase in the demand for agricultural produce.

The evidence for supposing an increase in the population of Europe between 1450 and 1520 has already been described (see pages 2–5). Similar evidence suggests that the trend continued unchecked throughout the sixteenth century. The number of taxed hearths in Naples went up from 315,990 in 1532 to 540,000 in 1595 and the Castilian census of heads of families showed that in 1594 the number had risen from 1,179,303 in 1541 to 1,340,320. The use of such figures can be criticised since they do not indicate the actual numbers of the people; moreover, as sixteenth-century governments evolved better methods of enumeration, it is possible that an apparent increase in the number of taxed hearths, for example, revealed the greater efficiency of civil servants rather than an increased number of mouths to be fed. Nonetheless, all the available statistics point in favour of an increase, and while there were many writers in the course of the sixteenth century who referred to the growth of population in order to grind a variety of political and social axes, none referred to a decrease.

The population of towns increased dramatically. Rome, Palermo, Messina, Marseilles, Lisbon, Seville, London, Antwerp all passed the 100,000 mark: Naples doubled its numbers from 100,000 to 200,000: Paris rose from 120,000 to 200,000, and Milan from

100,000 to 180,000: Venice having risen from 100,000 to 168,000 by 1563 subsequently lost 47,000 in the plague of 1576. From this it is possible to deduce an increase of the population at large because the urban mortality rate was so high that the rate of growth could only have been maintained by immigration on a vast scale from the countryside and this would not have occurred unless the pressure of population upon the land had intensified during the century. There is also evidence of widespread migration not only to the towns but also from one region to another. Franche Comté, devastated by 1559, was swiftly resettled from Picardy and Savoy; Granada, which lost much of its Morisco population between 1570 and 1580 filled up with farmers from northern Spain, and a south Germany chronicle, the *Zimmeriche Chronik* affirmed that 'in our times the people in Swabia as well as in all the other countries are greatly augmented and increased, whereby the land has been opened up more than within the memory of man; and hardly a nook, even in the bleakest woods and on the highest mountains, is left uncleared and uninhabited.'

The population of France rose from 10,000,000 to 18,000,000 by mid-century, falling subsequently to 16,000,000 as a result of the Wars of Religion, but it did not have to go far to seek new land. In the thirteenth century so much land had been reclaimed and colonised that Froissart described the country as 'the fairest kingdom of the world after the Kingdom of Heaven'. There was, therefore, plenty of land available when the population began to recover from the twin disasters of the Black Death and the Hundred Years' War. In contrast, the territories of the Holy Roman Empire were hard pressed to accommodate an increase from 12,000,000 to 20,000,000. Warfare was openly advocated as a means of population control, Sebastian Franck complained that the massacre of the peasants after the revolt of 1525 had not been sufficient to reduce the pressure on land, and Ulrich von Hutten even discovered a silver lining to the black cloud of Osmanli expansion: 'There is a dearth of provisions and Germany is overcrowded this age. What we all ought to have wished for – a foreign war whereby we could relieve ourselves of that multitude – has providentially come to pass; it is providential I say that war against the Turks should have become both warranted and necessary'. Switzerland attempted to solve its problem by exporting men for service in foreign armies. Between 50,000 and 100,000 were lost in this way in the fifteenth century and 250,000 in the sixteenth, yet still the local population rose in number from 800,000 to 1,000,000. In England where the population increased from 2,500,000 to about 4,000,000, Sir Walter Ralegh recognised the value of warfare in keeping numbers down, but Richard Hakluyt in his *Discourse of the Western Planting* preferred the more humanitarian solution of planned emigration to the New World.

All in all the population in Europe rose from approximately 50,000,000 in 1450 to 85,000,000 in 1600, and from this fact it is reasonable to suppose that the greater demand for food was the basic underlying cause of the persistent rise of prices throughout the sixteenth century.

The Social Consequences of Inflation

Since the rate of inflation and population growth in the sixteenth century was a dramatic one by the standards of the previous century, there has been a tendency to assume that the consequences of this must also have been dramatic. Historians have postulated both an industrial revolution promoted by profit inflation and the rise of a middle class with the acumen to exploit the situation, and there has been a prolonged debate whether or not the land-owning nobility failed to hold its own in the sixteenth century. Nonetheless, there is much to be said for a more cautious appraisal of the situation: many opportunities were created, some were seized but many others were let slip. There was, for example, an obvious demand for greater food production and certain profitable experiments in specialised farming were successful (see page 164). Yet it is equally obvious that remarkably little was done to improve agriculture throughout Europe as a whole until the eighteenth century. Many books were published to encourage improved methods of husbandry, but very few farmers could have read them and the system of production remained unchanged. Crop yields were desperately low. A ton of seed grain produced on average about five tons of harvested grain and from this the seed corn had to be put aside for next year's sowing. Attempts to expand the area of production usually involved the use of less fertile ground; consequently the average yield per acre was reduced.

Although the transport of grain surpluses was an important and lucrative industry, it could mitigate the worse effects of starvation only in areas accessible to shipping, and overall it accounted for less than one-fiftieth of the total consumption of grain. Not surprisingly the evidence indicates that the growing population of Europe had to accept an inferior type of diet: 'In my father's time', wrote the Sieur de Gomberville 'there was meat every day, food was plentiful, men drank wine as though it was water, but all that has quite changed today . . . the food of the most prosperous peasants is much poorer than the food which servants used to eat.' Nor was this mere nostalgia. Meat consumption declined significantly; pigs were produced in greater number than before but cattle became relatively scarce except in the Balkans and on the plains of eastern Europe, and, as a result, a vegetarian diet became the norm for most country folk. It was by eating less, not by producing more, that Europe sustained its increased numbers, and the food shortages of the last decade of the century indicated that this population growth was about to be checked by subsistence crises of increasing frequency and severity.

New techniques and sundry inventions improved the manufacture of soap and glass, the refining of sugar and the processes of ore extraction, but these were very minor industries in comparison with building, ship-building and textiles in which the basic pattern of production established by 1520 underwent little change in the rest of the sixteenth century. Of these three major European industries, textile production was perhaps the most expansionist. Production expanded to meet increased demands although there was no call for labour-saving devices since there was no shortage of labour. The guilds in fact were so preoccupied by the fear of unemployment that the entrepreneur who wanted to have greater control over the quality and price of his products went out into the countryside or into smaller towns to recruit his labour force outside the aegis of the established centres of production. The trend towards the 'new draperies' established in the fifteenth century (see page 19) was thus confirmed; and though the city weavers of Ghent and Bruges, for example, made periodic forays to smash the looms of the peasants in the surrounding countryside it was the lighter, cheaper says of Walloon Flanders, like those of East Anglia, which continued to capture the markets. The expansion in this area of production, however, was matched to some extent by the consequent decline of the ancient industries of the cities of Italy and the Netherlands.

Any consideration of an agricultural or industrial revolution is, therefore, quite inapposite with reference to the sixteenth century, but there is no doubt that inflation and population growth had an immediate effect on several classes of people. Too much attention has been paid, however, to the so-called rise of the urban middle classes. The most successful, most wealthy and most independent group of towns was to be found in the northern provinces of the Netherlands, and it is true that this region deliberately exploited the growth of population in Europe, supplying it with foodstuffs and other necessities by means of an expanding international trade. It was not typical of the rest of Europe however. As a result of the changing pattern of trade (see pages 169–83) and of the extension of a royal authority which regarded municipal autonomy with suspicion, the centres of the commercial middle classes declined both in wealth and political importance. The power of the Swabian and Hanseatic leagues was in decline while the Italian cities fell under the control of princes. Strasburg lost its former importance after the defeat of the Schmalkaldic league, Augsburg after the bankruptcy of Charles V, and Antwerp after the Dutch revolt. Moreover, the townsmen too, readily subscribed to the basic notions of their age; the ideal of republican Rome, temporarily revived in many Italian and German cities at the end of the fifteenth century, gave way in the sixteenth to the reassertion of aristocratic standards of behaviour. The successful merchants, therefore, sought ennoblement or at least to live like gentlemen on the terms laid down by gentlemen.

The sixteenth century was essentially an age which set tremendous store by land-owning and nobility and it was the landowners who were better placed than other classes to meet the challenge of inflation and the opportunity of more mouths to be fed. Although there was little improvement generally in European agriculture, landowners in various regions successfully developed profitable ventures of their own. The Roman nobility specialised in pastoral farming in the Campagna; the landowners of Holstein and Denmark grew rich from the sales of bacon, butter and cheese; in the Po valley they concentrated on the production of rice and maize and in the English Midlands and East Anglia they switched from arable farming to sheep rearing in order to meet the growing demand for English wool in the Netherlands. In Sweden the nobility were particularly fortunate in that their rents were traditionally paid in kind, so that as food prices rose so did the value of the income they received. Elsewhere other landlords tried to keep pace with inflation by exploiting the population pressure on land by raising rents, reducing the length of leases and increasing the fines paid for entry to a lease.

The most important development took place in north-eastern Germany and in Poland where vast estates, colonised before the onslaught of the Black Death, were admirably suited for the large-scale production of rye. The special condition of land tenure (*lassrecht*) which prevailed in these colonial regions allowed the landlords to demand greater labour services than were customary elsewhere, and the peasantry were unable to leave the land without permission. More valuable still, the nobility were granted special rights of lordship (*gutsherrschaft*), which went far beyond the usual powers of manorial jurisdiction (*grundherrschaft*) by treating the personal estates of the landlord as an administrative unit of the state while the landlord himself acted as a local representative of the sovereign. With plenty of land and a labour force as subservient as that of an *encomienda* in the New World, all that was needed was an efficient means of transportation to convey the grain to distant markets. This was provided by the lake and river systems of Poland, east Germany and the Baltic provinces, and the export of rye from Danzig increased by nearly fourfold between 1550 and 1600 and doubled again in the following twenty years. Further south in Bohemia and Hungary, where the land was similarly exploited for large-scale production, the lack of a river system for transportation was of no significance since the grain was sold in the region itself to feed the armies engaged on the Turkish frontier.

The landowning class, therefore, was able to protect itself from and even to exploit the rise in prices by adopting various courses of action, but many landowners did nothing of the kind. Ignorance of the changes taking place and simple inertia accounted for the relative decline of many families, others were too preoccupied with warfare and politics or too much embroiled in the crises of the Reformation to have time to husband their own resources: many were not sufficiently ruthless to interfere with the traditional customs of their manors, and a surprisingly large number were held back by paternal concern for the well-being of their tenants. Even when they tried to protect themselves they were not always successful. The introduction of large-scale grain production in Bavaria collapsed for the lack of a river system to convey the harvest to market. Enclosures for sheep farming in England ceased to be profitable in the later sixteenth century when the cloth trade fell into decline. Moreover, the peasants were often capable of organising a successful resistance to the introduction of new farming techniques or increased rents. Many of them prospered from the rise in food prices and could afford to invoke the protection of law, and in England, Castile and Saxony, for example, the governments deliberately intervened on their behalf both in the law courts and in the legislature. The elector of Saxony, Augustus I (1553–80), went even further to protect his subjects by buying up large estates in order to split them up into small peasant holdings, and in several German states it was declared illegal to raise rents or to convert long leases to short ones.

When the government and the law afforded the peasantry no protection there remained the powerful sanction of rebellion, and in Germany in particular there were peasant risings every few years in the half-century before 1524. Significantly the revolt of 1524 (see page 236) did not break out among the depressed peasantry of the north and east but among the more prosperous inhabitants of the south and west whose greater prosperity prompted them to resist the efforts of their landlords to interfere with their rights. The Articles of June 1524 protested against the enclosure of woods and common lands, the demand for more labour services on the demesne and the reduction of the length of leases, and, although the revolt was suppressed, the memory of its violence induced the landlords to behave with greater circumspection in the future.

Many landowners sought an easier way to counter the effect of inflation by acquiring more land since this provided them with additional income without the need to undertake more ruthless or imaginative methods of estate management. Some achieved this by litigation and there was a marked increase in the number of law suits involving territorial disputes; a few enlarged their properties by a successful marriage; others solicited the favours of their prince in the hope that some share of the estates which fell to him by escheat or forfeiture might be distributed to them. The frequency of civil war ensured a considerable traffic in land titles among those who backed the winning side, while in Protestant countries there were valuable opportunities to be exploited from the secularisation of Church land. Alternatively, the prince was petitioned for the award of monopolies, licenses and subsidies, and even more for appointment to lucrative positions in the army, the Church and the civil service. Indeed the landowning class was not only the principal beneficiary of royal patronage; it regarded this as nothing less than its due. Those who failed to receive the help they needed, therefore, became a source of disaffection, with the result that the final expedient in the struggle against inflation was very often a desperate gamble on the outcome of a rebellion.

Indirectly, therefore, inflation raised serious problems for the kings and princes of Europe since aristocratic discontent was a potent cause of political tension. Directly too they were as vulnerable as any other landowners to the effect of rising prices: nor could they, as responsible rulers, adopt any remedy such as the enclosure of common lands or the raising of rents, which might harm the interests of their own subjects and lead to widespread poverty and social unrest. Moreover, quite apart from the effect of inflation, the extension of royal administration in the sixteenth century and the greater scale of warfare – involving the employment of professional civil servants and the recruitment of mercenary armies, the provision of expensive weapons and the construction of more substantial fortifications – created a financial problem for which there was no easy solution. Most governments increased the revenue from existing taxes and invented new ones; they reinterpreted more strictly many of the conventions of feudal tenure in order to exploit more fully the fiscal obligations of their tenants-in-chief; they sold off much of their own land and in Protestant countries profited from the confiscation of monastic estates; they exploited the sale of titles, privileges, offices, licenses and monopolies; they frequently debased the currency; they sold annuities and bonds funded by revenues specifically assigned to provide the annual interest; they ran into debt. Finally, as a last resort, many of them went bankrupt.

For royalty and landowners alike the sixteenth century was an age of crisis. Some collapsed under the strain; others survived by a combination of good luck and resourcefulness; but it is impossible to generalise about the class as a whole. On the other hand it is clear that the poorest and most numerous sections of society, the peasantry and the industrial artisans, became still poorer. The considerable advantages which had been gained by them in the century following the Black Death had been forfeited by 1600, and the reciprocal relationships between lord and vassal which had given stability to rural society were eroded by the development of a less personal relationship based on the payment of rent or the provision of labour for wages. Those who were driven from their land by the loss of a lease, by an increase in rent or by an enclosing landlord, migrated to the towns where work became increasingly difficult to find. The exclusive corporations and guilds in a last ditch effort to protect their own workers refused to admit new members, and though mortality rates were high the constant pressure of new immigrants swelled the numbers of the under-employed.

The literary evidence of poverty and unrest in town and country alike is substantial but there is no need to rely solely on those writers whose compassion for the poor might conceivably have led them to exaggerate their sufferings. The introduction of legislation to combat the effects of poverty in many countries indicates that private and municipal charity was no longer able to cope with the problem and the most influential study of the subject, *De Subventione Pauperum* by the Spaniard Luis Vives, achieved international sales in the sixteenth century. Moreover, it is quite clear that although prices rose there was no corresponding rise in wages since there was so plentiful a supply of labour for hire.

One important attempt has been made to quantify the extent of the problem by a comparative study of the price of consumer goods in England and the wages paid in the building industry (E. H. Phelps Brown and Sheila Hopkins 'Seven centuries of the price of consumables compared with builders' wage rates' *Economica*, 1956). Its authors constructed a model of individual consumption, a 'basket of consumables' which included food (80%), textiles ($12\frac{1}{2}$%) and fuel and light ($7\frac{1}{2}$%). Having costed this against the wages paid in the period 1451–75, they discovered that in the next century, the wages paid in 1571, for example, were sufficient to purchase only two-thirds of the 'basket of consumables'. Similar studies have been made of the purchasing power of artisans in other countries and the overall impression emerges that the real value of wages declined by 50 per cent in the sixteenth century. The studies, however, exaggerate the extent of the problem because the majority of the population was not dependent on wages alone. Some were paid in kind or partly in kind, thereby reducing the effect of inflation; all, or very nearly all, lived on the land and their plots or gardens in the villages, and even within the confines of most towns, afforded them the opportunity to grow a measure of food for themselves. Significantly, perhaps, it was in Antwerp where overcrowding denied the working classes the possession of gardens, that the wages of the building workers followed the rise of prices more closely than anywhere else in Europe.

If the impact of inflation on the poorer sections of society cannot be evaluated precisely, it remains quite clear that the gap which widened in society as a whole between those who coped with inflation and those who did not was nowhere more evident than in that between the labouring classes on the one hand and the landlords and employers on the other. In western Europe their security of tenure was impaired; in eastern regions they were frequently reduced to a condition of serfdom; in the cities they found little relief from the poverty which had driven them from the land, and throughout Europe their standard of living was substantially reduced, both in terms of the clothing and furniture they could buy and of the food they consumed. Their profound dissatisfaction at a state of affairs beyond their comprehension expressed itself in a mood of suppressed resentment which underlay the history of the sixteenth century like a stratum of volcanic lava, erupting into violent demonstrations whenever the ordered structure of society was impaired by economic crises, political controversy or religious dissent.

Mediterranean Trade

The natural resources of the countries bordering the Mediterranean proved inadequate to meet the demands of a population which rose from 30 million to 60 million in the sixteenth century (F. Braudel *La Méditerranée et Le Monde Méditerranéen à l'Epoque de Philippe II*, 2nd edition, 2 vols. Paris 1966). This rapid growth destroyed the economic self-sufficiency of the region and provided northern shipping with an opportunity to compete on better terms with the local traders who had hitherto enjoyed a virtual monopoly.

The staple trade in grain, for example, was seriously affected by the failure of Sicily to maintain its traditional role as the 'granary of the Mediterranean'. Soil erosion began to take its toll of the crops, and the growth of population in the towns reduced the amount of grain available for export. Three bad harvests in succession between 1575 and 1577 created an unprecedented famine in the island; even more serious was the famine of 1591 – thereafter Sicily became an importer rather than a supplier of grain. The Italians and Ragusans, who had hitherto controlled the long-haul grain trade, searched desperately for new supplies in Egypt and among the islands of the Aegean, despite the heavy tolls levied by the Osmanli Turks, but the trade was suspended during the naval war of 1570–3 (see page 377). Even when peace returned to the eastern Mediterranean there was little improvement in the situation since the Turks themselves began to buy up the local surpluses to feed the growing population of Constantinople – which suffered famine between 1572 and 1581, and 1585 and 1589, and again in 1597 and 1600.

The traditional pattern of trade by which the western Mediterranean was supplied with grain from Sicily and the Levant was consequently destroyed, and the growing severity of famine in most Mediterranean cities in the latter half of the sixteenth century led to the arrival of northern ships with Baltic grain and barrelled herrings from the Netherlands. Grand Duke Ferdinand of Tuscany astutely recognised the changed conditions of trade and in 1593 declared Livorno to be a free port: within a decade 2,500 ships a year, most of them controlled by English, Dutch and Hanseatic firms, were visiting the port and made it the most important centre in the Mediterranean for the distribution of northern grain. For political reasons, Philip II of Spain tried to prevent this infiltration by placing an embargo on all English and Dutch ships visiting Iberian ports in 1585, 1595 and 1598, but the fact that on each occasion over five hundred ships were impounded demonstrated the strength of the northern challenge. Spain indeed could not survive without northern grain. Philip tried to circumvent his enemies, the English and the Dutch, by offering safe conducts to the Hanseatic league alone, but this proved valueless since most of the cargoes were eventually shipped from Amsterdam, and with the coming of peace with both England and Holland in the first decade of the seventeenth century, northern shipping sailed freely and in great number into the Iberian ports.

Apart from grain the Mediterranean region was running short also of the raw materials on which its industries depended. In the second half of the century hides had to be imported from Poland, from Russia and the New World, and wool supplies began to dwindle because of the expansion of the textile industries of the Netherlands. England sent most of her wool and unfinished cloth across the Channel and by 1550 over half the Spanish crop was being exported to the Netherlands. Subsequently, when Spanish production began to fall off, the Netherlands claimed an increasing proportion of what was available to the detriment of the Italian textile towns.

Timber, too, was in short supply with serious consequences not only for the shipbuilding industries, but also for the Italian trading fleets. On both counts Venice suffered badly. She derived her fir masts and larch beams from the Rheatian and Carnic Alps and from the Upper Adige, and her oak from Istria, but supplies were running out by 1550 and attempts to purchase timber from Dalmatia foundered on the difficulty of transporting it down to the Adriatic Sea. She was forced to adapt to the situation by making the best possible use of her limited resources. After 1520 oak was reserved exclusively for the arsenal, and galley production ceased altogether, except for the construction of warships, when the beechwood from which the oars were made became unobtainable. From a commercial point of view the loss of galleys was no bad thing since they were unsuitable as cargo vessels, but the private shipyards failed to notice the development of the galleon in northern waters and stuck to the traditional design of the carrack. Moreover, because of the lack of timber, they tried to economise by building fewer but larger carracks of anything up to 1,000 tons – larger in fact than most Atlantic vessels. These giant hulks were expensive, both to build and to operate commercially, and the northern interlopers with cheaper ships of more modest design – the three-masted *bertoni* – were beginning to compete successfully with the Italians long before the food shortages of the 1580s opened the ports to Baltic grain. Moreover, since production was limited to only five a year, the Italians were finally compelled to purchase ships from the Aegean islands, from Spain and even from northern Europe.

The changing pattern of trade in the Mediterranean threatened the commercial pre-eminence of Genoa and Venice. Genoa saved herself by adopting new tactics. Throughout the fifteenth century she had successfully competed with the Catalan ports for control of Spanish trade in the Mediterranean. When the Osmanli conquest of her colonies in the Black Sea and the Aegean destroyed the bases of her Levantine operations, Genoa began to exploit her commercial links with Spain so ruthlessly that in 1528 the Castilian *Cortes* complained that wool, silk, steel and soap, the principal commodities of Spanish industry, were being monopolised by Genoese firms. In that same year the Genoese staked their future on the Spanish connection by abandoning their alliance with the French, and offering the services of their famous admiral, Doria, to Charles V. Nor did they content themselves with dealing in commodities. The Ligurian aristocracy took up banking out of the proceeds of their trade and the Houses of Doria, Centurione, Pallavicino, Spinola and Grimaldi had outstripped the Fuggers by 1560 as the principal Spanish bankers. Instead of being hampered by the seasonal irregularity of its bullion imports from America, the Spanish government was able to finance its operation in Europe by means of Genoese loans; the Genoese for their part handled the sale of bullion on its arrival and so long as the silver continued to be mined in Peru they enjoyed a period of great wealth and luxury. Moreover, their agents were allowed to operate under cover in Seville at the heart of the Spanish-American empire, and when Portugal fell to Philip II in 1584 they also secured a privileged place in the colonial sugar trade, acquiring plantations and refineries in Madeira and the Azores.

The history of Venice was not so straightforward as that of Genoa. Her shipbuilding industry was paralysed, her war fleet of galleys was insufficient to protect her traders from attack by pirates based in Spain, Malta and the Barbary coast, and the changed conditions of the trade in grain and other commodities conferred advantages upon her northern competitors. In the Adriatic, the Aegean and the Levant, Venice retained something of her exclusive monopoly of trade, but she suffered badly from the Uskoks, a group of pirates based, impregnably it seems, at Segna near Fiume, and from the Osmanli Turks who seized both Cyprus and Negroponte during the sixteenth century and with whom the Venetians waged frequent and unsuccessful wars.

There remained the spice trade with the Arabs which had contributed so much to Venetian prosperity in the past (see page

7). The Portuguese discovery of an independent route to India had destroyed the European monopoly enjoyed by Venice, but the effect was not as disastrous as it first appeared. After an initial setback, when the Portuguese denied the Arabs access to the markets of India and thereby brought the Italian trade to a standstill, it became clear that the Portuguese, unable to maintain a permanent embargo on trade through the Red Sea and the Persian Gulf, could do no more than levy tolls on the Arab dhows. These tolls in addition to those imposed after 1520 by the Osmanli Pashas in Egypt compelled the Italians to pay a high price for their spices, but even so they succeeded in competing effectively with the Portuguese. Since the latter had nothing to offer the merchants of Goa but bullion, the profit from the spices had to cover the cost of both the outward and the return voyages, whereas the Arabs and the Indians were anxious to purchase the goods purveyed by the Italians in exchange for spices. In the long run, therefore, Portuguese pepper proved to be no less expensive than Italian, and was generally held to be inferior to it because sea water frequently contaminated the cargoes during the long storm-ridden voyages around the Cape. As a result the Italian trade recovered a good deal of its former vitality between 1550 and 1570, importing something like 2,000 tons of pepper a year from Egypt with a lesser amount passing from the Gulf to Aleppo and thence to Venice.

After 1570 the Levantine spice trade was once again disturbed, partly by an Arab revolt against the Osmanli Turks which temporarily closed the Red Sea to trade, partly by warfare between the Turks and the Persians which dislocated trade through the Gulf, and even more by the outbreak of war between Venice and the Turks in the Mediterranean. These circumstances compelled the Venetians to purchase their supplies from the Portuguese factor in Lisbon and prompted Philip II to offer them special terms, along with a share in the Sicilian grain trade, in order to bind them more closely to Spanish policies in Italy. Venice, however, refused to follow the Genoese into the Spanish camp and the decision was later justified by the return of peace to the Levant and the revival of the overland spice trade across Egypt. Moreover, for a while the advantage lay with Venice in the 1570s: Spanish and Portuguese shipping was frequently blockaded in the Atlantic ports by English and Dutch fleets and had to run the gauntlet of privateers and pirates between Lisbon and the Netherlands. By contrast, the overland route from Venice to south Germany was free from marauders and was protected by the south Germany cities which had grown rich from their connection with Italy. At the end of the century, however, this vital artery of trade was affected by a climatic change. The weather turned colder, the glaciers began to advance and the passes through the Alps were frequently blocked by snow even in the summer months. As a result the south German cities were compelled to turn to the Netherlands for supplies and Venice began to lose her commercial pre-eminence as a supplier of spices to Europe.

Despite the serious blow to her commercial and maritime pre-eminence Venice retained much of her prosperity in the sixteenth century. The textile industries of Florence and sub-sequently of the Netherlands, suffered from the Italian wars and the Dutch revolt respectively, and Venice profited from their discomfiture. The growing shortage of wool in the Mediterranean region as a whole did not prevent her merchants from gaining possession of a greater proportion of what was available, and the annual production of broad cloths increased: 8,563 pieces were produced on average every year between 1540 and 1549, 13,240 between 1550 and 1559 and 22,428 in the opening year of the seventeenth century. There was also a significant shift in investment from overseas trade to the Venetian mainland in the Po valley where land was acquired for building and for food production. Moreover, Venetians began to speculate more widely and indeed successfully on the bourses of Europe. Consequently, the decline in commercial wealth was matched by the profits to be derived from industry, land and finance, and the prosperity of Venice in the sixteenth century sustained the splendour of her art and architecture (see page 399).

Northern and Atlantic Trade

By the middle of the sixteenth century the age of south German prosperity had passed its peak. Cities such as Augsburg and Nuremberg suffered badly from the dislocation of trade which resulted from the Wars of the Schmalkaldic League (see page 240) and from the civil war which periodically flared up throughout the remainder of Charles V's reign as emperor. Moreover, their princely neighbours, who were jealous both of their wealth and their civic independence, used their influence in the imperial diet to hamper their activities by legislating against monopolies and money lending. Such a diet was held in Nuremberg itself in 1522 when it was decreed that the brunt of the imperial customs duties should be borne by the merchants and that the leading banks and international trading companies were to be disbanded. It was only on appeal to Charles V that the edicts were revoked, and the south German cities recognised that their one hope of survival lay in maintaining their traditional association with the Austrian Habsburgs. It was not surprising, therefore, that Nuremberg was the only Lutheran city to remain loyal to Charles V throughout the German wars. Augsburg was less fortunate. The Lutheran party backed by the support of the artisans and unemployed, forced the hand of the patrician merchants who ruled the city and compelled them to intervene in what turned out to be the losing side in the Schmalkaldic war. Only the intervention of the Fugger family with its intimate financial connections with the emperor saved the city from forfeiting its privileges.

Other and more serious problems arose meanwhile which meant that the Augsburg settlement of 1555 did not lead to a recovery of economic growth in south Germany. Chief among these was the flow of American silver into Europe. This not only rendered obsolete the mining operations on which the south German firms had based their other commercial actions, but put an end to the profitable arrangement by which the Germans exchanged their silver and Hungarian copper at Antwerp for Portuguese spices. After 1549 the Portuguese factor withdrew to Lisbon and, though the spice merchants could still make purchases there or at Venice, the production costs of the German and Hungarian mines priced their products out of the European markets.

There remained the business of speculation on the European exchanges and above all the provision of loans to the Habsburgs. Initially this proved to be a profitable undertaking. The Welsers, who were reluctant to abandon their main interests in commerce, increased their profitability at an annual rate of 9.5 per cent between 1510 and 1527: the Fuggers who concentrated on money lending increased theirs by 54 per cent. Jacob Fugger, for example, provided 543,000 florins towards the expenses of Charles V's election as emperor – against 143,000 supplied by the Welsers –

and in return secured further mining concessions in the Tyrol. He also supported the Habsburg policy of infiltration into Hungary where he had acquired control of the copper and silver mines at Neusohl and Kremnitz. This venture was terminated in 1524 when Louis II, at the request of his Magyar nobility, confiscated the mines, but after the Battle of Mohacs and the succession of Ferdinand of Habsburg to the Hungarian throne (see page 228) the mines were restored to the Fuggers. Jacob died in 1525 without sons, but his four nephews had been taken into the family business and of these Anton became the head of the firm. It was he who exploited his connection with Charles V to secure a lease on the estates of the three military orders of Spain, and subsequently on the silver mines of Guadalcanal in Andalusia and the mercury mines of Almaden. The price he paid was the provision of regular loans, some of them of extraordinary size; in 1536 for example he lent 100,000 ducats at 14 per cent to be repaid in American bullion; in 1537 he lent another 100,000 and in 1552, when Charles had been driven out of Germany by Maurice of Saxony, Anton joined him at Villach in Carinthia with 400,000 ducats.

The Welsers began to follow suit. They lent larger amounts to Charles, acquired leases on government revenues in Spain and became closely involved in the settlement of Venezuela. Meanwhile, the Nuremberg House of Kleberger played a similar role financing the operations of Francis I of France and of Henry II. Unlike the Genoese, however, whose loans to the Spanish government gave them the opportunity to take part in Iberian and colonial trade, the south Germans were particularly vulnerable to any suspension of interest. This happened in 1557. The Habsburgs suspended further payments on their debt, forbade the export of gold from Seville where 570,000 ducats were due to be sent to the Fugger's agent at Antwerp, and forced their creditors to accept non-redeemable government bonds, the *juros*, on which only 5 per cent was to be paid. The French bankruptcy in the same year showed that no royal creditors were safe. Nevertheless, there was no other business available for the south German bankers, and further loans were made until the bankruptcy of Philip II in 1576 finally put an end to their wealth.

In north Germany the decline of the Hanseatic League had begun by 1520 (see page 17). Yet Lübeck, though past her peak, was still the only city-state other than Venice to rank as a European power. She remained the staple market for much of Baltic and north German trade, she was still the principal carrier of grain, timber and fur to western Europe and her fleet was able to exert considerable influence in Baltic affairs. In 1522 it sailed to Stockholm (see page 301) to decide the outcome of Gustav Vasa's rebellion against Christian II of Denmark: in 1523 it helped Frederick, duke of Holstein, to drive Christian II from Denmark. As a result, both Gustav and Frederick had to renew the commercial privileges enjoyed by Lübeck throughout Scandinavia. In 1531, however, a small group of patrician families who had defended the city's interest so successfully in the past, lost control to a popular Lutheran movement led by Jurgen Wullenwever who immediately embarked upon an over-ambitious foreign policy.

In 1533 Wullenwever set out to destroy the kingdom of Denmark, to establish Copenhagen and Malmö as independent city-states, run by popular-based Lutheran parties similar to his own and to acquire control of Elsinore and Helsingborg, which controlled the Sound, and the Baltic islands of Bornholm and Gotland. In 1534 his flagship levied the Sound tolls and his agents engineered a series of popular revolutions in Rostock, Wismar and Stralsund, but the economic and social challenge to their power brought together an alliance among Lübeck's neighbours. Frederick I's son, Christian III, recovered control of Denmark, the Lübeck squadron was defeated by the fleets of Denmark, Norway and Sweden, and Wullenwever was compelled to resign in 1535 – to be executed two years later. The war ended in 1536 with the peace of Hamburg and with it the great days of Lübeck's power.

The Hanseatic League as a whole retained much of its commercial power and Hamburg, Bremen, Emden, Riga and Reval derived considerable advantage from the greater flow of trade from the Baltic to the rest of Europe. But the League no longer enjoyed its former monopoly. By the end of the century the Dutch had acquired control of nearly half the shipping in the Baltic and they exploited the loss sustained by the League's fisheries when the herring shoals began to migrate from Skane to the North Sea. Danzig, moreover, became an independent centre for the export of Polish grain on an ever-increasing scale.

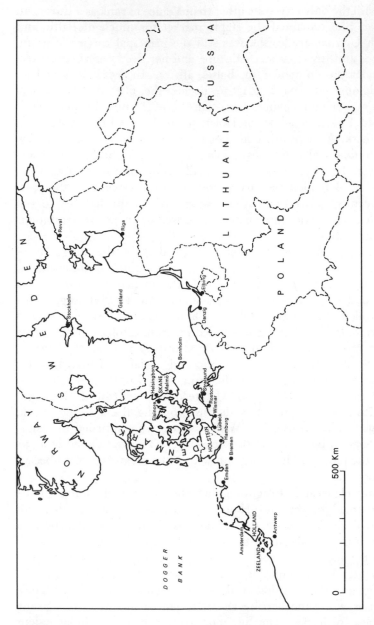

Centres of commerce in Northern Europe

28,000 tons were despatched from Danzig in 1555, 200,000 in 1600, and there was a significant increase in the export of timber, tar pitch, cordage, wax, flax, hemp, hides and furs. In return, the Poles imported luxury cloth, ·herrings, salt, wine and fruit. The English Eastland Company established its own staple at Elbing (Elblag) nearby on the Polish coast in 1579, but its challenge to Danzig was short-lived. Six years later the Danzig merchants persuaded their king to expel the English in return for making him an annual payment of half the income from the tolls levied on goods passing through their port.

Though the Hanseatic League and· the south German towns began to lose something of their former prosperity, Antwerp, established as a major commercial and banking centre before 1520, retained its preeminence for another fifty years. As the largest town of the most densely populated region of northern Europe, it imported in vast quantities the raw materials and the foodstuffs required by an industrial population and exported its products to the rest of Europe (see page 19). Of even greater importance was the fact that its fame as an international market made it the focal point of trade routes stretching out by sea to Mexico, Peru and the Phillipines, to Goa and Indonesia, to the Baltic and the Mediterranean and by land to the markets of France, Germany and Hungary. Its merchants did not have to seek for trade; they operated as commission agents, negotiating the exchange of produce between the merchants of other countries. So long as the foreigners chose to sell their goods in Antwerp, attracted in part by the privileges afforded them, but even more by the ease with which they were able to meet their customers from other lands during the twenty-two weeks of the international fair, so long would Antwerp continue to prosper.

As an international commodity market, Antwerp was well placed for the raising of loans and the Netherlands government of Charles V exploited the opportunity to finance its operations by borrowing from the wealthy merchants who traded in the city. Prominent among these, of course, were the agents of the Fuggers, the Welsers and the Hochstetters, but the international character of Antwerp attracted also the bankers of Florence, Genoa and Spain. Initially the loans were raised for specific short-term needs, and from 1516 their redemption was fixed according to the calendar of the four annual fairs. Initially, too, the demand was irregular and interest rates were therefore high: a government loan of 1520 carried a rate of $15\frac{1}{2}$ per cent, another of 1521 a rate of $27\frac{1}{2}$ per cent. As business grew and loans were negotiated for longer periods, the interest rates began to fall to between 12 and 15 per cent. The demand for money was at its heaviest and the flow of money to meet it at its steadiest between 1542 and 1557. It was in 1543, for example, that the equivalent of £500,000 sterling was provided for Charles V, an equal amount for the government of Portugal, and £1 million for Henry VIII of England.

One very typical figure of the 1540s was an Italian, Gaspar Ducci, who had established himself at Antwerp as a commodity broker and commission agent and then moved on to speculate on the exchange of Antwerp and Lyons. His skill in this field made him a useful agent for the fund-raising operations of the government of the Netherlands, and it was he who promoted the issue of bearer bonds – readily negotiable since they could always be redeemed by whoever was the bearer – against the anticipated revenues of government departments. So prolific was his business, so apparently successful, that other men with less resources than the great banking houses began to gamble on the profits to be made from government loans. The crash came in 1557 when the Netherlands government was unable to maintain the payment of interest and the new king, Philip II, was unable to help since his government in Spain had already suspended payments on its own debts. This was not only a blow to the major banking houses, whose loans were converted into state bonds – irredeemable and carrying an interest of only 5 per cent – but also to the lesser creditors who found it impossible to meet their own obligations to other traders. The total effect was to weaken confidence in the stability of Antwerp as a centre of financial and commercial exchange.

The damage though serious would have proved merely superficial and temporary had the commercial bases of Antwerp's prosperity been preserved, but in the same period the flow of international trade through the city began to falter. The Portuguese factor of spices had withdrawn to Lisbon in 1549 since the influx of American silver into Seville no longer made it necessary for his ships to hazard the storms and the pirates of the Atlantic coast. This in turn deprived the German merchants of the opportunity to sell their copper, silver, textiles and metal goods to the

Portuguese at the Antwerp fairs. The other basic staple, the sale of unfinished cloth from England, was disrupted by the devaluation of the English currency in the 1540s which so reduced its price in Antwerp that in the rush to buy it a glut was created. Subsequently the stabilisation of the currency in the 1550s sent up the price of cloth and threw the market once again into disarray. Opportunities for large-scale trade still existed however and Guicciardini, the Florentine historian who visited Antwerp at this time, was struck by the international influence exerted by the city. He estimated the total value of its imports at 16 million gold crowns; English cloth still accounted for 5 million crowns, Italian cloth and other products for 3 million, bulk wheat for just short of 2 million, French wine for 1 million and Portuguese spices, though radically reduced in quantity, for 1 million gold crowns. Clearly the pattern of trade had altered since 1520 but the city's importance as the principal market in Europe was still potentially very great.

A final blow, however, was struck by the social, religious and political unrest which beset the Netherlands in the second half of the sixteenth century (see page 357). The iconoclastic riots of 1566, the 'Spanish Fury' of 1576 and the rigours of war between the northern and southern provinces destroyed the wealth of Antwerp. Its population began to dwindle from 80,000 in 1550 to 42,000 in 1589, while its trade was stifled by the action of the northern rebels who blockaded the Scheldt. Those with initiative moved north to Amsterdam. By 1622, when the population there had reached 105,000, a half were newcomers or immigrants of one generation, and as one new arrival commented 'here is Antwerp itself changed into Amsterdam'.

The rise of Amsterdam reflected the growing commercial importance of the northern provinces of Holland and Zeeland, an importance based upon their success in the fishing industry. When the herring shoals deserted the fishing grounds off Skane in the Baltic for the North Sea, the Dutch were better placed than their Hanseatic rivals to fish the Dogger Bank and the Scottish coasts. By 1620 there were 2,000 *buizen* (see page 18) operating the 'Dutch gold mine' in the North Sea. Moreover, in order to keep the *buizen* permanently at work, the Dutch developed a new type of boat, the *ventjager*, a 'fast ship which sailed out to the *buizen* and brought the catch back to market. From Holland salted herrings were distributed to the rest of Europe and the profits of the trade provided the basis for Dutch expansion. Unlike the merchants of Antwerp, the Dutch did not wait for trade to come to them; they set out in the Baltic, along the Atlantic coast and eventually into the Mediterranean, to carry freight wherever it was to be found and their rates were ruthlessly competitive, undercutting the English, for example, by nearly half.

This was done not only by paying their crews less, borrowing money more cheaply and securing more advantageous rates of insurance, but also by stringent economy in ship-building: bulk purchases were made of timber, fir was used whenever possible in place of oak, and the shipyards were equipped with wind-driven saw-mills, winches and other labour-saving devices. They also designed a new type of freight carrier, the *fluyt*, which was virtually a long floating container with enormous holds. Its great length, often six times its beam, created longitudinal stress, but this was compensated for at the expense of the crew's quarters by reducing the superstructure fore and aft. Each *fluyt* was designed for its appropriate trade. Shallow drafts were needed for the silted estuaries of the Baltic, deeper drafts for the Atlantic, and the holds were specially modified for the timber and grain trade.

Consequently the Dutch began to monopolise sea-borne trade around the shores of northern Europe. Their main effort was directed towards the Baltic. The records of the Danish Sound dues recording the number of payments made by ships passing in and out of the Baltic revealed an increase in Dutch payments from 1,300 in 1500 to 5,000 in 1600. From the Baltic they swept down along the Atlantic coast and despite the long years of warfare with Spain, the Atlantic trade never slackened. Spain and Portugal could not do without grain, fish, metal goods and textiles for their own population and for their colonies. They also needed timber to build their oceanic fleets. There was oak in the interior but it was difficult to transport it to the coast and the expanding iron industry at Vizcaya competed with the shipbuilding yards of Bilbao for what was available. From 1570 therefore Baltic timber was imported. In return the Iberian merchants needed the Dutch vessels to transport Andalusian wool, high quality wool from Burgos and Castilian soap to the textile industries of England and the Netherlands, and salt from Setubal for the Dutch fisheries. In addition, they supplied the northern markets with fruits from the Mediterranean, wines from Seville and the Canaries, spices from India and silver from America. Nor was this the extent of Dutch commerce. The shortage of raw materials in the Mediterranean region gave them the chance to sail past Gibraltar and tap the rich markets of Barcelona, Marseilles, Naples and Livorno (see page 170), and by the end of the century they were about to embark upon the commercial exploitation of the Portuguese and Spanish discoveries around the world.

Portugal, the Estado da India and Brazil

The extent of the Portuguese empire in 1520, stretching as it did from the Atlantic coast of Africa to the Pacific coast of Asia, might well have seemed too vast to be effectively directed and defended by so small a country: on the other hand, because of the special circumstances of this area the presence of the Portuguese in great numbers was not necessary. There was no need for them to engage in production nor even to involve themselves in the collection of supplies for export to Europe. For centuries this had been handled most successfully by local producers and traders and all that was required of the Portuguese was to establish control of the principal trade routes. This was made relatively easy by the fact that the routes from China and Indonesia to India had to pass through the Malacca Straits or the Sunda Straits, and those from India to the Middle East were confined to the narrow waters of the Red Sea and the Persian Gulf. Once the Portuguese were able to establish bases in these regions they could divert into their own hands the trade which formerly had been controlled by others.

In order to maintain these bases a small garrison of Portuguese colonists could be supplemented by mercenaries, slaves and topazes – converts to Christianity – and Albuquerque (see page 29) had encouraged many of his men to settle permanently and marry local wives by granting them military fiefs in the new settlements. Two conditions remained to be fulfilled. The Portuguese had to remain resolutely neutral in all disputes between local rulers in order to husband their slender military resources. They had also to maintain an effective fleet to patrol the major sea routes and to defend any garrison which ran into trouble, for as Albuquerque had reported to his government 'if once

Portuguese bases in the Far East

Portugal should suffer a reverse at sea your Indian possessions have not the power to hold out a day longer than the kings of the land choose to suffer it'. In this respect the Portuguese were well favoured. The Chinese fleet was friendly. The fleets of local princes were unable to challenge the Portuguese on their own and the Arab galleys, powerful enough at close quarters in the Red Sea, were ineffective in the open waters of the Indian Ocean.

The problems of the Portuguese empire therefore were derived from reasons other than its size. One immediate difficulty sprang from the choice of Goa as the major Portuguese base in India. For this it was most unsuitable. The onset of the south-east and the north-east monsoons ensured that for three months every summer ships found it difficult to leave the port and for three months every winter difficult to approach it. Another difficulty was caused by the shortage of timber in Portugal. Because of this the Portuguese, like the Venetians, believed it to be more economical to use the supplies available for the construction of a few large ships rather than for several smaller ones. Moreover these ships, carracks, of the Mediterranean type, were designed primarily to 'carry the greatest possible amount of cargo and were unsuited to meet the challenge of defence and navigation on the high seas. As they became bigger – and over-laden – the sea increasingly took its toll of the annual fleets. From 1500 to 1550 one in eight ships was destroyed at sea: from 1550 to 1600 one in five. Those who survived the voyage had originally made their way to Antwerp to exchange their cargoes of spices for the products of the German and Hungarian mines. To do so however they had to run the gauntlet of Atlantic storms and European pirates and when the Spaniards began to import gold and silver from their American empire, Lisbon was made the major entrepôt of Portuguese trade. It was not so well placed as Antwerp and, unfortunately for Portugal, the Venetians contrived to maintain their own supplies of spices to Europe throughout most of the sixteenth century (see page 173).

From the Crown's point of view the profits of its imperial trade began to dwindle, not merely because of the withdrawal from Antwerp and the resilience of the Venetian trade, but principally because the Portuguese monarchy was unable to enforce a strict monopoly of trade throughout its empire as laid down in the India Ordinances of 1520. To some extent its hands were tied by the lack of a regular civil service in its overseas bases.

There was no formal hierarchy, no sense of corporate identity, and those who were appointed to positions of authority in Goa or Malacca regarded this as a reward for previous services to the crown and an opportunity to make a private profit for themselves. Worse still they compromised the Portuguese monopoly of the trading routes by conniving at smuggling with the Arabs in the Indian Ocean. A Venetian consul, whose concern it was to secure his country's supplies through the Middle East, reported that the spices were 'allowed to pass by the Portuguese soldiers who govern India in the Red Sea for their profit against the command of their king'. The eleven years of regency after the death of John III in 1557 left the colonial servants entirely to their own devices; and when Sebastian in 1570 abandoned his monopoly, requiring only that his subjects send all their cargo for sale in Lisbon where a duty would be levied, pirate contraband was still maintained throughout the empire.

In the course of the century the most profitable trade of all fell almost entirely into private hands: this was the 'country trade', begun initially to facilitate the collection of spices in Goa for collection by the annual fleet from Lisbon, and to pay for them by exporting Indian cottons to Indonesia for spices. Ultimately it became more profitable than the trade from India to Europe and expanded throughout the Far East where the Portuguese became agents for exporting Chinese goods to Japan. The Macao carracks enjoyed the greatest prosperity, sailing from Goa to Malacca and Macao where Indian cotton was exchanged for silks and porcelain from Canton: these were sold in Nagasaki for silver, and with the proceeds spices were purchased in Indonesia for resale in Goa. Other trade routes operated independently of the Portuguese government in the Bay of Bengal and along the east coast of India, between Mozambique and Goa and around the Persian Gulf. As a result the subjects of the Portuguese monarchy enjoyed the profits of the empire while their sovereign was condemned to bear the cost of defending it.

Increasingly these costs began to mount in the sixteenth century as it became more difficult for the Portuguese to maintain their monopoly of the spice trade. The capture of Diu after a long struggle between 1531 and 1535 strengthened their strategic position in the Arabian Sea, but the advantage gained was swiftly cancelled out by the appearance of Osmanli galleys in the Gulf and the Red Sea. Diu was attacked on several occasions and Portuguese activity at Ormuz and Aden was reduced to taxing the trade in spices instead of denying it altogether to the Arab and Osmanli traders. Elsewhere despite their resolute attempt to avoid entanglement in local disputes, the Portuguese increasingly found themselves at war with local princes in Ceylon, Bengal and Indonesia. Ternate, captured in 1522, was lost in 1574 and Malacca had to withstand five serious assaults, three of them by the Sultan of Achin. To add to the problem, the survivors of Magellan's expedition had to be bought off for 350,000 ducats by the treaty of Saragossa (1529), but Portugal and Spain remained in conflict over the settlement of the Philippines until the issue was resolved in 1580 by the union of the two countries by Philip II.

Towards the end of the century the English and the French had both established their own East India Companies but the major challenge to the Portuguese monopoly came from the Dutch who owed much to Jan van Linschoten, a Haarlem man in the service of the Portuguese archbishop at Goa. His *Itinerario*, a guide to navigation in Indian and Far Eastern waters published in 1595, had the immediate effect of prompting Cornelis van Hautmann to sail from Gouda to the east relying solely on Linschoten's advice. He returned with such profits that others were quick to follow. A few attempted the route through the Magellan Straits but all perished and the route most strongly recommended in the *Itinerario* was to avoid the Portuguese bases in India, Ceylon and Indonesia by sailing direct from the Cape of Good Hope to the Sunda Straits. This, though an excellent course, was dangerous to undertake in an age without chronometers since it was impossible to determine the exact degree of longitude and the ships were likely to be driven unawares upon the Australian coast. Nonetheless, between 1598 and 1602, fifty-one Dutch ships successfully made the voyage and in 1604 the Dutch East India Company was established by the States-Genéral. Within a few decades of the seventeenth century Portuguese power was destroyed.

For more or less one hundred years the Portuguese in the east were able to make use of and control a highly developed commercial organisation for the production and distribution of spices across thousands of miles of ocean. In the west – in the Azores, the Cape Verde Islands, Madeira, São Thomé and in Brazil – they had first to establish their own settlements and their own production before any commercial exploitation was possible. This was done by semi-feudal grants of land made to proprietory landlords, *donatorios*, who were required to cultivate and protect it at their own expense in return for extensive powers of jurisdiction over any colonists whom they could induce to emigrate with them. Another device was the introduction of slavery (see page 23). Already the Portuguese were expert in the purchase of slaves along the West African coast because the natives of the Gold Coast, having traded with or raided the hinterland to acquire gold dust and nuggets, would only part with these to the Portuguese in return for slaves. Slaves were available further along the coast between the Volta and the Niger where the civil wars of the kings of Benin produced a rich supply of captives for sale. As the coast was too unhealthy for permanent settlement the Portuguese had established themselves offshore on the islands of São Thomé and Fernando Po, and from there they ran a thriving business in slaves, importing them to work in the islands' sugar plantations, selling them on the Gold Coast or sending them on to the other islands of Portugal's Atlantic empire.

While sugar planting and vine production went ahead on the Atlantic islands, the Portuguese initially paid little attention to their mainland discovery of Brazil except for importing small quantities of the red flame-wood for use in the dyeing industry. It was not until the French began to land there for the same purpose that John III finally decided on effective action. In 1530 Martin Alfonso de Souza prospected 3,000 miles of coastline, expelled the French and established two colonies, one at São Vicente, near Santos, the other at Pernambuco. The land, divided into twelve captaincies, was granted out to *donatorios* but there was little to attract settlers to South America and the *donatorios* achieved only a limited success in producing dye wood, cassava, maize and sugar. Local labour was of limited use. The Indian was unable to reconcile himself to the sudden transition from a nomadic life to one of permanent settlement and daily labour. Moreover he had no resistance to the diseases – catarrh, smallpox, dysentery and syphilis – introduced by the Portuguese. If the colony were to prosper it needed negro slaves, but these were expensive and the profits of cultivation did not warrant the capital expenditure necessary to bring in a new labour force. Two things saved the colony; John III took it under direct control, appointing his own captain-general in 1549, and sugar production began to grow at such a rate that negro slaves could be imported in great number. By 1580 when the colony fell under Spanish control, the population of slaves had grown to 14,000, the number of Portuguese had reached 20,000, sixty sugar mills had been established and over thirty ships a year were hard pressed to ferry the cargo across to Europe.

Spain and America

The excitement which greeted Balboa's discovery of the Pacific in 1513 underlined the fact that the Spaniards regarded America not as a potential source of wealth but rather as an obstacle to navigation between Europe and the Indies. In 1519, therefore, the Spanish government of Charles V supplied five ships to complete the work first started by Columbus. The captain of the expedition was Ferdinand Magellan, a Portuguese who had served under Almeida and Albuquerque and who was present in 1511 at the fall of Malacca: his promotion however had not kept pace with his ambition and he offered his services to Spain. He guessed that the Portuguese would probably be already in possession of the Moluccas – they had in fact arrived there in 1513 – but he pointed out that so uncertain were the means of calculating the longitude, that the islands might well prove to be within the Spanish sphere of influence as defined by the treaty of Tordesillas.

Apart from the fact that the survivors could claim to be the first to have circumnavigated the globe, the expedition which set out in September 1519 was in every other respect a failure. One ship was lost in reconnaissance off the South American coast, mutiny broke out off Patagonia, and the passage through the Magellan Straits took thirty-eight days – a terrifying experience for the crews and one which led to mutiny aboard one ship and its loss as it vainly tried to turn back. Thereafter, by astonishing bad luck the surviving ships missed sight of all the islands of the South Pacific until they reached the Ladrones after ninety-eight days of thirst and near starvation, the crews being reduced to chewing the leather casings off the rigging. Magellan lost his life after getting involved in a local war and Sebastian del Cano, who took command, pressed on to arrive at the Moluccas in November

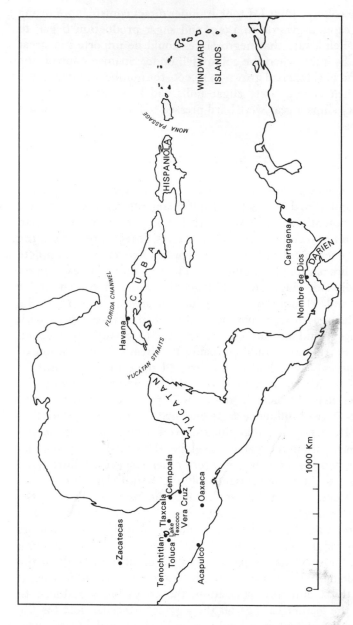

Central America and the Caribbean

1521. By this time one of the ships was no longer seaworthy and the party was divided among the remaining two, one to return across the Pacific, the other to complete the voyage around the world. The first was captured by the Portuguese but del Cano's ship evaded pursuit and eventually arrived home in 1522. Two other expeditions, one from Spain, the other from Mexico, were subsequently despatched to the Moluccas. Though they survived the elements they were swiftly destroyed by the Portuguese on arrival. Portugal was so evidently in control of the situation that Charles V finally acknowledged her claim to territory and trade as far as fifteen degrees east of the Moluccas in return for a consolatory payment of 350,000 ducats (Treaty of Saragossa 1529).

By 1529, however, the Spaniards had become rather more attracted by the profits to be derived from their American possessions. Diego Velasquez, the conqueror of Cuba (see page 35), subsequently despatched two expeditions to the Yucatan peninsula to explore the coastline, make contact with the natives and establish a new supply of slave labour. Neither party achieved much success but both returned with stories of an inland tribe of great power – the Aztecs who had built up a brutally efficient empire around their base at Lake Texcoco. More significantly the stories told of their great wealth, in particular of their gold, and Velasquez together with his secretary, Hernan Cortes, prepared an expedition to invade the Aztec empire. Velasquez however was denied his private hopes of fame and wealth when Cortes stole a march on him by absconding with the expedition in 1519 and made course for the Mexican mainland. He set up camp at Vera Cruz, seized whatever treasure he could find along the coast, despatched it to Spain, along with a demand for confirmation of his sole powers in Mexico, and settled the future of his expedition one way or the other by scuttling the remainder of his fleet.

This dramatic gesture was typical not only of Cortes but of all the other *conquistadores* who established the Spanish-American empire against enormous odds. They combined the qualities of bravery and greed, of brutality and missionary zeal, but more than anything else their spirit was epitomised by their passion for the execution of great deeds and of heroic gestures in self-conscious rivalry with the heroes of ancient legend. It was this spirit which held small bands of men together against the elements and the opposition of enemies who outnumbered them many times over. Such an undertaking now confronted Cortes. With 400 men, 15 horse and 6 cannon he set out in August 1519 to find the route to the Aztec capital of Tenochtitlan, which would take him through the territories of the subject races whose support he counted on enlisting. His first success was won just north of Vera Cruz at Cempoala. There he was well received and his daring in arresting five Aztec emissaries of Montezuma II who had arrived to demand the customary tribute enhanced his reputation to such an extent that the natives abandoned their idols and gave him over 1,000 warriors to accompany his march. From Cempoala he moved westwards through the most difficult mountain passes which taxed the strength even of men inured to the harsh life of the highlands of Castile or the sierras of Estremadura. After a month or so of endless exertion he arrived at Tlaxcala, only to find that the natives, though subject to the Aztecs, were unwilling to accept deliverance at his hands. After some fierce resistance, the Cempoalan warriors finally carried the day and Cortes was able to recruit Tlaxcalan troops also before pressing on with the last hundred miles of his heroic journey.

Tenochtitlan was a formidable city built in the middle of Lake Texcoco: three causeways, each one heavily defended, linked it to the shore and drawbridges at various points denied easy access to an invader. On this occasion there was no need of fighting. Montezuma, brave though he was, was astounded by the novel sight of horses, dogs and guns and superstitious enough to link the presence of Cortes in some way with the Aztec legend of the second coming of the god Quetzalcoatl. More to the point perhaps, Cortes was a persuasive talker and convinced the Aztecs of his friendly purposes to such good effect that on 8 November 1519, he and his followers were admitted to the city. For the time being Cortes felt safe enough among his hosts but he was afraid that Velasquez might have sent a punitive expedition to follow his tracks. Leaving some of his men in Tenochtitlan, therefore, he went back to the coast to meet the invading army he had anticipated, defeated it and persuaded many of its members by bribes and threats to follow him back to the capital.

During his absence the Spaniards in Tenochtitlan had outraged their hosts not merely by their greed for gold and land, but by their ruthless missionary endeavours to destroy the idols of the

Aztec faith. Cortes returned to find his men under attack and Montezuma, discredited for his failure to perceive the true nature of the Spaniards, was stoned to death by his own people. In a retreat across the causeway which cost him nearly half his men, Cortes escaped from the city, but the failure of the Aztecs to pursue him allowed him time to recover. His men found tin deposits from which to fashion bronze cannons, a dozen launches were made and in August 1521 by launch and by causeway a desperate attack was mounted against the capital. Numerically the Spaniards were outnumbered many times over, even with the aid of the Tlaxcalans who remained loyal to them, and on the advance along the causeways the Aztecs merely jumped into the water to let them pass before climbing back again to attack them from behind. Moreover, the morale of the Spaniards was not improved by the onset of torrential rain which mingled with the sounds of sacrificial drums within the city, beating in anticipation of the human sacrifice which would celebrate a victory. But the vigour and courage which characterised the *conquistadores* aided them in their hard-fought struggle across the causeways until finally they entered the city. There, with equally characteristic ruthlessness, they destroyed each building as they advanced until they stood victorious amid the rubble of a once great capital.

Cortes deliberately rebuilt the city to be the capital of a new empire and the centre of a new religion. Mexico City stood on the ruins of Tenochtitlan. The churches replaced the temples and Cortes with his *encomienderos*, among whom he apportioned the Indian settlements, demanded the tribute and the labour services which formerly had been supplied to Montezuma and his chiefs. This at any rate made for stability, and the problems of colonial rule in new Spain sprang not from native unrest but from disputes between the colonial officials. Cortes had been recognised by Charles V as governor and captain-general but in 1529 he returned to Spain to protest against the president of his *audiencia*, an old friend of Velasquez: the story of Columbus and of other *conquistadores* seemed likely to be repeated but Cortes received fair treatment. He was appointed member of a new *audiencia* and it was not until the first viceroy appeared – who consistently ignored his advice – that he finally gave up in disgust and went home for good in 1539. Nonetheless, he retained his dignities and the revenues from his *encomienda* in the rich valley of Oaxaca.

South America

Francisco Pizarro and his partner Diego de Almagra were *encomienderos* of Darien who had spent some years in exploring the Peruvian coastline and had heard stories of an Inca empire high up at Cuzco on the plateau of the Andes. In 1528 Pizarro took the precautionary step of returning to Spain to secure official recognition as governor of the Incas should his expedition be successful, and in 1530 he set out with Almagra to give substance to his new title. Unlike the other *conquistadores* both men were in their fifties and both came of peasant family, but they proved to be no less heroic and resilient than their younger rivals of nobler birth. They landed men and horses at Tumbes on the Peruvian coast and marched inland enduring the tropical heat of the foothills and the freezing storms of the Andean plateau. Their invasion coincided with a civil war between the Inca Huascar and his illegitimate brother Atahualpa in which the Inca was killed while Atahualpa made himself master of the northern provinces by capturing Cajamorca. There he was seized by Pizarro in a surprise attack and the *conquistadores*, exploiting their advantage among the leaderless enemy, sped southwards to take Cuzco, the capital, by November 1533.

Conquest was one thing, consolidation and control were another and the rough courage of Pizarro could not compensate for a lack of subtlety, nor for the fact that once the conquest had been made his subordinates drew attention to his peasant origin in order to challenge his authority. He forfeited any advantage he might have derived from his royal prisoner by having him murdered; unlike Cortes who had attracted the allegiance of the Mexicans by ruling in Montezuma's place from Montezuma's capital, Pizarro moved to Lima in order to shorten his lines of communication with the coast; moreover Almagra demanded Cuzco for himself and had to be sent off most reluctantly to explore the regions of Bolivia and Chile. While he was away, Pizarro tried to remedy his error of killing Atahualpa by appointing another Inca under his control but the puppet turned against its master, leading a rebellion which Pizarro was unable to suppress. Almagra returned to save the day in 1537 but again demanded Cuzco for himself and after a year of civil war was captured and killed by Pizarro. To complete the tragedy Pizarro himself was murdered in 1541 and his brother Gonzalo, who succeeded him, finally rebelled against Spain on account of the new native ordinances (see page 197) and was executed in 1548. By 1560 the new viceroy, Caneta, could claim to have removed the *conquistadores* from Peru – some in fact had already removed themselves to set up semi-autonomous states in New Granada (Colombia) and Chile – and established in their place a less personal, more peaceful form of government.

The replacement of *conquistadores* by royal officials was only to be expected when the government's policy switched from exploration and conquest to the consolidation of frontiers and the exploitation of the mines and other means of revenue production. The independent leaders whose ruthless vigour had made an empire could as easily destroy one; the new towns in which they had installed their followers enjoyed privileges unacceptable to a king who had suppressed the liberties of Castilian towns; and the system of *encomiendas* had entrenched them in positions of wealth and power which threatened the authority of the crown as well as flouting its declared intent to protect the Indian population.

As a result Charles V insisted on directly exercising his authority through the council of the Indies, a body which by 1524 had formerly evolved from the unofficial secretariat created by Juan de Fonseca (see page 33). It worked for several hours each day, it believed in the power of rational men to control circumstances by careful legislation, and demonstrated its overt suspicion of the tendency of local officials to exceed instructions. It was in short similar in character and composition to any other council of the Castilian monarchy, with the significant exception that the difficulties encountered in adjudicating a dispute in the Sierra Morena above Cordoba were magnified a hundred times when the region under discussion was located in the high Cordilleras or by Lake Texcoco. To meet this in part, the council sent out viceroys, one to govern New Spain from Mexico City, the other New Castile from Lima, but this delegation of royal authority was immediately followed up by the imposition of administrative checks on the viceroys' freedom of action. The *audiencia* with the means to discourage an independent-minded viceroy or governor was introduced into all districts of the Spanish-American empire; the *residencia*, the Castilian practice of demanding a judicial review of an official's conduct at the end of his commission, inhibited experiment and the frequent *visita*, the despatch of an agent from the council with powers to override all local decisions, resulted in the unfortunate consequence that conformity was only too often rewarded and initiative penalised. By its action therefore the council ensured that no one dared to emulate a Cortes or a Balboa; unfortunately, conscientious obedience to instructions which were often years out of date, led ultimately to the paralysis of the colonial administration.

A principal topic in dispute between the council and the colonists was the treatment of the native population. The *encomienda*, vital though it was initially for the organisation of labour, had aroused the indignation of Isabella, and the strictures of Las Casas (see page 35) had been officially adopted by the council. The bull *Sublimis Deus* (1537) declared that Indians were rational beings, capable of being good Christians and were not to be enslaved, and in 1542 the *New Laws of the Indies* required all government and ecclesiastical officials to surrender their *encomiendas*, confiscated those granted during the Peruvian civil wars, decreed that all remaining *encomiendas* were to revert to the crown on the death of their holders and reserved the direction of native labour to the *audiencia*. So damaging were these laws to the value of land ownership in the colonies that they provoked Gonzalo Pizarro to rebel, but by 1560 they had been enforced in New Spain. In New Castile the viceroy Mendoza secured a stay of execution for some years, but in 1573 a new series of edicts went even further in protecting the native population: 'discoverers by land or by sea shall not engage in war or conquest . . . nor become involved in quarrels with natives, nor do them any harm, nor take any of their property, unless it be given willingly or by way of barter'.

No government could have enforced such laws against unanimous opposition on the other side of the Atlantic and their acceptance during the course of the sixteenth century is largely explained by the development of new sources of livelihood for the colonists which to some extent made the *encomienda* less necessary. One such development was the *estancia*, the stock ranch, which embodied the Castilian's traditional preference for the grazing of nomadic herds and flocks to the cultivation of the soil (see page 142). Mendoza introduced the merino sheep to New Spain and, forty-five miles north-east of Mexico City, the Toluca valley became a centre of cattle ranching where over 150,000 head were being reared by 1555. For this type of farming the *encomienda* was irrelevant – but the Indians had no cause to celebrate the change. The migratory herds destroyed their crops so that the cost of maize in the Toluca valley went up eightfold and the heavy grazing in many areas led to soil erosion and ultimately to depopulation.

After the 1570s the flocks began to dwindle through overgrazing and the specialist role of the *estancia* was superseded by that of the *hacienda*, a comprehensive, vast and self-supporting estate which combined arable and pastoral farming with the production of textiles and other necessary industries. Its labour force, unlike that of the *encomienda* was free since the government refused to compromise the spirit of its new laws, but the freedom of the *hacienda* employees meant little in practice. Although the *hacendado* had to pay them wages, they had virtually no experience of money and were powerless to resist the attractive European goods which he offered them for sale: as a result most of them became burdened with debts which could only be cleared by a lifetime's service. Moreover, as the *hacendado* was vested with administrative and judicial authority, his power to control his labour force was virtually as great as any *encomiendero*'s.

In the silver mines the freedom of the workers was even more restricted since the colonial magistrates retained their authority through the *repartimiento* (see page 34) – known as the *mita* in South America – to undertake public works by forced labour. The charge of slavery was avoided by the payment of wages and it was by this means that the first great cities and churches of the conquest were erected. With the discovery of major deposits of silver at Zacatecas in New Spain and Potosi in Bolivia, mining was designated a public work, and so great was the demand for labour that the age of civic and ecclesiastical building came to an abrupt end. Towards the end of the century when the Spanish government was becoming ever more dependent on its silver imports and when the sinking of deeper shafts at Potosi demanded an ever-increasing supply of labour, over 14,000 families were being drafted to the mine every year, and though they received wages they were denied the freedom to seek work anywhere else.

Whether the *encomienda* prevailed or not, and despite the formulation of protective laws, the colonists found some way or another to exploit Indian labour and an age of economic expansion succeeded the age of discovery and conquest. The greater prosperity of the colonists led to a great increase in the volume of trade across the Atlantic – to the benefit of the Andalusian port of Seville. The city's monopoly of colonial trade confirmed by royal charter and regulated by the *Casa de Contratación* (see page 34), was exercised by the guild of merchants, the *Universidad de los Cargadores de las Indias*, whose tribunal, the *Consulado*, gave its name to the whole institution. Initially the monopoly served the interests both of the colonists who needed articles of daily use and supplies of wine, oil and flour, and of the Andalusians who could provide all these commodities from their own region – more or less to the amount of 10,000 tons a year in the period from 1520 to 1550. Then, for a decade, the volume of trade was significantly reduced, partly because of French piracy in the Florida channel, but even more because the looting phase of the colonial conquest was over while the production of goods for export had not yet got under way. Consequently, with less to collect and with a greater chance of losing it in any case to the French, the merchants of the *Consulado* lost confidence and in certain years – from 1554 – 1556 for example – no fleet was despatched at all. Subsequently the greater prosperity of the colonists, the greater amounts of silver to be collected, and the introduction of an efficient convoy system, encouraged a revival of Atlantic trade which then continued to flourish for the rest of the century.

Responsibility for the convoy system lay with Pedro Menendez de Aviles whose outstanding powers of organisation ensured the despatch of two separate fleets every year and their safe juncture and return in combination. The first fleet known as the *flota* left in May. From twenty to fifty ships would load up at Seville and slip down the Guadalquivir to Lucar where they formed convoy under the protection of two to six warships. Crossing the Atlantic they entered the Caribbean via the Mona passage and so along through the Yucatan Straits to Vera Cruz and the Gulf ports. Laden with Mexican silver the *flota* would then beat laboriously westwards against the trade winds to reach Havana by the following March. Meanwhile the second fleet, the *galeones*, had left in August and reached Nombre de Dios by way of the Windward Islands. There it disposed of its cargo, withdrew for the winter to the shelter of Cartagena and returned in the spring to take on board the Peruvian silver which had been shipped overland across the isthmus. It then sailed north-west on an easy reach to join up with the *flota* and together they went under protection through the Florida channel to reach Seville in the late summer. It was a brilliantly organised operation and although Menendez died in 1574, his system continued to work successfully until the seventeenth century. As a result French and English raiders were unable to disrupt the Spanish monopoly of trade and navigation in the Caribbean, and even Sir Francis Drake, for all the damage he did to Spanish bases and to Spanish prestige, could not capture the *flota*. Indeed the record of silver imports into Spain (see page 158) bore witness to the success of the convoys.

Further evidence of the expansion of Atlantic trade after the introduction of the convoy system is provided by the *Consulado*. Whereas its merchants had exported about 10,000 tons a year in the first half of the century, in 1580 the figure was 20,000 tons and in 1600 25,000. There was however a significant shift in the balance of supply and demand. The colonists were at last producing their own food and therefore looked to Seville not for the produce of Andalusia but for manufactured goods and luxuries such as silks, textiles, leather, swords and cutlery. Since Spanish industry could not keep pace with the demand, foreign merchants with access to the supplies required by the colonists infiltrated Seville under the cover of local firms and the city grew in population to 100,000 by 1600 as the sole purveyor of European goods to America. As a result, and to the consternation of the Castilian government, the silver imports began to drain away at the hands of Portuguese, Flemings, Germans and Genoese merchants in order to pay for the goods which Spain herself could not produce in sufficient quantity.

There were other foreigners who made no pretence of operating through the official channels of the *Consulado* but who supplied a service that the colonists were not able to refuse – the provision of slave labour. In the West Indies and on the mainland the Spanish conquest led to the destruction of the native population. The gentle Caribs made the only protest in their power against the intolerable conditions of work imposed upon them by the Spaniards by abandoning all desire to live: there were perhaps 300,000 in Hispanolia in the year of the island's discovery but by 1540 barely 500 remained. The mainland tribes were hardier and better able to endure the imposition of forced labour, but they could not withstand the epidemics of typhoid and smallpox which their conquerors brought with them. The evidence of the death rate has been variably interpreted but the local population of Mexico numbering somewhere between 11 million and 25 million in 1519 was reduced to 2½ million at the most by 1600. To meet this problem the Spaniards resorted to the slave trade, but as they had no sources of supply they had to depend on the Portuguese or on those who could negotiate contracts with them.

Two German traders were commissioned in 1528 to produce 4,000 slaves within four years but the Portuguese who supplied them smuggled many more on their own account from their bases in the Azores. The colonization of Brazil after 1540 reduced the flow of slaves to the Spanish colonies and it was to exploit this situation that John Hawkins set out between 1562 and 1568 to supply the colonists with slaves and European merchandise. He sold openly, paying all lawful dues and offering his services to the Spanish government as a privateer to keep other interlopers out of the Caribbean. For a while the local officials ignored their instructions and traded with him until finally he had the ill luck to run up against the *flota* in the port of Vera Cruz. Thereafter it was the Portuguese who renewed their activities on a much larger scale. Despite the union of their country with Spain in 1580 they were forbidden to meddle in the private empire of Castile, but so great was the demand for slave labour that by 1600 they were supplying as many as 13,000 slaves a year.

One other line of unofficial trade which the authorities in Seville could not control was the commerce of the Pacific. The Pacific was virtually inaccessible to Atlantic shipping since there were few who chose to emulate the adventures of Magellan, and so a special fleet was constructed on the Pacific coast. From Acapulco the Manila galleons followed the trade winds to the Philippines, where they traded American silver for the silks and spices brought by merchants from Macao. Although the outward journey lasted only ten weeks, it took anything from four to seven months to struggle back to Acapulco, but so valuable was the trade to the colonists, not only for the profits to be derived but also for the supplies themselves, that they shrugged off both the tedium of the voyage and the endless prohibitions of their own government against the export of bullion.

Capital and Capitalism

Several historians have been tempted to refer to 'the rise of capitalism' in the sixteenth century or to describe the period as 'the age of capitalism' on the grounds that capital was being employed on a greater scale than ever before in order to finance both the greater volume and the wider extent of European trade. But for all the novelty of its development, trade remained a totally exceptional feature of European life, engaging the activities of a very small section of the population. Most Europeans continued to live in rural isolation. Their lives were determined by the ancient calendar of the manorial system and their attitudes to money and money-making remained unchanged from those of the Middle Ages.

These attitudes sprang from an idealistic concept of society which regarded it as an organism whose members existed to serve each other: 'the health of the whole commonwealth' wrote John of Salisbury 'will be assured and vigorous if the higher members consider the lower and the lower answer in like manner the higher, so that each is in its turn a member of every other'. The existence of deceit and exploitation did not invalidate the ideal. If the gentry cheated their tenants or vice-versa, this reflected badly on them but not on a system of land-tenure based upon personal and reciprocal relationships; if craftsmen cheated their customers, manual production remained a necessary and an honourable occupation; even the guilds, which were often accused of mono- polist and self-seeking devices, proclaimed the importance of their social function in maintaining the principles of a fair wage and a just price. The merchant, however, was suspect. It was recognised that he served his fellows by supplementing the deficiencies of one region with the abundance of another, but it was feared that he endangered his soul by exploiting men's needs in order to make himself rich – and while wealth itself was accepted unquestion- ingly, the deliberate pursuit of riches, the *appetitus divitiarum infinitus* was universally condemned. Indeed the social ambitions and the commercial enterprise extolled in later ages were cate- gorised by medieval writers as manifestations of the sin of avarice. 'He who has enough to satisfy his wants and nevertheless cease- lessly labours to acquire riches, either in order to obtain a higher social position, or that subsequently he may have enough to live without labour, or that his sons may become men of wealth and im- portance – all such' wrote Henry of Langenstein in the fourteenth century 'are incited by a damnable avarice, sensuality or pride.'

If the *appetitus divitiarum infinitus* was abhorrent in medieval eyes, no means of satisfying it was more rigorously condemned than the traffic in money. On this subject canon lawyers, School- men, popular preachers, aldermen and privy councillors were all of one mind. To deal in commodities brought some advantage to society, even though it exposed the soul of the trader to considerable risk: to deal in money, however, was an unmitigated social evil and a mortal sin condemned without reservation by the third Lateran Council in 1175 and by succeeding councils at Lyons (1274) and Vienna (1312). The penalty for usury was immediate outlawry and excommunication leaving the poor sinner utterly defenceless, both in this world and the next.

This at any rate was the theory and as such was universally respected. 'He who commits usury goes to Hell' commented the cynic, 'he who does not goes to the almshouse', but such cynicism found little support among the public at large and when, as late as 1532, a group of Spanish merchants in Antwerp approached the Sorbonne for a ruling on the matter, they heard the old condemnations reaffirmed as stringently as ever. Yet in practice the later Middle Ages was a time of great importance in the development of international banking, and the papacy itself had become the centre of a complex financial system. For those who could see nothing but evil in Rome this was merely one among the many indications of corruption and profligacy at the very heart of the church, but in fact the church took great pains to justify its action.

The technical arguments of the Schoolmen to permit the payment of an interest charge were of less importance than the distinction which was tacitly drawn between those groups to whom the law should and should not apply. Professor Tawney's jibe that 'the distinction between pawnbroking which is disreputable and high finance which is eminently honourable was as familiar to the age of faith as to the twentieth century' contains much of the truth. But there was more to it than giving a respectable name to activities which elsewhere were regarded as criminal. Canon law deliberately attempted to protect the poor, that is the majority of the population, from the toils of the money lender because it was his nature to exploit a desperate man's plight at the moment when his crops failed or his cattle died. Such a protective role was inappropriate, however, to the operation of governmental finance by secular or ecclesiastical princes, capable of protecting their own interests, and the complexities of the international money market seemed to put it beyond the jurisdiction of canon law.

This was not a view that could be justified in terms of canon law, however, and the continued development of capitalism in an age when the Roman church continued to promulgate its strictures against usury led some historians to suggest that it must have been the reformation which made the whole thing respectable. It was not a novel idea. An English pamphlet of 1673 affirmed that 'it grew to a proverb that usury was the brat of heresy', but the full statement of the case awaited Max Weber's classic *The Protestant Ethic and the Spirit of Capitalism*. The thesis collapses, however, when set against the words of the reformers themselves. Luther reproduced in highly-coloured language the doctrines not of contemporary Schoolmen like John Eck who favoured five per cent in certain cases, but of those earlier writers who had condemned usury without reservation. Luther indeed was wholly out of sympathy with all manifestations of the commercial spirit. 'Foreign merchandise which brings from Calicut and India and the like places wares such as precious silver and jewels and spices, ... should not be permitted' – and as for usury, 'the greatest misfortune of the German nation is easily the traffic in interest. The devil invented it and the pope, by giving his sanction to it, has done untold evil in the world.'

John Calvin as a citizen of Geneva was more disposed than Luther to recognise the social value and the essential respectability of commerce: 'What reason is there why the income from business should not be larger than from landowning? Whence do the merchant's profits come except from his own diligence and industry?' Usury was a different matter and he opposed it. He recognised the necessity for credit in business transactions and reluctantly accepted that in such circumstances an interest payment up to five per cent might be in order, but in doing so he went no further than any Roman canon lawyer. Geneva indeed tended to follow a similar line to Rome in distinguishing between its opposition to money lending and its cautious acceptance of high finance. The ministers, for example, accepted the establishment of one municipal bank in Geneva but nonetheless opposed the foundation of a second in 1580. They reaffirmed the need to protect the poor against the operation of the money lender – though they specially excluded those 'who lend money to merchants for the furtherance of trade' – and launched a puritan assault on the evil examples of covetousness and immorality supplied by banking centres such as Paris, Lyons and Venice. It was a view shared by the Calvinists of the Netherlands who condemned the staid patrician merchant class of Amsterdam as 'libertines' because of their association with finance.

With caution and confusion evident in both camps, it is clear that capitalism developed in the sixteenth century not because of one church or another but because, thanks to the mines of Bohemia and later of America, more capital became available for investment in trade. Even this development, significant and important though it was, must not be exaggerated. It was not a period of economic revolution, but rather one of imitation and development, so that there would have been little to puzzle or astound a fifteenth-century Italian in the practice of his successors at Augsburg, Antwerp or Amsterdam. Towards the end of the century, however, he might have been interested in a novel way of putting capital to work in the operation of long-distance trade groups by chartered companies. Joint operations by merchants in the form of private partnerships were already well-established but they were ill-equipped to handle the expense and the risks involved in oceanic trade. Several merchants, recognising that without monopolistic rights their ventures would be profitless, petitioned their government for such rights under special licence or charter. In England the government approved the formation of such chartered companies to trade in Muscovy (1555), in the Baltic (1579), in the Levant (1581), in Africa (1588) and finally in 1600 in the East Indies. Dutch and Zeeland merchants were also rounding the Cape after 1594, sponsored by several competing *compagnien van verre* (companies for distant voyages) and in 1602 they decided to combine together to challenge the English. They formed their own East India Company with a charter from the States-General which granted them a monopoly of trade between the Cape of Good Hope and the Straits of Magellan.

The principal novelty about the chartered company was not in its monopolistic powers – though the granting of these offended the majority of Europeans who could see no good at all in monopolies and looked upon them suspiciously as agencies of exploitation – but in the use it made of its capital. The regulating company was the more conventional. Essentially a guild of merchants, it controlled the admission of new members and determined among other things the quantity of goods in which each might deal, but it left it to each member to run the risks of his own ventures and to decide his own lines of action. The joint stock company on the other hand was much less a guild of merchants than an association of capital because it included anyone at all who would put up capital for a chance to share in the profits of the company's collective activities. The novelty lay not in working with a common capital but in the relative permanence of that capital, though this was not a distinction which was fully grasped in the sixteenth century since it was essentially a period of experiment. Initially it was felt that each voyage should be regarded as a separate account and at the return of the expedition the profits would be divided among those who had subscribed to the venture.

For the first fifty years of its career, that is until half-way through the seventeenth century, the English East India Company treated some voyages as separate concerns, but on others it carried forward the balance to finance later voyages. In this way it employed both temporary and permanent capital and the Dutch East India Company began on similar lines. In 1612, however, it decreed that the joint stock of capital was to be regarded as a permanent fund and the members, instead of withdrawing their capital were obliged to sell their shares on the bourse. Even so the Company was still not a 'modern' company. Its structure reflected much of the rivalry of the earlier *compagnien van verre* since it consisted of six chambers for the separate towns of Amsterdam, Middelberg, Rotterdam, Delft, Hoorn and Enkhuizen. Each chamber could operate independently and in the long run it was only the ascendency of the Amsterdam chamber which ensured the unity and survival of the company. Even in the early seventeenth century, therefore, in the companies of the most advanced kind, the use of capital was still a hesitant process of trial and experiment and was conducted against a general background of popular disapproval and suspicion.

6

Charles V

The Burgundian Inheritance

'GOD has been very merciful to you', wrote one of Charles V's counsellors after the imperial election of 1519, 'He has raised you above all the kings and princes of Christendom to a power such as no sovereign has enjoyed since your ancestor Charles the Great. He has set you on the way towards a world monarchy, towards the uniting of all Christendom under a single shepherd.' The map of Charles's possessions would appear to give substance to this view (especially if we anticipate a few years and add to it Bohemia and Hungary), but in reality the position was much less simple. Charles's *monarchia*, as contemporaries called it to distinguish it from the Holy Roman Empire, was a personal union of crowns. Charles ruled, for example, as a king in Valencia, an archduke in Austria, a duke in Luxemburg, a count in Hainault, a landgrave in Alsace, a marquis in Antwerp – and each of these separate territories had its own separate constitution. Consequently, his ability to cope with the perennial problems arising from the French wars, the Osmanli Turks and the Reformation in Germany, depended in the last analysis upon his ability to govern by different means the different states which comprised his *monarchia*.

In 1506, at the age of six, Charles inherited the Burgundian provinces from his father, Philip the Handsome. For many generations the Burgundian dukes had tried to unify their separate and scattered territories by the introduction of common institutions (see page 95). The provincial estates of the Netherlands, for example, had been persuaded to send delegates to a common States-General and Philip the Good had introduced the order of the *Toison D'Or* (the Golden Fleece) which served not only to reward the nobles with an honour rivalling the English Garter,

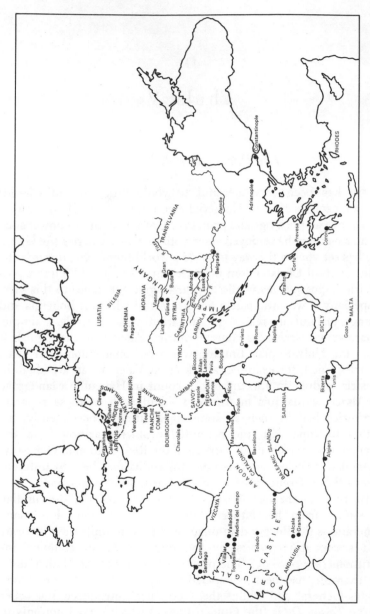

Europe in the reign of Charles V

but also to create an extra-provincial fellowship of ducal servants whether they worked in Hainault, Brabant or Franche Comté. Measures of this kind, however, could not unify the provinces overnight and the dukes' subjects had already surmised that the object was to make them more amenable to the ambitions of the dynasty – ambitions which under Charles the Rash, for example, had little to do with the true interests of the Netherlands.

Indeed the full dimension of the problem facing Charles V is indicated by the difficulty of defining what these true interests might be. When, for example, he sought to restore his brother-in-law to the throne of Denmark (see page 308), Brabant and Flanders were content to be bribed by Lübeck into opposing him, while Holland made it the principal object of its policy to destroy Lübeck's control of the Sound. In addition there was the perennial clash of interest between rival centres of trade and production, between Bruges and Antwerp, between Walloon and Fleming, between maritime and inland provinces, all of which was accentuated by the vigour of provincial politics. Not only did each province have its own Estates, but provincial affairs could not be concluded until each town had been canvassed for its views. Moreover, each town had its own constitution which generally afforded political power to an urban patriciate of well-established merchant families who were not readily amenable to ducal influence. The constitution of Delft was typical of many other towns by its 'Privilege' of 1445: the 'wise and rich' among the citizens were to choose forty of their number, 'the richest, most honourable, notable and peaceful' to be the regents of the town; they in turn were to draw up a short list of twenty from whom the duke might select the eleven aldermen and burgomasters. In these circumstances the duke's freedom of action was clearly restricted, and success or failure in governing the Netherlands depended to a large extent on his ability to maintain good relations with the regent class in the towns.

Charles could rely, of course, upon a measure of personal loyalty to himself as a Burgundian by birth and upbringing, but it was impossible to disguise the fact that his Burgundian interests occupied very little of his time once he came to manhood. Though he spent twenty-eight years of his life in the Netherlands, seventeen of these had been from birth until his departure for Spain, and for most of his effective reign his Aunt Margaret and later his

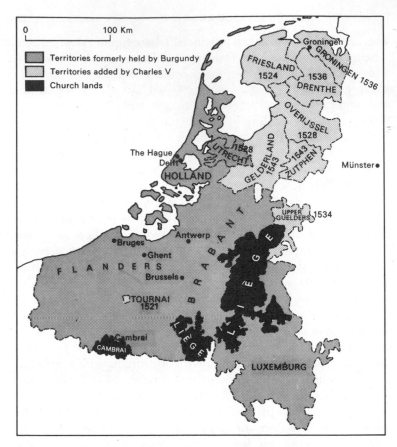

The Netherlands in the reign of Charles V

sister Mary acted as regents, maintaining a careful alliance with
the leading nobles of the *Toison D'Or* and the representatives of
the regent class in the towns. By and large it was a successful
reign. As a result of Charles's perpetual struggle with the French
(see page 221) the Netherlands acquired Tournai in 1521 and
Cambrai in 1543, and compelled the Valois kings to renounce
their claim to the suzerainty of Flanders. Moreover, Charles's
government in the Netherlands pursued a long and ultimately
successful campaign against Charles Egmont, duke of Guelders.
The duke had been greatly assisted not only by his alliance with
the French but also by the traditional reluctance of the northern

provinces to accept direction of any kind from the government in Brussels, and it was not until he had audaciously sacked The Hague in 1528 that any effective move could be made against him. Thereafter new provinces were created from the territories he vacated: Friesland (1524), Overijssel and Utrecht (1528), Drenthe and Groningen (1536), and finally, after the duke's death in 1538 and the defeat of his heir, William of Cleves, Gelderland and Zutphen were annexed in 1543.

The process of developing central institutions to unify the government and administration of the provinces made but slow progress. In 1531 the council of state set up a council of finance to co-ordinate methods of collecting taxes in the provinces, and a secret or privy council to administer certain areas of justice. More promising was Charles's plan to alter the character of the States-General, which was nothing more than an assembly of provincial delegates with no power to bind its members to any joint decision. In 1534, therefore, he proposed the formation of a defensive union of the provinces with regular financial contributions to be paid by each province for the maintenance of a standing army. The Netherlanders avoided the trap: they rejected the plan, 'for if we accept the proposal we shall undoubtedly be more united, but we shall be dealt with in the manner of France' – by which they referred especially to the French king's powers of taxation.

Despite their protests, however, the Netherlands proved to be remarkably generous in the supply of money, justifying the comment of the Venetian ambassador that 'these are the treasures of the king of Spain, these his mines, these his Indies which have sustained all the emperor's enterprises'.

Nonetheless, the Estates, the regent class and the abbots of the rich monasteries became increasingly restive as Charles continued to demand taxes to finance campaigns in Italy and elsewhere from which the Netherlands derived no advantage. In 1537 the city of Ghent refused to pay further taxes and within two years was in open rebellion. It was a close thing whether or not the other towns would join in, but Charles was saved by the fact that the rebellion, begun by the regent class, got out of hand and was taken over by the artisan guilds who instituted a system of municipal democracy. This so horrified the other towns that Ghent was left isolated before Charles's army in 1540, and was defeated.

Thereafter Charles continued to tax the Netherlands for purposes other than their own advantage, and during the crisis years of 1550–5 in the Holy Roman Empire he received the extraordinary amount of 8 million ducats. Although this served his immediate purposes it mortgaged the future for his son; not only was the fund of popular resentment augmented, but the government of the Netherlands was so hard-pressed to meet the demands which Charles so frequently laid upon it that within two years of his abdication it was forced into bankruptcy.

In one important respect – by his response to the threat of heresy – Charles revealed how much more effective he could be as a Burgundian duke than as Holy Roman Emperor, and the very first Lutheran martyrs in Europe were burned by him at Brussels in 1523. He had little assistance from the Church since the diocesan boundaries all overran into France and Germany, with the result that there were no resident bishops within the provinces to take action against the heretics. Consequently, Charles instituted his own Inquisition, endowing it with special authority to override diocesan boundaries and be free of canon law requirements. He also published the *Placarten*, a series of special laws against heresy, which, as the reign progressed, became increasingly savage in their penalties of death, mutilation and confiscation of property. The opposition to these policies reflected not only an Erasmian taste for toleration and a concern to do nothing which might interfere with trade, but also a considerable degree of alarm at the powers enjoyed by the royal inquisitors who showed scant regard for the traditional right of the towns and provinces to manage affairs in their own way. The opposition of the regent class was abruptly muted, however, when the Anabaptists of Münster (see page 240) threatened to unleash the forces of social dissension and democracy among the working class of the Netherland towns and especially among those whose wealth was declining as a result of the rise of Antwerp. As in the case of Ghent, the regents demonstrated that much as they resented any ducal interference with their particular liberties and interests, they feared more acutely the threat of social revolution, and in the last resort, therefore, were compelled to stand by Charles.

As a result Charles V's reign in the Netherlands ended satisfactorily enough so far as he was concerned. It was nonetheless clear that his son would find that his most difficult problem would

arise, not from foreign policy and finance, nor from the presence
of heresy – not even from the Calvinists who were beginning to
make their presence felt by 1555 – but from the jealous particularism of the regent class whose wealth and power were entrenched
behind the municipal and provincial administration of the
Netherlands.

The Kingdoms of Castile and Aragon

When Charles V arrived in Spain towards the end of 1517 in
order to accept the thrones of Castile and Aragon under the will
of Ferdinand of Aragon, he encountered a dangerous situation.
From the moment of Ferdinand's death the previous year royal
authority had collapsed. Cardinal Cisneros, a dying man, had
tried in vain to hold the fort until Charles's arrival, but his efforts
to restore authority by raising a militia force of 30,000 men had
been sabotaged by the nobles and the towns. The former were
involved in a variety of conspiracies to secure for themselves
territory and titles; the latter, following the lead of Toledo and
Valladolid, had demonstrated their independence by expelling the
royal *corregidores*. Charles himself made matters worse. He was
young and inexperienced, lacking the good looks of his father,
Philip the Handsome, and obviously ill at ease in his new environment. Worst of all, no Spaniard was able to break through the
retinue of Netherlanders which, led by his chief adviser, the Sieur
de Chièvres, monopolised his court, his council and his patronage.
Cisneros himself was rebuffed when, from his death-bed, he tried
to offer advice to the young king, and after his death his archbishopric of Toledo, the richest and most important in Castile,
was awarded to Chièvres' nephew.

The Castilian *Cortes* met in 1518 to recognise its new king.
Though it resented the presence of the Netherlanders, not least
because one of them had been appointed its president, it loyally
agreed to assist the king over the next three years with a *servicio*
(subsidy) of 600,000 ducats. There was less generosity in Aragon
and greater emphasis laid on the *fueros*, the traditional privileges of
the kingdom, but after long debates 200,000 ducats were finally
voted for the king. Equally protracted were the sessions of the
Catalan *Cortes*, and when they resulted in a *servicio* of only 100,000
ducats Charles decided to forego a visit to the Valencian *Cortes*.

Nonetheless, despite the reaction against royal authority which had followed Ferdinand's death, the situation began to improve very slightly when Charles showed himself more willing to identify himself with his new subjects by holding *audiencias* at Barcelona, and by appointing the first Spaniards to the order of the *Toison D'Or*.

It was then that Charles, learning of the death of the Emperor Maximilian, abruptly decided to leave Spain in order to secure his election to the imperial throne (see page 153). Such cavalier indifference to the sensibilities of those who had so far remained loyal to him provoked a universal outburst of protest, especially when his decision was followed by renewed demands for money. Chièvres summoned the Castilian *Cortes* to Santiago in 1520 to pay for Charles's voyage home and to assist with his election expenses, but most towns refused to authorise their representatives to commit themselves to any grant, and Toledo sent no representative at all. The *Cortes* was then adjourned to Corunna where Charles was embarking, and in great haste and under considerable pressure, eight of the eighteen towns represented grudgingly agreed to a *servicio*. It was of no value. The towns condemned the *Cortes* as an illegal assembly and exploited Charles's absence to defy the authority of Adrian of Utrecht, a Netherlander whom he had left behind as regent. In this way began the revolt of the *Comuneros*.

The revolt was not the work of artisans and unemployed but rather of city fathers in alliance with men like Juan de Padillo of the urban nobility. In August 1520 Padillo and Antonio de Acuna, the ferocious and ambitious bishop of Zamora, met in Toledo to establish a revolutionary government, the *Santa Junta,* and to publish their demands. These proved to be remarkably conservative; they combined the denunciation of foreigners who held Spanish offices with complaints against rising prices, and concluded with a demand that the *Cortes* should meet regularly and without royal interference. For the time being the grandees held aloof. They had no quarrels with the demands of the *Santa Junta* and for their own part they still smarted under the indignities imposed upon them by Charles and his retinue of Netherlanders. For them the final insult had been the appointment of Adrian as regent, and they were not displeased to witness his present discomfiture. The rebels, having forced him to take flight from

1 *The Foundling Hospital by Brunelleschi*

2 *Detail from* The Tribute Money *by Masaccio*

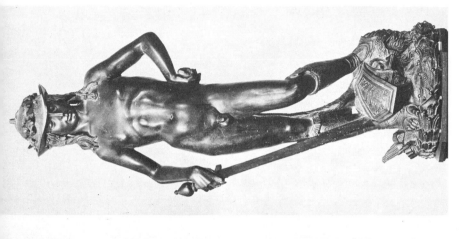

4 *David by Donatello*

5 The Birth of Venus *by Botticelli* (*opposite*)

3 *The Rucellai Palace, Florence, by Alberti*

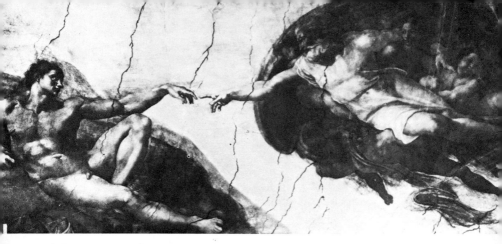

6 The Creation of Adam *from the ceiling of the Sistine Chapel by Michelangelo*

7 *Detail from* The Virgin of the Rocks *by Leonardo da Vinci*

8 The Madonna del Granduca *by Raphael*

9 *Detail from the altarpiece at Isenheim by Grünewald*

11 *The Chateau of Chambord in the Loire Valley*

10 The Nativity *by Dürer*

14 The Madonna of the Swan Neck by Parmigianino

13 The Rondanini Pietà by Michelangelo

12 The Pesaro Madonna by Titian

15 The Last Supper *by Tintoretto*

16 The Villa Rotunda, Vicenza, by Palladio

Valladolid, pressed on to Tordesillas where the old queen mother, Juana, still partially insane, was protected from the world in a convent. They hoped that Juana might be persuaded to join them, but whether she failed to comprehend their purposes, or understood them only too well, she refused to lend her authority to the *Santa Junta*.

Adrian, more perceptive than his sovereign, and recognising where Charles's best interests lay, appointed two important grandees to share his office – Fadrique Enriques, the Admiral of Castile with whom he had taken refuge, and Iñego de Velasco, the Constable. He also petitioned Charles to confirm his actions, to promise an end to the appointment of Netherlanders, to abandon his demands for a *servicio* and to return to Spain as soon as possible. Though Charles was slow to consent, Adrian's conciliatory gestures proved to be most opportune. The rebellion was undergoing a radical transformation, and, while Acuna seized Toledo and proclaimed himself archbishop, the poorer elements in the towns were demanding an end to the privileges enjoyed by 'grandees, *caballeros* and other enemies of the realm'. Whereas a rebellion against an absentee king who had alienated his subjects might have lasted for many years, a civil war between the grandees and the towns was soon over. In April 1521 Padillo was defeated by Castilian nobles at Villalar, and though his widow and Acuna put new life into the resistance of Toledo, the city fell in October.

Meanwhile a revolt of quite a different character had broken out in Valencia in 1519. When plague had hit the city and all the wealthier citizens and nobles had escaped to the country, the artisans, abandoned and resentful, had banded together in a revolutionary brotherhood or *germania*. Their objects were to destroy the privileges of the rich and to eradicate traces of Islam among their Morisco fellows – an explosive combination of social revolutionary fervour and crusading zeal, accentuated by the tensions created by the plague. Fondly proclaiming their loyalty to Charles, they knew little or nothing of events in Castile, and it was fortunate that there was no communication between the two rebellions. As it was, the Valencian rising proved to be a violent one and lasted for eighteen months, until it was suppressed by the efforts of the Valencian nobility.

When Charles returned to Spain he found himself happily secure on the thrones of Aragon and Castile, while the burden of suppressing the revolts had fallen on his own subjects. Thereafter he behaved with greater circumspection and there were no future rebellions – despite the fact that for the rest of his reign he proceeded to confirm the worst fears of the *Comuneros*, in that he was abroad for most of the reign and exploited the resources of Spain to finance his wars in Italy and Germany. Though the *Cortes* increasingly complained of his policies there was no question of arousing public opinion against him. The defeat of the towns left them abjectly obedient. Charles moreover had learned a great deal from the revolt. He identified himself more closely with the nobility to whom he owed his throne, and rewarded its suppression of the *Comuneros* with lucrative appointments to municipal offices. Moreover there was no lack of patronage available for those who elected to serve Charles in the New World or in his European campaigns. Indeed as a land-owning class meeting the challenge of rising prices by raising rents, free of taxes and assured of opportunities in government service, the Spanish nobility became well pleased with its king – and when royal land or government annuities were offered for sale they demonstrated their growing wealth by rushing forward to purchase them, in the teeth of competition from Genoese and German bankers. Charles recognised that so long as he left them alone his throne was secure. Consequently, although he never invited them to share in the administration, he avoided interference with their privileges, kept innovations to a minimum and demanded money only from the defeated inhabitants of the towns. Above all he wisely entrusted the administration to the careful hands of the Castilian Francisco de los Cobos, under whose skilful direction the years passed uneventfully.

With no powerful family to support him and no formal training in law, Los Cobos was fortunate to secure a minor position in royal service. When Ferdinand died he left immediately for Flanders, made himself agreeable to Chièvres, and was finally appointed as secretary to Charles. Though Charles reserved his closest favours for Burgundians such as his Chancellor Gattinara and Nicholas Perrenot de Granvelle, he valued Los Cobos very highly and wisely left the direction of Spanish affairs to the man who most thoroughly understood them. The king's absence from Spain made his secretary's rôle all the more important – sorting out reports, petitions and council minutes for Charles's attention and transmitting to the relevant councils the policies ordered by Charles. In this Los Cobos excelled. He built up a staff of men like himself, not *letrados*, but sons of the municipal nobility, and established a considerable degree of professional spirit among them. Even in one of the most vital functions of government, the distribution of royal patronage, Los Cobos did not abuse his position. He made a modest fortune of course, his son became a marquis and his daughter was married to a duke, but he served Charles both efficiently and loyally. He struggled to develop good budgetary procedures, but these were immediately invalidated by Charles's renewed demands for money. No *Cortes* tried to limit Charles's expenditure as critically as did Los Cobos, nor urge him so intensely to economise by making peace, but it was all to no avail and the secretary died in 1547 worn out by the demands of his office.

The ordinary revenues of the crown (see page 142) were raised from 380 million maravedis to 500 million, but this was quite insufficient to keep pace with prices which had doubled by the end of the reign. Similarly, the increases achieved in the contributions of the *mesta*, in the clergy's *subsidio*, in the *cruzada* which taxed the sale of indulgences to the remarkable extent of over 50 million maravedis annually, and in the *maestrazgos*, the revenues from the lands of the Orders, were not enough to meet the demands which Charles V perennially made upon his Castilian administration. One solution would have been to compel the nobles to pay something towards the expenses of their king, but an attempt in 1538 to secure their consent to a universal excise on foodstuffs had to be abandoned as politically inopportune. Instead, the government leaned more heavily upon the *Cortes* – which meant in effect on the towns – and the revenue from *servicios* rose from 37 million maravedis a year to 136 million. There was, of course, an additional source of revenue in the treasure from the New World, or rather, from the *Quinto Real,* the share of the treasure reserved for the crown, and the taxes levied on the remainder. To start with this was of little value. It did not reach an average of 30 million maravedis a year until the 1530s; it then rose to 120 million by 1540, slumped back for a short period, but reached a new peak of 326 million maravedis a year by the end of the reign.

Even the augmented *servicios* and the growing flood of bullion could not pay all the expenses incurred by Charles's European activities and by 1534 there was nothing for it but to plunge into debt. Loans from bankers however required securities in the form of anticipated revenues or supplies of treasure, and one after another of the crown's sources of income thus came to be alienated to the financiers. To the public at large the government sold *juros*, a form of annuity first sold during the crusade against Granada. These were now set against the revenues of the *encabezamiento* – a fixed payment made at the request of the towns to replace the *alcabala*. Eventually over two-thirds of the revenue from this tax had been pledged in advance.

There was a limit to the extent to which the revenues could be mortgaged, and just before his death Los Cobos wrote to Charles to inform him that the limit had been reached. He urged him 'to remember the importance of finding a remedy and relief for these kingdoms because of the extreme need, for otherwise there could not fail to be serious trouble, because the need is so notorious that not only are the natives of the kingdom aware of it and are refusing to take part in financial transactions, but even foreigners . . . are doing the same thing because they know that there is no source from which payments can be made'. Charles remained deaf to his pleas, even when his bankers refused him loans or demonstrated their lack of confidence by charging him interest at 43 per cent. His wars had still to be fought. The campaign against Metz in 1552 cost him 2 million ducats (750 million maravedis), and was only one venture among many. There could be no other outcome but disaster, and in January, 1557, the government of Castile, like the government of the Netherlands, acknowledged the true legacy of Charles's reign by suspending payment of interest on his debts.

With taxation at such a rate and with the towns the chief sufferers, the economy of Castile was not as healthy as it should have been. It is true that the Vizcayan iron exports prospered, the Basque ports profited from the sale of raw wool to the Netherlands, the fairs of Medina del Campo were of international importance and the opening up of the New World had greatly increased the wealth and size of Seville. But though there was large-scale migration to the Andalusian valley of the Guadalquivir to plant cereals, vines and olives to ship out to the colonies, the industrial centres were slow off the mark to meet the demands of the colonists for manufactured goods. Their craft was not in doubt but their industries had become dangerously underdeveloped, largely because the impoverished condition of the Castilian peasants had weakened their local market.

The peasantry suffered from heavy taxes, higher prices, raised rents and, wherever the *mesta* reigned supreme with its sheep, from unemployment. There was, of course, a greater demand for grain, but the nobility lacked the interest to invest capital in the irrigation schemes which were necessary to bring wealth to the land and to those who tilled it. With a declining local market, therefore, industry too had begun to decline, and awareness of this very fact had encouraged the guilds to be more restrictive than ever in their regulations. In these circumstances and with rising prices and taxes it is not surprising that investment had fallen to nothing. Spanish industry failed not only to meet the challenge of the colonial market, but also to take advantage of the bullion coming into the country. Indeed it soon became abundantly clear that the bullion quickly disappeared to other countries to purchase the goods which Spain herself was failing to produce.

If Charles V appeared to regard his Spanish kingdoms, and Castile in particular, as little more than a source of revenue to finance his policies in other regions of his *monarchia*, he did not fail to recognise his responsibility for the spiritual protection of his subjects. Initially he was less eager than his grandparents had been to promote the authority of the Inquisition. He disliked its arbitrary powers and secret methods of operation, and was prepared to argue that its relentless campaign against the *conversos* (see page 143) had succeeded to such good effect that there was no longer any reason for it to continue. This, however, was before other opponents of the Inquisition appealed against it to the pope, and at this attempt to involve papal authority within his kingdom Charles immediately sprang to the Inquisition's defence. The inquisitors for their part were happy to demonstrate to Charles that the *conversos* were by no means the only group to threaten the orthodoxy of the Spanish church. Since 1510 there had grown up a mystical movement among a group of Franciscans whose followers were known as *alumbrados* or illuminists. Believing that they had totally abandoned themselves to the possession of the Holy Spirit, they subsequently made the blasphemous assumption that in such a condition they were incapable of sin. By 1525 illuminism had been discredited so effectively that all the extremer forms of devotion were also under suspicion, and the modest mystical practices of a certain Ignatius Loyola led temporarily to his arrest (see page 267).

Lutheranism was easily dealt with. Once his heresy had been defined and condemned, Luther's books were banned and there was little, if any, response in Castile and Aragon to his doctrine. By 1558 barely a hundred cases had come before the Inquisition; two-thirds of these concerned foreigners, and of the remainder the presumption is that they had been confused with Erasmianism. This in no way affected the seriousness of the charge, since Erasmus himself and the humanism associated with his name had become the object of a witch-hunt in the universities of Spain. The great days of Alcala and the translators, the humanist reforms of Cisneros and the welcome given to Erasmus's early writings, were forgotten in the crisis of the Reformation, and it was Erasmus's ambivalent attitudes, both to Luther and to the monastic orders, which led to the Inquisition's attack on his followers. Charles V did not approve, but the first victims were carefully chosen while he was in Italy with many of his humanist courtiers in 1529, and by the time of his return in 1533 the Inquisition had so successfully confused the ideas of Erasmus with those of Luther that none could disentangle them. Even the seventy-year-old chancellor of Alcala was imprisoned as a heretic for beliefs which had won him respect twenty years earlier, and the humanist Luis Vives left Spain, commenting, 'We live in difficult times in which we can neither speak nor remain silent without danger.'

The Inquisition in fact was unnecessarily protective. Since the days of the *Reconquista* the Spaniards had developed a passionate attachment to their faith, and their zeal was maintained by the ever-present threat from Islam, both at home among the Morisco population and in North Africa. Of all the campaigns of Charles V the one they were most willing to support was to drive the Turks from North Africa. Indeed it was becoming clear that the success of Ferdinand and Charles in the Italian wars had made Spain the greatest power in the west Mediterranean, upon whom devolved its defence against the Osmanlis (see page 231).

As for the Italian conquests these were acknowledged with some pride since they were attached to the Spanish throne, and, as a result of the formation of a council of Italy by Los Cobos, it was to Castile rather than to Aragon that these were assigned. Sicily, rather like Aragon, was a poor kingdom whose institutions enjoyed great privileges, and despite the cost of protecting the island from the Osmanlis its taxes were the lightest in the *monarchia*. Naples had greater wealth and was, therefore, more exploited. For over twenty years its ruthless viceroy, Pedro de Toledo, encouraged factions between the city and the nobility in order to reign supreme over both, and secured increasingly large grants to supplement Charles's income – 150,000 ducats for example in 1543, 175,000 in 1544 and 500,000 in 1552 – quite apart from any raised for local administration. The conquest of Milan in 1535 was of less immediate value since it was so expensive to defend. The ambassador in Genoa commented that it would need the income of seven Perus to meet the cost of governing Lombardy, but it was rightly regarded by the duke of Alba and others as the strategic key to Italy and could not therefore be abandoned. Its true economic value was not appreciated until peace returned to Italy after Charles' death.

Habsburg-Valois Rivalry

The election of Charles V to the Holy Roman Empire began an era of intense rivalry between himself and the unsuccessful candidate Francis I; although personal jealousies played their part, the underlying causes of the conflict between the Habsburgs and the Valois were of dynastic and national importance. Charles began his reign as a Burgundian, ambitious to recover the lands lost to France, especially the former duchy of Burgundy, and thus one day to be buried at Dijon among his ancestors. Later he inherited the long-standing disputes between Spain and France for control of Navarre, Roussillon and, above all, Italy. Even before he became emperor he was advised from Spain that he must seize control of Milan: 'The first consideration is that the duchies of Milan and Genoa are the keys and doors to the possibility of holding and dominating all Italy, and Italy duly occupied and duly reduced to your subjection is the true seat and sceptre for dominating the whole world. And inasmuch as the French, your enemies, know it very well and hold this point in more estimation than the defence of their own kingdom, it must be contemplated that at all and any times when they find an opportunity to return there they will do so.' Once the imperial throne was his also, the importance of Lombardy became even greater as a means of communication between his German and his Spanish possessions.

Francis I held contrary views. Burgundy had been assimilated into its rightful place within the French kingdom; Naples had been legitimately held, however briefly, by both Charles VIII and Louis XII and might yet be held again; above all, the territories of the *monarchia* came near to engulfing his own. Charles threatened the French frontier from Gravelines, Artois and Luxemburg to Franche Comté, and again along the line of the Pyrenees. The only loophole was the duchy of Milan, and it was there that Francis knew that he must defy the emperor in order to protect his country from encirclement.

Charles advanced from the Netherlands to seize Tournai (1521), while with apparent ease his commander in Lombardy, Prospero Colonna, restored the Sforzas to Milan and defeated Lautrec, the commander of a Franco-Swiss army, in the following year at Bicocca. Charles's military success was matched by diplomatic triumph. Henry VIII of England, despite his pledges to Francis I at their much publicised encounter at the Field of the Cloth of Gold, joined the emperor by a secret agreement at Gravelines; Adrian of Utrecht, Charles's former regent in Spain, was elected to the papacy, and the Constable Bourbon of France declared for Charles. Bourbon had married the daughter of the Beaujeus, (see page 129) but when she died childless in 1521 the king had threatened to reclaim her appanage for the crown. As a result of this France was now threatened from three sides. In 1523 a Spanish army crossed the Pyrenees, Bourbon led the Imperialists from Milan into southern France and laid siege to Marseilles, while Henry VIII marched from Calais. Although Henry came near to Paris, which was always dangerously vulnerable to attacks from the northern frontier, he fell back after learning that his allies had achieved little success, and the year ended with Francis I still secure within his kingdom.

In 1524 it was the turn of Francis to seize the initiative, and the French successfully crossed into Lombardy where Milan and other cities fell to his attack. Pavia alone held out. During the winter, in February 1525, Francis unwisely abandoned the strong position held by his army in the park of Mirabello outside the city in order to challenge a relieving force arrived from Germany.

As a result the French were defeated and Francis himself was taken prisoner. Charles's dramatic triumph, however, did not guarantee him equivalent political advantages. The French defeat at Pavia did not mean the defeat of France, and the other European states were prepared to contest any major territorial changes. Already in fact, while Francis was taken off to Madrid, his regent, Louise of Savoy, was negotiating alliances with the Italian cities, with the new pope, Clement VII, with Henry VIII and even – so desperate was the situation – with the Osmanli Turks. It was not easy, therefore, for Charles to determine what terms might reasonably be demanded from his prisoner.

It was one thing to demand the renunciation not only of all claims to Italy but also to suzerainty over Flanders, Artois and Tournai, but this did not gain actual territory for Charles. More important was his dynastic ambition to recover Burgundy, and ultimately, after seven months in captivity, Francis agreed by the Treaty of Madrid (1526) to seek the permission of the States-General for the return of the duchy to Charles. In addition, while renouncing all claim to territories held by Charles, he pledged himself to reinstate the constable Bourbon to his dignities, to marry Charles's sister as a symbol of their future amity and to join Charles in a crusade against the Turks. It is difficult to imagine what else Charles might have secured; equally it is impossible to believe that he could have put much faith in Francis's promises. Although the king made solemn oaths before the Holy Sacrament and left two sons as hostages, he had no sooner returned home than he repudiated the treaty, sent further emissaries to the Turks and mobilised the Italian cities in the League of Cognac under the protectorship of Henry VIII.

If Charles was angered by Francis's lack of good faith he was even more enraged to learn that in the very year of Mohacs (see page 228), when Christendom had no other defenders save the Austrian Habsburgs, the pope should abandon him to ally with the French. He therefore ordered Bourbon to take Rome. This was done in 1527, but the troops got out of hand and, in an act of savagery notorious even in a savage age, the city was sacked. Clement fled to Orvieto but dared no longer demonstrate support for Charles's enemies. In no way disconcerted by the sack of Rome, the French army under Lautrec, whose record since Bicocca had been significantly undistinguished, marched upon

Naples and besieged the city. On this occasion the French had the invaluable support of Genoa whose admiral, Doria, blockaded the garrison in Naples and supplied the besieging army by sea. Unfortunately for Francis I his agents in Genoa failed to pay due deference to the proud families who ran the city, and Doria was recalled to drive them out in 1528. By this event, one of the most important in the whole history of the Italian wars, Charles V was provided with an invaluable ally who safeguarded his maritime communications between Spain and Italy, supplied his armies, reinforced his naval power against the Turks and supported him with loans from its wealthy banking houses.

The first immediate consequence of Doria's change of side was the failure of the French expedition to Naples, since Lautrec could not survive without supplies. Moreover his army fell sick of malaria and he died in company with many of his troops. Meanwhile another French army, seeking to recover Milan, was defeated at Landriano (1529) and Italy was once again securely under Charles V's control. This was a position of strength which he used to good effect in negotiating a general settlement with the pope and with Francis I. By the Treaty of Barcelona (1529) Clement was brought to heel. Charles promised to protect the interests of his family, the Medici in Florence, provided they agreed to respect his own – a pointed reference to their membership of the League of Cognac – and, since Naples was technically a papal fief, Clement was obliged to recognise Charles's right to rule the kingdom. Finally, he was required to wait upon Charles at Bologna in the following year in order to crown him, in a rare occasion of its kind, as Holy Roman Emperor.

Francis I by the Treaty of Cambrai (1529) renounced once again the claims he had foregone in 1526 and the marriage with Charles's sister finally took place, but he was spared the most humiliating clauses of the Treaty of Madrid. Bourbon, dead, required no restitution of territory and Charles no longer demanded the duchy of Burgundy; after three more years in Spain he was rather less of a Burgundian than in the past and as a matter of practical politics had come to recognise that the duchy could only be acquired by direct conquest. In payment for his broken promises, however, Francis had to ransom the sons he had left as hostages for two million gold crowns.

So powerful was Charles's position in Europe that Francis, in place of direct military action, began to seek alliances among those who for different reasons were opposed to the emperor; Henry VIII on account of his divorce, the duke of Cleves on account of Lutheranism, Pope Clement VII – who dared to meet him at Marseilles in 1533 and arrange a marriage between Catherine de Medici and the future Henry II – and Suleyman the Magnificent (see page 231). In 1535 before these policies had matured, the last of the Sforzas died in Milan and Francis reverted to direct attack. Claiming Lombardy for France he burst into north Italy but failed to take Milan. In 1538 therefore he agreed to the Truce of Nice, which left him in temporary possession of Savoy and Piedmont, and allowed a brief respite to his emnity with Charles, to whom he granted free passage across France in order to deal speedily with the rebels of Ghent (see page 211). By 1542 he was on the offensive again, attacking Luxemburg in alliance with Cleves, ceding Toulon to the Turks, joining his fleet with theirs in a raid on Nice, and renewing the campaign in Piedmont with a victory at Ceresole in 1544. The Osmanli alliance, however, discredited him. Charles isolated him from his European allies and another truce, negotiated at Crépy in 1544, restored the frontiers of 1538.

Francis died in 1547 and though his son, Henry II, showed less interest in Italy he was by no means less hostile to the emperor, bearing a special grudge for the three years he had endured as a hostage for his father. His strategy was well conceived. He recognised that for the time being his best interests lay not with the Osmanli Turks but with the German Lutheran princes. When Charles V seemed to be triumphant over them after the Battle of Mühlberg in 1547 (see page 243), Henry – who persecuted heresy more savagely in France than Charles could in any of his own dominions – decided to go to their aid. By 1552 a special agreement was negotiated at Chambord by which, in return for French military intervention on their behalf, the Lutheran princes would guarantee to Henry possession of Metz, Toul and Verdun, the three key fortresses of Lorraine. Metz was taken in 1552 and heroically defended by the duke of Guise against determined counter-attacks by Charles V who well knew the need to recover the fortress. 'From this city they will have a clear road to the Rhine' he wrote 'and so will be able to cut off my communications from south Germany to the Netherlands.' In vain he spent two million ducats on the enterprise and, when the German Lutherans rallied against him and drove him from the Empire, he finally decided to abdicate.

This left Charles's brother Ferdinand in Austria and his son Philip in his other kingdoms. The war, therefore, continued between Philip and Henry II, and with the election of Paul IV in 1555, a pope bitterly hostile to Spain, the French were again invited to intervene in Italy. Guise made a brave show of thrusting through to Naples but his campaign was cut short by the duke of Alba. By way of compensation, however, he captured Calais in 1558 from Philip's English allies. By this time the governments of Henry and Philip were both mortgaged to the hilt, and by 1559 had been driven into bankruptcy. There was nothing for it therefore, but to make peace by the Treaty of Cateau-Cambrésis. The French gains of the truce of Nice were forfeited, but France gained Calais and, unofficially, Metz, Toul and Verdun. Otherwise, after thirty years of sporadic warfare, the frontiers were the same as at the Treaty of Cambrai (1529).

Suleyman the Magnificent 1520 – 66

The particular characteristics of the Osmanli Empire (see pages 105–9) demanded special qualities of military leadership from its sultans, but Suleyman the Magnificent who succeeded Selim in 1520 was something more than a brilliant soldier. He ruled his subjects with such justice and humanity that he won from them the title of law-giver, and his administrative skill in organising the government of the empire, to whose expansion he contributed so much, ensured its stability for many decades after his death in 1566. Europeans, however, were too afraid of him to admire him, and their fears were well justified for he was both perceptive in determining his strategy and ruthless in carrying it out. Within a month or so of his accession he recognised that Rhodes and Belgrade were not only barriers to the expansion of his empire but bases from which Europeans might launch dangerous counter-strokes. He therefore decided to attack them both without delay. Neither target was an easy one. Rhodes, an island fortress whose Knights of St John had successfully withstood attack for several hundred years, was well nigh impregnable, and all previous Osmanli campaigns in the Balkans, even those led by Mehmed II, had foundered against the walls and towers of Belgrade.

Nonetheless, Belgrade was taken in 1521 and Rhodes had capitulated by the end of the following year, and the success in each case was due largely to the skill and the determination of the sultan. Against Belgrade he organised his supply columns witn great care; expeditions were despatched to isolate the city from the north and west, and when the citadel was besieged in earnest a flotilla of river craft was sent up-stream to deny the citizens the opportunity of relief by water. Against Rhodes it was more a matter of ruthless resolution than skill since it was impossible to take the fortress by storm. Losses were heavy and winter fell before success had been achieved, but Suleyman's determination to maintain the siege outlasted the resources of the defenders, who surrendered on honourable terms in December 1522.

Adrian VI declared in great alarm that as a result of Suleyman's victories 'the passages to Hungary, Sicily and Italy lie open to him' since from 1522 the Osmanlis were able to pursue their attack on two fronts, along the Danube valley or across the Mediterranean. In either case the responsibility for resisting Suleyman fell on Charles V; not only was he emperor and therefore morally committed to the defence of Christendom, but his territories were the first to be threatened whether by land or by sea. Part of this responsibility he delegated to his brother Ferdinand who, by the Convention of Brussels (1522), assumed control of Austria, Styria, Carinthia, Carniola and the Tyrol, and whose close alliance with Louis II of Hungary had involved him intimately in Danubian affairs; but the overall problem of the Osmanli threat to Europe was one which constantly demanded Charles's attention throughout his reign.

Suleyman had many administrative and military problems to occupy his attention after 1522, not least along the frontier with Persia, but his janissaries were growing restive at his failure to exploit the capture of Belgrade. Consequently, in 1526 he set out with 100,000 men to challenge Louis II for control of the Hungarian plain. The attack was delayed by bad weather, when bridges and roads were carried away by floods, but it was the Hungarians who suffered a more serious disadvantage.

The Magyar nobles were resentful at the growth of German influence in their country. The Fuggers of Augsburg were winning control of the mining industry, and Louis' sister Anna had married Ferdinand of Austria – provoking the anger of Jan Zapolya, the powerful *voivode* of Transylvania, who had hoped to marry her himself. Louis tried to placate public opinion by expelling the Fuggers but there was no going back on the marriage. As a result, when the Turks advanced into Hungary, Zapolya refused to join his sovereign against them. The armies met at Mohacs, midway between Belgrade and Buda: the janissaries stood firm as always against the vigorous charges of the Magyar cavalry, and the superiority of the Turkish artillery finally tipped the balance in Suleyman's favour. Louis was killed and the Turks swarmed northwards into Buda.

The invaders withdrew from the capital at the approach of winter, and the threat of a Persian invasion in the following year diverted Suleyman's attention from the Balkans. But he retained possession of all land south of Buda, including not only the Danubian plain but also the valleys of the Sava, the Drava and the Tisza (Theiss). Nor was he disturbed by any counter-attack since Ferdinand of Austria and Jan Zapolya were too busy fighting each other for the small strip of independent Hungary which remained north of Buda. Since Louis had left no son his brother-in-law Ferdinand was elected King of Bohemia and Hungary, but a rival party among the Magyar nobility had acclaimed the *voivode* as its king. The matter was settled for the time being when Zapolya was defeated at Tokay in September 1527. He fled to Transylvania and secure among the Carpathian mountains proclaimed his independence of Habsburg and Turk alike. Two years later he joined forces with Suleyman in the most dangerous assault yet made on Europe by an Osmanli army.

In spite of bad weather the invaders occupied Buda, overran the rest of Hungary and burst into Austria; by September 1529 they were encamped outside Vienna. The city was most resolutely defended. The suburbs had been razed to the ground to allow a clear line of fire from the walls, the gates were bricked up, save one which served as a sally port, and, while 22,000 troops fought off the 24,000 of Suleyman's army, Ferdinand stood by at Linz to send down supplies and to maintain contact with Charles in Italy. Moreover the nature of warfare in the sixteenth century gave some advantage to defence; rarely did cities fall to the initial assault and a long siege was necessary to induce surrender. This

Suleyman was unable to do. Although he had made arrangements for thousands of camels to stand by in the Danube to supply his army as it advanced, his lines of communication were so far extended that convoys took nearly a month to reach him. Meanwhile heavy rain storms continued to hamper his operations as winter approached. After eighteen days he was compelled to withdraw.

Despite their setback at Vienna the Osmanli Turks were no less dangerous than before and the Viennese were destined to experience for many years the rigours and alarums of life in a frontier town. In 1532 Suleyman renewed the attack but by an original route. Instead of following the line of the Danube north to Buda and west towards Vienna, he marched to Essek (Osijek) on the river Drava and there set off across open country in a direct line for Vienna. Sixty miles south of the city he was held up at Güns, and so effective was the resistance that his army began to retreat in some disorder. Charles V, who was there in person, wanted to exploit this advantage and dreamed of recovering the whole of Hungary, but the German troops in his army refused to cross the imperial frontiers and Charles himself was distracted by news of an alliance between the pope and Francis I (see page 225). Indeed a kind of stalemate had now been reached in the Balkans. If Suleyman could not advance into Austria the Habsburgs were unable to liberate Hungary. Vienna was too strongly defended to be taken at a blow, and north of Buda the Turks were more or less at the limit of their lines of communication. Suleyman himself was preoccupied after 1533 with the conduct of many campaigns against Persia, and it was not until Mosul and Baghdad had been taken that the Persians made peace in 1555. For his part Charles V was too busy in Germany and Italy to take advantage of the Sultan's difficulties and Ferdinand was left unaided to make what little advances he could.

The inability of both sides to strike decisive blows was recognised by a truce of sorts between Ferdinand and Suleyman in 1533, but neither the *ghazi* chieftains on the frontier nor the marcher lords who faced them paid it much attention. Nor did it settle the dispute between Ferdinand and Zapolya. In 1538 Ferdinand recognised Zapolya's life tenure as an independent ruler of Transylvania on condition that he himself should inherit it. In the two years that intervened before Zapolya's death, however, the *voivode* married Isabella of Poland and produced a son, John Sigismund, and it was to protect her son's interests that Isabella appealed to Suleyman: In 1541 the sultan marched again up the Danube, drove Ferdinand out of Buda which he had only just recovered, and installed John Sigismund as his vassal in Transylvania. Two years later he marched north of Buda and occupied Gran. Ferdinand was clearly unable to expel him but in 1547, since the Persian war threatened to flare up once again, Suleyman agreed to a five-year truce at Adrianople. Ferdinand was allowed to govern the little remnant of Hungary still in his possession but only as a vassal of the Sultan, paying 30,000 Hungarian ducats a year in tribute money.

From the truce until its renewal on identical terms at Prague in 1552, neither side launched any major campaign in the Balkans, and John Sigismund was left undisturbed in Transylvania. But Ferdinand used the time to excellent effect, improving the defences of the few Hungarian fortresses in his possession. The Osmanlis had not attempted to occupy the whole of Hungary but rather to establish garrisons at such important centres as Belgrade, Buda and Gran, whence to launch their attacks into Austria. The Europeans, however, were at last learning how to exploit the Turks' difficulties over their lines of communication and were resolved to delay an Osmanli advance by protracted sieges rather than incur the risk of a major battle. This was the strategy behind Ferdinand's defence work, but it was not put to the test in his lifetime. The truce was renewed in 1562. Ferdinand died in 1564 and Suleyman two years later.

Throughout these years of conflict in the Danube valley Charles V had been able to delegate much of the burden of defence to his brother. In the Mediterranean he had to bear alone the brunt of the Osmanli raids on Naples, Sicily and Spain. The Morisco population in Spain was potentially a fifth column whose Islamic loyalties might be exploited by the Turkish fleets who attacked the coastline every year; Sicily, the all-important granary of his Mediterranean empire, was always threatened with attack if not invasion, and the grain ships constantly ran the gauntlet of Osmanli raiders. Above all, the sea routes linking Spain, Naples and Milan, the lines of communication upon which depended Charles's mastery of Italy were dangerously exposed – especially to an enemy who subsequently found allies in North Africa and

France. The alliance with Genoa assured Charles of the invaluable services of its Admiral Doria who in 1532 captured Coron from the Turks in the Morea; and the Knights of St John, expelled from Rhodes in 1522, were garrisoned by Charles in Tripoli, Malta and Gozo in order to strengthen his defence of the central Mediterranean. Unfortunately for Charles, the Osmanli Turks found allies among the Moorish rulers of North Africa whose hostility to Spain dated back to the conquest of Granada. Chief among them was Khair ad-Din Barbarossa, a barbary pirate who had made himself master of Algiers and who, in 1529 expelled the Spaniards from the Peñon, the fortified rock at the harbour entrance which they had held since Ferdinand's reign. Immediately after the fall of Coron, Suleyman appointed him Pasha and Grand Admiral of the Osmanli fleet.

In 1534, after raiding southern Italy, Barbarossa seized Bizerta and Tunis from a rival Moslem pirate who was allied to Charles V. So great was the danger to Sicily and indeed to Charles's control of the central Mediterranean, that the emperor wasted no time in raising 400 ships and 30,000 men and leading them in person against Tunis in 1535. He seized the fortress in the harbour, and the captives within the city, hearing the attack, successfully rebelled against their masters. Although the victory was dramatic, its effects were short-lived. Charles could not afford to keep a permanent garrison in the city and had to entrust its defence to a Moslem ally whose reliability could not be guaranteed, while Barbarossa still continued to raid the shipping from his other North African bases. Worse still, the French, who had discussed the matter of an alliance with the sultan as early as 1526, had at last signed a formal treaty in 1536. John de la Forêt had been admitted to Constantinople in 1534 to negotiate trading privileges for the French, and under cover of signing a commercial treaty committed the French to support the Osmanli attacks on Charles V. Barbarossa was able to shelter at Marseilles during the winter of 1536–7, and in 1543 Toulon was formally and publicly made available to his fleet.

Meanwhile the Osmanli attacks on Otranto had led in 1538 to a coalition between Venice, Charles and the papacy. Andrea Doria, commanding the emperor's squadron, joined the allies off the coast of Corfu, but his interests as a Genoese were not those of Venice which hoped to recover control of its former Dalmatian bases. Consequently, when a relatively small Osmanli fleet engaged the allies at Prevesa, Doria's main concern was to keep his squadron in being in order to shield Italy from attack, and as a result of his caution the allies were defeated. Venice in great indignation withdrew from the coalition at the price of 300,000 ducats and made a separate peace with Suleyman. Charles gave up the attempt to beard the Turks in the eastern half of the Mediterranean and instead concentrated his attention on North Africa. Having failed to bribe Barbarossa to enter his service in return for a Tunisian throne, Charles launched an attack against another Moslem pirate at Algiers in 1541. This was a disaster. The expedition was thrown on to a beach by a storm and its commanders proved to be irresolute in the crisis; as a result 12,000 men were lost.

Encouraged by their victories at Prevesa and Algiers the Osmanli Turks broke into the western Mediterranean in 1543 in open alliance with France. From Barbarossa's headquarters at Toulon, in whose market place Christian prisoners were sold as slaves, the French and Osmanli fleets bombarded Nice. Dangerous though the situation was, the French were not happy to be so actively involved on the sultan's side, while the Turks discovered that even with the French bases available to them it was too hazardous a business to operate more than one thousand miles from home for long periods of time. After Barbarossa's death Piale Pasha took command of the Osmanli fleet and was greatly aided by Dragut, a former prisoner from the Spanish galleys whom Barbarossa had ransomed. In 1551 Dragut took Tripoli from the Knights of St John, and Charles was too old and too preoccupied with other matters to do anything about it. For nearly a decade Dragut roamed at will in the western Mediterranean, raiding the Spanish coast, Sicily and the Balearic Islands until Philip II could accept the situation no longer. In 1560 he sent a fleet under the duke of Medina Celi to seek out Dragut along the North Africa coast but, unhappily for the Spaniards, they ran into the full Osmanli fleet led by Piale Pasha and were routed off the island of Djerba. Spain's only success was the relief of Malta in 1565. Piale Pasha had landed 40,000 men on the island but the Knights of St John whom Charles had installed there fought with great courage. Dragut was killed in action and Piale Pasha recognised that the operation demanded a long and resolute siege. This was made impossible by the arrival of the Spanish fleet and the Turks withdrew.

Nothing was more calculated to bring home to Europe the reality of the Osmanli threat than the activities of Suleyman's fleet in the western Mediterranean. Yet despite the danger to European shipping very little territory was lost. Sicily and Malta were held securely and although the coastal raids on Spain and Italy caused much inconvenience and damage, they were never the preliminaries to an actual invasion. The greater danger came by way of the Danube valley where armies of many thousands could be mobilised under the Sultan's personal leadership to ride against Europe. The threat was never under-estimated in the sixteenth century – though it is clear that Europeans never realised how much they were protected from Osmanli invasion by the constant warfare which the sultan had to wage against the Persians. Nonetheless, the Osmanli army was operating at the very limits of its lines of communication and supply. Even if Vienna were to fall – her defences weakened perhaps by treachery, inefficiency or disease – the conquest of Austria would have presented the Turks with problems they were unlikely to have solved. It was one thing to hold the thinly-populated regions of the Balkans from a few selected bases, but quite another to hope to hold down Austria in the same way.

Yet the greatest problems facing the Osmanli Empire were not presented by any enemy; they sprang from its essential character as a nomadic fighting force inexorably committed to plunder on an ever wider scale. Any modification of this prime function was unacceptable to the Osmanlis, and though the sultans and their vezirs did a great deal to consolidate the frontiers of their empire and to develop administrative procedures for its government, they dared not forget that their basic role was to conquer not to govern. If the sultan failed in this he was deposed. Even Suleyman the Magnificent could not alter this and in 1526 for example, he attacked at Mohacs not out of any urgent desire to destroy Louis II but to silence the rebellious discontent which three years of peace had induced among his janissaries. Moreover, during Suleyman's reign a rift began to appear between the *sipahis* and the janissaries. The *sipahis* were the feudal cavalry, the descendants of the original *ghazi* horde which had swept across Asia Minor and whose fierce devotion to Islam gave added fervour to their desire to plunder the infidels of Europe and of Persia. Their rewards were the spoils of war and the accumulation of fiefs, but they had grown jealous of the special influence exerted at court by the janissaries. These were the *kullar*, the men of the sultan, privileged to serve him personally and rewarded by the highest appointments in the administration of the empire – despite the fact that few had been born Moslems and all were conscripted from the subject races of the empire. The rival factions sought leaders in Suleyman's own family, and his sons, jealous of each other and anxious to establish positions of strength before their father died, engaged in civil war. For Suleyman this was a personal tragedy; to safeguard his empire he was forced in 1533 to execute his eldest son, Mustafa, and the civil war was not ended until another prince, Bayezid, was executed in 1561.

Whatever the difficulties, however, the empire stood or fell by the military qualities of its sultan. Under Suleyman it had prospered, and if his immediate successors proved to be less talented, if the empire seemed to be beset with insoluble problems and if a limit appeared to have been reached in the Ottoman advance on Europe, the emergence of a vigorous leader could always alter the situation overnight – and as late as 1683 an Osmanli army was again encamped outside the walls of Vienna.

The Holy Roman Empire 1519 – 55

The throne of the Holy Roman Empire, for which Charles V ultimately sacrificed his best interests in Spain and the Netherlands, afforded considerable honour but little power. It has already been shown that the imperial princes were as determined as any ruler in France or Spain to be sovereign within their own territories and had succeeded to the extent that no emperor could impose upon them policies which they opposed (see page 148). The strength of an emperor's authority therefore depended either on the degree of unanimity he could achieve in the diet or on the extent of his private territories – since what could not be achieved by an emperor might sometimes be brought about by the resolute action of a duke of Austria. Charles indeed was better endowed with territory than any previous emperor, but so great was his *monarchia* and so varied the problems it presented that it allowed him little opportunity to concentrate his attention on German affairs. Moreover the problem was exacerbated beyond measure by the beginnings of the Reformation in Germany, since this compelled him to become the champion of one cause and the permanent foe of the other. In these circumstances it was impossible to hope for unanimity in the diet, nor could Charles look for support from the Catholic princes who at first constituted the majority. So great was their suspicion of the emperor, so close their fellow feeling with the other princes, that despite their anxiety to eradicate heresy they refused to do so under the emperor's banner, or on terms which augmented his authority at the expense of any Lutheran prince.

Charles faced his first problem at the Diet of Worms in 1521 when Martin Luther appeared before him at the insistence of Frederick the Wise, the elector of Saxony. Luther's opposition to papal authority had already been condemned by the bull *Exsurge Domine*, and the papal legate Aleander was angry that a secular tribunal should presume to examine an excommunicated heretic. The elector of Saxony, however, was equally angry at what he considered to be a deliberate insult to his newly established University of Wittenberg: though he never met Luther in person nor even adopted his doctrine, he firmly believed that his promising young professor had been shabbily treated by Rome (see page 88) and the emperor deemed it politic to humour him. Luther was, therefore, admitted to the diet under an imperial safe conduct. The proceedings were brief. When Luther acknowledged his publications and refused to withdraw them without further debate, he was declared to be an outlaw and Charles pledged himself wholeheartedly to enforce the decrees of the pope. 'To settle this matter' he said, 'I am determined to use all my domains and possessions, my friends, my body, my blood, my life, and my soul', but there was little he could do to override the privileges of a prince as strong as the elector of Saxony. Before Luther's safe conduct expired, the elector had him taken off into hiding and subsequently he returned to Wittenberg where he remained under the elector's protection.

Among the many supporters of Luther who had thronged the streets of Worms – to such extent that Aleander had feared for his life – were several of the *Reichsritter*, the imperial knights who constituted a dangerously depressed section of the community ready to take up any new cause if it could conceivably bring them advantage. As lesser gentry, claiming to be tenants-in-chief of the emperor, their class had been ruined first by the Black Death and then by the rise in prices. Warfare was their only occupation but when there was no one to employ them they turned to brigandage, and for many years the princes and the emperor had tried to suppress their activities. The most notorious of the knights was Franz von Sickingen. After many years of terrorising the duchy of Württemberg he declared himself a Lutheran, summoned other *Ritter* to join him at Landau in 1522, and began to attack the rich ecclesiastical principalities of the Rhineland. Significantly in this as in so many other crises of German history the emperor was powerless to act on his own authority but the princes, whether Lutheran or Catholic in sympathy, were not prepared to sanction private freebooting on such a scale. They mobilised their forces and defeated the *Ritter* at Landstuhl, where von Sickingen was mortally wounded and the so-called Knights' War was brought to an end.

Another dissatisfied section of society was the German peasantry which was angry at the measures taken by landlords who met the price rise by demanding greater labour services and higher rents. As a result there had been peasant risings in every decade for the past half century, but there were not so many among the poverty stricken and depressed inhabitants of the north and east as in the south and west where the peasants enjoyed greater prosperity and were all the more determined to protect it. In addition, whenever there was unrest, but especially in the Upper Rhineland, the sign of the *Bundschuh*, (the peasants' boot,) symbolised a revolutionary kind of millenarianism which found expression in visionary invocations of the 'law of God' and radical demands for restructuring society.

Revolt broke out in 1524 at Stühlingen near Schaffhausen, where the sixty-two articles issued by the peasants expressed the traditional protests against extra field work and the loss of common land, woodland and fishing rights. Because so many of the princes were at war in Italy the revolt spread swiftly across south Germany, to be joined by the tenants of the great abbeys and the unemployed of the towns. The *Bundschuh* too was raised, but on this occasion the millenarian tracts were given a specifically Lutheran character. The Twelve Articles of Memmingen in March 1525, demanded an end not merely to the abuses of villeinage but to villeinage itself, supporting the more radical propositions in Lutheran style by an appeal to the Gospels. There was nothing there they claimed to justify villeinage; rather, all men should be free, 'because Christ has delivered and redeemed us all, the lowly as well as the great, without exception, by the shedding of His precious blood'. Social revolution inflamed by religious frenzy was a potent mixture, and the revolt fell under the leadership of rabble-rousing prophets who employed fire and sword with missionary zeal. Chief among them was Thomas Münzer. A former Lutheran who had found his master's theology too moderate for his own extreme taste, he was now transported to apocalyptic heights by his own breathless cries for the massacre of the unrighteous – by whom he meant the landlord class and their bailiffs. In great alarm the German princes hurried back from Italy to defend their properties, and crushed the revolt at Frankenhausen. Münzer was tortured to death with great barbarity, and the deep anxieties of the victors found release in the massacre of the vanquished. The fury was short-lived however as the landlords soon recognised that they needed their peasants alive rather than dead.

The Peasants' Revolt and the Knights' War revealed that the suppression of internal disorder was a matter which only the princes could handle, and it was to the princes alone that Luther now entrusted the fate of his movement. He had had some sympathy for the tenants of the abbeys, but he was basically conservative and he abominated anarchy. Above all he was horrified by the polemics of Münzer, whom he had had expelled from Saxony for his extremist views, and he feared that he himself might be blamed for the peasants' appeal to the Gospels on the subject of villeinage. He rushed to vindicate himself in print: the offending article 'would make all men equal and so change the spiritual kingdom of Christ into an external worldly one. Impossible. An earthly kingdom cannot exist without inequality of persons'. The peasants were accordingly 'false to the gospel they professed to follow ... therefore whoso can strike, smite, strangle or stab, secretly or publicly, such wonderful times are these that a prince can better merit heaven with bloodshed than another with prayer'. His views, though hysterical, were conventional enough and his deliberate aim in writing was to save the

Reformation from anarchy and millenarianism on the one hand, and from Charles V and the pope on the other, by relying exclusively upon the princes.

This was a shrewd move which recognised that the outcome of the religious struggle in Germany would be settled neither by the emperor nor by the people but only by the princes. In a few cases, as at Augsburg, a popular Lutheran movement carried the day, but in most of the German states it was the confession of the prince which determined that of his subjects. Some princes genuinely embraced Lutheranism: others found it convenient to pretend to do so since in a Lutheran state the prince became head of the church and had the opportunity to secularise church lands (see page 252). The duchy of East Prussia for example was created by Albrecht of Brandenburg, master of the Order of Teutonic Knights, when he declared himself a Lutheran, dissolved the Order and appropriated its lands. On the other hand the mingling of religious zeal with self-interest was not confined to the Lutheran camp. In Bavaria, where the population had shown great enthusiasm for the publications of Luther, the devotion of the duke to the Catholic cause was immeasurably strengthened when the pope agreed to his retention of one-fifth of the ecclesiastical revenues of the duchy – and a similar arrangement was later negotiated with Ferdinand of Austria, the emperor's brother.

The emperor himself could do nothing. He left for Spain soon after the Diet of Worms, and the edicts against Luther were ignored. In 1526, however, strengthened by his victory at Pavia, Charles ordered Ferdinand to summon the Diet to Speyer and on his behalf to present the members with an unequivocal demand for the punishment of those who broke the laws of the empire. When this had been demanded against the *Reichsritter* the princes had not demurred, but they were not prepared to punish each other at the emperor's order. This did not mean that Catholic princes tolerated Lutheranism but rather that their fear of heresy could not outweigh their suspicion of the emperor: in no circumstances would they risk making Charles stronger by weakening the independence of their own order. Lutheran and Catholic alike, therefore, passed a unanimous resolution 'that each one should so live, govern and conduct himself as he hopes and trusts to answer it to God and to his imperial majesty'. As a precaution against the evil day, however, the Lutheran landgrave of Hesse showed considerable acumen by seeking out alliances with all the enemies of the Habsburgs – with France and Denmark and even with far distant Transylvania.

Three years later Charles arrived fresh from further triumphs in Italy, and the Diet was again summoned to Speyer where it was obliged to rescind its declaration of 1526. Despite this, the princes urged Charles to accept the presence of Lutheranism where it was already established, providing there was no more confiscation of church property and the Mass be permitted for Catholics in Lutheran states. Significantly it was not Charles but the Lutherans who objected. They claimed that it was unfair to debar Lutheran services in Catholic states, and their official protest won the name of Protestant for their movement. Charles left Germany in anger, but on his return from his triumphal coronation at Bologna (see page 224) his mood became conciliatory. He wanted to settle the Lutheran problem as peacefully as possible in order to rally the whole empire against the Turks, who the previous year had nearly seized Vienna. Accordingly he summoned the Diet to Augsburg, hoping to find grounds for agreement between the two sides. Luther as an outlaw was not permitted to attend, but his close friend and fellow theologian, Philip Melanchthon, was invited to present his doctrine before the emperor.

The *Confessio Augustana*, which later became the official version of Lutheranism, was deliberately couched in such moderate terms that Luther was in an agony of mind lest Melanchthon's conciliatory mood should lead him to abandon essential points; this he did not do, and the emperor's advisers were compelled to point out that any theological compromise between themselves and Melanchthon was out of the question. Campeggio, the papal legate, therefore urged Charles to set about the destruction of heresy without delay, and offered him a bull of deposition against the elector of Saxony – the brother of Luther's protector at Worms. Charles could not accept the proffered weapon. Perplexed by the apparent impossibility of getting his own way within the empire, yet worried too by the Osmanli threat to Austria, he merely announced that the Lutheran princes had six months' grace in which to reconsider their position.

The elector of Saxony and the landgrave of Hesse had no

intention of reconsidering anything, and with other Lutherans they formed the League of Schmalkalden:

Whereas it is altogether likely that those who have the pure word of God preached in their territory are to be prevented by force from continuing this service so pleasing to God; and whereas it is the duty of every Christian government to have the word of God preached to its subjects . . . Now we, solely for the sake of our defence and deliverance, which both by human and divine right is permitted to everyone, have agreed that whenever anyone of us is attacked on account of the word of God and the doctrine of the gospel . . . all the others shall immediately come to his assistance as best they can and help to deliver him.

The words were plain enough and there was military strength to support them, since the eight princes and eleven city states – which included the rich and strategically important cities of Lübeck, Magdeburg, Bremen, Strasburg and Constance – were pledged to field 10,000 men and 2,000 horse. For the moment they were not required to do so. 'Because of the common enemy of the Christian name', Suleyman, who was then on his way across country to Vienna, Charles summoned the Diet to Nuremberg to declare an imperial peace pending the decisions of a general council of the church: he then rode off to Güns with Lutherans and Catholics in his train.

Free from restraint, the Schmalkaldic League grew in size. Augsburg, Frankfurt, Hamburg and Hanover joined its ranks: it claimed it could raise 20,000 men; it was in alliance with France, and, to demonstrate its power, Philip of Hesse organised the invasion of Württemberg in 1543 in order to restore its exiled duke, Ulrich. Ulrich had made himself thoroughly unpopular with his peasants, townsmen and nobles, and had been expelled several years back by Charles V who had entrusted the duchy to Ferdinand of Austria. Since then, however, Ulrich had declared himself a Lutheran. The league conducted a brief and successful campaign to restore him, and the cost was met by secularising church lands in the duchy.

In the same year an Anabaptist rising broke out in Münster. The Anabaptists not only denied the validity of infant baptism, but represented a radical millenarianism which appealed greatly to depressed or unemployed labourers in Switzerland, Germany and the Netherlands. In a world in which the prince, the church,

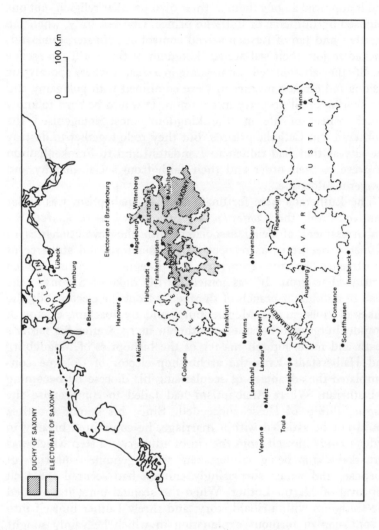

Germany in the reign of Charles V

the landlord and the employer were tightening their hold over the lives of ordinary people, Anabaptism gave explosive vent to the frustration and misery of the poor; it reaffirmed their individualism and it appeared among them as their own peculiar religion, not one imposed by Lutheran or Catholic prince. Consequently, when Jan Matthys and Jan of Leyden seized control of Münster, thousands flocked to join their self-styled 'kingdom of the world', to escape the life they abominated and to share in a society where apocalyptic visions and ecstatic mysticism were combined with polygamy and the sharing of all property in common. It would be hard to know which aspect of life in 'the kingdom' most antagonised the Lutheran and Catholic princes, but they rode together to destroy the city as they had ridden to Landstuhl and to Frankenhausen to preserve their order and their faith from social anarchy and dangerous doctrine.

The Lutherans were fortunate that as Anabaptism was so far removed from the *Confessio Augustana* they were spared the embarrassment of being associated with the revolutionaries of Münster. Secure in its respectability, therefore, and still free of interference by the emperor, the League of Schmalkalden continued to grow. It was joined by the duke of Saxony – the head of a different branch of the family from the elector – by the dukes of Holstein and Mecklenburg, and by Joachim, elector of Brandenburg, who became a Lutheran in 1538 after his father's death and made himself master of the bishoprics of Magdeburg and Halberstadt. Even the archbishop-elector of Cologne contemplated the advantage of secularising his diocese by becoming a Lutheran. Where Anabaptism had failed to compromise the league, Philip of Hesse succeeded. Since his sexual appetites could not be satisfied within marriage, he committed bigamy in order to save himself from the sin of adultery – a step which was remarkable for being undertaken with genuine sincerity of purpose, and which surprisingly enough had secured the tacit approval of Martin Luther. When the scandal burst it provided the Catholics with a ribald story, and threw Luther himself into a confusion of tortuous explanation in which he vainly sought precedents from the Old Testament patriarchs. More to the point it caused a rift between Philip and his allies. Sensing their disapproval and realising how dangerously isolated he was in an age which punished bigamy with death, he abandoned his membership of the league for the emperor's promise that he would not be prosecuted. This suited Charles's purposes admirably. In 1541 he was determined to make a final bid for unity, and if that failed, to resort to force: Philip's withdrawal from the league was therefore opportune should force prove necessary.

First, however, Charles summoned the Diet to Regensburg in 1541 in order to discover a measure of common ground between the two confessions. Despite a remarkable attempt to establish some pretence at unity over the doctrine of justification by faith, the venture failed as it was bound to do and Charles began to plan his military *coup de main*. The Truce of Crépy (1544) secured a respite for him from the war with France and released the Spanish army in Italy for service in Germany. Moreover Charles had at last found allies within the empire. William of Bavaria agreed on this occasion to support his action against the Schmal-kaldic League, and Maurice, the new duke of Saxony, was so determined to secure the electoral title for the ducal branch that despite being a Lutheran he promised to defect to Charles. When the duke of Alba crossed the Alps in 1546 the Schmalkaldic League was thrown into confusion by Maurice's invasion of electoral Saxony. Philip of Hesse agreed to fight but was no longer acceptable as a leader and no one could check Alba's triumphant progress down the Rhineland. The Lutheran cities surrendered in his path, the archbishop-elector of Cologne resigned his see, and in 1547, when Alba joined Maurice in Saxony, the remnants of the league were defeated at Mühlberg. Philip and the elector were taken prisoner and Maurice was awarded the electoral title.

Charles demonstrated at Mühlberg that when he could mobilise the resources of his *monarchia* to implement policies which as emperor he was unable to enforce, the independence of the German princes was seriously endangered. To follow up his victory he immediately summoned the diet to Augsburg and demanded the formation of a general imperial league financed by all the members to maintain a standing army capable of enforcing the laws of the empire. If he had succeeded in this, Charles might have reversed the well-established trend towards particularism in the empire. William of Bavaria knew this also and, though he was the emperor's best ally in Germany against the Lutherans, he vigorously opposed the introduction of constitutional changes of such importance. Led by him, the other princes took heart and the battle won at Mühlberg was lost amid the committees of the diet. All that Charles secured was an interim injunction enforcing Catholicism with a few modifications to placate the Lutherans – allowing priests to marry, for example, or the layman to take communion in both kinds. Compromises of this kind, however, satisfied no one; moreover the pope was opposed to them. The general council meeting at Trent since 1545 (see page 273) refused to countenance the sort of comprehensive settlement by which the emperor hoped to unite the members of the empire, and Charles was both angry and disheartened. In fact he chased a chimera. Doctrinal compromise was not possible as the Diets of Augsburg (1530) and Regensburg (1541) had shown and, if the emperor could not impose one single faith throughout the empire, then the princes would have to be free to determine their own. In other words a political compromise was the only kind possible.

Charles was now in trouble. The success of the Spanish troops made him realise that without Spain the empire could not be governed and he began to think that his son, Philip of Spain, should succeed him instead of his brother, Ferdinand of Austria. Ferdinand immediately withdrew to Vienna in high dudgeon. Maurice too was lost. He was too ambitious and too staunch a Lutheran to remain the emperor's ally for long, and after leading the imperial forces to recover the secularised diocese of Magdeburg for the church, he appropriated it for himself in 1551. In the following year he negotiated help from Henry II at Chambord (see page 225) by offering him the key fortresses of Lorraine (Metz, Toul and Verdun) and the title of Protector of German liberty. The French entered Lorraine, Maurice marched on Innsbruck, Ferdinand still sulked and Charles fled to Carinthia. After this matters became confused. Henry II wanted Charles's defeat but not the triumph of Lutheranism; Charles was reconciled to Ferdinand, squeezed one final loan from the Fuggers and made a desperate but unsuccessful attempt on Metz; the former elector of Saxony was released but immediately demanded his title from Maurice, and Maurice was fatally wounded after a skirmish with the margrave of Brandenburg-Culmbach with whom he was at odds. His death, Charles's abdication, Ferdinand's accession, and the impending bankruptcy, both of the Habsburgs and of the Valois, cleared the way for a political compromise at the Diet of Augsburg in 1555.

The settlement merely confirmed what had already come to pass: Lutheranism and Catholicism were recognised as the two official confessions of the empire as far as the princes were concerned, and by the maxim *cujus regio, ejus religio* their choice determined the confession of their subjects. Calvinism, the new and vigorous development in the Protestant camp, was not recognised, and ecclesiastical princes were forbidden (by a clause subsequently added by the emperor) to abandon Catholicism and to secularise their dioceses as family possessions. These two points were to give rise to great controversy in the future, but for the time being the German princes were thankful to have an end to the civil war.

By his own lights Charles had failed, and for this reason he took the unheard of step of abdicating in 1555. To some extent the fault lay in his having too elevated a view of his potential role in the world, one which even in the Middle Ages would have been impractical. Contemporaries distinguished between the empire and the *monarchia*, but in one sense Charles treated them as an integral unit giving him the leadership of Christendom as the heir of Charlemagne. Charles was not a man of great imagination nor was he in any way unbalanced; his gifts were those of practical commonsense, tenacity and the ability to learn from experience. It is likely therefore that the visionary ideal of empire was implanted in him during his youth by Mercurino da Gattinara. Gattinara, his Grand Chancellor was a Piedmontese, recruited into the international team of civil servants who administered what was left of the old Burgundian inheritance. He wrote enthusiastically of Charles 'following the path of the good Emperor Justinian, giving law to the whole of Christendom' – not by exercising dominion, since Gattinara did not advise the conquest of Europe, but by example and influence. Moreover, within the territories belonging to Charles, common institutions were to be developed as a means of centralising their government. Neither of Gattinara's policies was attainable. The pope, the Valois and the German princes vigorously refused to accept the leadership of Charles; the difficulty of communication between Brussels, Madrid, Naples and Frankfurt or Vienna made central direction difficult, and the well-established particularist institutions of each Habsburg kingdom and duchy were not to be overridden by an imperial council of state.

If Charles is judged by more practical criteria than those of Gattinara, it is clear that the Peace of Augsburg indicated his failure not only to eradicate Lutheranism within the empire but also to prevent the princes from determining the course of events. This was only to be expected. The constitution of the Holy Roman Empire encouraged the efforts of the separate princes to establish sovereignty in their own particular states, and militated against the desire of the emperor to establish a measure of central control. The Knights' War, the Peasants' Revolt and the Schmalkaldic League all indicated that the power of effective decision lay with the princes. The only authority Charles could enforce was as head of the Habsburg *monarchia* when the Spanish army, for example, gave him the victory at Mühlberg. But the resources of the *monarchia* could not be consistently nor constantly applied to Germany because Charles was involved in perpetual warfare with the French and the Turks in defence of his other territories. Consequently, he had little opportunity to concentrate on German affairs, and his frequent absence from the daily routine of political manipulation – bringing persistent pressures to bear on one prince or another – was a serious disadvantage for which the occasional appearance in strength was no compensation.

It would be easy on the evidence of German affairs and Charles's own act of abdication to paint a sad picture of failure, but it would be totally misleading to do so. Charles ruled many lands over many years and his fortunes fluctuated widely. The young prince of 1520, about to meet Luther at Worms while the revolt of the *Comuneros* still smouldered in Castile, must be set against the triumphal emperor of 1530, fresh from his coronation at Bologna and celebrating his victories at Pavia and Landriano, the withdrawal of the Turks from Vienna and the Treaties of Cambrai and Barcelona. Similarly his successes at Tunis, at Güns, at Ghent and at Mühlberg must be thrown into the scale against the defeat at Algiers and Metz. Unfortunately there is no simple table of points by which the degree of overall success or failure can be quantified. As ruler of the Netherlands and of the Spanish kingdoms Charles was undoubtedly a success. He won additional territory in Tournai, Gelders, Milan and the New World (see page 191), though he had to relinquish his family's ambition to recover Burgundy. He strengthened his government's powers to overrule local authorities and to centralise the making of decisions; heresy for example was vigorously attacked, despite the protests of those who sympathised with the persecuted or objected to the special powers of persecutors, and – a useful test of any government's success – taxes were paid on an ever-increasing scale throughout the reign. Indeed Charles would have done well if Spain and the Netherlands had been the full extent of his dominion. As it happened they were eventually plundered to finance campaigns and uphold causes in which they had no direct interest, while matters of importance, such as the state of the Castilian economy, were left in abeyance. Bankruptcy was a heavy price to pay for Charles's election to the empire.

Within the empire, for which so much was sacrificed elsewhere, Charles failed to achieve his objectives, yet as emperor he was certainly more influential than either Maximilian or Frederick had been. Moreover, in his dual role as Habsburg prince and Holy Roman Emperor he held his own against the Turks, denying them any conquests in the western Mediterranean and maintaining intact the frontiers of Austria. At the same time, and despite the handicaps of his commitments elsewhere, he drove the French out of Italy, and the net effect of all the treaties negotiated between 1526 and 1559 was to leave France isolated within an encircling line of Habsburg territories. On this foundation his son Philip was able to establish Spain's ascendency in Europe.

The German Response to Lutheranism

Luther's doctrines (see page 90), conceived at the very crisis of an intense spiritual agony and developed under the pressure of opposition and debate, had been more or less fully worked out by the time he appeared before Charles V at Worms. Moreover, thanks to the printing press they were well known throughout Germany and had aroused support in many quarters, not least among many of the common people. His vigorous condemnation of ecclesiastical abuses was in keeping with the strong tradition of practical piety which had been established by the mystic preachers of the fourteenth century (see page 82), and his attack on indulgences in particular was welcomed by those who were unhappy about the practices of Tetzel and his like. Above all, however, it was the nationalist response to his attacks on Rome which accounted for most of his popularity, so that at Worms his name was shouted in the streets to the great alarm of the legate Aleander. 'All Germany is in an upheaval. Nine out of every ten people shout Luther and the tenth, if indifferent to what Luther says, at any rate shouts death to the court of Rome.'

More important than the applause of the public was the support he received from the humanists who imagined him to be a second Reuchlin, falling victim to the same Dominican inquisitors. It was a reasonable supposition, since Luther's criticism of the mechanistic attitudes to religion seemed to echo the complaints of Erasmus, and his Greek scholarship was of a high order. Indeed, when Frederick the Wise sent him into hiding after the Diet of Worms, he passed his time at the Castle of Wartburg in producing a German translation of the Greek New Testament, using the language of the Saxon chancery as his model since it was intelligible to readers both of low and high German. The strongest body of academic support came from his own university of Wittenberg which became the centre of a considerable missionary enterprise. Luther's followers went out not only to other universities, but also to other countries, especially throughout Scandinavia and down into Bohemia and Hungary. Their action was assisted and followed up by a constant flood of literature from the Wittenberg presses. Each of the three great pamphlets of 1520 ran through more than fifteen editions, and an analysis of the publications circulating in Germany in 1523 reveals that 183 were by Luther or were ascribed to him, 20 were by his opponents and 215 by his friends.

Of all his friends none was more loyal nor of greater service than Philip Melanchthon, Reuchlin's great-nephew. Younger than Luther and more brilliant, both as a theologian and as a classical scholar, his appointment to Wittenberg had done much to enhance the university's prestige, and Luther had the greatest admiration for his ability. Melanchthon advised him on his translation of the New Testament, helped to give precise form to the expression of his doctrine and, despite being the younger man, did much to restrain Luther's pugnacity of thought and manner. At Augsburg in 1530, when he drew up the *Confessio Augustana* for discussion by the Diet, he was perhaps too ready, for Luther's peace of mind, to seek an accommodation with the Catholics, but Luther recognised that in the mild and scholarly Melanchthon he had an invaluable foil to his own very different character. 'I am rough, boisterous, stormy and altogether warlike, I am born to fight innumerable monsters and devils, to remove stems and stones, cut away thistles and thorns and clear away wild forests, but Master Philip comes along softly and gently with joy, according to the gifts which God has abundantly bestowed upon him.'

Although Wittenberg and Melanchthon remained enthusiastically loyal to Luther's cause, the German humanists soon lost their enthusiasm for him. They had made the initial mistake of assuming too readily that Luther was one of themselves. Erasmus, for example, had closely identified Luther's enemies with his own. 'I am deeply disturbed about the wretched Luther', he wrote when the Dominicans launched their first attack against him. 'If they pull this off no one will be able to bear their insolence. They will not be quiet until they have utterly ruined the study of languages and good letters'. Luther himself was not unaware that his actions had been misconstrued. Whereas the humanists' criticisms of the church had reflected their dislike of superstition or corruption, Luther's were the logical consequence of a radical theology. 'Others have attacked the life,' he wrote, 'I attack the doctrine'.

The humanists were alarmed to discover that Luther, for all his Greek scholarship, was no child of the Renaissance. His emphatic reliance on the sanctity of the individual conscience owed nothing to the self-confident humanist belief in the importance of the individual; its true derivation was to be found in the teachings of the German mystics and the concept of the 'inner light'. Moreover, while the men of the Renaissance proclaimed the dignity of man and the marriage of faith and reason, Luther remained an alien, tormented figure for whom reason was 'the devil's whore'.

The breach with the humanists came in 1525 when Luther published De Servo Arbitrio (On the Bondage of the Will). Mankind, he claimed, had no free will and salvation was impossible without the operation of God's own grace. 'Through His will which is immutable, eternal and indefectible, God foresees, foretells and realises all things. This principle is like a lightning flash, blasting and destroying human freedom absolutely.' This was too much for Erasmus. He had reserved his judgement, and thus endangered his own position while imperial and papal thunderbolts hurtled through the air, but on free will he could not be silent. 'If what is commanded be not in the power of everyone, all the numberless exhortations in the Scriptures and also all the promises, threatenings, expostulations, reproofs, asseverations, benedictions and maledictions, must of necessity stand coldly useless.' His conclusion was that 'God indeed preserves the ship but the mariner conducts it into harbour'.

Luther was not surprised to find himself deserted by the humanists but it was disconcerting for him to have to repudiate several of his original followers. Carlstadt, for example, had outstripped Luther in his radicalism. While Luther remained in hiding after Worms, Carlstadt managed to win control of the Wittenberg council and introduced his master's ideas pell-mell. He forbade the sale of indulgences and the singing of masses for the dead, he encouraged priests to marry and he administered communion in both kinds. In addition he imposed so puritanical a code of behaviour that the performance of works in observing it was made to seem more important than the faith which, as Luther had taught, could alone bring salvation. 'What a mess we are in with everybody doing something else' wrote Spalatin, and the elector too was angry: 'We have gone too fast. The common man has been incited to frivolity and no one has been edified.' It was a just comment and he forbade any more changes. Luther meanwhile returned to the city, instituted a more orderly reformation and expelled Carlstadt – who subsequently ended up in Switzerland, self-important, impetuous and troublesome to the end.

Carlstadt was less dangerous than the three laymen from Zwichau who arrived at Wittenberg claiming that the inspiration of the Holy Spirit made it no longer necessary for them to refer to the authority of the Bible. Having proclaimed the rule of the saints and the slaughter of the ungodly, they were expelled from Saxony at Luther's request and found their true vocation with Thomas Münzer, who had also plagued Luther at Wittenberg, in spurring on the peasants to murder and destruction during the Peasants' Revolt. Radical visionaries could be dispensed with and repudiated, but Zwingli was a different matter. As the leader of the Reformation in Zurich (see page 255) he preserved decency and order but repudiated the real presence. Luther stood firm. He met Zwingli at Marburg in 1529 at the request of those who hoped to prevent a rift in the reformed camp, but on this issue neither could give way and their churches remained separate.

As the humanists cut themselves adrift from him and the radicals compromised his doctrines, Luther also lost the support of most of the common people by his denunciation of the Peasants' Revolt. From this moment he entrusted the safety of his movement into the hands of the princes, the Very Christian Nobility of the German Nation to whom he had appealed in his pamphlet of 1520. In several of the towns, such as Augsburg, the work of the Wittenberg missionaries, reinforced by the stream of broadsheets from the printing press, led to something of a Lutheran landslide, which the authorities hastened to identify themselves with lest they be swept away. Throughout the empire as a whole, however, the success or failure of the Reformation became a matter for the princes to decide. Because of the particularist nature of the Holy Roman Empire Germany became a kind of draughtsboard; in the white squares, protected by such princely champions as the elector of Saxony or the landgrave of Hesse, Luther and his followers were free to move; in the black squares they faced arrest and execution. Why then, in view of the imperial ban, were there any white squares at all? What was the appeal of Lutheranism to so many of the German princes?

As a religious rebel Luther had the great advantage of being staunchly conservative in all other matters. Indeed he was almost out of touch with his time. He abominated capitalism and commerce (see page 204) and, ludicrous though it was at a time when Charles V threatened his life, he subscribed to a view of imperial authority which was wholly medieval. He advised Frederick the Wise for example that 'As a prince you should obey the emperor and offer no resistance', and he disliked the formation of the Schmalkaldic League, even though the survival of his movement depended upon it. In the course of time he followed the example of the princes themselves, and looked to each local ruler as the authority to whom obedience was due. He never idolised the princes, but he recognised the need for secular authority – 'The world cannot be ruled with a rosary' – and he preferred them to the *Ritter* or the rebellious peasants. Consequently he was ready to subject the Lutheran church in each state to the authority of the prince, thereby endorsing St Paul's advice that, 'the powers that be are ordained of God'.

Since the time was ripe for a reformation of some kind or other, it is not surprising that several princes were genuinely attracted by the doctrine. Frederick the Wise, though he saved Luther from destruction and allowed him to establish the Reformation in Wittenberg, never formally abandoned Catholicism, but his brother John (1525–35) and his nephew John Frederick (1536–54) became devoted Lutherans. So too, for all his faults, did Philip of Hesse, (see page 240). With many Lutheran princes, however, it is clear that the doctrine was enhanced by the material advantages to be derived from adopting it. All princes needed greater wealth to maintain their independence against their neighbours or against the emperor, and the doctrine of the priesthood of all believers provided a welcome opportunity to raise money by dispensing with monks and secularising their land. The long-term effects of this must not be exaggerated. Many princes were so short of money that they could not afford to retain the confiscated lands as a source of permanent revenue, but sold it off cheaply to their subjects. Others were controlled to some extent by the opinion of their own Estates, where there was often a powerful voice in favour of using monastic land for education and the relief of poverty. Philip of Hesse, for example, finally retained possession of 40 per cent of the land secularised in his landgraviate: in other states the princes had to settle for less. Nonetheless, whatever the percentage of his gains, the dissolution of the monasteries provided a prince at the very least with a valuable windfall.

Of much greater importance than money to many princes was the more effective jurisdiction which Lutheran princes enjoyed over their own subjects. 'Every man his own priest' did not, in Luther's view at any rate, convey the corollary 'every prince his own pope', but wherever the Reformation was established the church became subject to the princes' control. Luther disliked political interference with religion, since he believed in the unaided power of the Holy Spirit to direct the church, but in practical everyday situations he could not solve the problem of ecclesiastical authority without the aid of the princes. In a small region it was reasonable to invest authority with the local congregations, although there remained the danger of radicals gaining control as Carlstadt had done at Wittenberg in Luther's absence. For a larger area the Catholic answer was to appoint a bishop, but Luther could find no biblical authority for such a method of control and so, as a last resort, he looked to the prince or the civic authority to appoint a Visitor: from this it was a short step to the Erastian Church in which the temporal power enjoyed jurisdiction over the members of the clergy.

Whenever a prince adopted Lutheranism his subjects had to follow suit, but this caused surprisingly little discontent or upheaval. A prince's authority carried tremendous weight with his subjects – moreover there were very few obvious differences between the two confessions. Luther never liked to think that he had founded a new church but, rather, a reformed version of the old; the elimination of superstitious practices and abuses did not mean that the Catholic liturgy was abandoned. For most of the inhabitants of a small community the new pastor was but the old priest writ large; he still celebrated Mass, though he now did so in German and the sermon was given rather more prominence than before, but the structure of the Mass was unchanged and even the Elevation of the Host was retained by Luther until shortly before his death. What was novel was the emphasis on hymn singing. Luther loved music: 'It drives away the devil' he said 'and makes people sing', and it was he himself who wrote *Eine Feste Burg*, the battle hymn of the Lutheran Reformation.

By the time of Luther's death in 1546 the future of the Reformation was firmly in the hands of princes. Luther had never wholly forfeited public support in the south, where many congregations continued to meet in cities and remote country areas alike, but the future there lay with the Catholic dukes of Bavaria and Austria who were anxious to eradicate them. It was in the north, therefore, where Lutheranism was imposed by the members of the Schmalkaldic League, that the Reformation became entrenched, and it was here that Luther himself survived twenty-five years of public outlawry under the private protection of the electors of Saxony. In 1525 he had married a nun, Katherine von Bora, and for the rest of his life he enjoyed a happy marriage and an active career, settling disputes among theologians and princes alike by vigorous sermons, letters and publications. After 1546, however, without his energy and his personality to inspire and inform it, and with only the princes to determine its future, Lutheranism began to lose momentum, and the initiative passed to the more revolutionary reform movements being developed in Switzerland.

7

Protestantism and the Counter-reformation

The Swiss Reformers

THE political situation in Switzerland was similar to that in the
Holy Roman Empire, of which it had formerly been a part, in
that there was no central authority capable of enforcing a religious
settlement uniformly among the separate cantons. Moreover, the
cantons differed greatly in their character and outlook. Zurich,
Berne and Basle were relatively prosperous city-states, in complete
contrast to the forest cantons of Uri, Schwyz, Unterwalden, Zug,
Glarus and Appenzel, while Lucerne, Freiburg, Solothurn and
Schaffhausen were essentially communities of peasant farmers
grouped around small market towns. As a result, the Diet of the
Confederation passed resolutions rather than laws, and each
canton remained sovereign in matters affecting its own inhabitants.

In the early days of the Swiss Reformation the central figure
was Ulrich (Hudreych) Zwingli. He was born in 1484 at Wildhaus,
the son of the local bailiff and nephew of the priest; he studied
at Basle, Berne and Vienna, became proficient in both Greek
and Hebrew and returned to Switzerland to take Holy Orders.
He served for a time in the Italian wars as a chaplain to the
Swiss mercenaries – for which he was awarded a papal pension –
but eventually he revolted at the inhumanity of selling Swiss
lives to other princes, and in 1506 returned to a parish in the
forest canton of Glarus. When Glarus supported the French
alliance, which in Zwingli's eyes was the principal cause of the
traffic in mercenaries, he left in indignation for Zurich, where in
1518 he was appointed parish priest of the Great Minster.

By this time he had come to the conclusion that there was no
merit in works performed through faith. He knew of Luther's
theses of course, but in all probability his ideas had sprung

independently from his own studies of St Paul and St Augustine, from which Luther too had derived his inspiration. Apart from this the two men had nothing in common. Zwingli, a self-confident humanist in the Erasmian tradition and a cheerful man of the world, had experienced nothing of Luther's spiritual agony. They thus arrived at their doctrine by different emotional routes. Luther had been rescued from his dangerously morbid self-concern by the doctrine of justification by faith alone, to which he clung thereafter with emotional fervour as the answer to his own deep personal problems, and which he subsequently defended by denouncing all other authority but that of the Scriptures: Zwingli, in a more detached manner, began with the academic concept of the supremacy of the Scriptures and proceeded to deduce the rest from that. With much less passion than Luther he ultimately became the more radical of the two, but it was characteristic perhaps that his own public challenge to the sale of indulgences should have passed off with none of the furore which attended the Tetzel affair – since the indulgences were quietly withdrawn by order of the bishop of Constance.

In the space of the next six years – from 1519 to 1525 – Zwingli continued to develop ideas of an increasingly radical nature, but succeeded nonetheless in establishing them at Zurich in a manner which was wholly remarkable for its calmness, orderliness and quiet moderation. He exercised a discreet influence in the city council through the burgomaster, Hans Waldmann, and encouraged others by his sermons to initiate liturgical and other changes, but for his own part he avoided provocative or dramatic actions. In 1522, for example, a group of followers deliberately and with much publicity broke the Lenten fast but Zwingli, though he wrote and preached in their support, refrained from joining them. Similarly, after unsuccessfully petitioning the bishop of Constance in 1522 for permission for priests to marry, he himself took a wife but did not make the fact public until 1524. In 1523 the bishop was invited by the council to attend what he took to be an academic disputation at the Town Hall. To his indignation he discovered on arrival that he was faced with a public meeting conducted in the vernacular, at which Zwingli and his supporters had everything in their favour – including the open Bibles ostentatiously arrayed before them to which they were determined to appeal on every point.

Zwingli proposed 67 Articles which more or less followed Lutheran doctrine by rejecting the authority of the pope in favour of the exclusive authority of the Scriptures, by challenging the validity of monasticism and clerical celibacy, and by repudiating the value of the Lenten fasts, the worship of relics, the sale of indulgences and the invocation of the saints. There were also some interesting innovations. Zwingli rejected music, rather as Carlstadt had tried to do, as a sensual snare; moreover he denied the Real Presence and claimed that the Last Supper was a commemorative occasion only. The bishop could accept very little of this, but so moderate was the spirit, if not the content, of the debate that an open breach between himself and the council was averted. Subsequently the council declared that as the Articles had met with no effective answer they were to be adopted by the city, and in the quietest possible manner over the next twelve months the authority of the bishop and of the pope was gradually renounced.

The ease with which this happened is explained in part by the deliberate avoidance of animosity and of personal conflict by the city council on the one hand and by the bishop and the pope on the other: it is also possible that at this stage of the Italian wars the pope did not wish to prejudice his opportunities of raising Swiss mercenaries by a dispute with one of the cantons. Whatever the explanation, Zurich became a Protestant city without public scandal or excommunication. Daily services began to be replaced by what Zwingli termed 'prophesyings' – public readings of the Scriptures accompanied by detailed commentaries – and in 1525 the Mass was abandoned for the Zwinglian Lord's Supper. The repudiation of episcopal jurisdiction meant that the city council assumed the direction of religious affairs, a move which Zwingli endorsed. Unlike Luther he did not believe that the word of God could act unaided; indeed, like Carlstadt, he wanted to make the Church the arbiter of manners and morals, and for this to be done he required the closest co-operation between Church and State in 'one holy community'.

Although the papacy appeared to acquiesce in the Zwinglian Reformation, Zurich was afraid of its Catholic neighbours, and feared above all an alliance between the forest cantons and the Habsburgs. To forestall this, Zwingli advocated a preventive war, in alliance with Berne and Basle where the Reformation was beginning to be established. Fighting broke out in 1528, but the war proved indecisive until the Battle of Kappel in 1531 when Zwingli was killed and Zurich defeated. The Reformation however was not endangered. The Swiss cantons agreed to allow each canton to determine its own confession – an intelligent anticipation of the Augsburg principle of *cujus regio, ejus religio* – and in Heinrich Bullinger the city enjoyed an able and scholarly successor to Zwingli, whose gifts as a mediator were in demand throughout the Protestant cities of Switzerland and the empire.

Zwingli's influence had already spread northwards to Strasburg but the city was very much a refuge for Anabaptists and other radicals who disputed his identification of church and state. In 1527 the city came under the influence of Martin Bucer, a radical theologian of authoritarian temper. He shared Zwingli's taste for ecclesiastical discipline and expelled the radicals who rejected all authority save their own, but he insisted that the Church alone had power to enforce its moral control. In practice the Strasburg council worked in close harmony with Bucer, but in Bucer's *Commentary on St Matthew* (1527), he affirmed that the Church was necessarily independent of the state. He also maintained that within the Holy Roman Empire, of which Strasburg was a member, the emperor had no right to attack the Church, and that if he did so the lower or 'intermediate' political authorities, be they princes, magistrates, Estates or councils, had both a moral responsibility and a political right to resist him. Bucer's theory proved to be of considerable importance for other 'intermediate authorities', since it justified rebellion on moral grounds without giving encouragement to Anabaptism or anarchy.

Bucer's doctrine and his manner of administering affairs were to have considerable influence on John Calvin who came to Strasburg in 1538 at the age of 29, and spent the next three years in the city. Calvin had been born at Noyon, the son of a lawyer and educated at the College de Montaigu in Paris. He became a classical scholar and attached himself to the fringe of the humanist circle but, to please his father, he took up law at Orleans in 1528. Three years later when his father died, leaving him a reasonable inheritance, Calvin was free to return to Paris where he tried, vainly, to make his reputation with a commentary on Seneca's *De Clementia*. The humanists with whom he associated were in the Erasmian tradition, interested in theology and passionately concerned with the abuses then current in the church, and Calvin shared their views, until quite suddenly his whole outlook was altered: 'By a sudden conversion God subdued and reduced to docility my soul'. This left him painfully aware of his own sinfulness, but with equal speed and with none of the prolonged agony of Martin Luther he realised what he had to do. 'As if by a sudden ray of light I recognised into what an abyss of errors I had hitherto been plunged. Now, therefore, O Lord I did what was my duty and fearlessly I followed in Thy footsteps.' By this he meant that he became a Protestant. It was a dangerous moment to do so, since Francis I had just begun to enforce the laws against heresy (see page 320), and Calvin had to flee, first to Basle and then to Ferrara, where a group of emigré humanists and reformers had established themselves. There he wrote his *Institutes of the Christian Religion*. He returned to Basle for the publication of his *Institutes*, which was first published in 1536 but destined to be revised and expanded many times throughout Calvin's lifetime.

In the year his *Institutes* first appeared, Calvin made a swift visit to Paris and then decided to attach himself to Martin Bucer at Strasburg. He found the frontier closed, however, since war had broken out again between Francis I and Charles V, and so he made a detour to the south, arriving in Geneva at a moment of crisis in the city's history. For several years after the defeat of Zurich and the death of Zwingli, Berne had aspired to primacy among the Swiss Protestant cantons and had tried to bring Geneva under its control. Geneva, however, was being fought over by its city council, by its bishop and by the neighbouring duke of Savoy. Missionaries from Berne, among them a powerful French preacher, Guillaume Farel, succeeded in winning over the city council, and with military aid from Berne expelled the bishop and drove away the duke. The city then declared its independence, resolving, 'to live according to the Gospels and the word of God, as has been used since the abolition of the Mass and as is now practiced among us'. This was not easy however, since many rival factions appeared, and Farel in particular felt his position to be in danger. The arrival of Calvin, whose *Institutes* he admired, seemed to him to be most fortuitous and he invited him to share in the government of Geneva. Calvin was horrified. A literary man, a scholar rather than a preacher, with no taste for public life, he shrank from Farel's offer until the older man, with the vigour of an Old Testament prophet, convinced him that God would have it so.

Their partnership did not last long. Many of those who had helped to free Geneva from its bishop and from the duke of Savoy refused to accept the strict regimen which Farel required of them. These 'libertines' as Calvin called them won a great deal of support, not only at home but also in Berne where there was no desire to see the development of an independent church in Geneva. As a result they won the election of 1538: the new council imposed a Bernese liturgy and rejected Farel's demand for the excommunication of, 'men who were out of harmony with the union of the faithful and sowing dissension among them'. As a result the two reformers were banished from the city and Calvin, much relieved, was able to complete his journey to Strasburg. Three years later, however, the council asked him to return. Berne's influence had grown too great, 'libertinage' had gone too far and there was danger of a reaction towards Roman Catholicism. Calvin was reluctant to leave Strasburg where he had been extremely happy, but the appeal to his conscience could not be resisted: 'I submit my mind, bound and fettered in the obedience of God' he wrote, and returned to Geneva in 1541 to serve the city until his death in 1564.

Calvin reorganised the Genevan Church as an autonomous body with authority vested in four special Orders; pastoral care and preaching were assigned to the pastors, teaching to the doctors – 'We will call them the order of the schools' – poor relief to the deacons and moral discipline to the elders. This last assignment was accorded great importance and Calvin declared that 'no Church could exist unless a fixed rule of life were established, such as is made known to us by the Word of God'. His problem, however, was how to discipline the elders. Calvin's powers were extremely limited since for more than a decade after his return he had to work with, and all too often against, the city council. It was this authority which appointed the elders. As a result Calvin could secure the enforcement of laws against general licence and disorder; he could even replace the taverns with regulated drinking houses – where consumption was limited and Bibles were read aloud – until they lost money; but he could not secure jurisdiction over the private lives of the more important families. His main opponents were Ami Perrin and his father-in-law Francis Favre, who won control of the council in 1549. They valued Calvin's general influence in the city, but did not wish personally to be subject to his rules. Moreover they had reason to oppose his policy of offering citizenship to many foreign exiles, and to French refugees in particular, since this provided Calvin with an expanding base of political support.

These were years of frustration and weariness for Calvin, until the situation was resolved by the unaccountable appearance in the city of a notorious Spanish heretic Servetus, who denied the doctrine of the Trinity. Calvin wanted him burnt at the stake, the Perrins sought to protect him, and when Calvin finally triumphed, the whole balance of power was tipped in his favour. The Perrins were discredited and fled the city in 1555 leaving Calvin virtually in sole charge. In the last nine years of his life he admitted over 5,000 exiles to citizenship, and used the authority of the council to enforce the consistory's regulation of private morality – even private entertainment and manners of dress – by means of public rebuke, fines, tongue piercing, flogging, exile and even by death. It was a harsh code, harshly enforced, yet it proved to be remarkably acceptable to the majority who found positive advantage in having a code of behaviour to obey. Though Luther might have been alarmed by this apparent revival of the importance of works, John Knox called Geneva 'the most perfect school of Christ that ever was in earth since the days of the Apostles'. It was also a school in the more formal sense too, providing an excellent programme of primary and secondary education, crowned by an academy of some distinction under Theodore Beza.

Under Calvin's vigorous leadership Geneva eclipsed Berne and Zurich, and even Wittenberg, as the centre of the Protestant cause. The basic tenets of Lutheranism were retained. Calvin believed with Luther in justification by faith, the priesthood of all believers, the authority of the scriptures and the omnipotent power of divine grace; he denied, as Luther did, the validity of indulgences, of celibacy, of pilgrimages, and of all sacraments not instituted by Christ; he used the vernacular as Luther did and shared his love of music. On other matters there were differences of emphasis. Calvin rejected the scholastic complexity of consubstantiation, but his admission of a spiritual presence in the Eucharist divorced him also from Zwingli's wholly commemorative doctrine. Moreover, whereas Luther denied free will, Calvin concentrated on the other side of the coin by preaching predestination in all its rigour – 'The eternal decree of God whereby he has determined His will in respect of every man. For He did not create them all alike but ordained some to eternal life, the rest to eternal damnation'. Though Calvin agreed that there was something disturbing about God's eternal decision (*decretum quidem horribile*), he nonetheless found it a source of spiritual comfort, since it freed him from the nagging moments of doubt which periodically overcame Luther, and left him serenely aware that he was helping to fulfil God's pre-ordained plan.

Both Luther and Calvin were in many respects socially conservative, despite Calvin's less respectful attitude to secular authority. Luther was out of touch with his age when he denounced trade as well as usury (see page 204) but Calvin, though he lived in a more commercial environment, refused to allow Genevan banks to adopt the interest rates demanded in Catholic Genoa and Lutheran Augsburg. He insisted on a limit of five per cent and enforced a rigorous control over profiteering. Where the two leaders differed was not so much in their view of what was desirable in human behaviour, but whether or not it should be regulated by the Church. Luther was reluctant to supply a code of behaviour lest he encourage a revival of the doctrine of justification by works. Calvin, by a paradox, restored works to importance by teaching that God's Elect were obliged to show themselves worthy of their calling by the manner of their lives. So that they should never be in doubt, therefore, he supplied them with a code to follow – and it was perhaps the puritanical element latent in Calvinism which led him to require that the code should apply also to those who were not of the Elect, lest they offend the Elect by the scandal of their lives.

Of considerable importance was Calvin's more positive concept of the role of the Church and its relation with the state. For Luther the Church was not an institution to mediate between man and God but a community of people bound together by faith. Although Calvin would never have dreamed of challenging this doctrine of the priesthood of all believers, he distinguished the invisible Church – the transcendent spiritual community of all God's Elect throughout the ages – from the visible Church, manifest in history and serving as a formal institution to train and govern the Elect. To perform its role adequately, therefore, the Church could not accept direction by princes or elected magistrates: following Bucer, Calvin taught the separation of function between church and state but, in practice, by winning control for the consistory over the council, he established a theocracy in Geneva, where the magistrates served as the agents of God and of His Church. Outside Geneva, however, in a world where Calvinists did not control the secular authority, Calvin reluctantly adopted Bucer's view that, to prevent the persecution of God's Elect, the secondary or 'intermediate' authorities might take arms against superior powers, rather as the City Council of Geneva had once done against the duke of Savoy.

In France, Scotland and the Netherlands it is true that the spread of Calvinism was accompanied by social turmoil and political upheaval, and attempts have been made to account in political and social terms for the success of the new church. Some have suggested that an ambitious middle-class responded warmly to Calvin's frank recognition of commercial activity, while its members enjoyed the opportunity for self-importance afforded in church affairs by the authority given to the elders. It has also been suggested that a discontented proletariat adopted Calvinism to profit not only from the spoils of image-breaking and church-wrecking but also from the subsequent breakdown of order which made possible the looting of grain warehouses. Although the iconoclasm in the Netherlands must be seen against a background of two years of exceptional poverty, unemployment and hunger (see page 361), and although the great urban families dominated the Calvinist provinces of the Union of Utrecht, neither explanation will serve as a general rule. The middle classes throughout Europe were no more given to Calvinism than to Roman Catholicism, and against the Calvinist burghers of Amsterdam, La Rochelle and Heidelberg must be set their Catholic counterparts in Brussels, Paris and Munich. As for poverty, no region of Europe was spared in this respect, and many of the poorest in France, Spain, Italy and Germany remained devoutly Catholic.

The only group of any importance which may properly be termed self-seeking in its support of Calvinism was the lesser nobility, a class which was aggrieved by the extension of royal authority and frightened by the consequences of inflation. Many of its members seized upon Calvinism as an opportunity to profit from the secularisation of church property and hoped for a new deal from a new order. Such men were perceptively described by the French chancellor, L'Hôpital: 'Several take shelter beneath the cloak of religion even though they have no God and are more atheistic than religious; among them are lost souls who have consumed and wasted their all, and only survive on the troubles of the realm and the possessions of other men'. Yet even this point does not bear detailed examination. In France, for example, it was not the self-interest of lesser nobles which mattered so much as the genuine conversion of leading members of the Bourbon and Montmorency families (see page 322). In the Netherlands it is true that the nobles of the compromise (see page 361) were down-at-heel but it was the great lords of Scotland who joined with John Knox to drive out Mary of Guise.

It is abundantly clear that different particular factors affected the spread of Calvinism in different particular states, but two overriding factors are apparent. Calvinism could not spread successfully against the opposition of an efficient government, as in Spain or Bavaria – or, for that matter, in Lutheran Saxony. Secondly, when a government, as in France or the Netherlands, was unable to silence the Calvinist missionaries these achieved most of their converts by the power of their preaching. The missionaries were highly trained, their rhetoric swayed mass audiences and if they did not always convey the pure essence of Calvinism they successfully exploited the latent anti-clericalism of the crowds and aroused them to anger at the inadequacies of the unreformed Catholic church. After years of neglect by priest and bishop the people readily responded to those who spoke with enthusiasm, authority and direct simplicity about judgement and salvation.

For those converted, the attractions of the new faith were easily defined. It was a highly confident movement, taking its text from St Paul: 'If God is for us, who can be against us?' Moreover it offered a more coherent body of doctrine than the other Protestant sects: Lutherans indeed sometimes felt uneasily that they were closer in spirit to Rome than to the radical centres of Zurich, Strasburg and Geneva, and the confusion in their minds was to be skilfully exploited by the Jesuits.

Calvinists, furthermore, were strengthened by a well-ordered theology, the product of a French lawyer's able mind, which separated them from all other confessions and provided them in addition with a firmly regulated manner of life. Wherever congregations were established, they were linked together with their nearest neighbours, and all of them, in whatever country they might be found, maintained the closest contact with Geneva from which they received a constant flow of instructions and guidance. Above all, they enjoyed the firm conviction that they were predestined to be saved. Consequently, they not only refused to compromise with their enemies, but were better able to withstand persecution by them. Whereas Lutheranism became almost exclusively a German movement, dependent for its survival on the goodwill of German princes, Calvinism spread throughout France, Scotland and the Netherlands and parts of England and Germany, winning converts and threatening governments – the most vigorous, the most highly organised, the most disruptive and the most successful missionary force of the Reformation.

The Foundations of the Catholic Reformation

The Catholic Reformation was not simply a Counter-reformation, a deliberate reaction to the challenge posed by Luther, Zwingli and Calvin, but the response of Catholics themselves to the unhappy condition of their Church at the end of the fifteenth century. Consequently, it began long before Luther was appointed to Wittenberg, and it was not until the second half of the sixteenth century that it became preoccupied with combatting the spread of Protestantism. Nor was it a coherent movement, since it represented the spontaneous efforts of many individuals, or groups of individuals, who acted coincidentally but independently of each other to remedy the inadequacies and the corruption within their Church. Its origins were various and varied. They can be found in the *devotio moderna* of the Netherlands, or the reformed Augustinian canons of Windesheim, in the diocesan reforms of Cisneros, in the witty and scholarly criticism of Erasmus and the humanists, or in Savonarola's impassioned denunciation of clerical greed, in the revival of Thomist studies by Cajetan or in the attention focused on the writings of St Augustine and St Paul.

One important characteristic of the Catholic Reformation was the emergence in Italy of new or reformed orders who made it their business to operate in the world rather than withdraw into closed communities. The Capuchins, for example, a reformed branch of the Franciscans, made a deliberate attempt in the spirit of their founder to meet the spiritual and material poverty of the Italian working class. Their lack of worldliness made many clergy suspicious of them, and their reputation was almost destroyed when one of their leaders, Bernardino Ochino, became a convert to Lutheranism, but the austerity of their lives won the respect of the masses, and the direct simplicity of their preaching made them an evangelising force of great potency. Others who tried to combine the ordered life of the religious with a missionary desire to operate directly in the world were the new orders of clerks regular; they were neither monks nor friars but communities of secular priests who lived together under monastic vows, and whose life was devoted to action rather than contemplation. The Barnabites, for example, founded in Milan in 1533, combined a strict penitential life with a practical concern for the education of the poor, while the Somaschi, from Somasco near Bergamo, established orphanages.

Rather different in their long-term effect were the Theatines, founded in 1524 by two contrasting characters, Gaetano di Tiene, a gentle saintly priest who was eventually canonised as St Cajetan, and Pietro Caraffa, a vigorous, impatient and relentless churchman who became Pope Paul IV. Their purpose was to serve and to reform the world, but they operated in a rather special manner. Though each member lived in strict obedience to the vow of poverty, most came from wealthy families, whose wealth sustained the Order and removed the need for begging alms. There was also a certain self-conscious aristocracy of the spirit among them. Candidates for admission were rigorously tested, and membership was deliberately restricted to the few whose devotion and sense of service were beyond doubt. Not surprisingly the Order, because of its social connections, its spiritual prestige and its reforming zeal, became a nursery from which were recruited many bishops of the Catholic Reformation.

The two founders of the Theatines also shared in the membership of a long-established and pious confraternity, the Oratory of Divine Love, which without the formality of taking vows brought together about sixty priests and laymen to perform the services of the Church which were so negligently performed elsewhere. Its members were men of singular devotion and scholarship, including the humanist Jacopo Sadoleto, Reginald Pole from England and a Venetian noble, Gasparo Contarini, whose sympathy with Luther's idealism took him to Regensburg in 1541 in the hope of seeking a genuine settlement. Paul III was so impressed by their quality that he appointed six of them cardinals between 1536 and 1542, and commissioned the Oratory to prepare a scheme of church reform. The report, *De emendenda ecclesi*, which appeared in 1538, was brutally outspoken; it condemned the role of the papacy in the sixteenth century and singled out for particular criticism its preoccupation with raising money: 'And this is the source, Holy Father, from which as from the Trojan Horse, every abuse has broken forth into the Church. The first thing needed is that the laws should be observed and no dispensation should be granted save on the grounds of strict necessity. But still more important is it that the Vicar of Christ should never consider himself at liberty to use the powers of the Keys (i.e. of St Peter) for gain.' It then proceeded to identify all the abuses current in the Church so perceptively and so abrasively that the report was never published.

A very different order and one much opposed by Caraffa, since it presumed on one occasion to criticise his Theatines, was the Society of Jesus. Ignatius Loyola, its founder, was born in 1491 and after serving as a page to Ferdinand of Aragon, fought for Charles V in Italy. In 1521 he was so badly wounded that he had to spend many months in hospital. For want of other reading he picked up some devotional works to pass the time, and was so profoundly moved by these that he left hospital to go as a pilgrim to the Image of the Blessed Vision at Montserrat in Aragon, despite the fact that his wounds had left him permanently crippled. He then retired as a solitary to Manresa where for nearly a year he tried in vain to achieve a sense of personal salvation by a life of rigorous austerity and self-denial. He was saved from total despair by a mystic experience in which he felt himself miraculously enabled to distinguish the promptings of the devil from the voice of God; once he had identified the devil as the author of all his agonies of remorse, he immediately took his salvation for granted.

Unlike Luther, for example, Loyola could not attribute the overwhelming conviction of deliverance which he experienced to any particular Scriptural authority. It was rather the direct result of a personal and mystic vision of the truth. 'He thought to himself' wrote his colleague Lainez, 'that, even if no Scriptures had been given us to teach the truths of faith, he would nevertheless have determined to give up life itself for them solely on account of what he had seen with the soul.' This did not mean that he wanted to dispense with the Scriptures, nor indeed with the mediatory role of the Church. He valued above everything else the celebration of the Mass as the richest experience of communion with God, and he sought to express his mystic devotion in practical terms. In 1523 he made a long and difficult pilgrimage to Jerusalem and then, recognising that an uneducated soldier was of little use to the Church, he returned to Spain to study at the universities of Alcala and Salamanca. Throughout this time he felt compelled to preach in the streets, and many people came to him for spiritual direction, but the mystic phraseology he employed caused him to be identified with the *alumbrados* (see page 220) and in 1527 he was arrested by the Inquisition. Although he was quickly released he decided to avoid further trouble by moving to Paris where he entered the College de Montaigu – which by a strange coincidence had also been the college of Erasmus and Calvin.

Although he was not a gifted scholar, this 37 year-old ex-soldier exercised such tremendous authority over his fellow-students, that several of them were to follow him for the rest of their lives. In 1535 Francisco Xavier, Diego Lainez, Alfonso Salmeron from Spain, Simon Rodriguez from Portugal, Pierre Lefèvre from Savoy and other Frenchmen and Spaniards joined him in taking vows of poverty and chastity in preparation for a private crusade to the Holy Land. When they discovered that the eastern Mediterranean was in a ferment because of warfare between Venice and the Turks, they moved around Italy for several months before finally settling at Rome. Their practice of frequent communion and their regular preaching aroused suspicion and resentment, but no one denied the value of their work among the sick and the poor. Pope Paul III himself heard of their reputation and was impressed by their desire to be of particular service to the papacy. In 1540, therefore, he allowed them to form a new order, the Society of Jesus, and its members vowed obedience not only to their elected general Loyola, but also to the pope and his successors – 'To go without demur to any country where they might send us, whether to the Turks or other infidels in India or elsewhere, to any heretics or schismatics as well as to the faithful.'

One of the most remarkable features of the Jesuit Order was its rigorous programme of training. New members had to serve a novitiate lasting two years, in which they worked in hospitals, begged for alms and went on pilgrimage. In addition, they followed a programme of *Spiritual Exercises* designed by Loyola. Although the *Exercises* were not published until 1548, Loyola had been developing them since his own experiences at Manresa. They represented a series of meditations through which the novice progressed, slowly and thoroughly, under the guidance of a skilled director. Their purpose was revealed by their full title of *Spiritual Exercises for overcoming oneself and for regulating one's life without being swayed by any inordinate attachment*. They involved a process of self-examination and of confession, recognition of God's glory and righteousness, meditation upon the life of Christ and especially of His passion, and contemplation of the joys of Heaven. They did not, however, stop at this peak of mystical exalta-tion, but led the novice to prepare himself for total obedience to the service of Christ through obedience to the Order and the service of mankind. So important were they in the spiritual development of the Jesuit that he renewed the *Exercises* every year of his life.

After the novitiate there succeeded the scholasticate, a period of study lasting, according, to circumstances, from five to twelve years. It was a demanding course designed to prepare the Jesuit for the three primary tasks of his Order, preaching, teaching and the hearing of confession. The vows of poverty and obedience were then renewed and the Jesuit began his work in the world. A very small proportion of them – one in fifty – went on to take the four vows taken by the founders in 1540, but for all of them obedience to the Order was the keynote of their training and of their work. Their purpose, as the *Exercises* put it in vivid terms was, 'in order that we may be altogether of the same mind and in conformity with the Church herself, if she shall have defined anything to be black which to our eyes appears to be white, we ought in like manner to pronounce it to be black'. For men of considerable intellectual ability, seasoned by up to a dozen years of university studies, this degree of intellectual obedience demanded the greatest test of self-denial and humility, compared with which obedience to orders directing them to journey to Japan or to Elizabethan England was a relatively simple matter. The significance of this was well expressed by Loyola in his *Letter on the Virtue of Obedience*: 'We may easily suffer ourselves to be surpassed by other religious Orders in fasting, watching and other austerities of diet and clothing, which they practise according to their rule, but in true and perfect obedience and the abnegation of our will and judgement, I greatly desire, most dear brethren, that those who serve God in this society should be conspicuous.'

Their main sphere of operations was initially confined to Italy and the Iberian peninsula. There they established a reputation for preaching and hearing confession, for pastoral work and for winning the ear of influential laymen. Rodriguez in Portugal attracted the attention of King John and was entrusted with the education of the heir to the throne, Sebastian. It was from Portugal, moreover, that Xavier travelled to Goa and thence to the Moluccas, Japan and China, where he died in 1552. In Spain the Jesuits were less well received. The special privileges granted by the papacy to the Order to enable it to act more effectively in the world – absolving its members for example from the need to meet together for the common recitation of the offices, or from securing the permission of local diocesan authorities before preaching or hearing confession – along with their international character, aroused a great deal of jealousy and nationalist resentment. The Dominicans, who were already entrenched in the Spanish Inquisition and in the universities, were not disposed to abdicate in their favour, and the Spanish court was suspicious enough of Rome's foreign policies to be equally suspicious of those who seemed to be the agents of the Vatican. Nonetheless the extraordinarily high quality of Jesuit preaching and scholarship could not be gainsaid, and the Order's first triumph in Spain came about when Francisco Borgia, duke of Gandia and viceroy of Catalonia, set the seal of his approval upon the Order by establishing the first independent Jesuit university at Gandia.

This event turned out to have important consequences for the Order, prompting Loyola to think out afresh his whole policy in the sphere of education. So far he had concentrated on training his own members; now he began to conceive of education as a means of winning over the world at large. More colleges were founded and places were offered to those outside the Order: in this way the Jesuits became a powerful force in secondary and university education throughout Europe, although the full curriculum, the *Ratio Studiorum*, was not defined until later in the sixteenth century. So excellent was the quality of the teaching that the colleges attracted pupils from many of the most influential families in Europe, and trained them, if not for entry to the Order, at least for the defence of Roman Catholic doctrine. This development led in turn to the training of missionaries specifically prepared to meet the challenge of Protestantism. The *Collegium Germanicum* in Rome sent out missionaries into the Holy Roman Empire, and Pierre Lefèvre, who led the attack, did much to strengthen the resolve of Catholic princes to have no truck with Lutheranism. The dukes of Bavaria, for example, helped them to establish colleges at Ingolstadt and Munich, and Lefèvre's pupil, the Dutchman Peter Canisius, won renown for his work in the Habsburg territories. With indefatigable energy he travelled 1500 miles a year, and his *Summary of Christian Doctrine* became one of the most famous books of the Catholic Reformation.

When Loyola died in 1556, fourteen provinces had been created and the Order counted 1500 members; eleven years later on the death of his successor, Lainez, four more provinces had been added and the membership had risen to 3500. Even more important was the fact that the Jesuits were now becoming almost totally committed to what had been originally only one aspect of their work – the attack on heresy. By mid-century the champions of Catholic reform had discovered for themselves a special rôle as the 'shock troops of the Counter-reformation'.

The Papacy and the Counter-reformation

The Catholic Reformation was inspired by a fervent determination to remedy the weaknesses which corrupted the Church and offended its most devoted adherents: it was not designed as a missionary enterprise against Protestantism. Heresy, of course, was an evil to be dealt with in whatever form it manifested itself, whether among the Moriscos, the *alumbrados*, the anti-trinitarians, or the Hussites, but only as part of a more general pastoral concern · to root out blasphemy, superstition, ignorance and indifference. Little or no attention was paid to Protestantism before the first Jesuit missionary went to Germany, and the concern of the new Orders had been to reform and to strengthen their Church by reaffirming the pastoral role of the priesthood, and by reasserting the value of the sacraments and services of the Church, rather than to prepare it specifically for an anti-Lutheran crusade. The two matters eould not, of course, be separated when the full extent of the Protestant challenge to Rome came to be appreciated, but those things which had served to bring about a measure of Catholic Reformation could not of themselves bear fruit in an effective counter-attack on Protestantism. For this it was necessary that the piecemeal and unrelated efforts of the different orders be mobilised under a central direction, and this by the very nature of the Catholic Church could be supplied only by the papacy itself.

Such an event seemed at best unlikely in view of the nature of the Renaissance popes. Their reputation for immorality, their cultivated enthusiasm for the fine arts, their perpetual involvement in warfare and diplomacy and their all-consuming anxiety to augment their finances, had perverted the spiritual character of their office. They knew moreover that nothing effective could be done unless they summoned to their aid a General Council of the Church, and this they feared would represent a greater threat to their authority than any yet presented by Lutheranism (see page 147). With the election of Adrian of Utrecht in 1522, however, the succession of politicians, warriors and connoisseurs was suddenly broken. The austerity of the new pope's life, while it alarmed his court, gave promise of a new type of leadership from Rome, but Adrian was an old man at his election and with his death a few months later the opportunity of finding a successor of similar piety was passed over. Instead the papacy was given to Clement VII (1523–34) who exerted all his efforts to manipulate to his own advantage the struggle for power in Italy between Francis I and Charles V. The Sack of Rome, at which he nearly lost his life, left him a virtual prisoner of the emperor, and his one consolation was to evade his captor's demands for a General Council, which he knew would depose him for being of illegitimate birth.

Clement's successor, Paul III (1534–49) was another worldly figure; a humanist and a patron of the arts, he was also the father of illegitimate children whose promotion in the world was a matter of great concern to him – so much so that his son, Farnese, was made duke of Parma, and two teenage grandsons were appointed cardinals. Yet Paul's pontificate from 1534 to 1549 proved to be a period of considerable reform. Paul approved and indeed en-

couraged the foundation of the Barnabites and the Society of
Jesus, he maintained a close connection with the Oratory of Divine
Love and went so far as to commission its members to prepare a
scheme for reforming the Church. Unhappily he dared not accept
its findings. Contarini, whom he admired sufficiently to appoint a
cardinal, despite his being a layman, urged him to reform some of
the fiscal departments at an estimated cost of between 20,000 to
30,000 ducats a year, but the revenues of the Papal State had been
so depleted by the Italian wars that Paul was more dependent than
ever on the sale of dispensations, indulgences and offices.

A more serious dispute arose between Paul and Contarini
when the cardinal went to Regensburg in 1541 (see page 243)
to seek some kind of settlement with the Lutherans. Paul was
angry at the thought of any accommodation with heresy, and from
their conflict there emerged a novel element in the Catholic
Reformation which can properly be identified as the first indication
of a Counter-reformation. Caraffa, despite his close association
with Contarini in the Oratory, supported the pope's refusal to
have any truck with heretics, and when Paul decided in 1542 to
revive the Roman Inquisition – it had lapsed in the previous
century – Caraffa was appointed one of the first Inquisitors. So
keen was he to take action that he furnished his house at his own
expense with a private prison in order to interrogate suspects,
and the full vigour of his relentless pursuit was soon evident.
Caraffa directed his attack against the important and the well-
connected, since heresy was obviously more dangerous in such
quarters than among the ignorant poor; it also suited his particular
nature to conduct the kind of campaign which created scandal
in high places. There was scarcely any trace of Lutheranism to be
found in Italy but, not to be outdone, Caraffa mounted a witch-
hunt against anyone whose unguarded statements about papal
authority or the efficacy of indulgences exposed them by association to the charge of heresy.

Like many other authors of witch-hunts, Caraffa was inordinately
fortunate to stumble by chance upon a genuine and highly-placed
victim, Bernardino Ochino. This head of the Capuchin Order
had been attracted by Luther's doctrine of justification by faith –
as indeed had Contarini – and he finally declared himself a
Lutheran at the time when Caraffa's investigations were getting
under way. His flight to Germany, and that of several other Italian
bishops and priors whose views were not wholly orthodox, gave

Caraffa the excuse he needed to launch a full-scale campaign against the Italian universities. He was able to call upon the help of the Spanish governments in Italy, and because of the long tradition of private feuds and factions in many cities there was no lack of malicious accusations by enemies and rivals to keep Caraffa's agents fully occupied. The University of Modena disbanded itself in 1546 as a result of his investigations, and academic freedom was compromised throughout Italy.

By accident or design, therefore, Paul III had helped to establish the fundamental bases of the Counter-reformation – the first official enquiry into the weaknesses of the Church without which no reform could ever be achieved at Rome, the Inquisition to seek out heresy in Catholic lands, and the Society of Jesus to challenge it abroad. The next step was to summon a General Council of the Church. Paul had reluctantly promised to do so on his election to the papacy, but to his secret delight the prolongation of the Habsburg-Valois wars had made it impossible for many years to summon an international assembly of this kind. In 1545, however, Europe was at last at peace and Charles V insisted that the council meet without further delay at Trent, an Italian town within the Holy Roman Empire where he could keep an eye on its delibera-tions. Charles's intentions were perfectly clear. The council was to reform the abuses of which the Lutherans complained, and draw up a doctrinal statement acceptable to both parties: once this was done he could then hope for peace within the empire. This was the last thing Paul wanted to happen. Reform by a General Council would inevitably compromise his finances, and a settlement with Lutheranism, his authority. Much depended, therefore, on the resolution of a procedural matter. If the council members voted 'by nations' as at Constance, the pope would be left at the mercy of the Spanish and German delegates directed by Charles V; if they voted individually then, of the 270 bishops in attendance at Trent, the 187 Italians would represent a permanent majority only too susceptible to papal cajolery and bribes. By securing the adoption of the latter course, Paul ensured a greater measure of control over the council, and was assisted throughout by his three legates, Reginald Pole, the future Julius III, and the future Marcellus II, who steered the discussions so skilfully that papal authority was not brought into question.

Paul's major triumph at Trent was to secure a restatement of Catholic doctrine which made compromise with Lutheranism impossible. Luther's teaching on free will and justification by faith was rejected categorically, the validity of the seven sacraments was reaffirmed, and the tradition of the Church was held to be of equal authority with the Scriptures. The price the legates had to pay for this resounding victory was an agreement on certain reforms, none of which really threatened Paul's position. Bishops and priests were ordered to preach regularly, and if a bishop was absent from his diocese without good cause for more than six months he was to forfeit one quarter of his revenues. Since this at the worst could only mean non-residence on half pay, the penalty was not over-severe. Paul himself agreed to order all his cardinals to give up any diocese held in plurality – though not without offering them some private compensation.

For Charles V the reforms were too insubstantial, the doctrinal statement too exclusive, and in high dudgeon he offered the Lutherans at Augsburg an interim settlement of his own (see page 244) in a vain attempt to heal the schism. Meanwhile, when the pope withdrew the council to Bologna on the pretext of plague in Trent, Charles forbade his bishops to go and the first sessions ended inconclusively. The council did not meet again during Paul's pontificate, but his successor, Julius III (1550–5) recalled it to Trent in 1551. Charles V insisted that the Lutherans be represented though it soon became clear, even to Charles, that their contribution to the debates on penance and transubstantiation did nothing to reconcile the two sides. In any case the council dispersed in alarm after the emperor's flight from Germany.

After Julius III and his successor Marcellus had both died in 1555, Caraffa was elected Paul IV. In many ways he seemed to be the most obvious candidate to lead the Counter-reformation, but he was now seventy-nine and there was more than a touch of hysteria about his determination to root out unorthodoxy. Heresy indeed became identified with opposition of any kind to his views: Philip II was excommunicated because of his intervention in Italy, Reginald Pole, one of the legates at Trent, fled for his life from Paul's irrational hatred, and the talented cardinal Morone, one of the best negotiators in the curia, was imprisoned for being too accommodating to opinions other than the pope's. The Inquisition of course was more active than ever, and, in the Dominican Michele Ghislieri, Paul found a man of even greater severity than himself to direct its operations. Special campaigns were launched in Venice, where Paul had good reason to suspect the influence of foreign merchants, and in Ferrara, whose duchess, Renée, had made her court a refuge for Protestant exiles from France and Germany. More sinister, however, and less justifiable was the renewed attack on the universities when, in order to strengthen its control, the Inquisition compiled an Index of prohibited books – the 'list of authors and books against which the Roman and universal Inquisition orders all Christians to be on their guard under the threat of censure and punishment'. The works of Erasmus and of other Catholic humanists were banned outright, sixty-one Italian printers had their licences rescinded, and the enforcement of the Index destroyed the little that was left of academic vitality in Italy.

There was a reaction of sorts after Paul's death in 1559. The Inquisition was sacked by the Roman mob, and the college of cardinals, seeking a pope of more moderate character, elected Pius IV (1559–65). He was not a strong theologian, however, and he left the defence of orthodoxy to the Inquisition whose power was therefore unabated; on the other hand he released Morone from prison and sent him to negotiate with the leading representatives of the French, German and Spanish Churches the terms on which the General Council was to be recalled to Trent in 1562. Without Morone's diplomatic skill the Council would have ended with the national churches going their own way independently of the pope and of each other. Ferdinand I wanted to follow his brother's policy of finding common ground between the Catholics and the Protestants, and he had a powerful ally in the Cardinal of Lorraine who was seeking some accord with the Huguenots (the French Calvinists). The Spaniards, no longer influenced by Charles V, opposed all talk of compromise so violently that their retainers were frequently involved in street brawls with those of the Cardinal of Lorraine. Identification with papal policy on this issue however did not prevent the Spaniards from demanding greater reform within the Vatican, nor indeed from questioning the pope's authority. They asked, for example, if the residence of bishops within their dioceses was required by divine law or ecclesiastical law; if the former, then the bishop could be held to be independent of papal authority and answerable to God alone.

It was impossible for such conflicting views to be accommodated, but the worst manifestations of a divided church were eventually avoided. Lorraine went home after his brother had been murdered in the streets, but an appointment as papal legate to France mollified him in part. Ferdinand I was eventually silenced with vague assurances that the pope would consider the question of clerical celibacy along with the introduction of communion in both kinds as a possible means of reconciling the Lutherans, and a certain promise that his son Maximilian would be recognised as heir to the Holy Roman Empire. As for the Spanish ploy, the question of episcopal jurisdiction was, after many stormy sessions, finally referred to the pope for a ruling, and papal authority was thus preserved intact.

Despite appearances the General Council did not altogether collapse under the weight of political, personal and theological antagonisms, and historically its sessions proved to be of the greatest significance in the development of the Catholic Church. In terms of practical reformation it seemed to have achieved very little. The requirement to preach regularly and the punishment of episcopal non-residence represented a step in the right direction. Even more important was the decision taken at the third session to set up seminaries in every diocese for the training of the clergy. What mattered most in this respect was the determination of the local bishop to do his job properly and, even more, the example set by the pope. To a large extent, though the council was steered away from discussing the subject, the popes themselves initiated a programme of reform in Rome. Paul IV, one of the authors of the Oratory's report, did much in his violent way to implement those points which did not ruin the Vatican's finances: he rounded up the criminals and prostitutes who had made the city of Rome a scandal in the eyes of the world, he sent the wandering monks back to the discipline of their monasteries and began to check the extent of simony in the matter of clerical appointments. Pius IV maintained the momentum of these reforms, and under the austere and irreproachable Ghislieri, who ruled the church as Pius V (1566–72), the process was continued, if not to a triumphant conclusion, at least to such good effect that the finger of scorn could no longer be pointed at the papacy. Monastic discipline and clerical residence were strictly controlled throughout Italy, and, of particular significance, Pius abolished the collection of annates, reduced the sale of indulgences and checked the expenses of his court.

Whether or not the General Council should claim responsibility for the reforms which followed, its role in determining the nature of Catholic belief cannot be questioned. This was a matter of vital importance, without which the Inquisition and the Society of Jesus would have been powerless to operate effectively, and if the council's decisions were not those which would have pleased an Erasmus or a Contarini, the pressures of the Protestant challenge were so great by mid-century that it was only by adopting an uncompromising line that the Catholic Church could hope to save itself. Augustinian and biblical humanism, both associated in some measure with Lutheranism, were in part repudiated, to be replaced in the universities and seminaries by a revived form of Thomism. This was not an obscurantist decision. Thomism, the scholastic tradition founded by St Thomas Aquinas, had foundered in the fifteenth century on the shoals of inconclusive and unrealistic debates. Thomist studies, however, had revived in the sixteenth century inspired by Cajetan, Luther's opponent at Augsburg, and sustained by the profound scholarship of such Spaniards as Suarez and Dominigo Soto. It was Soto who carried the day at Trent in reducing the importance of the individual's interpretation of the Scriptures and in restoring the value of the commentaries.

Although it framed no resolution to this effect, the Council of Trent had in fact established the supremacy of papal authority. By skilful manipulation of its proceedings, the popes had avoided any repetition of the challenge to their authority which had characterised the Conciliar Movement in the past and it was significant that papal reform was undertaken by the popes themselves independently of any council resolution. This tacit recognition of papal supremacy was of value to the post-Tridentine Church: in the struggle that was being joined between the Society of Jesus on the one hand and the Calvinist missionaries on the other, it was necessary that one voice should speak for the Church, and one authority reign supreme. Equally important was the council's decision to close the door to conciliation and compromise. Although this paved the way for intolerance and persecution, there was no other means to meet the needs of the ignorant and the perplexed than by re-defining for them the precise differences between orthodoxy and heresy. This the council did with great éclat, and because of this its sessions marked a new era in the history of the Church, albeit an era in which the Church of Rome lost its universal character and became only one among other Christian denominations.

8

Eastern Europe and the Baltic

Poland and Lithuania 1444 – 1609

ON the eastern frontiers of the Holy Roman Empire lay the
territories of Poland and Lithuania, stretching from the Oder to
the Dnieper, from the Baltic to the Black Sea. As the two states
shared a common frontier and were ruled by members of the same
family, the Jagiellos, they had agreed in 1413 to work more closely
together, but no common institutions had yet been evolved to
bring coherence to the government of so vast an area. The
principality of Lithuania was ruled by its grand duke, and the
kingdom of Poland itself was nothing more than an amalgamation
of several duchies, such as Great Poland, Little Poland, Kujawia
and so on, from which others such as Mazovia, were to remain
separate until as late as 1526. Nor was Poland a kingdom in the
usual sense of the word, but a self-styled *rcez pospolita* or republic
in which the nobles elected the king and dominated the national
assembly or *sejm*. A few great families, by virtue of their traditional
right to occupy the major offices of church and state, controlled the
senate and selected the representatives of the lesser nobility, the
szlachta, who sat in the lower house. In the regional assemblies,
the *sejmiki*, however, the *szlachta* attended freely without selection.
Lithuania on the other hand had no *sejmiki*, its *sejm* had only
limited powers, and political authority lay exclusively with the
council which, like the Polish senate, was dominated by a few great
families.

In addition there were serious problems due to racial diversity
and religious rivalry within the kingdom and the principality.
Poles, Lithuanians, Latvians, Germans, Jews and Armenians
mingled with Russians from the provinces seized when Russia had
collapsed in the thirteenth century (see page 290), and, in addition

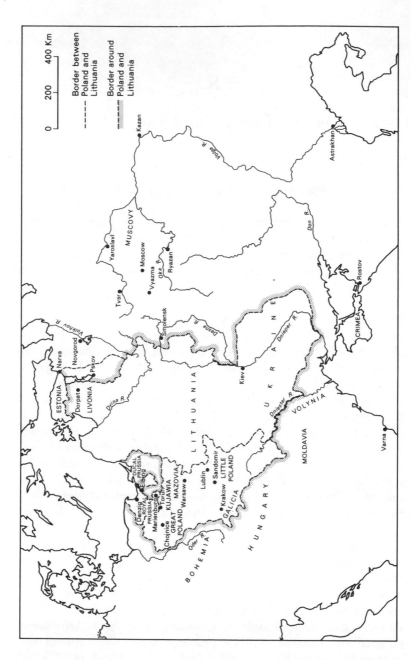

Poland-Lithuania and Muscovy

to the minority faiths of Jews and Moslems, there was a profound gulf between the Roman Church and the Orthodox Church to which the former Russian provinces retained their allegiance.

The first step towards the creation of a more centralised government was the election in 1444 of the Lithuanian grand duke Casimir to succeed his brother as king of Poland. Before he could do much to improve the administration of his territories, however, he faced the greater task of defending them. The Order of the Teutonic Knights in Prussia and Livonia threatened him from the north, the Osmanli Turks from the south; in the south-east the Crimean Tatars ravaged the steppes between the Dnieper and the Dniester and in the east, the new kingdom centred on Moscow was working to recover the territories which formerly had belonged to Russia.

In the circumstances it was an additional embarrassment that his wife Elizabeth, daughter of Albert of Habsburg and sister of Ladislas Postumus, should have looked upon Bohemia and Hungary as rightful inheritances for her sons. The Jagiellos had in fact been influential in both kingdoms before Albert's reign and there was, therefore, plenty of scope for diplomatic intervention in the events involving the emperor, Frederick III, George Podiebrad and John Hunyadi (see page 150). As a result Casimir gave support to Podiebrad, who in turn secured the election of Casimir's eldest son, Wladislav, as his successor in Bohemia in 1471. In the event there seemed to be no advantage gained for Poland. Wladislav was an ineffectual ruler and when Matthias Corvinus of Hungary seized most of his territory and claimed his title, Casimir was too preoccupied elsewhere to send him help. When Matthias died in 1490, however, Wladislav's reputation for weak ineptitude made him an ideal candidate for the Hungarian throne, for the Magyar nobility was anxious to preserve its liberties; he therefore ended up as king both of Hungary and Bohemia.

While chance and diplomacy finally won the day in the west, in the north Casimir was engaged from the beginning in direct military action against the Teutonic Knights, a crusading Order which had established itself along the Baltic coast from Danzig to Estonia. In 1454 Casimir went to the aid of a group of dissidents in the Order who had formed their own Prussian League, but he was defeated at Chojnice. Three years later, assisted by the rich city of Danzig, which had become the centre of the league's resistance, Casimir succeeded in buying out the mercenaries in the Order's pay and won a victory at Marienburg. After a lull lasting several years both sides returned to the attack in 1462, and Casimir was ultimately victorious at the Peace of Torun (Thorn) in 1466. Danzig, Elbing, Marienburg and the diocese of Varna were ceded to Poland, the whole region to be known as Western or Royal Prussia; the rest of Prussia remained within the Order, but the Grand Master paid homage to Casimir and opened the Order to Polish knights. In the east there was no such success. Ivan III (see page 291) recovered Novgorod and other frontier districts which had once been part of Russia, and won the Tatars of the Crimea to his side. As a result the Poles were denied access to the Black Sea, and their south-eastern and southern territories were subjected to marauding expeditions by both Tatars and Osmanli Turks.

When Casimir died in 1492 Wladislav was left undisturbed in Bohemia and Hungary, his brother Jan Olbricht was elected to Poland, and a third brother Alexander was elected to Lithuania. In 1494 they met together in an attempt to pool their resources against their enemies, but the attempt came to nothing since none of the three princes had much ability and it was impossible to establish a coherent strategy for the three kingdoms. When, for example, the Polish campaign against the Turks was side-tracked into Moldavia, the Magyar nobility, who regarded Moldavia as a Hungarian sphere of influence, jealously refused to let Wladislav go to his brother's aid and the Poles were therefore defeated. Alexander meanwhile lost Vyazma and the region of the Upper Oka to the Russians. Jan Olbricht died in 1501 and Alexander, if anything more indolent than his brother, succeeded him until his own death in 1506 when Poland and Lithuania at last came under the rule of Sigismund, Casimir's most able son.

Sigismund's inheritance had been made the more difficult because his father and his brothers, in order to win support for their campaigns, had been obliged to make important concessions to the lesser nobility, the *szlachta*. The *szlachta* were beginning to exploit the opportunity to sell corn in Europe (see page 3) and as a result their estates had to be organised to produce substantial surpluses, which in turn required the provision of a labour force under their direct control. The peasantry had hitherto enjoyed the right of free migration, and those who lived in areas which two centuries earlier had been colonial settlements had been allowed considerable powers of self-government. Under pressure from the *szlachta*, the Jagiellon kings abolished these rights by new laws in 1493 and 1511, and further legislation destroyed the peasants' right to appeal to the king from a seigneurial court. With the peasantry delivered into their hands, the *szlachta* enclosed land at will, confined their peasants to their villages and imposed heavier burdens of field work. In addition to their monopoly of economic power the *szlachta* had also made progress towards achieving greater political power, demanding that the *sejm*, a consultative assembly, should become a more positively legislative body. To guarantee the victories they had won from Casimir and his sons, their final act in Alexander's reign had been to secure a new constitution, in which the king was compelled to declare that, 'from henceforward nothing new may be established by us or our successors, without the full consent of the Council and delegates of the lords, which may be harmful to the republic or to the harm or injury of any private person or directed towards a change of the general law and public liberty'.

The *szlachta* had thus become the self-appointed custodians of a constitution which enshrined the advantages they had acquired over king and peasants – nor was this to be the end of the story. In 1520 Sigismund was forced to agree that the membership of the lower house of the *sejm* should not be determined by the great noble families but controlled by election from the *sejmiki* where the *szlachta* were dominant, and furthermore that those elected should be paid for the trouble of representing their regions. In the same decade the *szlachta* formulated three new demands – for their exemption from ecclesiastical courts, for the 'execution of the laws' which in effect meant the right of the *szlachta* to codify and enforce those laws which best suited their interests, and for an assurance that the king repurchase alienated crown lands, which in the main had been sold cheaply to the greater nobles, and thereafter live of his own without appealing to the *sejm* for money. Sigismund resisted these demands as best he could but his position quickly deteriorated. Despite the military expense of defending Poland, the *sejm* refused to provide him with regular grants, and to meet particular crises he had to purchase ad hoc grants by making further concessions. Finally, in 1538, he was so anxious to secure the election of his son, Sigismund Augustus, that he agreed to a new rule that after his son's reign all new kings were to be elected not by the *sejm* alone, but with the participation of the entire nobility.

With problems of this kind to face at home, Sigismund for all his general ability was at a disadvantage in conducting his campaigns abroad. On the Russian front things went badly. An opportunity to inflict defeat on Vasily III was destroyed by the defection of Michael Glinsky, a Lithuanian prince, and in 1514 the Poles lost Smolensk. Many attempts were made to recover the city, but at length it was recognised by the truce of 1522 that a kind of equilibrium had been established along the frontier, and that neither side could hope for further victories in the immediate future. Smolensk might possibly have been recovered if Sigismund had had more help from Poland, but the Russian campaign was regarded with indifference as a Lithuanian affair, and Poland was in any case entangled in a dispute with the Teutonic Knights. In Jan Olbricht's reign the Grand Master of the Order had refused to pay the homage required by the peace of Torun: in 1511 a new Grand Master, Albrecht of Brandenburg, not only followed suit but allied with the Russians, as well as winning the support of the Emperor Maximilian who sent an embassy to Moscow to add to Sigismund's difficulties. At this stage, Wladislav, for once, proved useful to his brother: because of his close alliance with the emperor and the double marriages between their families, he persuaded Maximilian to withdraw diplomatic support from Albrecht. Albrecht therefore declared his conversion to Lutheranism, secularised the lands of his Order, constituted himself duke of Prussia and, in order to guarantee his new status, paid homage to Sigismund for his duchy.

For the last decade or so of Sigismund's reign his kingdom was more or less at peace with his neighbours. When his nephew, Louis, was killed at Mohacs he was tempted to intervene in Hungary, not only to drive out the Turks but also to support Zapolya, his brother-in-law by his first marriage, against Ferdinand of Austria (see page 228). Zapolya, however, complicated matters by allying with Suleyman, and Sigismund, though watchful, remained inactive. It was a fair conclusion to a difficult reign. Smolensk had been lost, but in most other respects Sigismund had safeguarded his frontiers, and though he had had to abandon a considerable degree of royal authority to the *szlachta*, it was some consolation to him that his son should be assured of an unchallenged succession in both Poland and Lithuania. In 1548 he died and Sigismund Augustus inherited his crowns and his problems.

Sigismund Augustus was a man of broad culture and great humanity, who shared his father's political and administrative ability. Nonetheless he was unable to withstand the demands of the *szlachta*, and between 1562 and 1565 he capitulated on virtually every point. The 'execution of the laws' was accepted in principle; ecclesiastical courts, though not deprived of their jurisdiction over the *szlachta*, could no longer call on the king to execute their judgements, and it was finally worked out after long debate that the holders of mortgaged crown lands were to assign one-quarter of their revenues to the royal treasury for the defence of the kingdom. In this respect therefore Sigismund Augustus was better off than before since he now had a regular income, sufficient to maintain an army of 40,000, but the real gains achieved by the *szlachta* were of such obvious value that the lesser nobility of Lithuania demanded to be similarly privileged. This was done in 1569 when, by the Union of Lublin, Lithuania and Poland became one kingdom under one king and one *sejm*, in which all the nobles had equal rights.

The unity achieved at Lublin was to some extent already compromised by the divisive consequences of the Protestant Reformation. Sigismund, in 1526, had had to take swift and vigorous action to safeguard the Catholic church, and indeed his own authority, both in Danzig and royal Prussia, but elsewhere the problem was less acute; the conversion of the nobility rarely affected the peasantry, and the differences between the Protestant confessions left their adherents vulnerable to the attack of the Jesuit missionaries whom Sigismund Augustus introduced in 1565. Four Jesuit colleges were established in as many years, and the rate of conversion to Rome was so great that the Protestants met at Sandomir in 1570 to demand that all confessions be guaranteed certain rights. The demand was met. The king was not strong enough to risk civil war, and Poland, with its successful experience of coexistence between the Roman and Orthodox churches, was the one European country where a measure of toleration was acceptable. Sigismund Augustus himself disliked persecution, accepting the advice of his humanist secretary, Andreas Modrzewski, that, 'what belongs to the mind and the spirit cannot be forced out of anybody by torture or threats', and most of his subjects were prepared to concur with this sentiment.

These important developments in Poland were played out against the background of a renewed conflict with Russia. Personal temperament and political necessity alike inclined Sigismund Augustus to remain at peace with his neighbours: he avoided entanglement in the affairs of Transylvania, he offered no challenge to the Osmanli Turks in Moldavia and the Crimea, and he tolerated, though never trusted, his vassal, the duke of Prussia. Nevertheless he recognised that the expansion of Russia, if allowed to go unchecked, would one day engulf Lithuania, and for Ivan IV he could only feel the distaste of the humanist for the barbarian. His major concern was both to discourage diplomatic contact between Ivan and the governments of England and Sweden and also to establish a Polish fleet in the Baltic in order to deny him access to Europe by sea. For this reason both sides became interested in Livonia, a Baltic province which had been colonised by the Order of Sword Bearers, an offshoot of the former Teutonic Knights. The master, Gothard Kettler, well aware that the Order was incapable of resisting a Russian attack, had opened negotiations with Sigismund Augustus to cede his lands to Poland in return for the duchy of Courland. A Russian invasion in 1560 settled the matter quickly, and by 1561 Poland and Russia were committed to war for the possession of Livonia. The issue was complicated by the fact that Eric XIV of Sweden also wanted Livonia, and had already seized the neighbouring province of Estonia, in temporary alliance with Ivan. In 1568, however, his successor Johan married Sigismund Augustus's sister and abandoned the campaign. This left the Poles free to check the Russian advance, but by 1572, when Sigismund Augustus died, the issue was still uncertain.

For nearly two centuries a Jagiello had been elected to the Polish throne, but as Sigismund Augustus died without heirs, the field was left wide open. Maximilian II wanted the succession for his son, Ernest, and was well placed to organise a military coup, but he hesitated, and the general mood of the nobility, hostile to the Habsburgs, swung in favour of a Valois prince, Henry of Anjou – despite Protestant fears engendered by news of the massacre of St Bartholomew's Eve. The general mood was of particular significance on this occasion because, as a result of the concessions made by Sigismund in 1538, the entire nobility had been enfranchised. The task of bringing over 40,000 voters, to say nothing of their attendants, into one place, was organised with remarkable skill and good order; each was free to state his case – 'not force, not gold, not acclamation but fair argument, the common good and persuasion, should hold sway' – and when Henry emerged as the candidate of the majority, the minority very properly gave way because they did not want 'our country to be ruined and ourselves to be the cause of bloodshed'. A similar unanimity was demonstrated in drawing up the terms to be presented to Henry, the *pacta conventa*, which listed his more obvious obligations to provide an army and to pay his debts. In addition he was required to preserve peace between the rival confessions by signing a charter known as the Warsaw Confederation, and to accept the *Articuli Henriciani* which rehearsed the privileges of the *szlachta* along with the threat that, 'if a king act against these laws, liberties, articles and conditions, or does not fulfil them, he thereby makes the nobles free of the obedience and fealty they owe him'.

Henry, who was wholly taken aback by the terms required of him, refused to sign them and abandoned his new kingdom with relief and alacrity when the French throne passed to him a few months later on the death of his brother Charles IX. A second election was held in 1575, less well-organised than before and much more divisive in its effect. Maximilian II put himself forward on this occasion with the backing of the senate, but the *szlachta* settled for a Transylvanian prince, Stephen Bathory. When Bathory was crowned in 1576 in Danzig, other areas declared for Maximilian, and civil war was only averted by news of the emperor's death.

Stephen, though he scrupulously observed the terms imposed upon him, made a spirited attempt to govern vigorously. He used his position as the source of all patronage to good effect; he summoned the *sejm* regularly as required, but also used his own rhetorical skill to influence its decisions, and reminded its members that they too had public duties and obligations to perform; he stood firm in demanding financial aid and was assisted in his stand by the assurance that the mineral wealth of Transylvania would help him out in lean years. Stephen's determination to work within the letter of the constitution won him the support of Jan Zamoyski, a most influential noble whose anxiety to protect the interests of his class was matched by a deep concern for good government and the promotion of his own family. Both men moreover were anxious to promote the Counter-reformation without persecution; they helped to found more Jesuit colleges, but were politic enough to retain Protestants in the administration of government affairs. This combination of forces had the unfortunate effect of alienating another family, the Zborowskis, who had initially supported Stephen and resented the loss of influence at court – so much so that they entered into treasonable relations with the Habsburgs – but the combination of king and Zamoyski proved to be sufficiently effective. Order was maintained within the kingdom, and the Russians were attacked so vigorously in Livonia that Ivan was forced to concede the Baltic provinces by the Treaty of Yam Zapolsky (1582).

As a Transylvanian prince, Stephen was more eager to fight the Turks than the Russians. When Ivan died he made his successor a remarkable offer of alliance and perpetual friendship – in order to mobilise a joint crusade – going so far as to contemplate the union of Poland and Russia under one sovereign and to suggest means for protecting the minority races and religions in each country. The Russians were too suspicious to agree immediately, however, and in the troubled times which followed (see page 299) the idea was abandoned once and for all.

The feud between Zamoyski and Zborowski led to civil war after the death of Stephen Bathory in 1586. Zborowski backed the candidature of Maximilian, son of the former Emperor Maximilian II, while Zamoyski supported Sigismund, heir to the Swedish throne, whose wife was a Jagiello and sister to Sigismund Augustus. In 1588 the war ended with the capture of Maximilian, and Sigismund began a long reign which lasted until 1632. When Sigismund inherited the throne of Sweden in 1592 his firm stand against Protestantism had won Zamoyski's approval, but forfeited the loyalty of his Swedish subjects who rebelled in 1598 under the leadership of his uncle Karl (see page 313) and deposed him in 1604. In the meantime Sigismund succeeded in transferring Estonia from Sweden to Poland, and Zamoyski, who strongly supported this action, fought loyally for him in defending the province against the Swedes.

Yet Zamoyski's confidence in Sigismund had already been undermined. Before the Swedish rebellion occurred there had been rumours that the king would retire to Sweden, having sold the Polish throne to the Habsburg archduke, Ernest. Zamoyski was understandably angry, not so much at the details of the plot which never came to anything, but at the notion that, 'foreigners should negotiate over us between themselves'. Moreover, loyal Catholic though he was, he felt that Sigismund's encouragement of intolerance by Catholic corporations was alien to the spirit of the Warsaw Confederation. 'I would give half of my life to bring back to Catholicism those who have abandoned it, but I would give my whole life to prevent them from being brought back by violence.' Nor was it a matter only of the Warsaw Confederation. Zamoyski also stood firmly by the *pacta conventa* and the *Articuli Henriciani,* and just as he had supported Stephen Bathory when the king had governed effectively within the terms of the constitution, so he was ready to turn against Sigismund if these terms were in any way modified. In 1605 Sigismund showed his hand at a meeting of the *sejm* when he demanded greater powers, justifying his case on the legitimate grounds that the peasantry required his protection, and pointed out that the practice of seeking a unanimous rather than a majority decision in the senate led to oppression by the minority. In all probability the demand would have been deemed unacceptable in any case, but Sigismund, who lacked the rhetorical ability of Stephen Bathory, presented his argument badly. Zamoyski publicly declared his opposition to the king, hoping to make him withdraw without the need for force, but his own death soon after merely left the way clear for more extremist opponents to declare that a king who violated the constitution forfeited the loyalty of his subjects.

Civil war raged for several years, with the Protestants supporting the constitutional party against the Catholic king, but since a large section of the nobility preferred Sigismund to any other candidate the rebels were defeated in 1609. This did not mean, however, a victory for the king: an amnesty was required for all his enemies, and the constitution, as drawn up after Sigismund Augustus's death, was reaffirmed. It was clear that elective monarchy had come to be associated with ineffectual government, but the *szlachta*, with its vested interest in the constitution, refused to see in this a source of national weakness. Poland accordingly was ill-equipped to meet the challenge to her frontiers which was renewed by Russians, Turks and Swedes in the seventeenth century.

Russia 1462 – 1605

Before the Mongol invasion of Europe in the thirteenth century, the ancient kingdom of Russia was based on the Ukraine with its capital at Kiev. Thereafter it was dismembered, not only by the Tatars of the Golden Horde from the south-east, but also by the Lithuanians from the west, leaving only a few isolated Great Russian principalities of which Muscovy was ultimately to become the nucleus of a new Russian kingdom. Cut off from Europe in the backwoods of the middle Volga and the Oka, and tributary to the Mongols, the principality was nonetheless intensely conscious of a Christian tradition, derived from the Orthodox Church of Byzantium. As a result the Muscovites regarded the Roman Catholics of Lithuania not only as politically treacherous but also as schismatic. Out of respect for this tradition, the niece of the last of the Byzantine emperors came to Moscow to marry the prince who, as Ivan (John) III succeeded to the throne in 1462. Ivan adopted the two-headed eagle of her family as his own heraldic device and, self-consciously and deliberately, set out to make his country the heir to Byzantium. Muscovy was indeed well placed to be the centre of an empire; it lay, at the juncture of forest and steppe, at a central watershed where the Volkhov and the Dvina flowed into the Baltic, the Dnieper and the Don to the Black Sea and the Volga to the Caspian. What was needed was a ruler resolute enough to drive his armies along these river routes.

In 1462, however, the forces of the Tatars and of the Lithuanians lay barely seventy miles from the frontiers of Muscovy, and the independent Great Russian principality of Tver was only fifty miles away. Ivan began cautiously in 1467, leading a series of reconnaissance expeditions to secure his eastern frontier against the Kazan Tatars, and when, after two years, he had forced an armistice favourable to Moscow, he then turned westwards to the rich and autonomous republic of Novgorod. The small circle of families who governed the city had close links with Lithuania and immediately appealed to Casimir (see page 282) to incorporate them within his territory and to bring them ecclesiastically under the authority of the Roman archbishop of Kiev. This in turn antagonised the mass of the population which was devoutly Orthodox; thus, when Ivan advanced upon the city in 1471 he found many of its citizens looking to him for deliverance from their oligarchs.

The fine summer of that year left the ground in excellent condition for campaigning and when Ivan advanced into the areas around the city, thereby depriving it of food supplies, the population rose against its governors and capitulated to him. The terms of the settlement left the north-eastern territory of Novgorod in Muscovite hands but the city itself was to remain more or less independent under Ivan's rule. Riots in 1477 and a conspiracy to bring in Casimir in 1479 gave Ivan the opportunity to establish his absolute rule within the city; those who were known to be in contact with Lithuania were executed in great number, and over the next ten years 8,000 or more of the wealthiest citizens were deported to Moscow leaving Ivan in complete control. During this same period, moreover, Ivan annexed not only the territories of Novgorod but those of the surviving great Russian principalities; Yaroslavl fell to him in 1463, Rostov in 1474, Tver in 1485 while Pskov and Ryazan retained a merely nominal independence.

Inspired by the memory of Russia's former greatness, Ivan was determined to recover the Ukranian territory which had once been its heartland: when the Jagiellon princes complained that Ivan was attacking their patrimony he retorted, 'But what do they call their patrimony? The land of Russia is from our ancestors of old our patrimony', and later, 'And do not I regret my patrimony, the Russian land which is in the hands of Lithuania – Kiev, Smolensk and the other towns?' Casimir of Poland reacted by encouraging Ahmed, khan of the Kazan Tatars, to terminate his armistice with Ivan and thus distract his attention from the Ukraine. As a counterstroke Ivan sought an ally further south in Mengli-Girey, khan of the Crimean Tatars. It was not an easy alliance to negotiate since neither side had anything in common, but in 1480, after Ahmed's horde had trespassed into the Crimea, Mengli-Girey duly signed a pact.

The alliance was concluded at an opportune moment. In that

same year Ivan's brothers, Andrey and Boris, defected to Casimir (see below) and Ahmed invaded Muscovy. Ivan was ready to panic. His wife, Zoe, with memories of her family's staunch resistance at Byzantium – 'my father and I lost our patrimony rather than submit' – urged him to make a stand, but, having sent her off to Archangel, he was preparing to follow when his council shamed him into staying. In the event, Mengli-Girey kept Casimir occupied by invading the Ukraine, Andrey and Boris, finding no great welcome for them in Poland, returned to help their brother drive out the Tatars, and Ahmed, once he had been forced to withdraw from Muscovy, was set upon by other Tatars from east of the Volga who murdered him in 1481 and sacked Kazan. This marked the end of Moscow's humiliation by the Golden Horde, and Ivan signified his new status as an independent sovereign by declaring himself to be Tsar, Sovereign of all Russia and Autocrat. His position was further strengthened in 1487 when Mengli-Girey's stepson, with Russian assistance, established himself in Kazan.

With his southern and eastern frontiers secure Ivan invaded Lithuania in 1491. Alexander, who succeeded Casimir in 1492, was unsuccessful in resisting the attack and in 1494 he ceded Vyazma and the region of the upper Oka, south-west of Moscow. He then made matters worse for himself by trying to impose the Roman liturgy on the Orthodox inhabitants of the frontier districts, and the disturbances which this provoked tempted Ivan to renew the war in 1500. He defeated the Lithuanians on the River Vedrosha, near Dorogobuzh, and in 1502 laid siege to Smolensk. It was a moment of high triumph for Ivan though it could not be sustained. His Crimean allies, ravaging the Polish district of Galicia and Volynia, were too far south to be of assistance at the siege which eventually was raised; on the strength of his successes, however, Ivan secured a six-year armistice in 1503, which left him in possession of territory, bounded by the Desna and the Dnieper and midway between Smolensk and Kiev, from which both cities would be vulnerable to future attack.

Within his growing empire Ivan II consolidated his authority over his subjects. The rulers of Moscow had for many years been regarded more or less as *primus inter pares* by their relatives, by the many princely families who had entered their service and by the traditional nobility, the boyars. All of them, for example, had enjoyed the 'right to depart', a tradition of free service by which they could transfer their allegiance at will from one prince to another. Ivan's military success gave him the opportunity to demand recognition of his sovereign status, and the 'right to depart' was considerably reduced. Prince Daniel Dmitrievich Kholmsky, for example, one of the great boyars, was compelled not only to swear publicly that he would never depart from Ivan's service, but also to find eight guarantors who stood to lose 8,000 roubles if he defected. It was declared to be an act of treason for anyone to abandon the tsar for one of his relatives, and it was this which led to the defection of Andrey and Boris. Ivan had deliberately refused to honour the old tradition of regarding his brothers as his equals. He reduced not only the powers of independent jurisdiction they enjoyed within their own territories, but also the extent of the territories themselves. When Yuri, the eldest of his brothers, died in 1472, Ivan took possession of his estates instead of sharing them with Andrey and Boris, and when a boyar 'departed' from Ivan to Boris in 1480 the tsar had him arrested for treason, despite the fact that he was on Boris's own territory and supposedly immune from Ivan's jurisdiction. In 1480 the brothers, therefore, fled to Casimir, but returned to assist Ivan in the struggle against the Tatars. This did not deter Ivan from seizing Andrey's estates after his death in the following year, and another brother, also named Andrey, was arrested in 1491 for being too slow in sending aid when Ivan required it. He died in prison.

In order to strengthen his authority, Ivan increased the number of boyars in his own service, and rewarded them by granting them the life tenure of certain royal estates. As the number of these *pomeschiki* grew, however, it became increasingly difficult to find sufficient land. In 1503 the tsar invited the Russian church to give him some of its property, reinforcing his case with the view of many of the clergy who believed the monasteries to be corrupted by their great wealth. The leaders of the church retaliated by claiming that no worthy recruits of noble birth would come forward to be ordained in landless churches and monasteries and, therefore, the tsar would be depriving Russia of its future archbishops and abbots. It was not the church's logic but its strength which carried the day: Ivan was aware that his clergy proclaimed from their pulpits a greater authority for him than he dared to claim for himself, and church property was of less value than the stamp of divine approval which the church bestowed upon him. Nor did he wish to compromise the crusading spirit of his war against the Roman Catholic Lithuanians by a dispute with his own church. Instead he looked to the territories won by these crusaders to provide the rewards for his own followers. 1600 or more *pomeschiki*, for example, moved in to occupy the land left by the 8,000 families who were moved from Novgorod to Moscow, and the frontier regions in general were parcelled out among men whom Ivan had come to trust.

At the end of the reign Ivan III's achievement was imperilled by a dispute over the succession. When his son Ivan died in 1490 his grandson Dmitry was regarded by the boyars as the likely heir to the throne. The *pomeschiki*, however, preferred the claim of the tsar's second son, Vasily (Basil) and in 1497 they organised a plot to take Dmitry prisoner. Outraged by this challenge to his authority Ivan executed the ringleaders and had Dmitry crowned, but in 1502 he changed his mind and appointed Vasily as his heir. He also assigned to him over two-thirds of the royal estates so that not having to share his patrimony, Vasily would be stronger than his brothers. Vasily, in fact, went further than Ivan had done in exalting his own authority at the expense of his relatives: after his accession in 1505 he treated them with humiliating contempt and denied them a place in his counsels. He also demonstrated his suspicion of the boyars as a class, giving his favours instead to the *pomeschiki* who had initially supported his claims. By his conquests he was able to provide them with generous rewards, with the result that the boyars grew increasingly restive as the reign progressed.

Meanwhile the Muscovite empire continued to grow. Pskov and Ryazan forfeited the last traces of their independence under Vasily's rigorous rule, and war was renewed against Lithuania. Just as there were many Muscovite families who had in the past 'departed' into the service of the Lithuanian grand dukes, so many Lithuanian nobles of the Orthodox Church transferred their allegiance to the tsar, including Michael Glinsky, a very powerful landowner into whose family Vasily had married. With their assistance further attacks were directed against Smolensk which fell in 1514 and, despite the most spirited counter-attacks, remained in Russian hands until its transfer was officially conceded in the armistice of 1522.

In the south and east the defeat of the Kazan Tatars and the installation of Mengli-Girey's stepson had assured the Russians of peace in that quarter, and the current ruler, Shah Ali, maintained his father's alliance with the tsar. Without the Kazan Tatars to keep them in check, however, the Crimean Tatars joined with the Osmanli Turks and prepared to advance northwards. Mengli-Girey did not altogether abandon his alliance with the tsar, but his son, Mehmed-Girey, sent a force to drive Shah Ali from Kazan and then invaded Russia in 1521. Moscow itself was besieged when, quite coincidentally but most opportunely for Vasily, the Astrakhan Tatars invaded the Crimea. Mehmed-Girey withdrew to face them, was killed in battle in 1523 and, after another eight years of confused fighting, Shah Ali's brother, Djan Ali, recovered control of Kazan.

When Vasily died in 1533 the frontiers were temporarily secure, but within their confines civil war and anarchy were to last for fifteen years. So great was the dissatisfaction of the boyars with the manner of Vasily's government that when he was succeeded by a three-year-old prince, Ivan, they seized the opportunity to plunder the royal estates and to settle old scores among themselves. At length a reaction of a kind set in, and when Ivan proclaimed an end to the regency in 1547 he was able to count upon the more public spirited boyars, led by Alexei Adashev and a priest named Sylvester, and the *pomeschiki*, who, as a service nobility, had felt remarkably at a loss with no one to serve. Ivan's 'Chosen Council' became an instrument of reform: provincial governors were denied authority over the *pomeschiki* in 1549, and a year later were forced to share with them the presiding chair at the provincial assizes. In 1555 many of the governors were dismissed, the dues paid to them were passed to the Chosen Council in Moscow, and their duties were undertaken by elected representatives. At the same time some progress was made in setting up new ministries, nearly half the members of the central administration being resettled in and around Moscow.

Not surprisingly, the long period of anarchy in Russia had had repercussions in Kazan where Djan Ali was murdered and where, after six rulers had been eliminated in as many years, Safa-Girey of the Crimean Tatars at last established his authority. When the Chosen Council and Ivan set off for Kazan with 100,000 men the Tatars launched a diversionary attack on Tula in 1552. Ivan moved across to meet them with half of his army, and, having defeated them, joined the others at the siege of Kazan. Both sides imbued their forces with religious fervour: 'It is better that I die here' said Ivan, 'than live to see Christ blasphemed, and the Christians, entrusted to me by God, suffering at the hands of the godless Kazans.' The Tatars were equally committed to their cause. When 340 of them had been taken prisoner they were tied to stakes before the city walls to induce the garrison to surrender but instead they were killed by the arrows of their own people who declared, 'it is better that you die by our clean hands than by the dirty hands of the Christians'. When the city was no longer defensible the inhabitants chose to rush out in a desperate fight to the death rather than surrender.

After the fall of Kazan the whole region was reduced to order in the next five years, a major achievement of some consequence for it led directly to the submission of the neighbouring Tatars of Astrakhan whose territory was annexed in 1566. Finally, the great Nogai Horde of Tatars, who held the Caspian depression east of the Volga, recognised the tsar as their suzerain, and so the whole of the Volga river and the great continental trade routes to central Asia were brought under Russian control. To the south the Tatars of the Crimea remained hostile but Ivan feared to commit his troops against them since it would stretch his lines of communication too far: moreover the khan was in alliance with Suleyman the Magnificent. Instead, Ivan planned to push out his northern frontier towards the Baltic so that he might outflank Lithuania and benefit from the opportunity of trade with western Europe. In 1558, therefore, his troops occupied Dorpat and Narva in Estonia, and in 1560 he invaded Livonia.

It was at this juncture, when Russia was about to challenge not only the power of Poland but also that of Sweden, that a serious upheaval took place at Ivan's court. For some time he had been growing increasingly suspicious of his Chosen Council, partly because Adashev and Sylvester wanted to stake everything on a crusade against the Crimean Tatars instead of attacking the Baltic Provinces, but even more because Ivan was particularly sensitive to any criticism of his wife Anastasia and of her family, the Zakharins. In 1553, when Ivan was dangerously ill and seemed to be on the point of death, his advisers had been reluctant to accept his baby son, Dmitry, as heir-apparent for fear of the anarchy which might once again attend a royal minority, especially as the Zakharins would be prominent among the regents. They therefore proposed to Ivan that he should nominate his cousin, Prince Vladimir of Staritsa. From his sick-bed Ivan could view this only as a gross betrayal of the trust he had placed in them, and his anger was so intemperate that Adashev and Sylvester hastily swore allegiance to the baby Dmitry. The damage had been done nonetheless. Ivan never again confided in them freely, and in the years that followed, every petty incident of the court, every disagreement in the council, fed his suspicion until in 1560 he dismissed them from office.

This unhappily was not the end of the affair. Anastasia died shortly afterwards and Ivan, who had loved her deeply, began to convince himself that some of the boyars had conspired to poison her. Suspicion and mistrust corrupted the mood of the court and the failure of the Livonian campaign did nothing to dispel the gloom. In 1564 Prince Michael Kurbsky, one of Ivan's most trusted servants and his commander of the army in Livonia, defected to Poland because Ivan refused to accept his advice to recall Adashev and Sylvester. This was too much for Ivan. His physical condition had been deteriorating, and the loss of weight and hair indicated something of the inner torment he had experienced since Anastasia's death. On hearing of Kurbsky's betrayal he fled from Moscow and went into hiding for a month. He then sent two letters to be read out in the capital: the first assured the people that he regarded himself as their ally and bore them no malice, the second attacked the boyars and the clergy for diminishing his authority, and both implied that he had abdicated. The citizens were greatly alarmed, both at the loss of their tsar – 'He is our Sovereign, given to us by God; we know no other' – and at the prospect of anarchy and civil war. They, therefore, sent a delegation to bring Ivan back on whatever terms he chose to make, and in this manner Ivan returned to Moscow.

He was a changed man. The tensions of the past five years had not only developed a capacity for morbid suspicion to the point of insanity, but had also released a latent streak of horrifying brutality. This was evident from his savage persecution of all who, by family ties or past friendships, had been associated with Kurbsky; more fundamentally it was reflected in his refusal to acknowledge the traditional machinery of government, maintained and supported by the boyars and *pomeschiki*, by creating alongside it a new corps of servants known as the 'Special Court', the *oprichnina*. Initially Ivan recruited a thousand or so *oprichniki*, settled them in and around Moscow, evicting *pomeschiki* and other tenants to make room for them, and clothed them in a distinctive uniform of black robes. Thereafter they grew in number and authority until the officers of the traditional administration – the *zemshchini* – controlled only the outlying and less productive regions of Russia. Their role was not clearly defined. They carried a symbolic broom of reform at their saddlebows, but their brutality in dealing with anyone whom Ivan feared or suspected – which included all the members of the *zemshchina* – left little doubt that they were instruments of terror, royal executioners, rather than agents of royal administration. When Novgorod, for example, was suspected of withholding taxes, Ivan committed it into the hands of the *oprichniki* for six weeks of torture, mutilation and murder; 60,000 citizens were said to have died and the river was choked with their bodies. Since none dared to oppose him publicly Ivan's subjects had no option but to conspire in secret – even his cousin Vladimir, who had been nominated by the Chosen Council to succeed him in 1553 was involved – while Ivan, mistaking the effect for the cause, ordered the arrest and execution of suspects on an ever-increasing scale.

Russia, in short, appeared to be torn apart in a bloody civil war between the *oprichniki* and the rest of the population, but in 1571, to add to the confusion, the Crimean Tatars swept northwards with over 100,000 men. The *oprichniki* were unable to check their progress: Moscow was sacked and burned and, two years later, the Tatars were checked only fifty miles south of the city by the efforts of those boyars and *pomeschiki* who were still prepared to serve a tsar who had repudiated them. Ivan reacted characteristically: he purged the *oprichnina*, renamed it the *dvor*, reduced its powers, and those of the *zemshchina* who had rallied to his defence were re-settled on their original estates in and around the capital.

There was, however, an entirely new problem which was beginning to affect boyars, *pomeschiki, oprichniki* and indeed all who served the tsar in return for land. Since the fall of Kazan the peasantry had been colonising the eastern frontier: like the

Cossacks of the Don and the Dnieper, they formed themselves into nomadic hosts under an elected leader, pressing on restlessly eastwards, 'serving for grain and water, not for lands and estates', so that by 1581 they had crossed the Urals, and were eventually to reach the Pacific coast, 7,000 miles from Moscow, in 1639. As a result of this massive emigration to the east, fewer peasants were left to work the land, and, without an efficient agrarian economy to support it, the success of the entire administration was endangered. In the sixteenth century the problem was only beginning to emerge, but before Ivan's death it was reported that in the Novgorod region, for example, nearly nine-tenths of the land was being left to lie fallow for lack of labour.

Of more immediate importance to Ivan was the failure of his campaign in the Baltic Provinces. He knew that European states like Poland and Sweden, unlike the Tatars of the Golden Horde, had economic and technical resources superior to his own, and for this reason he sought alliances with Austria and with England. Chancellor arrived from England in 1553, and Ivan quickly granted him special privileges in order to make use of his country-men's skills in mining, metallurgy and medicine. It was for this reason that Sigismund Augustus of Poland appealed to Elizabeth of England to withhold her aid from Ivan: 'Up to now we could conquer him only because he was a stranger to education and did not know the arts.' In the event it was the inadequacy of the Polish constitution rather than the fruits of western technology which gave Ivan the advantage during the years following Sigismund Augustus's death, but, once Stephen Bathory had consolidated his position, the Poles recovered Livonia and compelled Ivan to renounce his claims in the Treaty of Yam Zapolsky (1587).

In the midst of failure in the north and unrest at home Ivan's mood alternated between bouts of depression and fits of rage. It was in one of these fits that he killed his favourite son, Ivan, in 1582, and two years later he too died, full of remorse, leaving his country to be engulfed in a Time of Troubles more serious and more prolonged than that of his own minority. Initially some semblance of order was preserved, not by Ivan's son, Fedor, a weak and melancholy prince, but by Fedor's brother-in-law, Boris Godunov, who had the energy, the resolution and the ambition to suppress those who would challenge the tsar. When Fedor died in 1598 it was Boris who was elected to the throne by an assembly of the boyars. He was respected for his vigour, he had won the support of the clergy by elevating the see of Moscow to patriarchal status in 1589, and his measures to restrain the emigration of peasants from the land were acclaimed by the landowners. It was necessary for him nonetheless to arrange the murder of Fedor's half-brother Dmitry, and it was symptomatic of the general uncertainty and anarchy that before long a false Dmitry had appeared to claim the support of many followers. When Boris died in 1605 Russia was convulsed in a civil war which was to last for nearly a decade, while Sweden took possession of Novgorod, and Polish armies entered Moscow.

Gustav Vasa and Swedish Independence

The Union of Kalmar (1397) between Denmark, Norway and Sweden under the rule of the Danish king was similar to the Union of Lublin between Poland and Lithuania in that it represented a merging of aristocratic republics under one king. Each country was governed by its own nobility, which was content to maintain a nominal allegiance to the king of Denmark provided there was no interference in its administration of local affairs. Only in Sweden were a few dissidents to be found. Many of the free peasantry and miners cherished a romantic, but nonetheless passionate devotion to the legends of their former independence, and from time to time a Swedish noble would lead them in a rising against the Danes – and indeed against the members of his own class.

Such a man had been Karl Knutson, 1434–70, whose memory was kept alive by the peasants of the Dalarna valley and the iron miners of the Bergslag, and whose nephew, Sten Sture, led them to victory against Christian I of Denmark in 1471. After the battle Sture had still to contend with his fellow nobles who preferred to retain their allegiance to a distant sovereign than obey an ambitious member of their own order. Since the nobles controlled the *rad*, the ruling council, Sture had to bolster up his authority by frequent appeals to the peasants and miners, and for many years an uneasy balance of power was maintained. In 1497, however, Hans of Denmark invaded Sweden, and the nobles rallied to him until they discovered that he shared none of their fears about Russian expansion into Finland. At this the *rad* reluctantly withdrew its allegiance and declared for Sture.

When Sture died in 1503, Svante Nilsson, his nephew, retained control of the administration and governed in alliance with the *rad* until his own death in 1512. His son, however, to whom he had deliberately given the name of Sten Sture the Younger was too ambitious to win a royal title to remain for long at peace with the *rad*. Matters came to a head in 1514 in a dispute over territory between Sten Sture the Younger and Gustav Trolle, the newly-appointed archbishop of Uppsala. Sture put his case before the *riksdag*, the assembly of the Swedish Estates, in which the nobility and the clergy were joined by representatives of the towns and of the peasantry, on whose support Sture and his ancestors had traditionally relied. Trolle on the other hand had appealed to Christian II, who invaded Sweden unsuccessfully in 1517, but with better fortune in the following year. After a Danish victory in 1520, Sten Sture died of wounds and Christian II was able to consolidate his position by punishing resistance to his government. Trolle, now firmly committed to the king's party, informed him of his likely opponents of whom eighty-two were killed on 8 November 1520 – a massacre to be known for ever as the Blood-bath of Stockholm – and many others were executed or exiled as Christian made a royal progress through his long-lost kingdom.

Within weeks the Dalarna peasantry was in revolt, led by Gustav Ericsson, an angry and embittered young noble of the Vasa family. For many years the Vasas had been related to the Stures and had identified themselves with the cause of independence: for this reason Ericsson had been taken hostage for a while in 1518, and subsequently his father, his brother-in-law and two uncles were murdered in the Stockholm Bloodbath. Meanwhile the *rad* itself was contemplating revolt. Christian's brutal treatment of his enemies had brought home to the nobles for the first time in many generations the full implications of the Union of Kalmar, and when Ericsson defeated a royal army in 1521 and seized Uppsala, many of the most senior nobles went to join him, hoping thereby to exercise some control over his actions. Ericsson realised, however, that while Christian held the principal fortresses, he needed more aid than the *rad* could muster, and with this in mind he opened negotiations with the city of Lübeck, headquarters of the Hanseatic League.

The League was already at odds with Denmark. Its monopoly of Baltic trade, shipped overland to Hamburg via Lübeck, had been impaired by the opening of the Danish Sound to Baltic shipping, and Danish and Dutch merchants had been the first to seek trade concessions from Ivan III after he had expelled the Hanse from Novgorod. It was, therefore, without difficulty that the Lübeck merchants were persuaded to support Ericksson, and an expedition of 750 trained soldiers and ten warships, along with the necessary supplies, was swiftly paid for by private contributions. Christian meanwhile was distracted by a rebellion in Denmark itself. His vigorous methods of government had become increasingly unpopular there, and in his place the Danish nobility had put forward his uncle Frederick of Holstein. By the midsummer of 1523, therefore, Ericksson had succeeded in liberating the provinces of central and northern Sweden, and on 6 June he compelled all his followers, peasants and nobles alike, to recognise the logical conclusion of his rebellion by declaring himself to be Gustav I of Sweden.

His kingdom was small, threatened from Norway in the west, and from Halland, Skane and Bleking in the South. Its population was less than 750,000, most of whom lived in village settlements, isolated from each other by lakes, mountains and forests. Small quantities of silver were mined at Sala, and copper north of Falun, but the only town of any consequence was Stockholm where furs and hides, and the iron from the Bergslag, were exchanged for textiles, food and luxuries supplied by the Hanse, to whom after 1523 Gustav was obliged to allow monopolistic rights and the privilege of trading free of all tolls. One special feature of Swedish society was the independence of the peasantry. They owned just over half the land, governed themselves in a simple form of village democracy and were represented as an Estate in the *riksdag*. The four hundred or so noble families were more or less indistinguishable from them except that they held their land, about one-fifth of the country, free from taxation, and it was only an inner group of twenty-five to thirty families which was influential in the *rad* and in provincial government. With the Church owning another fifth of the land, this left barely six per cent for the king, who was poorly provided for in other respects too, since there was no civil service to support his government beyond a few clerks in a chancery and the bailiffs of his estates.

But Gustav had more serious problems to face than the lack of a civil service. His most difficult task was to retain the support

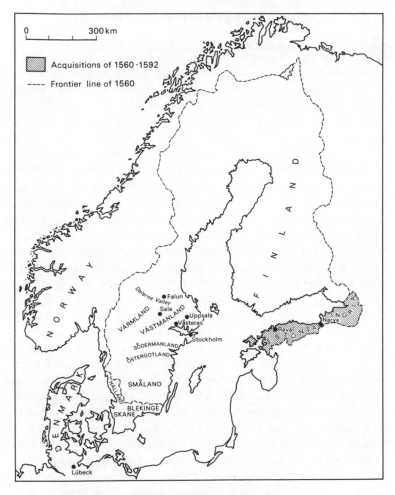

Sweden under the Vasas

of his followers once the days of fighting for independence were
over. Those who had fought for him could not understand why
men of ability who had formerly served Christian II should be
needed in Gustav's service; furthermore, the Sture family,
jealous of the royal status he enjoyed, encouraged dissension in
the Dalarna valley where it was claimed that, 'all those who
faithfully served the lords and realm of Sweden has Gustav hated
and persecuted, while all traitors to the realm ... these has he

favoured'. For a dangerous period in 1524–5 Kristina, widow of Sten Sture the Younger, was in conspiracy with both former friends and former enemies of Gustav, and it needed a ruthless parade of force in the Dalarna valley to restore order; but the danger from that source was not at an end.

In the meantime Gustav fell foul of his bishops. Urgently needing money to meet debts of over 120,000 marks, mostly owed to Lübeck whom he could not afford to antagonise, he turned to the Church. The Church was well endowed, owning fractionally more land than the nobility, and the bishops enjoyed such wealth that they were able to call out more horsemen for knight service than any great noble, and had not hesitated to do so in the past when they imagined their interests in danger. Despite the opposition led by Hans Brask, bishop of Linkoping, Gustav began to appropriate certain church properties, raised forced loans from the clergy and quartered troops in the monasteries. In 1526, having demanded two-thirds of the entire income of the clergy for that year, he agreed to be content with a grant of 15,000 marks, but the growing opposition to his activities meant that many of the clergy refused to pay. At the same time there was trouble over the question of church reform. The Swedish Church, though wealthy, was not as corrupt as in other countries, but Lars Andreae, Gustav's chancellor, had claimed, as a Catholic reformer, that the Church's property belonged to the people, for whom the king rather than the clergy should be the trustee; eventually he became more of a Lutheran under the influence of Olaus Petri, a priest who had studied at Wittenberg. Gustav, himself, as yet unaware of the political implications of Lutheranism for royal authority, nonetheless took pleasure in protecting Petri from the hostility of Brask and, by making the printing press a royal monopoly, secured for him an opportunity to publish his books and translations unhindered. Indeed, few other books were published at all.

Gustav's seizure of church property and the charge of encouraging heresy led to a crisis in 1527 which coincided in part, and in part was connected with, further trouble in the Dalarna valley. The peasants were deeply suspicious of Gustav's church policies, and their old devotion to the Stures was re-awakened by the appearance of the so-called *Daljunker*, the Dalesman, who claimed to be the son of Sten Sture the Younger. Under his banner the peasants were once more in rebellion. It was a crisis which Gustav was well equipped to tackle and, as Sten Sture might have done, he gambled everything on an appeal to the *riksdag*, which was summoned to meet at Våsteras. His rhetoric was powerful: in a speech of great authority he explained his problems and his debts, condemned the Church for selfishly hoarding its treasure, insisted on a public disputation in order to clear himself and Olaus Petri of the suspicion of heresy, appealed in ringing terms for national unity, and threatened to abdicate if his wishes were not obeyed.

The Dalarna rebellion, dangerous as it was, worked in Gustav's favour for at such a crisis no one dared look for an alternative ruler. Consequently, his demands were met. The bishops were required to surrender their castles, to retain only as many knights as the king desired and, since they would, therefore, require less income than before, to relinquish their 'superfluous revenues' to the king. Monasteries, though not abolished, were virtually appropriated by the appointment of lay administrators, and all lands given to the Church since 1454 were restored to the families of the donors. In addition, a disputation not only cleared the king and Petri, but by the wording of its resolution – 'that God's word may be purely preached everywhere in the realm' – left the door open for Lutheran preaching based on the sole authority of the Scriptures. After the *riksdag* had dispersed, Gustav compelled the *rad* to endorse its decisions, relying on its members' reluctance to consider his abdication and their awareness of the advantages they could look for from the appropriation of Church property. The ordinances in fact, prompted by Gustav, acknowledged the king's right to interfere in the appointment to benefices and, without one word of criticism of Rome, introduced injunctions of a Lutheran kind on the matter of clerical status, clerical fees and ecclesiastical courts.

In the next few years events moved quickly. Dalarna was suppressed, Brask fled the country, Olaus Petri exploited his monopoly of the printing press to issue Luther's works in full, and his brother, Laurentius, fresh from Wittenberg, was installed as archbishop of Uppsala without the pope's consent. In 1530, in order to settle his debts with Lübeck, Gustav ordered all urban churches to surrender their largest bell, or its equivalent value in cash; in 1531 he applied the order to all rural churches, and once again the Dalesmen of Dalarna rose in protest. It was a dangerous moment since Christian II had suddenly appeared in Norway with the backing of the emperor, Charles V, and Gustav was forced to temporise by promising to put the matter before the *riksdag*. The citizens of Stockholm, close allies of the Dalesmen since the fifteenth century, but much influenced by their commercial contacts with Lutheran cities in Germany, eventually declared their support for Gustav's policies and the rebellion immediately subsided. Two years later Gustav marched through the valley. Although he had owed everything to its peasants in the rising of 1521, their subsequent behaviour had destroyed his affection for them and by executing their ringleaders and abolishing their traditional right of self-government he hoped to ensure peace there in the future. In the meantime, Frederick of Denmark had joined with Gustav to defeat Christian, and had taken him back to Copenhagen where he remained a prisoner until his death in 1559.

One further complication in this complex pattern of events was provided by the revolution of the Lutheran proletariat in Lübeck, and the attempt of Jurgen Wullenwever to overthrow Denmark and establish control of the Sound (see page 177). Sweden itself was not directly involved, though Gustav followed Wullenwever's progress with alarm, and when the German merchants in Stockholm were suspected of conspiring with Lübeck in 1535, he swiftly executed the ringleaders and abolished the city's tradition of supplying its own defence force.

Now that his enemies at home and abroad had been defeated or reduced to order, it was time for Gustav to consolidate his power by establishing the administrative machinery to enforce it. Without a civil service too much depended on the person of the king: the chancery was nothing more than the office where the clerks wrote letters at his dictation, and the exchequer merely the place where his bailiffs handed in the returns from their estates. Gustav had no ambition to revolutionise his administration, but he wanted secretaries of greater importance and ability, and he recognised that to find them he would have to look outside Sweden. In 1538 he found Conrad von Pyhy, who had been trained in the service of the Habsburgs, and in 1539, George Norman from the University of Greifswald. Neither was given free reign to create a new administrative structure. Pyhy, however, created a Council of Government which could meet permanently to deal with affairs of state, whether or not the king was present, and he established the chancery and the exchequer 'out of court' where they could develop their own formal procedures. Norman, on the other hand, was employed in church affairs. Although Gustav approved the teaching of the Petri brothers they had angered him by claiming that the Church should be a self-governing body, and he looked to Norman to make it, in effect, a department of state, appointing him 'superattendant' with the absolute power of a vicar-general. The Petris were condemned for treason in 1539, and although the sentence of execution was never carried out – indeed the brothers were restored to office in the church – the lesson of royal supremacy was quickly learned.

In 1540 Norman sent out commissions to take an inventory of all church property and to assess its value, an obvious preliminary to further spoliation if not to outright confiscation. In the southern province of Småland, where Catholicism was more deeply embedded in the hearts of the people, where services in the vernacular were disliked and where there was genuine anger at the amount of church plate which had already been seized, the arrival of Norman's commissioners provoked a rebellion, led by a peasant farmer, Nils Dacke. Pyhy, too, was as unpopular as Norman since his new administrative measures were regarded as meddlesome interference, and the rebellion represented in effect a conservative reaction to the policies and the pace of Gustav's government. Dacke turned out to be highly successful in waging guerilla war against the regular troops sent against him, and his forces advanced north into Östergotland. Gustav sought to temporise, summoned the *riksdag* to give his case the maximum amount of public support, and appealed to the southern provinces to forget their temporary disagreement with him, but to remember the Stockholm Bloodbath: it was effective propaganda and it carried the day. Dacke lost support and in 1543 he was defeated, betrayed and killed. In the long run, however, the rebels could derive some comfort from the fact that Pyhy too in the same year was disgraced for quite separate reasons, and his administrative policies were not developed.

Pyhy's fall was occasioned by an incident in foreign affairs. Christian III of Denmark was alarmed that the emperor, Charles V should continue to promise aid to Christian II, who was still living in a Copenhagen prison. Gustav too shared some of his anxiety and agreed to a defensive alliance between their countries. Old habits died hard, however, and so great was his suspicion of Denmark that Gustav could not bring himself to trust Christian III, even though the latter was most scrupulous in honouring the terms of the alliance. Pyhy, unaware or heedless of his sovereign's reservations, went abroad to raise troops on behalf of the alliance, and exceeded his brief by promising too much money and committing Gustav too firmly to a hostile stance against Charles V. When he returned in 1543 he was disgraced and imprisoned for life. Thereafter Gustav could please neither Christian nor Charles V and was extremely fortunate to be spared an attack by either.

In 1544 Gustav summoned the *riksdag* to assist him in three important matters. Dissatisfied with the quality of foreign troops, and in particular with those who had fought so badly against Dacke, he proposed to create a new type of peasant army, to which the *riksdag* agreed. The idea was to train the peasants for a short period in the essentials of drill and fire power, and then send them back to their villages in readiness for any crisis. Initially the reserve was to be voluntary, but later it would take one in ten of the free peasants and one in twenty of those belonging to a noble. In this way Sweden, one of the poorest and smallest countries in Europe, became the first to establish a native standing army. A more controversial matter was that of church reform and it was typical of Gustav that he should specially invite the bishops and the clergy to join the debates in order to rally them to his side, or to demonstrate to them that the other estates were not inclined to oppose him. The *riksdag* in effect confirmed the Reformation in Sweden by accepting Lutheran leadership in the church, though without any precise formulation of doctrine and without any abuse of Rome. Bishops were replaced by superintendents, and Norman began to play a less dominant role, working in tactful co-operation with Laurentius Petri.

Most controversial of all was the question of the succession. Despite opposition to Gustav's policies, and despite the claims of other families and the natural jealousies to be expected, the *rad* was ready to agree that Sweden's interest required an hereditary succession vested in the Vasa family. This decision, remarkable if seen in the light of events of 1520–7, is explained by Gustav's careful conciliation of their number: his second and third marriages were with their families, his firm stand against the Dalarna peasantry had established his respectability, and his readiness to redistribute church land gave the recipients a vested interest in preserving his government. Above all, and this is why the *riksdag* also added its assent to the Succession Pact, it was clear that Gustav had indeed maintained Swedish independence, and that the struggles with Denmark and the development of a Swedish Lutheran church had done much to create a greater sense of national identity.

For the last decade or so of his reign Gustav remained unchallenged at home and abroad, and was free to do much to strengthen his country's economy. His methods were universally criticised as meddlesome, but Gustav had no high opinion of the commercial instincts of his subjects and he found that the only way to create a successful enterprise was to run it himself. By his own investment in forges and in German workers, and by subsidies for the manufacture of arms and armaments, he set the iron industry on its feet; he ran his farms with such skill that, instead of leasing them out for rent, he transformed them into production units supplying his standing army. His own fortune he handled with great care and, being quick to see that rents in kind were of greater value than cash in a period of rising prices, he therefore reversed the general pattern of commuting goods for cash. Most of his wealth, of course, came from the Church, and nothing could conceal the fact that the royal supremacy had been used as a licence to plunder. Six and a half tons of silver were appropriated during his reign, two-thirds of all the tithes, and the extent of his confiscation of land can be assessed from the following census of farms in Sweden in 1520 and 1560:

	Peasantry	Nobles	Clergy	King
1520	35,239	13,922	14,340	3,754
1560	33,130	14,175	—	18,936

Gustav died in September 1560. It was his misfortune, if not his tragedy, to have forfeited the affection of the free peasantry of the Dalarna valley, with whom he had initially fought against the rule of Denmark. Nevertheless, it was his triumphant achievement to have established an independent kingdom. Gustav of course was a violent man, and one less ruthless would never have survived against his enemies; yet he also had the rare gift of basing much of his power on the strength of public opinion, never shrinking from going to the *riksdag* to win approval of his policy. As a result, Sweden was made independent, and his own family was assured of the succession to a throne which commanded respect among the nobility and was supreme in the Church.

Sweden and the Vasas 1560 – 1600

Gustav's eldest son Erik had acquired views about the nature of monarchy which went considerably further than those of his father. This was partly due perhaps because he had had to wait dutifully to inherit the throne instead of seizing it by his own strength and wits, and partly because of a growing strain of insanity which increasingly clouded his judgement. Whatever the cause, he deemed it inappropriate that his right of succession should have been derived from a decision of the *riksdag* and, therefore, in order to demonstrate a line of descent from the long forgotten former kings of Sweden he chose to call himself Erik XIV.

Trivial though this was, it was nonetheless significant since it indicated that Erik had misread the situation. Gustav had pretended to no divine right, and the succession had been vested in his family because he had been careful to establish an identity of interest between himself and the nobles of the *rad*. Most of them had been his companions-at-arms in one campaign or another, and they had shared with him the sense of a common achievement. He, too, had shared with them the lands of the Church, he had married into their families and it was generally recognised, even by those most jealous of him, that no one else could have been found to replace him. Erik, however, deliberately disassociated himself from the *rad* by refusing to marry into the nobility, and made a great deal of fuss about selecting a foreign princess worthy of his blood – an Elizabeth of England or a Mary Queen of Scots. Moreover, he set out to discredit the nobles as a class. He used the *riksdag*, not as a convenient counterweight to the power of the *rad*, but as a public platform from which to denounce the nobility, and he appointed a High Court under the direction of Joran Persson whose brief it was to charge one noble after another with treason, conspiracy or negligence.

At the same time he intervened unwisely in a dispute between

Reval and Russia by attempting to blockade Narva. Warfare excited him. He had the money to indulge his interest, and had personally supervised the training and equipment of his army as well as commissioning many new ships for the navy. The war, however, went badly, being complicated by Polish objections to Erik's interference in the Baltic Provinces (see page 286), and by a civil war with his own brother Johan, who had married a Jagiellon princess and was pursuing his own interests in Livonia. Johan was arrested and imprisoned in 1563, Poland declared war on Sweden, and Denmark, too, joined in, partly out of traditional hostility to Swedish independence but also because Erik's blockade of Narva had disrupted Danish trade. For seven years the Swedes kept up a desperate defence of their southern provinces and survived a blockade which ran them perilously short of supplies. The new navy then began to show its paces and with honours more or less even, peace was made in 1570.

By this time Erik was no longer king. His insanity had become more evident during the war years, and his wild denunciations of imagined conspiracies only served to ferment them in reality. In 1567 he held prisoner most of the Sture family, a family of which his father too had been suspicious, and after a special visit to their prison to seek an emotional reconciliation with them, returned two hours later to murder one of them himself and order the immediate execution of the others. The next six months revealed the bewildered action of a broken mind. Persson was arrested and then released, Johan was released, the surviving Stures were given blood money which was then demanded back, and finally in 1568 Erik announced his marriage to a peasant girl. Since there was no other action open to them, Johan and the *rad* deposed him, and he remained their prisoner until his death in 1577. Johan himself was declared king, but in terms which emphasised the elective nature of his succession, and relations between the king and his nobles were never easy. It was not simply a matter of jealousy or greed. The nobility was quite genuinely seeking a role for itself in the government of the country, while Erik and Johan seemed to govern almost exclusively through the agency of their own secretaries, who were rarely of noble birth. Johan moreover was such a lazy man that he rarely bothered to check what his secretaries did in his name, and the nobility was justified in its complaints against the authority of petty officials. They demanded in 1585, for example, that their sons be recruited and trained in administrative work, and that there should always be two nobles on hand to whom the secretaries were to refer matters if Johan were not available, but the king merely temporised and refused to bring them into full partnership with him.

A direct clash between the king and the *rad* was probably averted by the presence in Swedish affairs of a third force represented by duke Karl, the third of Gustav's sons. He was a cautious man who had exploited Erik's deposition and Johan's elevation to make himself virtually sovereign within his provinces of Södermanland, Västmanland and Värmland. He claimed absolute rights of jurisdiction over his people, raised his own taxes, issued his own coinage, and by 1580 was on the brink of civil war over Johan's religious policy. Johan had married a Jagiellon princess who was, therefore, a Roman Catholic, but he was neither Roman Catholic himself nor so naive as to believe that compromise was possible. He was, however, ready enough to discuss matters with Rome and this compromised him altogether in the eyes of his puritanical brother. Erik had restored bishops to the Swedish church and Johan was prepared to allow them considerable autonomy in church affairs, provided they indulged his preference for the older rituals, and, in the so-called *Red Book* of 1577, he authorised a new liturgy which embodied much of this ritual. His own clergy followed his lead without trouble but Karl was fiercely opposed to the liturgy. He prohibited the *Red Book* in his own provinces and when Johan outlawed the clergy who obeyed his brother, Karl retaliated by threatening civil war.

The members of the *rad* felt it necessary to reconcile the brothers and, despite their disputes with Johan, concluded that the king was in the right. In 1582 the *riksdag* condemned Karl's assumption of independent powers, but as the duke did not attend the session he paid no heed to its strictures. Matters finally came to a head in 1586, but as neither Johan nor Karl wanted to see the issue resolved by the *riksdag*, they arrived at a private settlement in which Karl gave way on everything but the new liturgy. This was not the end of the affair. After the peace settlement with Denmark in 1570 and Russia's acceptance of Swedish control in Estonia in 1583, Iohan had strengthened his alliance with Poland by securing the election of his son Sigismund to succeed Stephen

Bathory (see page 288). With the heir-apparent permanently absent in Poland, two of the leading nobles, Hogenskild Bielke and Erik Sparre persuaded the *rad* to appoint a committee to act as regents in the event of Johan's death, and deliberately excluded Karl from its membership. Karl interpreted this as a conspiracy by the nobles to reduce the importance of the Vasa dynasty, but Johan, for the time being, sided more with the *rad* than with his brother. Within a few months, however, Sigismund wanted to renounce his Polish throne, and it was arranged that the matter be discussed with Johan and the *rad* at a meeting in Reval in 1589. Johan was apparently only too happy to have his son home again, but Bielke and Sparre warned both of them that abdication would precipitate a war with Poland. Sigismund took the point and returned to Warsaw, but Johan was so vexed at the outcome that he turned against his advisers – 'the men of Reval' – and interpreted their action as a device to keep Sigismund away from Sweden for ever so that they might rule in his place.

In such a mood he found a ready ally in Karl and together they began deliberately to discredit the members of the *rad* before the *riksdag*, dismissed Bielke and Sparre from their offices and humiliated the remainder by demanding new oaths of loyalty which bound them to silence if they disagreed with their king. Whereas Karl was ready to attack the *rad* out of policy, Johan did so only out of vindictiveness and his mood softened as the years went by. Indeed, by the time of his death in 1592, he had to some extent reconciled himself with the 'men of Reval'. Sigismund's arrival, however, brought about yet another twist to events, the *rad* and Karl finding themselves unexpectedly in alliance in defence of their Lutheran faith. The alliance did not last long. Once Sigismund had returned to Poland, Karl's ruthless determination to be the Regent and the sole source of power in Sweden drove the *rad* into opposition, and Sparre and Bielke fled to join Sigismund. In 1598 they returned with him, supported by the Polish fleet, but Karl had united the rest of the country behind him in the name of Lutheranism and independence. Sigismund gave up the struggle and returned to Poland. Less honourably, he abandoned his supporters into Karl's hands and in 1599 after a public trial before the *riksdag* Bielke, Sparre and their colleagues were executed. It was not a question of right or wrong but rather a trial of strength, and Karl's victory led to his coronation in 1600 as Karl IX of Sweden. He had thus to defend his country against Poland as his father had done against Denmark, and, in so doing, to establish his family's right to govern Sweden in the century which followed.

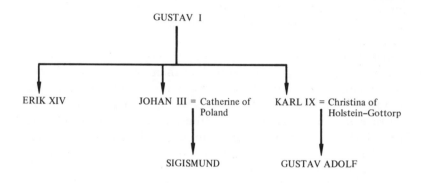

The House of Vasa

9

France 1515-98

The Reigns of Francis I and Henry II

FRANCIS I and Henry II paid little or no attention to the day-to-day business of government which had so occupied the time of Louis XI and Louis XII. Their temperament inclined them to live lavishly in the public eye, and their inclinations were reinforced by a profound desire to conform to popularly accepted notions of royal behaviour. They quizzed their ambassadors about the physical appearance and athletic prowess of their international rivals, Charles V and Henry VIII, and it was in self-conscious imitation of the courtly style of Italy that they bestowed their patronage on the arts. Francis indeed showed considerable interest in the New Learning. His sister, Margaret of Navarre, was one of the best educated women of the sixteenth century, and she ensured for many years that humanists who strayed across the border into heresy were protected by the king from the consequences. Poets and humanists, of course, were maintained at little cost, but Francis also showed himself willing to spend considerable sums on the employment of artists and architects, (see page 401). Leonardo da Vinci, Andrea del Sarto and many other Italians were brought to France, and the so-called First School of Fontainebleau was established under the direction of the Florentine artist Giovanni Battista Rosso. Henry II continued his father's work of building in the Loire valley at Fontainebleau, commissioned a new façade for the Louvre by Pierre Lescot and employed many artists to immortalise his mistress Diane de Poitiers.

Neither Francis nor Henry, however, had any doubt that the occupation most appropriate to their royal status was the conduct of warfare, and for this they were well endowed by nature. Indeed,

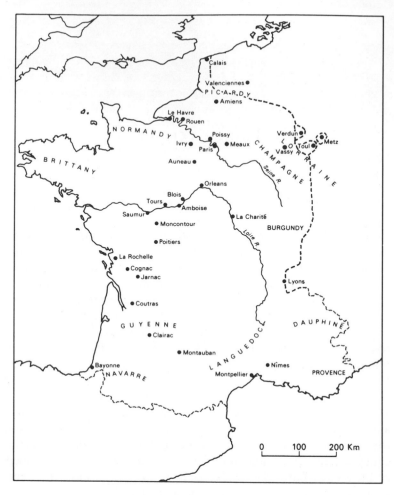

France during the Wars of Religion

whenever an unwelcome truce disrupted a campaign their aggressive instincts had to be released in the pursuit of wild beasts or the mock combat of the tournament – at which Henry lost his life in 1559. For nearly half a century, therefore, France was governed from a saddle, yet, surprisingly perhaps, royal power was enhanced rather than diminished. The capture of Calais, Metz, Toul and Verdun could scarcely compensate for the French kings' repeated failure to dominate Italy, and was dearly paid for at the price of bankruptcy, but the warfare itself served an invaluable purpose in satisfying the ambitions of a restless nobility for more than two generations, and by bringing the clergy into greater dependence upon the crown as a result of the Concordat of Bologna (see page 120). More important still was the fact that by their military leadership Francis and Henry succeeded in embodying, no matter how imperfectly, a growing sense of nationhood among their subjects, and this, combined with the impressive dignity, indeed the glamour of their courts, engendered something of the all-essential mystique of monarchy without which royal government was powerless against the entrenched traditions of social pressure groups and provincial 'liberties'.

The foundation of royal government had of course already been established. The king was recognised as God's anointed representative, the source of all justice and the fount of all patronage whether cultural, ecclesiastical, military or civil. At the centre of the administration was the council, variously referred to as the *Conseil du Roi*, the *Conseil Privé* or the *Conseil d'Etat* (see page 132). Certain nobles were invited to attend its meetings, but their presence merely masked the influence of lesser-born experts who worked indefatigably and obscurely to strengthen royal authority, extend its jurisdiction and improve its revenues. Chief among these were the *maîtres des requêtes*. Their office, unique to France, allowed them to exercise a general commission on the king's behalf, especially in matters which did not fall traditionally within the competence of established courts. Their overriding powers made them so useful an instrument of royal government, that the eight *maîtres* of 1493 had been increased to more than sixty in 1559. Moreover, the relative sophistication of the royal administration in France was revealed by the fact that whereas in other countries the institutionalised secretaryship of state could only be evolved by an extension of the function of the king's private secretary – a Los Cobos or a Thomas Cromwell – Henry II was able to appoint four *secrétaires d'état* ready-made from the ranks of his *maîtres des requêtes*.

The *maîtres des requêtes* wielded exceptional powers for exceptional purposes: the more humdrum, day-to-day administration of France was conducted under the direction of the four sovereign courts (see page 134). Chief among these was Paris *Parlement* whose members advanced the king's interests and their own employment by extending and centralising the jurisdiction of the crown. On occasion they became too jealous of the duties they performed on the king's behalf, claiming a degree of privileged independence of the royal council and of the *maîtres des requêtes* which could only lead to conflict, but Francis and Henry had their measure; summoning them to their presence, in a ceremony known as a *lit de justice*, they reminded them forcibly of their origin in the royal council and commanded them to complete their business in accordance with the royal will. In addition both Francis and Henry deliberately developed the competence of the other sovereign courts in order to reduce the tendency of the *parlementaires* to monopolise the king's business. The *Chambre des comptes* and the *Cour des aides* established an almost exclusive right to deal with appeals in disputes over taxation, as well as with the general administration of royal revenues, and the *Grand Conseil* was specifically instructed by Francis I to co-ordinate the administration of justice by sorting out, and overriding where necessary, the conflicting claims of local seigneurial and ecclesiastical courts. This, of course, was already a well-defined function of the work of the *parlement*, but so much still remained to be done that both courts were able to operate in the king's interest without challenging each other's competence.

Throughout the provinces, the work of extending royal authority had been considerably eased by the elimination of the great apanages – even Louis XII's unwise creation of Bourbon had been terminated in 1523 (see page 222) – but many problems remained. If the king could usually impose his will whenever he himself intervened in local affairs, the small number of his *officiers* – about one for every 1,250 of the population – did not permit him to intervene everywhere and at all times. Diversity and separatism, aggravated by the difficulty of maintaining efficient communication across vast distances, made it virtually impossible to treat France as a united kingdom; some of the provinces behaved at times as though they were independent members of a federal union, and there were many regions of France where a man could live without fear of the king's *officiers* provided he did not fall foul of the local great family. The Guises in Champagne and Burgundy, the Condés in Picardy, the Albrets in Guyenne or the Bourbons in Languedoc, monopolised not only the chief offices of the province but established their clientele in positions of influence at all levels of

provincial life, so that in a moment of crisis their role of military
governor could be transformed into that of military dictator – as
indeed happened in the second half of the sixteenth century.

Nonetheless, within the traditional boundaries of the provinces
and the traditional spheres of influence of the great families,
royal agents continued to make headway in extending their
sovereigns' authority and jurisdiction. Within the towns, of course,
the appointment of *contrôleurs des deniers communs* (see page 132)
had ensured that the wishes of the royal council were listened to
with some respect, and it was within the bailiewicks that the new
advances were achieved. The *baillis* indeed became so influential
that in order to share the burden of their work, as well as to
prevent them establishing too great a personal ascendency within
their bailiewick, *lieutenants-criminels* and *lieutenants-civils* were
attached to their office, and the number of *procureurs du roi* and
avocats du roi continued to grow steadily until 1559. The flow of
appeals from the *bailli*'s court to the local *parlements* became so
great in fact that in 1552 a new tribunal, the *présidial*, was appointed
to deal with the less important of these, and to establish yet
another influential group of *officiers* to represent the council in
provincial life.

None were more important, however, in the life of the average
Frenchman than those whose task it was to improve the flow of
revenue into the royal treasury, in order to sustain the armies
perennially engaged in Italy. The administration of assessments
and collection was improved in part. A central treasury was created
in 1523 under a *trésorier de l'épargne*, so that income from royal
land need not be treated separately from that derived from taxation:
in 1543 the boundaries of the four *généralités* were redefined,
creating sixteen tax districts in all, each with its *receveur-général*
and answerable, after 1551, to a *trésorier-général*. Changes such
as these were merely incidental and superficial since there was
much that needed comprehensive reform, not least the fact that
the treasury derived the bulk of its revenue from the poorest
section of society. To alter this, however, was beyond the ability
of the Valois government, nor indeed could any fundamental
changes be achieved until the privileged classes who were exempt
from taxation had been overthrown in the revolution of 1789.

A more immediate problem, and one which presented a serious
challenge to royal authority, was the spread of Protestantism from

Germany and Switzerland. French humanists, of course, had been quick to welcome Luther's publications, and Lefèvre d'Etaples (see page 65) had already come very near to expounding the doctrine of justification by faith in the commentary he supplied for his own edition of St Paul's Epistles in 1512. His pupil, Guillaume Briconnet, became an ardent reformer who, as bishop of Meaux, was anxious to root out the evils of non-residence, ignorance and corruption among the clergy of his diocese: in addition, however, he allowed his court to become a centre for those like Guillaume Farel whose enthusiasm for reform was swiftly leading them into heresy. The Meaux group, as it was called, enjoyed the protection of Margaret of Navarre, and through her of her brother Francis I – to the extent that Zwingli felt it appropriate in 1525 to dedicate to him his *Commentary on the True and False Religions*. Since the French kings, however, were already masters of their own church through the Concordat of Bologna, there was no political incentive for Francis to embrace the new faith, nor was he in fact anxious to do so. He protected a few favoured scholars from the anger of the Sorbonne, whose privilege it was to defend orthodoxy, but he supported the burning of Lutherans and, as the climate of opinion began to harden against heresy, the Meaux group ran for cover. Briconnet, after appearing before the Sorbonne, returned to his diocese to hunt out Lutheran publications, Farel fled to Basle in 1523, and Lefèvre, after publishing his translation of the Gospels, took refuge in Strasburg in 1525.

A mild reaction followed Francis's release from his Spanish captivity in 1526, and Lefèvre returned home to publish a translation of the Old Testament, but the need to raise money for his ransom compelled the king to reassure the nobles and clergy of his orthodoxy by giving a more vigorous lead to the persecution of heretics. It was the heretics themselves, however, who finally determined their fate. On the evening of 17 October 1534, Lutheran placards condemning the Mass were posted throughout Paris and in many other towns, and one was fixed to Francis' bedroom door. So angry was the king at this insult to his authority that he set about an immediate programme of repression. Two hundred arrests were made, twenty-four were burnt at the stake, and in the following years the Lutheran movement in France collapsed. Briconnet died in 1534, Lefèvre in 1536 and the Meaux group retreated into orthodoxy. Meanwhile the duke of Guise and his brother, the cardinal of Lorraine, established a firm hold over the provinces adjoining the empire from which the contagion was most likely to spread; and though Henry II was prepared to win Lutheran allies to suit his purposes abroad, at home he was resolute in persecuting their co-religionists.

The defeat of Lutheranism in France was soon made irrelevant by the emergence of Calvinism which presented the government with a much less tractable problem. The bishop of Winchester, in his sermon at the funeral of Mary Tudor, said that, 'the wolves be coming out of Geneva . . . and have sent their books before, full of pestilential doctrines, blasphemy and heresy to infect the people': exaggerated though his fears might have seemed in England in 1558, his words aptly described the situation in France. The first French edition of the *Institutes* appeared in 1541 and a French psalter appeared in the following year which was possibly even more effective in its missionary effect. By 1547 the government was alive to the problem, and the edict of Fontaine-bleau specifically banned Swiss as well as German books unless they had the approval of the Sorbonne. By this time however 'the wolves' themselves had arrived – Frenchmen who had been trained at Geneva to preach their faith and to withstand persecution, and whose missionary efforts were so successful that Calvinist congregations were swiftly established across France. This success is not easily explained but, since there was neither political advantage nor social gain to be derived from conversion to Calvinism during the persecution of Henry II's reign, the issue must have been decided by religious conviction. In other words, conversion was achieved by preaching, and though the manner of preaching must have been singularly effective, the subject matter was the vital factor. Calvinist teaching was so well thought out, so clearly demonstrated, so brilliantly designed to exploit the weaknesses within the Roman Catholic church, that for the hundreds of Frenchmen who felt at all deeply about the unreformed condition of their own church, there was nothing they could do but conform to what they knew to be inadequate or to accept the direction of Geneva.

The peasantry was mainly indifferent to the new faith. It could not read the books, and it rarely enlisted in the Calvinist congregations unless prompted to do so by its feudal overlords. At Montpellier in 1560, for example, the rural labourers, comprising one-fifth of the local population, constituted barely one-twentieth of the Calvinist community, which was largely dominated by artisans. The most important group of converts, however, was found among the nobility. Many of the missionaries were of noble birth, and many of their first converts were ladies of rank who sent their children, future leaders of society, to be educated in Geneva or brought up at home under a Calvinist tutor. Theodore Beza, before his return to Geneva to run the Academy, achieved remarkable success among the lesser nobility of Burgundy, and also converted Jeanne d'Albret, the wife of Antoine de Bourbon who was head of one of the three great families of France. Bourbon's brother Louis, Prince of Condé, was converted too, though Calvin was never wholly satisfied that his conversion was genuine. Unlike the other converts, some of the nobility did indeed look for political or financial advantage, as described by L'Hôpital, the royal chancellor: 'Several take shelter beneath the cloak of religion even though they have no God and are more atheist than religious; among them there are lost souls who have consumed and wasted their all, and can only survive on the troubles of the realm and the possessions of other men.' Against this kind of man, however, must be set the figure of Gaspard de Coligny, Admiral of France and a member of the Châtillon family of the House of Montmorency. He was a devout and serious man who struggled to resist conversion, but, once won over, his loyalty to his new beliefs became a source of inspiration to all his followers.

The presence of the nobles in what came to be called the Huguenot movement in France was a fact of great significance. Since they were soldiers by profession they organised themselves on military lines. At the Huguenot Synod of Clairac in November 1560, for example, the province of Guyenne was divided into seven *colloques*, each with its own colonel to organise the defence of the local congregations. Similar measures were adopted in Languedoc, Provence and Dauphiné, and, rather more sketchily, across France. When Henry II died the Huguenots had the support of the Bourbon and Châtillon families, a Protector-General in Condé, and a National Assembly which successfully met in Paris in defiance of the edicts. Inspired as they were by a burning conviction of the righteousness of their cause, they were thus well placed to threaten not only the Roman Catholic church in France but also the Roman Catholic monarchy.

The Wars of Religion to 1572

When Henry II died from wounds received in a tournament his eldest son, Francis II, was wholly unfit, by reason of his youth and his poor health, to govern the country on his own. Accordingly the three major families of France entered into competition for the privilege of assisting him.

Best placed to do so were the Guises (see family tree), a family with great estates in Lorraine which had made its fortune in the service of the Valois. Francis, duke of Guise, the captor of Calais, was a warrior whose wounds had earned him the honourable nickname of *le balafré*; his brother Charles, cardinal of Lorraine, was an experienced diplomat who carried great weight both at court and at the Council of Trent; above all, his niece, Mary, Queen of Scots, was married to the king. The family in short enjoyed great wealth and influence: it was also staunchly Roman Catholic in contrast to its greatest rival, the Bourbon family (see family tree), which had more or less adopted the Huguenot cause. The Bourbons boasted royal blood in their veins, not merely as kings of Navarre but as relatives of the Valois – a fact which had traditionally allowed them to behave more irresponsibly than any other subjects of the crown, but which had nonetheless failed to save the Constable Bourbon from the penalties of treason (see page 222). The head of the family, Antoine de Bourbon, was a timid and poor-spirited man, preoccupied with the Spanish threat to Navarre and the safeguarding of his estates in south-western France and Picardy: his Huguenot brother Louis had all the courage in the world but lacked the qualities of reliability and leadership, and the moral strength of the family lay with Antoine's wife, Jeanne d'Albret, a determined and vigorous adherent to Calvinism.

Guise and Bourbon alike, however, were *parvenus* compared with the Montmorencys. Anne de Montmorency, head of the oldest noble family in France, Constable of France since the disgrace of Bourbon and overlord of vast territories in the Midi and the Ile de France, was by tradition and temperament loyal to his king and to his church. His nephews, however, the Châtillons, had joined the Huguenots, and his own sons were at least sympathetic to their cause. Territorially, therefore, as well as in its divided religious affiliation, the Montmorency family stood midway

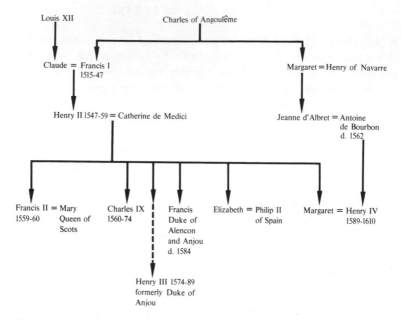

The House of Valois

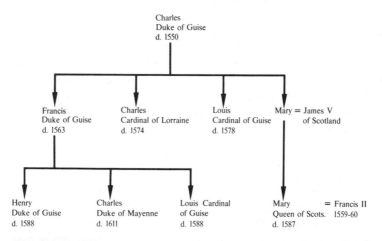

The House of Guise

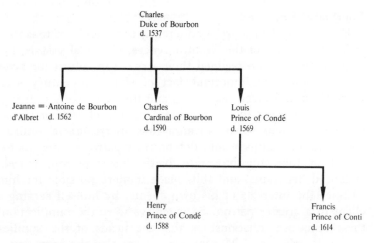

The House of Bourbon

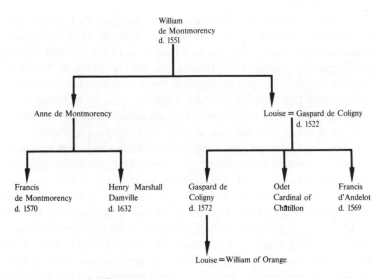

The House of Montmorency

between the Catholic Guises of the east and the Huguenot Bourbons of the west.

Each family had its own adherents, not merely of tenants, nor even, in the case of the Montmorencys, of feudal vassals, but of client families, who pledged their services in return for favours. Patronage was an important fact of sixteenth-century society. The patron advanced his clients and their relatives, securing for them employment in the royal service, the church or the army or helping them to an advantageous marriage: in return the client and his family would defend their patron's interests to the extent of following him into battle. Each patron, moreover, enhanced his status, and thus made it more possible for him to advance the interests of his own clients, by himself serving as a client to a greater patron. So extensive were the ramifications of these reciprocal relationships that the heads of the families of Guise, Bourbon and Montmorency were also the apex points of three vast pyramids built upon favour and obligation – and since the clients tended to follow their patrons' lead in the matter of personal and religious loyalties, the issues of French political life in 1560 were therefore polarised in the conflict between its three greatest families.

The situation, which was in no way peculiar to France, did not necessarily endanger the monarchy. Rulers of the quality of Francis I and Henry II – or of Charles V, Philip II and Elizabeth of England – were able to exploit the rivalries between their most powerful subjects by making them compete for those favours which only the sovereign could dispense, and by keeping them in suspense over the outcome of an award. Manipulative ploys of this kind were beyond the ability of Francis II, though not of his mother, Catherine de Medici, on whose shoulders the defence of royal interests accordingly devolved, but her skills of political management could not disguise the fact that her title to exercise them was none too sound. The neglected wife of Henry II, driven from the limelight by the glamour of Diane de Poitiers, Catherine had been regarded for nearly thirty years with scorn or compassion, but never with respect. Moreover, it was widely felt that her foreign birth, and especially the commercial associations of her family, made it inappropriate that she should exercise authority over the proud nobility of France. In any case, there was no question of her doing so in 1559 when Francis II became king, since, as everyone anticipated, he at once capitulated entirely to the Guises.

Two problems confronted the government: the treasury was over forty million livres in debt, and the Huguenots had grown in strength to the extent that in some areas they constituted a rival organisation within the state. To meet both these problems the Guises took the rare step of summoning the States-General, which had not met since the fifteenth century, only to find that the Bourbon clientele in the Third Estate could exercise enough influence to prevent both the granting of additional revenue and the persecution of Huguenots. The Huguenots, indeed, were not prepared to await persecution. One of their nobles, La Renaudie, staged a plot at Amboise in March 1560 to kidnap the king and thus release him from the control of the Guises. The 'Tumult of Amboise' failed in its purpose, but the Guises were sufficiently alarmed to accept a suggestion by Catherine that the leading nobility be summoned to an enlarged council at Fontainebleau, to discuss the question of church reform and the possibility of some toleration for Huguenots. The Bourbons boycotted the meeting. A second royal summons resulted in Antoine's appearance, but when Condé remained obdurate the Guises, in a remarkable show of strength, had him arrested and sentenced to death for treason. Blood royal or no, Condé's life was saved only by the death of Francis II in December 1560: as Charles IX was yet a minor, Catherine was able to claim full powers of regency and release Condé from prison.

At last Catherine was at the centre of affairs, but she could hardly have chosen a worse time for her triumph. Throughout the provinces there was a marked reaction against the general tendency towards greater administrative centralisation and, in particular, against the century-long erosion of seigneurial jurisdiction. In addition, the conflict of the leading families, exacerbated by religious rivalry, threatened to swamp the crown's authority in the flood-tide of civil war. Catherine's objective was simple: she sought by all the means available to protect and maintain royal authority until such time as her son Charles IX should be capable enough to assume the throne himself. Since bankruptcy prevented her from creating her own forces to match the power of the leading families, she tried to contain the situation by short-term diplomacy. Initially she hoped to ally with the Montmorencys and thereby keep the Guises and the Bourbons in check: in addition she sought to simplify the game to some extent by discovering some form of compromise between the Catholics and the Huguenots. The cardinal of Lorraine, disenchanted with the lack of progress at Trent, had suggested to Catherine that some means might be found for establishing locally a measure of doctrinal reconciliation and, to this end, she summoned a colloquy of theologians to Poissy in September 1561. It soon became clear that Catherine had misread the situation. The Jesuit Lainez and the Calvinist Beza immediately demonstrated that though each was anxious to enlist the favour of the queen mother, neither would accept her as an arbiter between themselves, and the search for a *via media* was abandoned. Anne de Montmorency moreover was so antagonistic to the spread of heresy that, in preference to the queen mother's offer of an alliance and to the friendship of his favourite nephew Coligny, he chose to side with his enemies, the Guises, in the defence of Catholicism.

To demonstrate their opposition to the queen mother's policy, Guise and Montmorency left the court, taking with them their relatives and clientele, and so great was the threat of a Catholic rebellion that Catherine immediately turned to the Huguenots for aid. Coligny assured her that there were 2,150 Huguenot communities who would rise to her defence if she would only grant them a measure of toleration. Accordingly, in 1562 the Edict of January allowed them to hold their own synods, to worship freely in private and to hold public services in the country areas and in the suburbs of the towns. Two months later the duke of Guise, passing with his retinue through the town of Vassy, chanced upon a Huguenot service held illegally in the centre of the town, and in the fracas which resulted his retainers killed thirty of the Huguenots. The Massacre of Vassy had not been engineered by Guise, who had earlier avoided Vitry where he knew the Huguenots to be breaking the law, but he was quick to exploit it by marching direct to Paris in order to seize the royal family. Condé, who might well have held the capital against him, lost his nerve and fled to the Midi, leaving Catherine and her children defenceless. 'The taking of the king or Paris is half the victory in civil war', wrote a contemporary commentator on the French wars of religion, and in this case the Guises had won both.

If Condé had had only his own wits and his own family to sustain him the war would have ended there and then. The

Calvinist pastors, however, were ready to summon their congregations to defend their faith with their lives. As a result the Huguenots
seized control of Lyons, Tours, Blois and Rouen, levying troops
and organising the purchase of supplies. In addition, Beza arranged
the transmission of money from Geneva to raise mercenaries in
Germany, and Elizabeth of England offered her support if Le
Havre were released to her as a base for English operations. The
central conflict took place in the valley of the Loire: Condé
advanced from Orleans, Guise and Montmorency from Paris,
while Catherine de Medici attempted to negotiate with both sides.
Fortunately for her, the opening encounter led to the death or
capture of the principal protagonists; Antoine de Bourbon was
killed at Rouen, Guise was captured and assassinated, Condé and
Anne de Montmorency were both taken prisoner. As a result it was
a straightforward matter in 1563 to arrange the Peace of Amboise
between them and bring both sides together to drive the English
from Le Havre.

The Peace of Amboise granted liberty of conscience 'pending
a General Council and the majority of the king', and liberty of
worship to all noble households. Bourgeois worship, however, was
restricted to one service in each *baillage* or *sénéchaussée*, with the
result that Condé and the other noble patrons of the movement
appeared to have won the privilege of liberty of worship for
themselves at the expense of the urban congregations upon whose
support they had depended. Coligny alone had opposed the
settlement, and he alone retained the confidence of the pastors,
who denounced the Peace of Amboise as a betrayal of their movement and prepared themselves for a further contest. In the
Catholic camp, too, there was indignation at the failure to check
the spread of heresy, and it was clear that warfare would soon
be resumed. In a desperate bid to restore national unity by rallying
the country round the young Charles IX, Catherine set out
with him in 1564 on a royal progress throughout France. At
Bayonne in 1565 she met her daughter Elizabeth (married to
Philip II) but the presence of the duke of Alba prompted the
Huguenot leaders to suspect that something sinister was being
plotted against them. In 1567, therefore, when the Spanish
army began to move along the French frontier towards the Netherlands (see page 364), they feared that Alba was to be used against
their own forces. In September, therefore, they staged an attempt

to kidnap Charles IX at Meaux: the Surprise de Meaux was a failure but, like the Massacre of Vassy, it proved to be a signal for the renewal of civil war in France.

The second war proved as indecisive as the first. Nothing significant occurred save the death of Anne de Montmorency, and the Peace of Longjumeau in 1568 repeated the terms of Amboise – but the shock of the Surprise de Meaux had driven Catherine to side openly with the Guises. She repudiated her previous policy of conciliation and compromise, dismissed those of her servants who had advised her in this and listened instead to her favourite son, the young Henry of Anjou, who was eager to demonstrate both his orthodoxy and his ability as a soldier. Within a few months the civil war had been renewed.

The third of the Wars of Religion was fought more bitterly than its predecessors. Coligny and Condé eluded attempts to seize them, and fled to La Rochelle which thereafter became one of the principal centres of Huguenot resistance. The Catholic armies led by Henry of Anjou pursued them and in 1567 defeated Condé's men at Jarnac. Condé was killed. Later, at Moncontour, the struggle for Poitiers was resolved when Henry defeated Coligny, and the Huguenot cause appeared to be destroyed. Coligny, however, with another Huguenot noble, Francis la Noue, escaped into the Midi, moving from one Huguenot community to the next, recruiting men, raising supplies and keeping one step ahead of the pursuing Catholic army. Their aim was twofold: to prevent themselves being drawn into a final and possibly fatal encounter with Henry of Anjou and, by prolonging the campaign, to deny to the government an opportunity to exploit the victories of 1569. In both they were successful. Not only did Catherine's youngest son, Francis, duke of Alençon, become jealous of the glories won by his brother Henry, but several nobles, sympathetic to Coligny's cause, began to ally with his cousins, Francis de Montmorency and Henry, Marshall Damville. These men, later to be categorised as *politiques*, represented no organised party, still less were they Huguenots, but they had come to believe that the acceptance of a measure of toleration was preferable to the dominance of Guise intolerance at court. Their neutrality impeded the action of the government, while Francis's jealousy led to the creation of a rival faction at court, and when Catherine realised that she could neither hope for an immediate victory nor finance a prolonged campaign she decided in 1572 to treat with Coligny at St Germain.

The Peace of St Germain allowed freedom of worship in noble households and within two towns in each *baillage*. More valuable was the promise to protect the interests of the Huguenots against the prejudiced judgement of the *parlements*, and to declare them eligible for civil and military appointments in the royal service. Most important of all, and the true measure of Coligny's military strength, the Huguenots were given four towns of great strategic importance, La Rochelle, La Charité, Montauban and Cognac, in which their garrisons might be posted to serve as sureties for the treaty.

Catherine was so impressed by the strength of Coligny's position that she decided he was too dangerous to be allowed out of her sight and invited him to the court. She was even prepared to accept in part his policy of uniting the Huguenots, Catholics and *politiques* by reviving their traditional fears about Spanish encroachment on their frontiers, and by seeking alliances with William of Orange and his brother, Louis of Nassau, who were vainly trying to overthrow the duke of Alba in the Netherlands (see page 364). Where Catherine underestimated Coligny was in her failure to discern behind the patriotic fervour of his policy, the equally fervent determination of the Calvinist who sought to create an alliance of Protestant states which might, by destroying Spain, destroy also the Counter-reformation. Catherine herself was too fearful of Spanish power to countenance any such policy, but, for the time being, the concerns of her own children distracted her attention from Coligny's true purposes. His proposed alliance with England became for her a golden opportunity to seek in Elizabeth a worthy bride for her favourite son Henry; another royal marriage, of inferior status but nonetheless acceptable, was arranged through Coligny's aid between her daughter Margaret and Henry, the Huguenot king of Navarre. Meanwhile, Charles IX, a poor-spirited prince, hitherto under his mother's thumb but desperately eager to emulate the tough vigour of his forebears, fell more and more under the spell of Coligny's bluff personality and, through his admiration for his mentor, began to emancipate himself from his dependence on his mother.

In April 1572 a treaty was made with Elizabeth of England, but it was only a defensive treaty and Henry's courtship of Elizabeth hung fire. In the Netherlands the Calvinist Sea-Beggars seized the port of Brill (see page 365), Louis of Nassau invaded Brabant from Germany and seized Mons, while a volunteer force of Huguenots, led by Coligny's companion, Francis La Noue, took Valenciennes. Catherine recognised at last that France was on the brink of war with Spain, with nothing more to rely on than a few Netherlands rebels and a purely defensive treaty with England. Her fears of Alba were reinforced when another Huguenot force, sent to relieve Louis in Mons, was intercepted and destroyed by the Spanish commander, and her own maternal pride was piqued by the realisation that Coligny's influence with her son Charles outweighed her own. In August she tried to reinstate herself in Charles's regard, but Charles declared his independence on 11 August by promising to commit 15,000 men to invade the Netherlands. In despair at the way things were going, Catherine appealed to the Guises to assassinate Coligny and thus remove the cause of her concern. Their plot miscarried. Coligny was merely wounded and Charles IX publicly declared his determination to avenge his friend. There was nothing left for Catherine but to gamble everything on one final confrontation with her son; in the event her tempestuous nature triumphed over Charles's new-found independence and, in a scene of emotional intensity, she convinced him that their lives were in danger from Coligny and the Huguenots. Under pressure from his mother the king agreed to sign an order for the murder of Coligny and certain other leaders, excluding Henry of Navarre, and the execution was committed to Henry of Anjou, Henry of Guise and the Provost of the Merchants of Paris.

The matter swiftly got out of hand. The citizens of Paris, angry at the presence of so many Huguenots for the wedding of Margaret and Henry of Navarre, were ready to run amok: so too were the Guises, who had scores in plenty to settle with those who had followed Coligny to court. As a result, on the eve of St Bartholomew's Day, the planned assassination of a few Huguenots became within a few hours the massacre of thousands, and the madness spread to several other cities. Taken aback though she was by the enormity of the violence she had unleashed, Catherine had nonetheless achieved her objectives. Coligny's baleful influence was removed and with it the likelihood of war with Spain. The price she had to pay, however, was to accept once again the direction of the Guises and the outbreak of further civil war.

The Later Wars and the Accession of Henry IV

The war which followed upon the Massacre of St Bartholomew's Eve took the form of a struggle for La Rochelle. The city refused admission to a governor sent from court and held out for seven months under the direction of Francis La Noue. The war then came to an abrupt end because of Catherine de Medici's urgent determination to see her children crowned or married to reigning sovereigns: her plan to marry Henry to Elizabeth of England had already failed, but as compensation of a sort the Polish throne was up for election. Henry of Anjou, therefore, had to leave France for Poland (see page 286) and abandon his campaign against the Huguenots. Indeed he had to go much further than that in order to reassure the Polish electors of his willingness to tolerate different religious confessions, and the Peace of La Rochelle in 1573 granted freedom of worship not only in all noble households, but also to the citizens of La Rochelle, Montauban and Nîmes.

The terms of La Rochelle demonstrated that the massacre had failed to destroy the Huguenot movement. It had nonetheless altered its character by killing off many of its leaders and by frightening away scores of its former protectors among the nobility. To some extent, therefore, the movement reverted to its earlier character of a missionary crusade sustained by ordinary folk, townspeople in the main, and led by its pastors. This meant, however, that its numbers and its influence were substantially reduced: it was largely confined to areas in the south, and its ultimate survival depended less on its own strength than on the weakness of the crown.

The crown indeed was becoming significantly weaker, and many nobles, their estates impoverished by inflation and war damage, were beginning to exploit the anarchic conditions created by the civil wars by taking to banditry. More dangerous still were the *politiques*. Although they never constituted a formal political group, the term is usefully applied to those who, out of humanist philosophy or personal indifference, preferred toleration to persecution, who hated the Guises, who were appalled by the massacre, who were alarmed by the ever-growing threat of anarchy, and who very often looked for an answer in the revival of local government free of central interference. Francis of Alençon counted himself among their number, hoping to use their support to strengthen his position against his brother, Henry, but the most dangerous *politique* was Henry Montmorency-Damville, Marshall Damville, Coligny's cousin and second son to Anne de Montmorency. From his family's great estates in Languedoc he was in a strong position to establish his personal ascendency in the province, and in alliance with the Huguenots and with those who resented the centralisation of administration in Paris, he made himself virtually independent of the crown.

This was immediately apparent when war broke out again in 1574 after the death of Charles IX and the return from Poland of Henry of Anjou as Henry III. The most able soldier, and the most intelligent of Catherine's sons, he lacked the emotional stability to employ his talents to good effect. At times he gave way to moods of religious hysteria, behaved with exaggerated piety and suffered the pains of extreme self-mortification: at other times he indulged in bouts of dissipation, accompanied by effeminate companions whose behaviour affronted the rest of the court. His accession marked rather than caused a renewal of the civil war when Damville seized the occasion to summon to Nîmes in December 1574 an assembly of Huguenots and *politiques*. As a result the southern provinces of Languedoc, Provence, Dauphiné and Guyenne began to form a self-regarding, self-directing community whose leader Damville negotiated as an equal with the royal council in Paris. Henry of Navarre, whose marriage to Margaret had saved him from the assassins on St Bartholomew's Eve, escaped from the court to join Damville and, by virtue of his independent sovereignty in Navarre, declared himself Protector of this new state within the state. Other nobles deserted the court, embarrassed perhaps by Henry III's behaviour and perhaps by the incompetence of his administration, and finally the king's own brother, Francis, now duke of Anjou, joined the *politique* camp.

Henry III had no option but to negotiate with his brother, and the treaty of 1576 was accordingly referred to as the Peace of Monsieur after the official title accorded to the brother of a king of France. Under its terms the Huguenots were granted complete freedom of worship except in Paris, their synods could meet openly, special tribunals of Huguenots and Catholics, *chambres mi-parties*, were appointed to protect their interests in the *parlements*, military guarantees were provided by assigning them eight garrison towns, Henry of Navarre was made governor of Guyenne, the young prince of Condé governor of Picardy and Damville was tacitly left supreme in the Midi. These in effect were the terms Coligny had always sought for, representing not, as in 1563, a compromise with the nobility but the wholesale concession of toleration to the entire Huguenot movement. In the long run, however, the treaty was worthless. Its terms could only be enforced and defended against Catholic opposition by a strong monarch, yet it was precisely because the monarch was so weak that the treaty had been forced from him. Indeed, the success of the Huguenots and *politiques* in coercing the king encouraged the Catholics to follow suit.

Their immediate reaction was to form a Holy Union or Catholic League with its stronghold in Paris and its leadership vested in the Guise family. To some extent it was very similar to the Huguenot organisation of the 1550s: its members were passionately devoted to their faith, the friars and monks fulfilled a role similar to that of the Calvinist pastors in sustaining the zeal of their followers, and the noble families provided the movement with military backing. It posed a direct threat to the type of monarchy which had slowly been evolving in France, since the League declared its opposition to the concept of a centralised administration, promising to restore to the provinces the liberties they had formerly enjoyed – 'as in the time of King Clovis'. It was also a highly organised body, requiring total obedience to its leader, the duke of Guise, and demanding the payment of contributions and the provision of men and arms. In short it became, like Damville's creation in the Midi, effectively a state within the state, and even entered into independent negotiations with Philip II of Spain.

The League was able to exert sufficient pressure upon Henry III to secure the summoning of a States-General to Blois in 1576: it also secured the election of a large majority of members who were prepared to support its views. Accordingly, the Huguenots and *politique* members withdrew in protest, but this only drove Henry III more firmly into the arms of the League. Skilfully he made a virtue of necessity: he issued the Edict of Poitiers which annulled the more generous terms of the Peace of Monsieur and then, in a move to win control of the League, declared himself to be its leader. The Leaguers retaliated by disbanding their organisation, and in the civil war which broke out in 1577 as a result of the Edict of Poitiers, they gave the king no assistance. Fortunately for Henry, the Huguenots and *politiques* were temporarily at odds with themselves. La Rochelle refused to admit Condé and his men within its walls, Damville led a campaign against his own nephew, Châtillon, Coligny's son, and, so inconclusive was the conflict, that within a few months Henry III was able to procure a settlement at the Peace of Bergerac. The number of Huguenot garrisons was reduced to six, freedom of worship was restricted to one town in each *baillage*, but nothing was done to weaken the independent position of the *politiques*. As a result, since no one, neither king nor *politique*, neither Catholic nor Huguenot, could hope at that time to secure better terms, the country was allowed to settle down for what was to be in effect a seven-year truce.

During this time Henry III forfeited what little respect he had once earned before his coronation, and his ambitious favourite, the duke of Epernon, was able to fill the court with his clientele and to secure control of an increasing number of important towns and fortresses. Francis of Anjou played little part in French affairs; he wasted his energies, as his brother had once done, in seeking to marry Elizabeth of England, and then engaged himself in an act of pointless intervention in the Netherlands revolt (see page 371). Catherine herself tried to compensate for the incompetence of her sons by travelling the country, seeking to settle old enmities and to bully or cajole the different factions into accepting compromises. The truce was disrupted temporarily in 1580 by a short-lived campaign by Henry of Navarre, concluded by the Peace of Fleix which merely repeated the terms of Bergerac, and the situation might well have dragged on indefinitely – to the ultimate advantage of Catherine's policy – when in 1584 it was transformed by the news of Francis of Anjou's death.

As a result of Anjou's death, Henry of Navarre became the heir-apparent to the throne, to the great alarm of the Catholic party. A secret society of Catholics in Paris, having won control of the Paris guilds, and thus of the city's government, made an alliance with the Guises and reconstituted the League of 1576. The League's power spread swiftly throughout the north and east, and wherever it established control it not only persecuted the Huguenots, but replaced royal officials and commanders with its own men. Furthermore, by the Treaty of Joinville, the League committed itself to support the international plans of Philip II to destroy heresy in France, England and the Netherlands, to defeat the Dutch rebels, to replace Elizabeth of England by Mary, Queen of Scots, to destroy the Huguenot *politique* party in France and to prevent the accession of Henry of Navarre. Henry III and Catherine were therefore trapped between two armed camps with neither the power nor the opportunity to arbitrate between them. Accordingly, since each side demanded their submission, they could, as Catholics, submit only to the Catholic League, and in 1585 they made the Treaty of Nemours with its leader, the duke of Guise. All edicts of toleration were rescinded, League officers were appointed to all positions of authority in the government and Henry of Guise became more powerful than his king.

The civil war which resulted from the League's triumph was ostensibly a conflict between Henry III and the League on the one hand, and the Huguenots and the *politiques* on the other; in fact, contemporaries correctly diagnosed the situation by referring to it as the war of the three Henrys, since Henry III, Henry of Navarre and Henry of Guise had ambitions which could only be satisfied by the destruction of the other two. As nominal leader of the Catholic armies, Henry III positioned himself in the valley of the Loire in order to prevent Henry of Navarre from joining with a force of German mercenaries raised at the orders of Elizabeth of England, whose own interests urgently required the destruction of the Catholic League. Henry III's plan, however, involved other considerations since his one hope of safety lay in the defeat not of Navarre but of Guise. He therefore persuaded Guise to advance against the Germans, in the hope that he might be defeated, while one of his favourites, Joyeuse, was despatched to look for Navarre in the hope that he would fail to bring him to battle. The stratagem collapsed. In 1587 Joyeuse was defeated and killed at Coutras, while Henry of Guise was victorious over the Germans at Auneau. News of this victory led to a tremendous surge of popular support for Guise throughout the north of France – a mood characterised by hatred not only of the Huguenots, but also of Henry III himself. Since 1574, when Damville had brought about the formation of an independent state in the south, the northern provinces had had to bear the entire burden of the royal taxes, with the result that they were as hostile to the king as to his Huguenot heir-apparent.

Nowhere was this mood more intense than in Paris, and violent riots broke out against the king and in favour of Henry of Guise. Henry III then alienated the Parisians still further by offering, in the year of the Armada campaign, what little assistance he could to Elizabeth of England by appointing his own remaining loyal commander, Epernon, to govern Normandy, in the hope that on the Channel coast he might possibly do something to embarrass the Spaniards. Mendoza, the Spanish ambassador in France, immediately conspired with the Catholic League to distract Epernon from his task by seizing the capital: accordingly, when news came through that the armada had finally sailed, fresh riots were fermented, Henry of Guise entered the city with his own troops and, though Henry III was able to summon royal troops to his aid, the Catholic preachers who were active among the people persuaded them to throw up barricades in all the streets so that the king was trapped within his own capital. Mendoza's plan worked admirably: Henry III fled the city, Epernon left Normandy to join him, and the Catholic League was able to move its forces into Picardy to cover the flanks of Parma's army in the Netherlands (see page 374).

None of this, however, could save the armada from the English fireships and the Channel storms, and the news of Spain's defeat so delighted Henry III that he resolved to risk a further encounter with the League by summoning the States-General to Blois in October 1588. Unfortunately for the king the southern provinces sent no representatives, while those from the north were dominated by the League. As a result the three Estates were unanimous in demanding a reduction in taxes and greater vigour in the persecution of Huguenots. Most dangerous of all, they proposed that resolutions of a States-General should have the force of law, and it was clear that the Guises were about to make the assembly a powerful instrument for their own government. In a wild moment Henry nerved himself to eliminate his enemies. On 23 December, Henry, duke of Guise, was summoned to the Chateau of Blois and there, suspecting nothing until the final moment, he was murdered: on the following day his brother, the cardinal, shared the same fate.

With the death of Henry of Guise, the Catholic League fell under the control of his younger brother, Charles, duke of Mayenne, who mobilised all the support he could muster to destroy the king. Henry III was dangerously isolated, his authority confined to the Loire valley, and his mother, Catherine, the only person capable of attempting any form of negotiation, was ill and dying. He, therefore, turned for support to Henry of Navarre, and together with their armies they marched north to besiege the capital. Paris was in the hands of a central committee of fifty, known as the Sixteen because they represented the sixteen quarters of the city, who were in alliance with the Catholic League and with revolutionary communes in other cities. Though their fervour was high, their military defence lacked skill, but when victory was in sight for the besieging armies, one of the League's friars infiltrated the enemy lines and murdered the king. Henry of Navarre immediately claimed the throne but, since he refused to renounce his Huguenot faith, the royalist army deserted and thus, with only his own troops to command, he had to abandon the siege.

Henry's claim to the throne was impeccable, but his refusal to abandon the Huguenot church forced the Catholic League to cast around for an alternative successor to Henry III. The cardinal of Bourbon was of little use since he was Henry's prisoner: moreover he died in 1590. Philip II, the mainstay of the Catholic League, therefore proposed that either his own candidature be adopted or that of his daughter, the Infanta Isabella Clara Eugenia, for whom he would act as, 'Protector of the Catholic Religion'. When Pope Sixtus V, who refused to accept this proposal, died in 1590, the Spaniards secured the election of Gregory XIV, who gave money to the Catholic League and denounced the Salic Law which threatened to give the kingdom of France to a Huguenot rather than to Philip II. He died within a few months, however, and was succeeded by Clement VIII who, though friendly to Spain, had not been the Spanish candidate and was therefore free, when occasion arose, to negotiate independently with Henry of Navarre.

Henry meanwhile had defeated Mayenne at Ivry in March 1590, going on to besiege Paris where he came very close to success. It was said that 13,000 inhabitants died of hunger and disease, but the exhortations of the League's preachers, and the reign of terror conducted by the Sixteen, discouraged any talk of surrender. At length, in September, the city was relieved by a Spanish army sent from the Netherlands under the duke of Parma (see page 374). The Spaniards were now increasingly committed to the support of the Catholic League; an army of 3,500 established themselves in Brittany in alliance with the duke of Mercoeur who had seized the province for himself, while another army invaded Languedoc. Others too were making the most of the situation: Charles Emmanuel of Savoy overran Provence, the duke of Lorraine prepared to seize Champagne, Damville was already master of the south and Mayenne held Burgundy. It was not surprising therefore that many of the League's supporters began to weaken in their opposition to Henry IV. They feared the partition of their country at the hands of ambitious nobles and foreign princes, they found it impossible to reconcile themselves to the claims of Philip II and the Infanta, and they refused to abandon the principles of the Salic Law. Moreover, they were horrified by the radicalism and ruthlessness of the Sixteen in Paris. 'Democracy threatens you', was the shrewd thrust delivered by an anti-Catholic pamphleteer, 'the beggars are in command'. As if to give substance to the charge, the Sixteen appointed a Committee of Public Safety, which deliberately selected its victims from the professional and noble classes in the city and ended up by executing the leaders of the Paris *Parlement*. Mayenne could no longer leave the capital to go its own way. In December 1591 he hanged some of the Sixteen and disbanded some of its agencies, but he could not prevent the preachers from stirring up the mob in riots aimed as much at the social system as at the Huguenots.

Within a few more months most of the opponents of Henry IV were only too anxious to abandon the League, the Sixteen, and the Spanish alliance, and to negotiate a settlement with him. Henry for his part had waited patiently for such a situation to develop, and in 1593 he declared his conversion to Rome – a brilliantly timed stroke which removed the principal bar to his accession and opened to him the gates of Paris. From there he was able to make a fervent appeal to the patriotism of his subjects, urging them to drive the Spanish troops from the country.

It was a bold gamble which almost failed. Many Catholics refused to accept Henry's conversion as valid until Pope Clement had given him absolution in 1595, while most Huguenots were so outraged by it that they refused any longer to fight for him. As a result the great families which had seized control of the different regions bided their time, leaving Henry with little military support against the Spaniards. He lost Calais in 1596, Amiens in 1597, and was also very nearly at war with most of his own subjects; nonetheless, he held on grimly in the faith that a war of conquest was beyond Spain's resources, and aware that Philip II had no alternative candidate to propose for the French throne. Moreover, Philip was old, his government bankrupt and his best general, Parma, had died of wounds. With all the money and troops he could scrape together, Henry recovered Amiens after a siege of six months, upon which Philip II agreed to negotiate. The Treaty of Vervins signed in 1598 restored Calais; France had thus survived the civil wars without losing any territory to her greatest enemy.

Meanwhile, the nobles of the Catholic League were handled with care. Like Philip, they were unable to find any alternative ruler to Henry, whose conversion to Catholicism had undermined the whole basis of their opposition. Henry exploited their predicament by meeting them singly to promise them indemnity, pensions and titles. This skilful, if undramatic, policy served the best interests of the king and of France by bringing an end to the civil war, and in 1598 the last of Henry's opponents, the duke of Mercoeur, came to terms for the sum of 4 million livres.

In winning over his enemies, however, Henry forfeited the affection, and very nearly the loyalty, of the Huguenots. His conversion had angered those who had genuinely fought for religious principles, and the remainder were jealous of the generous pensions awarded to the Catholic nobles. Without substantial concessions the Huguenots would have renewed the civil war, and the measure of their strength may be judged from the terms they secured in 1598 in the Edict of Nantes:

(i) The Huguenots were allowed full liberty of worship in all places outside Paris where their faith was already established.

(ii) The Huguenots were accorded the same civil rights enjoyed by Catholics, and provision was made for the establishment and protection of their schools and colleges.

(iii) Over one hundred fortified towns, many of them, like Saumur, La Rochelle, Montauban and Montpellier, of great strategic importance, were leased to the Huguenots for eight years, to be garrisoned by them at the royal expense.

(iv) The provincial synods of Huguenot clergy and laymen were to meet freely, and even a national assembly could be summoned with royal permission.

(v) *Chambres mi-parties* made up of Catholics and Huguenots, to whom all breaches of the edict were to be referred for adjudication, were established in every *parlement* of France.

Not one of these concessions was made as an act of grace to former colleagues and comrades; still less was Henry giving currency to any theory of toleration. Each article represented a serious limitation of royal authority, and the Edict as a whole established the Huguenots as over-mighty subjects, whose political and military privileges gave them the power to defy the crown if they chose. Spain had gained nothing from the wars, the Catholic nobles had to rest content with royal favours and pensions, but the Huguenots had driven one of the hardest bargains that a king of France had been forced to accept. Nonetheless, privileged though they were to be, their numbers had fallen badly since 1559; the 2,000 or more congregations claimed by Coligny had dwindled to less than 800, and the action of the Catholic League had more or less driven them out of the north and east. Furthermore, the terms of the Edict made it virtually impossible for the Huguenots to expand again in those areas, while no such limitation was put on a Roman Catholic recovery in the south.

With Huguenot garrisons established in one hundred towns, with Damville still supreme in Languedoc and the Midi, Mercoeur in Brittany, Mayenne in Burgundy, and countless other noble families entrenched in positions of authority, it could be said that France resembled not a united kingdom but a confederation of French provinces, but Henry was not discouraged. He regarded the settlements of 1598 with Philip II, with Mercoeur and with the Huguenots both as a necessary step towards securing the general recognition of his title and as an opportunity to draw breath after decades of civil war: 'La France et moi' he said, 'nous avons besoin de haleine'. Moreover, having fought and bargained his way to the throne from a position of relative weakness, he was determined in the years ahead to make possession of that throne a worthwhile attribute. He had proved himself as a soldier and as a leader; above all he had the gift of inspiring the loyalty of ordinary Frenchmen, a loyalty perhaps he rarely deserved but which he readily exploited to promote a return to peace and order. With the recovery of royal authority the age of the Bourbon monarchy had begun.

10

The Habsburgs in Europe, 1555-1600

The Government of Philip II of Spain

ONE measure of the importance of Philip II has been perhaps the intensity of the judgements which his reign has evoked. English and Dutch historians have found it difficult to regard him as anything but a dangerous tyrant who came perilously close to destroying their liberties. Spaniards, however, have acclaimed him as *El Prudente*, the king of their country's Golden Age. Moreover, while Protestants and liberals still tend to see him as a reactionary bigot, the Catholic tradition portrays him as the generous crusader of the Counter-reformation and the champion of Christendom against the Turks. Behind the rival interpretations of his reign the man himself is likely to be lost.

Two things about him are beyond question, his extraordinary capacity for hard work, and his devout resolution to answer to God with his own soul for the well-being and good government of the subjects entrusted to his care. So firm-minded was he in this respect that he allowed himself neither respite from work nor opportunity for personal advantage: 'Doctor take note and inform the council,' he once wrote, 'that in cases of doubt the verdict must always be given against me'; and despite his love for the members of his family, revealed in letters of great affection which passed between them, the duties of a king overrode the considerations of a father in the matter of his son Don Carlos. Carlos was both physically and mentally abnormal, the strain of madness in Juana having been intensified, since both his parents were descended from her, by two generations of inbreeding within the Habsburg family. As a private individual Carlos would have presented a serious enough problem since he was not only subject to murderous rages but crafty enough in his sane moments to elude surveillance. As heir to the throne, however, he endangered the state and in 1568, after evidence had come to light of his treasonous correspondence with the king's enemies in the Netherlands, Philip was obliged to order his arrest. Six months later, when attempts to hunger strike had been succeeded by bouts of gluttony, the young prince died in prison.

Resolute though he could be – and indeed as he tried to appear to be – Philip was handicapped by a sense of his own inadequacy. He felt himself to be unworthy of his father Charles V, and he shrank from contact with strong successful personalities like his half-brother Don John, the soldier duke of Alba, or the sailor Santa Cruz. To conceal this weakness he cultivated a façade of cold, regal detachment, and the man who could write lively and affectionate letters in private became the king who deliberately refrained from smiling in public. In the end, as the Venetian ambassador recorded at his death, 'he displayed great calmness and professed himself unmoved in good or bad fortune alike . . . he held his desires in absolute control and showed an immutable and unalterable temper . . . no one ever saw him in a rage, being always patient, phlegmatic, temperate, melancholy'.

It was partly to cultivate further this sense of detachment, partly to satisfy a bureaucratic tendency in his personality, that Philip, unlike Charles V who had travelled ceaselessly from one kingdom to another, chose to live permanently in and around Madrid. As though to emphasise the point, he had a palace built twenty miles north of the city in an isolated spot on the edge of the Guadarrama sierras. The Escurial proved to be a fine grey stone edifice whose classical lines admirably embodied the terms of Philip's commission to Herrera, which required him to achieve 'simplicity of form, severity in the whole, nobility without arrogance, majesty without ostentation'. It was in part a mausoleum for the bones of Charles V, in part a monastery, and in part a private residence to which Philip could retreat in the summer months. There in welcome isolation he could hear Mass, enjoy his superb collection of Titians and Tintorettos and work undisturbed at his papers.

In Aragon, Italy and the Netherlands, Philip's determination to remain in Madrid was taken to mean that, unlike Charles V, he no longer regarded the *monarchia* as a collection of kingdoms to be governed individually and separately, but as an empire subordinate to and dominated by Castile. In fairness to Philip this was not his intention. He scrupulously observed the separate traditions of his kingdoms, and, with the exception of the Netherlands, each was governed separately through its appropriate council, such as the Council of Aragon, the Council of Italy or the Council of the Indies. Moreover, when Portugal fell to him in 1580 (see page 351) Philip rejected the idea of incorporating it into Castile: instead he treated it like Aragon as a separate kingdom and bound himself by the Oath of Thomar to respect its separate institutions and traditions. It was only in matters of finance that Philip, like his father, imposed any form of central direction, but even this was done both hesitantly and irregularly, and there was much truth behind his request to the Council of Italy, when asking for money in 1589, that, 'except in the most urgent cases it is not the custom to transfer the burdens of one kingdom to another'.

Naturally enough, perhaps, Philip's subjects were not inclined to believe his protestations, but their suspicions might well have been allayed to a greater extent had Philip followed his father's example by visiting them from time to time. The political value of Charles V's perennial peregrinations was that all his subjects could live in the hope that their sovereign might periodically descend upon them to experience their problems, receive their petitions in person, remedy their grievances and, most important of all, distribute rewards for their services. By governing his kingdoms separately, but by doing so from Madrid, Philip pleased no one. The Castilians complained that the responsibility and the expense of defending the interests of the *monarchia* fell almost entirely on them, and that they enjoyed no compensatory authority over the other kingdoms; the others for their part contended that their interests were neglected and subordinated to those of Castile.

The centralisation of the administration of the *monarchia* upon Madrid was of course altogether different in character from, say, the action of the Valois in strengthening the importance of Paris, since the *monarchia* was in no sense a kingdom. Its constituent kingdoms, speaking different languages, were widely separated from each other, and the sheer difficulty of communication between them was in itself enough to make the enterprise inadvisable. Unfortunately, there were personal inadequacies in Philip's own temperament which aggravated the situation, in particular the weakness which encouraged him to live in aloof isolation from his subordinates. Charles V, it is true, had advised him that, 'in the presence of a prince, councillors do not disclose their objects and intentions so fully', but this had never prevented the emperor from engaging in vigorous debate with his own councillors. Philip by contrast shrank from such a confrontation, preferring to work in the solitude of his study, reading the reports of councils he never attended on matters affecting countries he never visited.

The flow of *consultas*, memoranda and reports kept Philip inordinately occupied and, to make matters worse, he found it difficult to sort out those matters which most urgently required his attention. 'There is no order of precedence in the cases that come before it' complained the count of Barajas about the Council of Castile under his presidency, 'so that it is necessary for all who have suits to be tried to pace up and down the courtyard and struggle with one another to get nearer the door of the Council in the hope that they may be the next to be called before it'. Within the privacy of Philip's study the situation was no better. *Consultas* relating to the bridging of an Andalusian stream, the repairs to a fortress, the preparation of the Armada or a discussion with the pope about the details of clerical dress, were all methodically worked through as they arrived, and Philip's far-flung ambassadors, viceroys and commanders were moved to despair by his inability to establish priorities. Yet even this was not his greatest weakness. Philip suffered agonising changes of mind before arriving at a decision: indeed, it is clear that he deliberately immersed himself too often in the trivial details of routine administration in order to escape the need to deal with intractable issues requiring a decision. 'If death comes from Spain' commented one of his viceroys, 'we shall all be immortal.'

The bureaucratic life which Philip imposed upon himself was not entirely a device to escape from the burden of allocating priorities, making decisions or challenging in debate the contrary views of others: he believed so firmly in his personal accountability to God that he could not consider delegating his responsibilities to others and, perhaps for the same reason, he was handicapped by a passion for secrecy. The machinery of government was, therefore, made more cumbersome and slow since no one might act without the king's written authority and few could ever know exactly what was happening. Meantime, the king himself worked ever longer hours in the secrecy of his study to the exclusion of his family, the abandonment of his favourite pursuits and the astonishment of observers. 'Having so many subjects and trusting no one', wrote the Venetian ambassador in 1581, 'and insisting that everything pass under his own hand and eye, he is so perpetually preoccupied with this business, with so great labour and toil, that I have heard many people say that they would not for the world be the ruler of so many states as is his majesty, if it means living the kind of life he lives.'

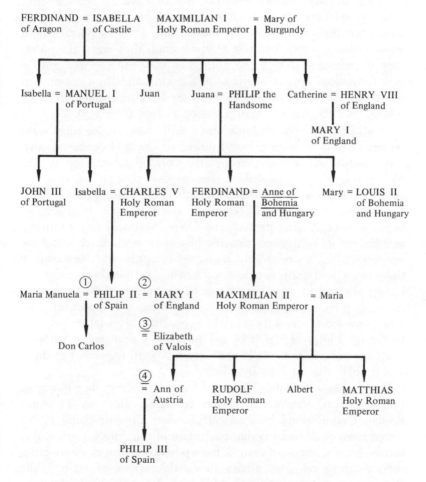

The House of Habsburg (including the rulers of Spain, Portugal and the Holy Roman Empire)

No matter how much he disliked delegating authority, however, Philip could not manage without some assistance, and for this purpose he employed secretaries, men subservient or diplomatically obsequious, who filed his correspondence, transmitted it to the appropriate councils, attended the discussions, edited the memoranda and added their own reports. In Gonzalo Perez he inherited a first-class assistant, trained by Los Cobos, and when he died in 1566 his illegitimate son, Antonio, was appointed to share the most important work with Gabriel de Zayas. Since the work was divided between them, neither could be privy to the whole truth, but both men knew far more about Philip's policies than anyone else at court. Humble clerks though they were, therefore, they were sought out by the noblest in the land seeking crumbs of information, appointments with the king and the presentation of petitions. Not surprisingly, too, they became entangled in the intrigues of the leading families at court (see page 353).

Of all Philip's Spanish kingdoms Castile was the one most subservient to his authority. Royal power was not, of course, in any way absolute but operated through the working partnerships which had already been established (see pages 139–43) between the crown on the one hand and, on the other, the nobility, the clergy, the *mesta* and the *corregidores* of the towns. The one institution capable of organising protest, the *Cortes*, was still free to do so, and indeed its complaints provide historians with much information about Philip's reign, but its power to apply sanctions against the crown had more or less vanished. Its members were no longer allowed to refer back financial matters to their towns – a device which formerly had permitted them an opportunity to resist new taxes – and its refusal to consent to legislation held no threat for Philip II: 'If it be my pleasure I shall annul without the *Cortes* the laws made in the *Cortes*; I shall legislate by edicts and I shall abolish laws by edicts.'

Yet it was a Castilian affair which, at the very beginning of Philip's reign, almost drove him to panic. Both as a devout Roman Catholic and as a powerful ruler, the one thing Philip feared most of all was any demonstration of religious unorthodoxy. Protestant historians, of course, have portrayed him as a hypocrite, subordinating religious affairs to considerations of state, while Catholics on the contrary upheld that he defended his faith at the expense of his country's best interests: religious zeal and national self-interest were, however, so inextricably interwoven in Philip's mind that the dispute about them is misleading. In a thoroughly genuine if simple manner he identified himself and his country as the agents of God's work – so totally indeed that any threat to Spain by Turkish galleys, by Protestant pirates, or by Roman Catholic armies represented a threat to God's self-appointed champions and, therefore, by extension, to God's own plans. Moreover, it was clear to him from his observation of Wyatt's rebellion against his first wife, Mary Tudor, and of the Schmalkaldic League's operation against his father, that heresy endangered not only the soul but also the state. As a result he was horrified beyond all measure to learn in 1558 that Protestant groups had been discovered in Valladolid and Seville.

The panic was hardly justified. Neither group was numerous and although there was evidence that some books and pamphlets had been secretly imported from Geneva, it seems more than likely that these people had more in common with the *alumbrados* of Charles V's reign than with the followers of Luther and Calvin. The Spanish Inquisition had in any case already demonstrated its inability to distinguish between mystics, Erasmians and Protestants (see page 220). Heterodox the groups may have been, and in Charles's day no doubt they would have done penance: Philip, however, launched the Inquisition in full cry after them, and his first public ceremony as king of Spain was to preside at the *auto da fé* at which the leaders were burned. Nor did the panic cease with the executions. All foreign books were banned from entry into Spain, all those printed in Castile had to be licensed by the Council of Castile, and a new Index, which excluded the works of Erasmus, was published to guide the rigorous efforts of the Spanish bishops in searching through both public and private libraries. As a result, Spanish intellectual life was slowly throttled under the bleak direction of the Inquisitor-General, Hernando de Valdes, and his ally, the Dominican theologian, Melchior Cano.

To make matters worse they enjoyed the inestimable advantage of discovering – indeed of inventing – a victim in high places. Cardinal Carranza, a man who had established for himself a sound reputation at the Council of Trent and who had advised Mary Tudor on the persecution of heresy, was appointed by Philip in 1558 to the archbishopric of Toledo, the most senior and wealthy office in the Spanish church. A year later he was arrested by

Valdes. It is true that since he was humbly born there were many who reckoned the appointment to have been too good for him, and they were joined by others, such as Cano, who had wanted it for themselves: moreover, his reputation as a theologian had been established at an international level, rather than within the Spanish church. Whatever the real cause, Carranza was arrested while his accusers ransacked his published works for evidence of unorthodoxy. The pope protested that the Inquisition had no jurisdiction over an archbishop, but the case was not transferred to Rome until 1566. Even then the papacy was too afraid of antagonising Philip, who in this matter stood firmly behind his Inquisitor-General, and another ten years elapsed before the case was heard and Carranza acquitted, to die immediately following his release from nearly twenty years of imprisonment, interrogation and fear.

Strict orthodoxy within Spain did not of course preclude the possibility of conflict with the papacy. Philip had been excommunicated during the Italian campaign of 1556–7, although thereafter the presence of Spanish power in Italy tended to be welcomed by the papacy for its value in maintaining the Counter-reformation. Philip, for his part, was glad to enjoy the ecclesiastical revenue specifically allowed him by the popes, the *cruzada* for example, (see page 140) and the *excusado* of 1567 which was awarded for his work in suppressing heresy in the Netherlands. Nonetheless, he who trusted few people never trusted a pope; nor did he believe there was any need of papal direction in matters affecting Spain. The Tridentine decrees were promulgated with some reluctance and with many provisos safeguarding the king's ecclesiastical jurisdiction and his powers of appointment. All bulls were subjected to royal scrutiny before publication and, after 1572, no Spaniard could be summoned to Rome in an ecclesiastical case without Philip's consent.

Spanish indifference to the authority of Rome and the Council of Trent, and the deep mistrust of international scholarship, even when most impeccably orthodox, reflected the ever-growing mood of insularity which had befallen Spain since the great days of Cisneros. It also reflected a growing hostility to all things foreign and a preoccupation, typical of many withdrawn and isolated communities, with purity of race, *limpieza de sangre*. In these circumstances the presence of the Morisco population was a perennial affront to the cause both of orthodoxy and of racial purity. Despite the laws passed earlier in the century, the Moriscos continued to speak Arabic and to wear their traditional costume: moreover, their conversion to Christianity was open to doubt. In Granada where they were most numerous they had been protected to some extent by their ability to purchase exemption from the laws, by the ineptitude of the local clergy, and by successive captain-generals from the family of Mondejar, who were permanently at loggerheads with the *audiencia* and looked to the Moriscos for support. A new archbishop, Guerrero, back from the Council of Trent, looked at his diocese with dismay and called an assembly of his clergy to bring about a series of much-needed reforms. All they would agree to, however, was a resolution demanding the enforcement of the laws against the Moriscos, and though Guerrero believed it would be better to reform the clergy first and the Moriscos thereafter, the *audiencia* and the Inquisition supported the resolution and urged Philip to take action.

Philip, believing he could safeguard the *Reconquista* only by enforcing the laws against the Moriscos, gave the appropriate orders in 1567. By 1568 the Moriscos were in revolt, though, fortunately for Philip, they did not seize the city of Granada nor were they reinforced by the Osmanli Turks. The current captain-general began to restore order with commendable efficiency, but the members of the *audiencia* jealously reported to Philip that the Mondejar family was not to be trusted where the Moriscos were concerned. Philip, therefore, sent Don John to supersede Mondejar, and thereby prolonged the rebellion by two years. Once the revolt had been crushed, Philip ordered the Moriscos to be dispersed throughout Castile. As many as 150,000 were therefore transported north, and 50,000 settlers moved in to take advantage of the land which for centuries they had worked and irrigated. Efficient though the operation was, it solved nothing: what had formerly been an Andalusian problem was made a national one, and the way was prepared for the final and tragic solution of the following reign – the expulsion of the Moriscos from Spain.

A much happier achievement of Philip's reign was the unification of the Iberian peninsula by the acquisition of Portugal. In this operation Philip was indebted to the advice of Cardinal Granvelle, a Burgundian from Franche-Comté who had already

served him loyally, though not with great success, in the Netherlands (see pages 358-9). Castile and Portugal were already bound by
close family ties (see genealogical table, page 347). Charles V had
married a Portuguese princess and Philip's sister, Juana, was the
widow of John II and mother of the young King Sebastian.
Sebastian, along with many of the Portuguese nobility, was killed
in battle against the Moors at Alcazar-Kebir in 1578, and Granvelle
was quick to exploit the opportunity to acquire for Philip the long
Atlantic seaboard of Portugal together with its overseas empire
and its merchant fleet. Sebastian's successor was an elderly uncle,
the cardinal Henry, whose early death was universally anticipated:
Granvelle nonetheless used his influence at Rome to prevent any
dispensation being made to allow Henry to marry and thus,
possibly, to produce an heir. Within Portugal itself he struck a
shrewd blow by ransoming the survivors of Alcazar-Kebir and
made skilful use of Cristobal de Moura, a Portuguese noble in
Juana's service, who built up a party favourable to Philip's
succession by stressing both the power of Spain to defend the
Portuguese empire and also the generosity of Philip in rewarding
his supporters.

By the time of Henry's death in 1580, therefore, the Portuguese
council was ready to support Philip, but it dared not declare its
opinion publicly because of the general enthusiasm for the
illegitimate claimant, Antonio, the prior of Crato, and the traditional hostility to Castile. Granvelle accordingly advised Philip
to invade before public opinion in Portugal could be mobilised
against him and before any other European government might
interfere. Swift and decisive action of this kind did not come easily
to Philip, and it is a fair measure of the influence then enjoyed by
Granvelle that Philip should have agreed not only to the invasion
of Portugal but also to Granvelle's suggestion that the duke of
Alba be recalled to direct the operation. In June 1580 Alba crossed
the frontier with 20,000 men, brushed aside a few token acts of
resistance and entered Lisbon in August. This gave the Portuguese
nobility and council the excuse they needed to accept Philip as
king, and in 1581 he appeared before them at the *Cortes* of
Thomar. Granvelle urged him to incorporate the kingdom with
Castile, but Philip clung to what he believed had been his father's
concept of the *monarchia*, and treated Portugal as a separate and
individual entity. By the Oath of Thomar he promised that

Portugal's traditions should be preserved, that government appointments should be reserved for Portuguese subjects and that the Council of Portugal, though remaining in attendance on Philip in Madrid, should be entirely Portuguese in composition and its deliberations conducted in the Portuguese language. Moreover, the Portuguese empire was to remain closed to Spaniards.

It was strange that Philip should have rejected Granvelle's advice since, by treating Portugal as a separate kingdom, he must have recognised that this was likely to create for his successors problems very similar to those he himself had inherited in Aragon, Catalonia and Valencia. Much as he disliked the traditional liberties of these kingdoms, their *fueros*, Philip scrupulously respected them; nonetheless he was regarded there with great suspicion and disfavour because, unlike Charles V who had attended a joint *Cortes* of the three kingdoms nearly every five years, Philip rarely visited them and lived rather too obviously in the midst of Castilians. Matters finally came to a head after a prolonged and complex prelude, in which local rivalries played as important a part as suspicion of the king. For many years the administration of Aragon was paralysed by a feud between the treasurer-general and the duke of Villahermosa, head of one of the most powerful families in the kingdom. Philip was at last compelled to intervene, and in 1588 appointed a Castilian, Almenara, to adjudicate between them. With his usual solicitude for local traditions, Philip selected a Castilian only to demonstrate official impartiality in a dispute concerning two local families and, furthermore, he made sure that the appointment carried the support of the Aragonese *Justicia* (see page 144). This, however, did not reassure the local nobility and townsmen who suspected a conspiracy to make Almenara viceroy of their kingdom.

It was at this moment that the affairs of Aragon were complicated by the belated consequence of conflict and intrigue at Philip's court. The privileged position enjoyed by the king's private secretaries had tempted them to intervene in the rivalry of the great families (see page 348). Perez, for example, had made himself useful to the prince of Eboli, while de Zayas had become the ally of the duke of Alba. The game was played out initially against the background of the Netherlands (see pages 365–73) where Eboli advocated conciliation, Alba coercion. Alba carried the day and was sent to implement his own policy but when, to some extent unfairly, he was recalled in 1573 Philip's half-brother Don John was ordered to carry out Eboli's policy.

Responsibility for the correspondence with the Netherlands was immediately transferred from de Zayas to Perez, who tried to strengthen his position by private communications with Don John's secretary, Escobedo, and with several Netherlanders, not all of whom were in favour with Philip. In the event Don John became so frustrated that he abandoned his instructions, seized Namur and sent Escobedo to Madrid to persuade Philip to raise an army in his support.

If Philip was embarrassed by the *volte-face,* Perez feared for his job. Eboli was no longer alive to protect him, and Escobedo could not be criticised in public lest he expose the fact of Perez's secret correspondence and thus discredit him with Philip II. Perez therefore denounced him secretly to the king, describing him as Don John's evil genius, and finally secured the king's permission to arrange his murder. Philip, however, disliked having his hand forced by his own secretary and after the murder he became mistrustful of Perez's intentions, especially when Escobedo's family, with the backing of the duke of Alba, began to clamour for vengeance, publicly blaming the murder on Perez and Eboli's widow. Sensing a first-class scandal and anxious to wash his own hands of it, in 1580 Philip arrested not only Perez but also the princess of Eboli for the murder, and appointed a new secretary, Mateo Vazques la Leca, who skilfully avoided being drawn into intrigues and with quiet efficiency survived the reign.

Perez, however, was not to be silenced for ever. After ten years of imprisonment in Castile he escaped and fled to Aragon where he claimed the traditional privilege of *manifestación* by which any man threatened by royal officials could seek the *Justicia's* protection and have his case heard before him. Philip was acutely embarrassed. Throughout his confinement, and even under torture, Perez, who had willingly confessed to Escobedo's murder, refused to implicate the princess of Eboli, and had insisted that he had acted solely on Philip's instructions. Since this was more or less true, Philip dared not bring him to trial: now, however, by his flight into Aragon and his appeal to the *Justicia,* Perez was ensured of an open trial and one, moreover, which allowed the accused considerable freedom in presenting his defence.

Since even the *Justicia* dared not defy the Inquisition, Philip had only one course of action left to him: he charged Perez with heresy and ordered the *Justicia* to release him to the Inquisition in Saragossa. The townspeople rioted at the news, killed Almenara and restored Perez to the *Justicia's* prison: riots again broke out at the second attempt to transfer Perez, but on this occasion the mob released Perez, who used the opportunity to mobilise a rebellion by the local nobility. With the situation entirely out of hand, Philip was compelled to send an army of 12,000 to restore order. Perez fled abroad, to be a constant embarrassment to Philip. Villahermosa spent the rest of his life in a Castilian prison, and the *Justicia* was executed, ostensibly for failing to deliver Perez safely to the Inquisition, but in fact because through his office he epitomised the most powerful tradition of Aragonese independence. Philip then summoned the *Cortes* to Tarragona in 1592 and there required it to accept the appointment of a Castilian viceroy, some minor changes in the procedure for giving approval to royal taxes, and an alteration in the terms of appointment of the *Justicia* so that he could be removed from office by the king. Having made these points Philip thereafter remained as scrupulous as before in observing the *fueros* of Aragon.

One thing which contemporaries found difficult to understand was the apparent impoverishment of Spain and the series of royal bankruptcies at a time when the empire overseas was producing gold and silver in unheard-of quantities. The bankruptcies, of course, sprang directly from the fact that Philip II committed himself to a foreign policy he could not afford. The first bankruptcy of 1557 was scarcely his fault but a legacy of Charles V's Italian and German campaigns: that of 1575 was more serious. Philip, who was perturbed by the predominance of Genoese bankers among his creditors, hoped to profit from disaster at least to some extent by opening the door to other bankers. He failed. The principal Spanish financier, Simon Ruiz of Medina del Campo, the Fuggers, the Florentines and the Lombards could not supply the enormous sums he needed: meanwhile the army in the Netherlands went unpaid, the Castilian fairs were momentarily paralysed, the fleet could not leave for the Indies for lack of money, two Seville banks collapsed, and the Genoese had only to wait a few months before Philip returned to them to negotiate a new settlement of his debts.

Thereafter the bullion imports began to increase dramatically (see page 158), but this in turn only encouraged Philip to undertake ever more ambitious and expensive projects. The Armada campaign finally cost him 10 million ducats, and by the mid-1590s he was spending over 12 million ducats a year on warfare alone. Moreover, the bullion imports, substantial though they were, represented even at their height barely a quarter of Philip's total revenues: the rest came from loans and Castilian taxes, and because the revenue from existing taxes was ultimately pledged for years to come in order to secure the loans, a new tax, the *millones*, had to be introduced in 1590. By the end of the reign, with the other kingdoms producing barely enough to cover their own expenses, Castile was supplying annually 2.7 million ducats from the *encabezamiento*, 3 million from the *millones*, 400,000 in subsidies from the *Cortes*, 1.6 million in ecclesiastical taxes, and 2 million in bullion imports. The burden could not be endured indefinitely, especially as Philip would not reduce his commitments, and in 1596 he was forced to go bankrupt for the third time.

Royal bankruptcies, serious though they were in their impact on the conduct of foreign policy, were usually remediable in that they did not betoken the collapse of the country as a whole and it was only a matter of months before the bankers would come round to negotiate a fresh agreement. But Castile itself grew poorer. The failure to develop agriculture, partly because of the *mesta*, and even more because the landowners refused to invest capital in irrigating their land (see page 219), led to a fall in food production and the drift of impoverished peasants to the towns. Trade and industry were also in decline. The bankruptcies had had serious consequences by disrupting the commerce of the fairs, but more serious still was the annual tax burden imposed by Philip which made investment difficult and industrial expansion virtually impossible. What aggravated the problem in the eyes of the *Cortes* was that poverty should increase while more and more bullion was imported from America, but no one could see that the terms of Atlantic trade had altered to the disadvantage of Castile. In America the colonists had begun to produce their own cloth, grain, wine and oil, and no longer needed the goods which the Andalusian market had formerly been evolved to supply. In short, the agricultural produce which Castile offered to her colonists was no longer wanted, and the manufactured goods which the colonists required, Castile was unable to produce. Consequently, in order to purchase these goods elsewhere, the bullion had to be exported as soon as it arrived and neither the *Consulado* nor the *Casa de Contratación* showed the slightest understanding of what was happening. In this state of economic stagnation and decline, the defeat of the armada and the failure to defeat the Dutch dealt a crippling blow to the morale of the Castilians: it only needed the devastating plague of 1599 which carried off at one stroke the total increase in the population since 1500, to reduce the country at the end of its Golden Age to a state of total disillusionment and of fatalist acquiescence in disaster.

The Revolt of the Netherlands 1555 – 72

The government of the Netherlands presented Philip II with a serious problem. The dukes of Burgundy and their successors, the Habsburg emperors, had acquired the seventeen provinces at different dates and by different means. As a result the inhabitants spoke different languages (French, Dutch or German, with several local dialects), cherished different traditions and not infrequently regarded their neighbours in other provinces as foreigners and former enemies. If Charles V (see pages 210–211) had aggravated the problem of diversity by his own extensive conquests in the north-east, he had also attempted to promote a sense of common identity by developing the use of such common institutions as the Council of State and the States-General of all the province. Nonetheless, the political life of the Netherlands remained centred in the assemblies of the provincial Estates and the council chambers of the cities. Any attempt to override these local institutions by treating the seventeen provinces as one administrative unit was certain to arouse deep-seated passions.

The regent class (see page 209), the patrician oligarchy which governed the towns and dominated the Estates of the southern provinces in particular, was especially sensitive to any challenge to its authority. The regents, of course, affirmed their loyalty to the sovereign in whose name they exercised their power. They even looked to him for protection from the craftsmen's guilds which demanded a greater share in municipal government. On the other hand they resolutely resisted any attempt to strengthen the powers of the Council of State, of the States-General or of any other institution designed to centralise the government of the Netherlands. Charles V, therefore, had regarded the regents with a wary eye and had looked instead to the provincial nobility to assist his plans.

The nobles were, generally speaking, an impoverished class with much to gain from such an alliance. The urban regents, whose wealth they envied, paid little deference to their threadbare nobility: only in the royal service were public honour and material rewards to be secured. Even the few wealthy landowners, like the duke of Aerschot for example, found it desirable to seek preferment from the crown. The wealthiest of all was William of Orange. The son of a Lutheran prince of Nassau, he had inherited the principality of Orange in the Rhône valley and owned a quarter of the rich province of Brabant. After entering the service of Charles V he became a Catholic, married the daughter of one of Charles' generals and proved to be his most useful agent in defending Charles' efforts to bring about a greater degree of unity in the Netherlands. As a reward he was appointed governor, or *stadt-holder*, of Holland and Zeeland, and it was on William's arm that the emperor leaned when he appeared in the Netherlands for the ceremony of his abdication.

Philip II, who was present in the Netherlands when Charles abdicated, was unpopular from the start. Reserved by nature and speaking no language but Spanish, he isolated himself from his new subjects as effectively as Charles himself had done on first visiting Spain in 1517. Moreover he ignored the existence of the Council of State which, within three weeks of his accession, protested at its exclusion from affairs, thus demonstrating that Philip had antagonised the very men on whose services his father had relied. Instead Philip consulted exclusively with the Sieur de Granvelle who, though a native of Franche Comté and experienced in Burgundian affairs, was immediately regarded in the Netherlands as a Spanish agent.

The most pressing problem was to stave off bankruptcy and to this end Philip summoned the States-General. The representatives of the seventeen provinces seized the occasion to complain forcefully of the Spanish troops, the *tercios*, billeted in their midst, but after petitioning Philip to replace them with local recruits they ended by voting him a nine-years' aid of 800,000 florins a year.

Hatred of the *tercios* seemed more important at that moment than matters of religion and taxation because it symbolised the Netherlanders' anxieties about Philip as a Spaniard and, by extension, about his methods of government. As Granvelle later explained: 'People here universally display discontent with any and all Spaniards in these provinces. It would seem that this derives from their suspicion that one might wish to subject them to Spain and reduce them to the same condition as the Italian provinces which are under the Spanish crown.' Indeed when Philip had returned to Spain in 1559 and the signing of the Treaty of Câteau-Cambrésis allowed him to recall the *tercios*, these anxieties found new expression in the general hatred of Granvelle.

Philip had appointed his half-sister, Margaret of Parma, to act as Regent but it was immediately obvious that her authority and that of the Council of State were subordinate to that of Granvelle, and that he in turn received his instructions directly from Madrid. In the circumstances, therefore, any policy associated with Granvelle would have met with suspicion, and his particular plan to re-organise diocesan boundaries aroused widespread anger. The scheme was in fact an admirable one, drawn up in Charles V's time as a necessary preliminary to ecclesiastical reform. Since all four diocesan boundaries overran into France and Germany, with the result that there were no bishops resident in the Netherlands, it was impossible to deal effectively with the problems of clerical ignorance and non-residence. Under the terms of the bull of 1561, therefore, the number of dioceses was increased from four to eighteen, their boundaries were drawn to approximate more closely with those of the Netherlands and three archbishoprics were created at Cambrai, Utrecht and Mechlin (Malines), of which Mechlin was to be the metropolitan. The government was empowered to appoint the new bishops, and their salaries were to be paid for by appropriating some of the revenues of the wealthier monasteries.

Much of the opposition to the scheme stemmed from the secrecy which, quite unnecessarily, had surrounded its inception, but there were other reasons for the intensity with which it was opposed. Its very novelty offended traditionalists. The abbots objected to the reduction of their revenues, Antwerp disliked the prospect of having a bishop within its walls to contest the jurisdiction of the city council, and many nobles lost valuable powers of patronage which had in the past allowed them to provide for their impoverished children with church appointments. The government, on the other hand, was provided with twenty-one lucrative and prestigious offices with which to reward its supporters, and Granvelle himself, with the additional dignity of a cardinal's hat, was appointed archbishop of Mechlin. Above all it was feared that the scheme heralded the introduction of the Spanish Inquisition, a more rigorous and powerful institution than that already introduced by Charles V, and the wholesale subordination of the Church in the Netherlands to the dictates of Spain.

William of Orange resigned in protest from the Council of State. He had in the past worked closely with Granvelle in Franche Comté and had expected to be promoted to the inner ring of Philip II's councillors. Granvelle, however, distrusted him – 'he is capable of any underhand deed that might be inspired by an unlimited ambition' – and took care to exclude him from matters of any importance. Indeed the fact that he had not been consulted about the diocesan reforms accounted more than anything else for William's hostility to them. The count of Egmont, as influential though not as wealthy as William, was similarly piqued and resigned at the same time. Their action was applauded by the people in general and the Estates of Brabant threatened to withhold taxes until the matter was resolved. So intense was the public hostility to Granvelle that Margaret of Parma persuaded Philip II that he would have to be recalled. Granvelle left the Netherlands in March 1564 and the diocesan reforms were quietly shelved.

So far there was nothing very unusual about the situation: the chief dissidents were not attempting to overthrow the government but rather to monopolise it, and Philip reluctantly gave them their opportunity. With Granvelle's departure the Netherlands were to be governed, as in Charles V's day, by the Regent and the Council of State, and both Egmont and Orange returned cheerfully to their duties. On one issue, however, Philip was adamant. He wanted to eliminate Calvinism before it could establish itself as securely in the Netherlands as it had done in France, and he ordered the Regent to enforce the *Placarten* (see page 212) with greater rigour. William of Orange opposed this. The Council agreed and sent Egmont to Madrid in 1565 to persuade Philip to delay matters. Egmont was graciously received and returned home confident of success, only to be followed by despatches to Margaret of Parma which ordered her to apply the *Placarten* without more ado. Philip moreover ordered that the duke of Aerschot, William's chief rival and one of the few Netherlanders to have been in Granvelle's confidence, should be appointed to the Council of State.

When William and Egmont once again resigned from the Council many of the lesser nobility met in defiance of the Regent's orders to protest against the *Placarten*. Their proposals, published in December 1565 as the *Compromise of the Nobility*, were signed by four hundred nobles, including Calvinists, opportunists and Roman Catholics averse to persecution. The following April three hundred of them rode into Brussels to present the *Compromise* to the Regent. Since the lesser nobility were generally speaking an impoverished class their appearance excited a courtier's criticism of their dress. 'Quoi madame,' he said to the Regent, 'peur de ces *gueux*?' – 'Afraid of these *beggars*?' The phrase caught on, not in its derogatory sense but as a badge of protest, and protest not only against the *Placarten* but against foreign influences, heavy taxation and the centralisation of government in Brussels.

Emboldened by the Regent's inability to prevent their descent on Brussels the Beggars offered their protection to the Calvinists and a flood of exiles returned from England and north Germany to address mass meetings throughout the Netherlands. Their preaching, conducted under the guns of the Beggars, may not have won many converts for Calvinism but it succeeded remarkably in arousing widespread anger at the obvious abuses of unreformed Catholicism. The cult of the saints in particular came under general attack and the ministers incited their audiences to destroy the images which filled the churches. Thereafter it was but a short step from image-breaking (iconoclasm) to general riot.

'The town of Ieper, among others,' reported a member of the Council of State, 'is in turmoil on account of the daring of the populace inside and outside who go to the open-air services in their thousands, armed and defended as if they were off to perform some great exploit of war. It is to be feared that the first blow will fall on the monasteries and clergy and that the fire, once lit, will spread, and that, since trade is beginning to cease on account of these troubles, working people – constrained by hunger – will join in, waiting for the opportunity to acquire a share of the property of the rich.'

Poverty indeed proved to be a potent ally of the Calvinists. The winter of 1564-5 had been the coldest of the century, the harvest of 1565 failed and the Baltic war between Sweden and Denmark (see page 311) closed down the vital grain trade with Danzig. Prices rose sharply, accompanied by famine and unemployment throughout the winter of 1565-6. In these circumstances the iconoclastic riots afforded an opportunity for every conceivable type of protest – theological, political or social, and the Calvinists fed the flames of agitation by hiring bands of the unemployed to join the image-breakers.

'Everything is in such disorder,' wrote Margaret in a panic, 'that in the greater part of the country there is neither law, faith nor king.' While individual members of the Council made local agreements with the Beggars, securing a return to order by the promise of toleration, Margaret herself urged Philip II 'to take up arms . . . or to make concessions'. Her reports confirmed Philip's worst fears about the folly, as he saw it, of entrusting responsibility in the Netherlands to the Council of State, and since he had no intention of making concessions he discussed with his advisers how best to take up arms. Alba urged the despatch of 10,000 *tercios* to teach the Netherlanders a lesson they should not forget. Eboli, on the other hand, advised Philip to go himself with only a small force, believing that Philip's own presence would be interpreted as a conciliatory gesture and thereby reduce the need for military intervention. In the event it was Alba who was sent to carry out the plan he had proposed.

There were many reasons apart from the growth of heresy which made it necessary for Spain to maintain her hold over the Netherlands. Antwerp, where the Spanish colony numbered over 300, was vital to Spain's economy, the market for sixty per cent of its wool and, in 1570, for most of its silver. It supplied Spain with the Baltic naval stores she required for her fleets, the weapons, textiles and other manufactured goods which she herself could not produce for her colonists, and the Polish grain which she needed in greater quantities every year to eke out her dwindling imports from Sicily (see page 170). Moreover the wealth of the Netherlands made it an indispensable source of revenue. Finally, there was the military advantage of having a base only eighty miles north of France, a base which completed the encirclement of

France with Habsburg territories and which also served, as Charles V's advisers had once said, 'as a citadel of steel, a shield to receive the blows of England, France and Germany far away from the head of the *monarchia*'.

In the light of the Regent's initial reports, Philip's action in sending Alba to deal with a riot-torn country was wholly understandable. What he failed to recognise was that Margaret had exaggerated the danger. In the event the response of the local authorities was exactly what Philip would have wished: within a few months the leading nobles in alliance with the urban regents had mobilised their forces to suppress the rioters. The Beggars, resentful of the manner in which the Calvinist clergy had siezed the initiative from them, backed down once they had been promised that the *Compromise* would be submitted for Philip II's consideration. Only William of Orange stood apart. He had helped to drive rioters out of Antwerp but within his own provinces of Holland and Zeeland he was noticeably less active than the other *stadtholders*. He then took everyone by surprise by abandoning his vast estates and high offices and fled to Nassau. It was a desperate move, and his motives have not been made clear. He had certainly been warned that he was on Alba's list of suspected persons but so too was Egmont, and while William fled the country Egmont and his friends renewed their oaths of allegiance to the Regent, confident that their world would not change.

This too was the hope of Margaret herself. By the spring of 1567 she had recovered her nerve and was able to report that order had been restored. Spanish troops, she claimed, were no longer needed and their presence might indeed stimulate further unrest. Philip II, however, was disinclined to temporise any further. Alba's orders to treat the Netherlanders as rebels and heretics remained unchanged and he began his march in April 1567. It is possible to argue that Philip had blundered by failing to distinguish Calvinist rioting from sedition and by failing to discern that the Regent and the Council had ultimately done their work well. On the other hand the Netherlands were too valuable for him to risk a second crisis and it was clear that the suppression of heresy would never be executed as he wished if it were left to the local authorities. Moreover, if hindsight is to be avoided, Alba might well have settled the matter once and for all, and thus have reduced the importance of the episode to that of, say, the revolt of the *Comuneros*, or the Aragon rebellion of 1591, in which, after a critical beginning, the situation was finally resolved to the advantage of the government. And indeed this was very nearly what happened. In the September of 1567 Margaret resigned in protest at the powers conferred on Alba but this made no difference to the resolute unfolding of his plans. First he arrested Egmont and a few others as hostages. He then appointed a Council of Troubles, a tribunal entirely under his control and under its jurisdiction began the prosecution of heretics according to the most stringent terms of the *Placarten*. He also put into operation the reorganisation of the dioceses.

In March of the following year there was a significant new development. Alba arrested 500 or so burgomasters, pensionaries and other members of the regent class, thereby transferring his attention from the Calvinists, who were after all a very small minority, to the class most powerfully entrenched in the government of the Netherlands and the one most likely to resist his policies. Those arrested were not immediately replaced, Alba affirming that 'putting in new men one by one is like throwing a bottle of good wine into a vat of vinegar. The wine will instantly turn into vinegar.' This combination of ruthlessness and military strength proved irresistible. No one dared move against the *tercios*, and when William of Orange and his brother, Louis of Nassau, invaded the Netherlands from Germany in June, Alba, by executing Egmont and the other hostages, ensured that no one rose to join them. It was then a simple matter to drive the invading forces out, and Alba erected a statue of himself as the hero, 'who extirpated sedition, reduced rebellion, restored religion, secured justice and established peace'.

Thus successful, Alba hoped that his task was done. He had proposed the policy but he had never sought the appointment, and now plagued with gout, he looked to be honourably released of his responsibilities. This he hoped would come about if Philip came in person to the Netherlands to crown the victory, but the King never came. Nor did he send the 4,000,000 florins Alba needed annually to maintain his administration and his troops. In March 1569, therefore, Alba summoned the States-General and secured 4,000,000 florins by a single, once for all, *aide* of 1% on all capital. He then demanded more, seeking a permanent income by a 5%

levy (the Twentieth Penny) on the sale of land and 10% (the Tenth Penny) on all other sales. The members of the States-General, frightened of Alba, yet as fearful of those they represented, took refuge in prevarication. Over the next two years they offered a second, and subsequently a third, *aide* but held firm against the Tenth Penny. When Alba ordered nonetheless that all sales be registered in preparation for the tax the merchants and shopkeepers of Brussels went on strike. It was a shrewd move. Alba could scarcely restore the flow of commerce by sending in his troops, and as trade and industry virtually ceased in the winter of 1571-72, unemployment and discontent mounted.

Alba, however, remained securely in control since no one dared challenge his authority. Not only in the matter of taxation but also in the persecution of heresy and the overriding of the traditional forms of provincial government, Alba had gone further than any previous ruler had ever dared: the opposition he aroused was passionately felt but it was powerless against his ruthless spirit and his 10,000 *tercios*. Offenders and suspects alike were arrested, often on the strength of secret denunciations, and the Council of Troubles dealt with over 12,000 cases in the years 1567-73. Its sentences were invariably harsh. 'It is not intended to uproot this vineyard', Alba said, 'only to prune it', but the pruning was severe and more than a thousand victims were exiled or executed. The population relapsed into sullen obedience, and Orange's now-annual incursions from Germany were invariably overwhelmed by Alba's army.

In 1572, however, Orange found an ally in the French government (see pages 331-2). Coincidentally and independently, on 1 April, a force of Calvinist privateers occupied Brill, a fishing port on one of the islands of the Rhine delta. The privateers called themselves Sea Beggars (*Water Gueuzen*) in conscious imitation of the nobles of the *Compromise* and in 1568 had secured *Letters of Marque* from William of Orange who, as an independent prince, was able to authorise them to recover from Spanish shipping the value of his confiscated estates in Brabant. The exiled consistories in London, Dover and Emden organised the sale of the prizes they took and recruited crews for what became a fleet of over thirty vessels. By 1572 William himself had broken with them since they paid little heed to his instructions. Nor were they on good terms with anyone else since the ships they raided were not confined to those sailing under Spanish colours. The city of Emden found them too hot to hold, France denied them access to her ports and Elizabeth of England, in March 1572, ordered them out of Dover. After roaming the Channel without purpose they adopted the suggestion of a former citizen of Brill to try their luck there – and found that it had been temporarily vacated by its Spanish garrison.

A few days later the inhabitants of Flushing, another port in the delta, rioted at the approach of *tercios* who were taken to be collectors of the Tenth Penny. Protesting its allegiance to Philip II, Flushing at first refused offers of aid from Brill but on 22 April it admitted a fleet of fourteen to strengthen its defences. Spanish troops would no doubt have coped with the problem, but in May these were recalled from Holland and Zeeland to meet Orange's invasion. Louis of Nassau occupied Mons while a force of Huguenots seized Valenciennes. A French force sent to support Mons was ambushed and defeated by Alba but Charles IX then gave permission for an army of 15,000 to enter the Netherlands. To William's horror and disappointment the Massacre of St Bartholomew's Eve intervened and destroyed his hopes. 'Confess, Sire,' said the French ambassador to Philip II, 'that it is to the King my master that you owe your Netherlands', and William would have echoed his words.

In fact the situation was not so simple as that. In the absence of the *tercios* the long pent-up hatred of Alba's government had found expression in revolt not only throughout Holland and Zeeland but even in Utrecht and other provinces. In July the rebel towns of Holland sent representatives to Dordrecht where it was agreed to recognise Orange as Stadtholder of Holland, to fight in the king's name against the usurped authority of Alba, to allow full toleration and to vote 500,000 florins for the campaign.

With the fall of Mons in September Alba was able to despatch troops to put down the rising. Mechlin in Brabant was sacked, partly to compensate the *tercios* for lack of pay, partly to intimidate the rebels. Zutphen in Gelderland was similarly treated and Holland and Zeeland awaited their fate. Naarden was the first victim and Alba had it razed to the ground. At this desperate moment William of Orange, in no less desperate straits after the failure of his invasion, decided to stake everything on one final throw by joining the Sea Beggars. It was his last resort: 'I am bent on going to Holland and Zeeland, being resolved to maintain the affair as long as possible and to find there my grave'.

The Revolt of the Netherlands 1572 – 1609

William's decision to join the Sea Beggars was to prove crucial to their success. The one man capable of uniting others against Spain had now joined the one group capable of sustaining the revolt. The Beggars could move at will along the coast and through the waterways of the Rhine delta. They were moreover wholly committed to Calvinism and determined to settle for nothing less than total victory for themselves and for their faith. This did not make them popular, and not even the presence of William of Orange could disguise the fact that they were pirates and heretics who disrupted trade and, when given the chance, persecuted

The Netherlands in the reign of Philip II

Catholics. With William at their head, however, they represented the only alternative to Alba and his Tenth Penny – and his *tercios*. Sometimes the Sea Beggars brought a city into the rebellion by force of arms but throughout Holland and Zeeland it was general practice for the regent class to negotiate its terms of alliance in advance.

Since the Sea Beggars would not venture beyond reach of the waterways Alba was compelled to come to them. It was a difficult campaign, a war of attrition in which the rebel towns were strongly defended and easily supplied by water; but Alba fought vigorously and successfully throughout the winter of 1572–3 and might conceivably have won the day had he been given the time, the ships and the supplies he needed. By one means or another he had raised nearly 9,000,000 florins from the Netherlands in 1570–71, and 1,000,000 from Spain. In the following year the conduct of the campaigns made it impossible for him to raise as much as 2,000,000 florins and 7,000,000 had to be sent from Spain. Philip II, however, had a war on his hands against the Turks (see page 376) and was being persuaded by the Prince of Eboli to regard Alba as a failure. No more money was sent, the Spanish troops began to mutiny and, by mid-1573, Alba's campaign had been stopped in its tracks.

Luis de Requesens, the governor of Milan, was counting the days to his retirement when in November 1573 he was appalled to learn that Philip had appointed him to replace Alba in the Netherlands. His one consolation was that his orders required him to attempt a general reconciliation, and in pursuit of this he halted the proceedings of the Council of Troubles and offered a pardon to all who surrendered. The Sea Beggars ignored him. Their main concern at that moment was the siege of Middelburg, a town of considerable strategic importance on the island of Walcheren which had declared its loyalty to Philip II and had in consequence been subject to attack since the summer of 1572. Its capitulation in February 1574 gave the Sea Beggars control of the North Sea shipping lanes and Requesens had no choice but to resume the war.

He had just embarked on the siege of Leyden when he had to withdraw his forces to meet an invasion by Louis of Nassau. Louis was killed at Mook on the Maas and his army was defeated. The *tercios* mutinied, however, for lack of pay, and marched on

Antwerp, holding the city to ransom for 1,000,000 florins. When Requesens succeeded in buying them off and resumed the siege of Leyden, the Sea Beggars opened the dykes and saved the city by flooding the countryside. Again the *tercios* mutinied, and Philip II urged Requesens to find a solution by negotiation since 'we are running out of everything so fast that words fail me'.

For several months in 1575 discussions were held with the representatives of Holland and Zeeland but the demands of the Sea Beggars could not be met by Spain no matter how serious the lack of money. Forced once again to resort to arms, Requesens began an impressively successful campaign to split the forces of Holland and Zeeland and, as the main thrust of his strategy, advanced across the central islands of the Rhine delta to lay siege to the outermost port of Zierickzee. Requesens and William alike believed that on the outcome of the siege depended the success or failure of the Revolt. They both reckoned without Philip II's declaration of bankruptcy in September 1575. Although the *tercios* continued the siege, unaffected by the death of Requesens in March 1576, until the town fell to them in July, they immediately abandoned their prize, marched into Brabant, sacked the town of Aalst and demanded their arrears of pay.

In this crisis the duke of Aerschot took control. He arrested the Spanish members of the Council of State and restored to membership the Netherlanders who had been imprisoned. Through the Estates of Brabant he raised troops in an effort to contain the mutineers and summoned the States-General of all the provinces. This appropriation of royal prerogative, this seizure of authority by those who governed in the king's name and through royal institutions, was not the work of pirates, heretics, adventurers or opportunists. It represented an aristocratic, conservative and Catholic reaction to the excesses of Alba's autocratic government, forced into the open by the fear that the Spanish mutiny was about to engulf the whole country in a reign of terror.

In the meantime, after many weeks of discussion, Holland and Zeeland had settled their future in June 1575 by an Act of Union. Aerschot could not therefore ignore them, though he held them to be as dangerous as the mutineers, and began negotiations with his old rival William of Orange. The Sea Beggars respected William as their leader but wanted no truck with any Roman

Catholic, Spaniard or Netherlander, and William was therefore at a disadvantage. He had moreover become passionately inspired by a vision of a united Netherlands. He had always worked to this end for Charles V but now the object was not merely unity but freedom too. This he knew he could not gain without making substantial concessions to Aerschot, while these in turn would forfeit him the loyalty of Holland and Zeeland.

All mutual suspicions were suddenly dashed aside by the news that the Spanish mutineers had finally run amok in Antwerp. The 'Spanish Fury', which destroyed over 1,000 houses and took 8,000 lives, aroused in all Netherlanders a sense of urgency and unity which, in November 1576, found expression in the Pacification of Ghent. In effect the Pacification was a peace treaty between the States-General on the one hand and Holland and Zeeland on the other. Under its terms all property confiscated since 1567 was to be restored, the *Placarten* were to be suspended, Catholics were not to be attacked in Holland and Zeeland nor Calvinists in the other provinces. In conclusion, both sides agreed to stand together against the *tercios*.

No reference was made to independence, and to some extent the constitution which Aerschot and William were prepared to accept was essentially very similar to that of 1564 – when Granvelle had withdrawn, leaving matters in the hands of the Council of State. Philip, too, for the time being, was prepared to accept the situation. The Eboli family remained influential and persuaded him that conciliation was still the best policy: unfortunately, in sending his half-brother, Don John, Philip chose the wrong man to implement it. Don John, the victor of Lepanto and the Morisco campaign, was a man of action and ambition. He tried nonetheless to fulfil his brief. He accepted the terms of the Pacification of Ghent and sent home the *tercios*, but the Netherlanders suspected the worst of him, and their suspicions were confirmed in 1577 when, in embodying the Pacification in a Perpetual Edict, he also included a declaration about the restoration of the Catholic faith.

Holland and Zeeland had in any case gone their own way. They had renewed their Act of Union in April 1576, repudiated their allegiance to Philip II and entrusted sovereignty to William until some other sovereign authority be found. Don John was thus required to wage war against them with neither troops nor money to hand. To make matters worse, the States-General refused to afford him assistance. By the summer of 1577 he had become so frustrated, humiliated and angry that he broke the settlement, seized Namur with his own bodyguard and ordered the *tercios* to be recalled. Thus reinforced he defeated the army of the States-General at Gembloux in January 1578, but was unable to break through to take Brussels.

In the confused stalemate which followed, William tried desperately to defend the Netherlands from the *tercios*, to maintain the authority of the States-General and to prevent the secession of Holland and Zeeland. It was a thankless task, and one soon overtaken by events. Class warfare, stimulated by Calvinist clergy and made more bitter by the hard times, had been evident since the mob invaded the chamber of the States-General in October 1576. Throughout 1577 riots in Brussels, Antwerp, Ghent and a score of other cities resulted in the overthrow of the regent class by Calvinist preachers in league with the artisans' guilds. So extreme was the radicalism of the new civic leaders that even William was denounced by them as a reactionary: so powerful were they that even William dared not withhold recognition from them.

In an effort to salvage the authority of the States-General and provide it with a leader of royal blood, William persuaded Francis, duke of Anjou, to let himself be elected Defender of the Liberties of the Netherlands. Henry III of France was only too glad to have his brother off his hands (see page 334) but Elizabeth of England saw things differently. Alarmed by the extension of French influence in the Netherlands she commissioned a German mercenary, John Casimir, to raise 12,000 troops on behalf of the States-General. It proved to be the last straw. The States-General was still burdened with the cost of the troops raised in Brabant in 1576 and could not pay the new arrivals – who promptly mutinied and added to the general confusion.

Throughout 1578 Gelderland had been in discussion with Holland and Zeeland about proposals for their mutual defence and in January 1579 the Union of Utrecht was formed, comprising Holland, Zeeland, Gelderland, Utrecht, Friesland and the province (though not the city) of Groningen. Each member of the Union retained its independence but agreed that in matters of war and peace they would act in perpetuity, 'as if they were a single person'. This left William in a quandary, still hoping for reconciliation under the States-General and still putting his faith in the duke of Anjou. Meanwhile as the northern provinces broke away under Calvinist leadership, so did the Catholic provinces of the south. As the Calvinist riots spread across the Netherlands, Aerschot and his Walloon colleagues decided that they had had enough. Ignoring the protests of those towns where Calvinists had seized control, the provinces of Hainault, Artois and Walloon Flanders drew up their own Union at Arras in January 1579. What they sought was the enforcement of the Pacification of Ghent – by which they meant to return to what seemed to them to have been the halcyon days before Alba's arrival – and in the new Spanish governor, Alexander Farnese, duke of Parma, they found a man to reassure them. He was a good soldier, an excellent negotiator and one of the few men of strong character to have won Philip II's confidence. The Union of Arras accepted his authority on condition that Spanish troops were not employed by him and that the terms of the Pacification, insofar as they affected the Catholic south, should be enforced.

By this agreement Parma established himself firmly in Artois and Hainault, and set out to win over the rest of the southern provinces by a combination of military strength and political tact. It was an exercise in which he excelled. He approached town after town in strength, offered generous terms, executed very few rebels, and allowed the Calvinists time in which to take refuge in the north. He skilfully exploited both the real strength of Catholicism in those areas which had suffered Calvinist control since 1577, and the hatred of the social revolution which had displaced the regent class. It was typical of the reputation which he established that when the Union of Utrecht sent troops to capture the city of Groningen the civic authorities appealed to Parma rather than to the States-General to protect them. In fact the States-General of the Netherlands was no longer a political force. It offered sovereignty to Anjou and in July 1581 published its Act of Abjuration, repudiating Philip II, but it was an empty gesture which had no effect on the Unions of Arras and Utrecht. Anjou felt ill at ease and tried to seize Antwerp for himself in 1583; after this fiasco his influence dwindled to nothing and he died unmourned in the following year. William cast his lot with the Union of Utrecht, but in July 1584 he was murdered by a Catholic.

William's death occurred at a critical time for the Union of Utrecht. So well had Parma won the confidence of the Walloon nobility that in 1582 he was permitted to strengthen his army of local recruits with Spanish *tercios*. Thus reinforced he cleared the Walloon provinces of northern troops and then moved up the coast. His strategy was to take possession of the ports and compel, by economic blockade, the surrender of the hinterland of Flanders and Brabant. Most of Flanders fell to him in 1584 and in the following year he made himself master of Brabant. At the siege of Brussels, and again at Antwerp, the Catholic population rose against their Calvinist masters and admitted the Spanish troops.

In this manner Parma re-established Spanish authority within the borders of modern Belgium, and there seemed little reason why he should not similarly deal with the Union of Utrecht. William's death had deprived the Union of its natural leader, and there was dangerous dissension among the Calvinists themselves. The regents, who had adopted Calvinism in order to preserve their monopoly of power in the days of the Sea Beggars, were profoundly suspicious of the Calvinist clergy, who wanted to establish greater control over the social and moral behaviour of the citizens. The clergy, moreover, appealed to the working classes to support them in challenging the exclusive authority of the regents, and they were reinforced by refugees from the south who had taken part in the socio-religious riots of 1577.

In this crisis in their affairs the Dutch cast around for foreign help. Henry III declined to intervene but in August 1585 the Union signed the Treaty of Nonsuch with Elizabeth of England. The Earl of Leicester with 4,000 men was to join the Dutch army, provided Flushing, Rammekens and Brill were handed over to England as sureties for the expenses incurred by the English force. Leicester arrived in December, too late to save Antwerp, but with a wonderful effect on Dutch morale. War-weariness was dispelled, and regents eager for the war replaced those who had been advocating negotiation. In 1580, in consequence, the States-General of the Union was able to field more troops than ever and appointed Leicester Governor-General. Unhappily, Leicester became embroiled in a bitter dispute about trade with Spain and the southern provinces. The Calvinist clergy denounced trade with the enemy as treason; the regents retorted that it was only by such trade that they could afford to finance the war. Leicester not only agreed

with the clergy but intervened directly in Utrecht to remove the
regents from power, and a direct clash with the regents of Holland
and Zeeland was averted only by his failure to perform the
principal task entrusted to him, the defence of the frontier.

Parma had reached the Waal, then the Maas and finally the
Rhine. From there he invaded the north-eastern provinces whose
resistance was less likely to be effective. Leicester went home in
December 1586. In his absence his commanders at Deventer and
Zutphen betrayed their cities to the Spaniards, and he himself on
his return in 1587 attempted a *coup* by siezing towns in Holland
and Zeeland. Even his Calvinist allies abandoned him. Dismayed
at the lack of help from England, they suspected (correctly) that
Elizabeth was more anxious to negotiate than to fight with Parma.
Leicester had no option but to return to England. His loss was an
unacknowledged blessing for the Dutch which prompted them to
rely no longer on foreign help but to invest sovereignty in their
own States-General. It was a brave resolution but, with Parma
poised to invade the last strongholds of the seaboard provinces, it
seemed an irrelevant one.

In the event the Union of Utrecht was saved by none other than
Philip II himself. In order to form a support group for the Spanish
Armada against England he recalled Parma's army to Dunkirk.
There it waited throughout the summer of 1587 and again, thanks
to Drake's raid on Cadiz (see page 381), throughout the whole of
1588 without making a move against the Dutch. When at last the
Armada came, the Dutch fly-boats, specially designed to operate
in shallow waters, prevented Parma's barges leaving Nieuport and
Dunkirk. Once the invasion of England had failed Parma renewed
the assault on the Dutch, but the situation had changed to his
disadvantage. It was not simply that defence works along the river
line had been strengthened. Spain was so overburdened by her
commitments that Philip could no longer send Parma the money
he needed: in consequence a section of the army mutinied – the
first of forty mutinies which handicapped the Spanish war effort
between 1589 and 1601. In addition Philip ordered Parma in 1590
to rescue Paris from the clutches of Henry of Navarre, and again
in 1591 to save Rouen. These incursions into France served
Philip's strategy well, but they destroyed Parma's own hopes of
completing his task in the Netherlands, and in 1592 he died of
wounds received at Rouen.

In the meantime the Dutch had discovered an able administrator in Jan van Oldenbarneveldt, the Advocate of Holland, who exploited his position as the senior civil servant of his province, and his province's commanding position in the Union, to exercise considerable influence in the States-General and especially in its executive committees. He was an experienced politician, well skilled in manipulating the members of the regent class to which he belonged, and in placing his allies in key positions in the administration. As a result, he enjoyed an unchallenged position of effective primacy throughout the war with Spain, and his contribution to the success of the revolt was invaluable. He persuaded the constituent provinces, which had been traditionally hostile to any centralisation of the administration, to accept the decisions of the States-General, and established the republic's finances on a firm basis, relying especially on the growing wealth of Amsterdam and the general expansion of Dutch trade in the final decade of the sixteenth century. Above all he brought forward William's son, Maurice of Nassau, to lead the new administration. Maurice had already been elected *stadtholder* of Holland and Zeeland in succession to his father, and it was Oldenbarneveldt who persuaded the Estates of Utrecht, Gelderland and Overijssel also to accept him. By this means the military command of most of the provinces was vested in the princely house of Orange.

Maurice was a brilliant soldier. When Leicester left for England, Maurice was only twenty years old, but he had already begun to demonstrate a remarkable degree of professionalism. Coached by his cousin, William Louis of Nassau, in Roman and Byzantine military studies and in mathematics, he acquired an academic approach which supplemented rather than detracted from his innate practical ability as a soldier. He devised battalions of 550 men in order to manoeuvre more speedily against the blocks of *tercios*, six times their size; he relied on military engineers in a manner unique in the sixteenth century and organised a special corps of pioneers to strengthen his defensive position whether in camp or on campaign: above all he drilled his troops regularly and, thanks, too, to Oldenbarneveldt's efforts in seeing that they were paid regularly, created a well-disciplined, reliable fighting force. Maurice's talents of course were not immediately apparent at the age of twenty, but the short lull afforded by Parma's preoccupation with the Armada and then with the French war gave him a few years in which to develop without having to meet the Spanish army at full strength. He seized Breda in 1590 and by a spectacular offensive through Zutphen, Deventer and Nimwegen, restored communications with the north-eastern provinces in 1591. In 1592 he cleared Gelderland and Overijssel of Spanish troops and captured Groningen in 1594. As a result the Dutch were in possession of all land north of the river line, and from Breda Maurice now burst through into Brabant and Flanders.

South of Breda, however, in the area controlled by the Union of Arras, Maurice was unable to make much headway, despite a brilliant cavalry victory at Turnhout in 1597, and thus the war settled down to a form of stalemate. If the Dutch were now secure above the river line, the Spaniards were impregnable below it. Philip died in 1598 leaving the Netherlands to his nephew, the Austrian archduke Albert, and the making of peace with England and France allowed the new government to concentrate its forces against the Union of Utrecht. Moreover, in its new Genoese commander, Spinola, it had a soldier who was something of a match for Maurice. The Spanish government, however, handicapped by the final bankruptcy of Philip's reign, went bankrupt yet again in 1607, and was unable to finance further campaigns. The Dutch too were on the verge of bankruptcy. Despite the wealth of many cities, the States-General had been overspent every year since the formation of the Union of Utrecht and the time had come to retrench. As a result there was a strong party in the States-General led by Oldenbarneveldt which was prepared to negotiate, despite the opposition of the Calvinist ministers, and of Maurice himself, who could not see that if Spinola was too weak to attack the north, he was also too strong to be expelled from the south. After two years of negotiation, therefore, a Twelve Year Truce was signed in 1609, by which Spain recognised the virtual loss of its northern provinces and the creation of a new independent state in the Dutch Republic.

Philip II and International Conflict

After nearly fifty years of conflict between France and Spain for the domination of Italy, the Peace of Cateau-Cambrésis in 1559 awarded the victory to Spain, and Philip accordingly began his reign from a position of relative strength in Europe. Yet, for the next decade or so, he showed himself to be extremely nervous in his handling of other powers. France remained his most dangerous enemy and, although the death of Henry II had brought to the throne a series of inadequate youngsters, Philip dared not relax his watchful survey of French affairs. The barrier of Spanish territories which encircled France from the Pyrenees, via the Alps and the Rhineland, to the Channel, could be regarded in two ways: the French certainly thought of it as a strategic stranglehold inhibiting them from undertaking a war with Spain, but Philip could only notice how vulnerable it was to attack by an enemy who enjoyed interior lines of communication. Stories of Huguenot infiltration from Navarre into Catalonia, though without substance, threw him into a panic in 1569, yet his fears in general were not entirely groundless. The Guises who had led the French armies against him in Italy were able, through Mary, Queen of Scots, to influence events in Scotland, and thus in England too, while the ability of Coligny in 1570 to arrange a French invasion of the Netherlands (see page 332) was certainly no figment of Philip's imagination.

The true measure of Philip's anxiety about France is to be found in his policy towards England. England was not a great power, but her cloth trade was important to the economy of the Netherlands, and he feared above all that the French might one day gain control of the island and thus disrupt his lines of communication by sea. The death of his first wife, Mary Tudor, in 1558 robbed him of a useful ally there, but her sister, Elizabeth, seemed anxious to remain on good terms with him, and her successful venture against the Guises in Scotland (1559-60) was of special value to Philip. Over the next decade, therefore, Philip had to tolerate Elizabeth's rejection of a Catholic settlement for the Church of England and her tacit acquiescence in the raids conducted by English pirates on his shipping. Indeed, as trouble began to build up in the Netherlands, Elizabeth's friendship became so important to him that he failed to see that Elizabeth was in fact as anxious as he was to keep Coligny and the French from gaining possession of the Netherlands. When in 1569 she appropriated a shipment of bullion which was blown into her harbours while en route to Alba, he dared do no more than impose an embargo on trade, which ultimately did more harm to Spain and the Netherlands than to England, and he tried in vain to prevent the publication of the bull of excommunication which, if enforced, would have replaced her on the throne of England by the Guise princess, Mary, Queen of Scots.

Although Philip was spared his father's preoccupation with German problems, and in particular with the defence of Austria from the Osmanli Turks, he could not overlook the fact that in alliance with the French, the Turks and the Barbary corsairs threatened his hold over the Western Mediterranean. In his view this was the most urgent problem confronting him and immediately he had made peace in 1559, and thereby ensured French neutrality in the Mediterranean, he decided to seek out Dragut along the North African coast (see page 232) and recapture Tripoli, a base of great importance in controlling the sea routes between Spain, Sicily and Naples. Instead of the swift raid which he had planned, however, the expedition took six months to assemble under the duke of Medina Celi, and was further delayed by winter storms before it finally disembarked on the island of Djerba in March 1560. By this time the Osmanli Turks had been alerted. Dragut, with inferior forces, kept well out of the way, but Piale Pasha left Constantinople in April with the Osmanli fleet and arrived off Djerba in the following month, taking the Spaniards by surprise. Leaving 6,000 men abandoned on the island, they rushed in a panic for their ships, and had scarcely reached open water before the Turks bore down upon them, destroying 27 of their 49 galleys.

Philip responded to the disaster by ordering a new fleet to be built: timber was in short supply (see page 182), but by 1564 Garcia de Toledo, the new Captain-General of the Sea, had 70 galleys and 30 other ships under his command. He took Peñon de Velez, a corsair base between Oran and Tangier, and in 1565 prepared to go to the relief of Malta where Piale Pasha had landed 40,000 men. Philip was in two minds about the operation: he was alarmed at the prospect of the Turks in Malta, but he was even more afraid of losing his fleet. Finally, after hesitating throughout the summer, he decided against an attack on the Turkish fleet, but allowed Don Garcia to land supplies on the island without engaging the enemy. The operation was brilliantly conducted and helped to save the island. The courageous resistance of the Knights of St John throughout the summer had convinced Piale Pasha that the garrison could only be reduced by starvation, and since Don Garcia's arrival made this a profitless undertaking, the Turks withdrew.

Encouraged by the relief of Malta, Philip ordered more ships to be built and developed a plan to immobilize the North African corsairs and deny the Turks access to the Western Mediterranean. At this moment, the Turks attacked Cyprus. Suleyman no doubt would have assisted the Morisco revolt, then at its height in Granada, but his successor, Selim the Sot, lacked his bold spirit. Instead he made Cyprus his target in order to give greater security to the sea route from Alexandria to Constantinople. Pius V appealed to the European powers to form a Holy League, but Philip was unwilling to sacrifice his fleet to save Venetian interests in Cyprus. When the Moriscos had been defeated, however, and the pope had promised him further taxes if he undertook a crusade, he agreed to provide half the League's forces – the pope supplying one-sixth and Venice one-third – and even more important to supply the expedition with Spanish grain. His half-brother, Don John, was made Commander-in-Chief and set out in 1571 to seek the enemy with about 300 ships, 50,000 seamen and oarsmen and 30,000 soldiers. It was too late to save Cyprus, which damped the enthusiasm of the Venetian squadron, but in October Don John ran up against the Osmanli fleet at Lepanto near the Gulf of Patras. He drew up his force in a line extending five miles across the mouth of the Gulf: the Turks attempted to outflank him and succeeded in drawing off the right wing, but in the centre where the galleys were locked together with grappling irons, the Europeans won the day. Uluj Ali, the king of Algiers, who had drawn off the right wing escaped with 35 galleys, but Ali Pasha, the commander, was killed and most of his ships were destroyed or captured.

The immediate results of the battle were disappointing. Cyprus could not be recovered, the fleet was in need of repair and the national commanders, despite the euphoria of victory, were very nearly at each other's throats. Their governments were no less divided. While Venice wanted to organise a spring offensive into the Levant, Philip was anxious to clear the Moslem corsairs from North Africa, but eventually he acceded to the protests of his own commanders by reluctantly agreeing to a joint sweep along the Morean coast in 1573. When this achieved nothing Venice withdrew from the League in disgust and Don John was sent to capture Tunis. As a result, the Turks suffered no permanent loss by their defeat and even Tunis was recovered a year later by Uluj Ali. In the long run, however, the battle was of tremendous importance. By their victory at Lepanto the Europeans had at last destroyed the legend of Osmanli invincibility, and the Turks themselves were less eager in future to hazard their fleets too far from base. Indeed, since both sides now found it too expensive, too difficult and too dangerous to maintain naval campaigns over any great distance, they tacitly agreed to a form of stalemate. Negotiations between Philip and the Turks began when captives were exchanged in 1574, and a secret truce was agreed to in 1578, which more or less left the western Mediterranean to Philip and the eastern half to the Turks.

Elsewhere, the 1570s proved to be difficult years for Philip. The Sea-Beggars established themselves securely in Holland and Zeeland, the bankruptcy of 1575 was a major disaster, and Drake's raids on Spanish bases in the Caribbean and South America became more serious and disruptive. In the 1580s Philip's overall position began to improve slightly as the result of a rapprochement between himself and the Guises. The Guises had been among his most spirited enemies in France, but their loyalty to Catholicism, their disillusionment when the Massacre of St Bartholomew's Eve failed to destroy the Huguenot movement, and their anxiety at the prospect of an international alliance between heretics in France, England and the Netherlands, led them reluctantly but inexorably into Philip's camp. Anjou's death in 1584 and the likelihood of a Huguenot, Henry of Navarre, inheriting the throne was the final straw, and in 1585 the Guises signed the Treaty of Joinville with Philip II. In return for Spain's diplomatic aid and a subsidy of 50,000 ducats a month, the Guises pledged themselves to deny the throne to Henry of Navarre, and promised Philip that Mary, Queen of Scots should henceforth be regarded as an agent of Spain.

Reassured on this vital matter Philip II was, therefore, free to plan the downfall of Elizabeth. Parma urged him to concentrate his efforts in the Netherlands alone, but Philip in a mood of unusual self-confidence appeared to believe that England, and possibly France too, lay within his grasp, and if he were right the fate of Holland and Zeeland was indeed of minor importance. His confidence sprang in part from the recent successes he had enjoyed by the defeat of the Moriscos, the battle of Lepanto and the conquest of Portugal: it was strengthened by the greater wealth available to him from the increased shipments of bullion from America (see page 158). It was not only the royal share of the treasure which mattered, but the fact that much of the sudden influx of the 1580s went to the banking firms who thereby accumulated capital out of all proportion to their needs. Since the war in the Netherlands and piracy in the Channel made commercial investments temporarily unprofitable, the only way for them to employ their surplus capital on any scale was by lending it to Philip, who accordingly insisted on a relatively low rate of interest.

Responsibility for invading England was entrusted to an experienced sailor, Santa Cruz, who asked for a full-scale invasion force sufficiently well-equipped with soldiers and supplies to land directly on the English coast and rouse the local Catholics to its side. The cost of this was regarded as too great, even in Philip's eased circumstances, and the whole affair was drastically scaled down by a decision to make use of the army which was already in the Netherlands, and to employ the fleet merely to transport it across the Channel. Parma knew that his men could not embark unless he gained possession of a deep-water port, but when he failed to capture Flushing, neither Philip nor his council could understand that from that moment the enterprise was doomed. Drake's raid in 1587, which destroyed much of the shipping and supplies in Cadiz harbour, simply aggravated the problem by delaying the expedition for twelve months. Santa Cruz died in the following February, to be succeeded by a less competent sailor in Medina Sidonia, and Parma was kept inactive in the Netherlands for the second year running.

Medina Sidonia in fact did an excellent job. He led his fleet of 130 ships, laden with 22,000 men, in perfect order up the Channel, brushing off the English attack until he had gained Calais Roads, but here the lack of a deep-water port proved fatal. The Armada could not come inshore without running aground, and Parma's barges dared not venture out to the fleet because the Dutch fly-boats, swift vessels of shallow draught, would have shot them out of the water. Medina Sidonia was, therefore, stuck without a port and the English had the weather gauge. Drake's fireships scattered the fleet, and though the Spaniards recovered manfully from the confusion, they were finally swept by southwesterly gales on to the Netherlands coast, or up the North Sea from whence they made a laborious voyage round the British Isles and back to Spain. Only four of the galleons were lost, but many armed merchantmen were destroyed, and of the surviving ships only half were fit for action again. More serious perhaps was the great loss of life suffered by the Spaniards, and worst of all was the effect of the disaster on Spanish morale.

Parma hoped that as a consequence of the Armada's defeat he might at least be free to take up the campaign in the Netherlands, but, as Philip wrote to him, 'the affairs of France are at this moment the principal thing'. Henry III had murdered the Guises, and had himself been murdered, leaving Henry of Navarre to fight for his throne. To prevent him from seizing Paris in 1590, Parma was sent to relieve the capital and again, a year later, to save Rouen from his hands. 3,500 Spanish troops moreover were landed in Brittany, a manoeuvre which so alarmed Elizabeth that to save the Channel ports from falling to Philip she had to send Norris to Brittany in 1590 and Essex to Normandy in 1591. Meanwhile in Rome the count of Olivares had used every diplomatic device of intimidation and bribery to secure the election of Gregory XIV, who was pledged to give full support to the Catholic League. When Gregory died a few months later, however, the conclave of cardinals had had enough of Olivares, and found in Clement VIII not an enemy of Spain but a pontiff unafraid to go his own way; from Philip's point of view this came to mean that Clement was willing to negotiate with Henry of Navarre and thus accept the notion of his possible conversion to Rome.

In a desperate attempt to win the French throne for himself Philip tried to lobby opinion in France against the sanctity of the Salic Law which debarred him, but discovered that even the most fervent enemies of Henry of Navarre could not bring themselves to abandon one of the few fundamental laws of the kingdom. The case was lost, and the Spanish ambassador Feria was tactless to harangue the States-General of 1593 like an angry creditor. Henry timed his conversion to a nicety, Paris opened its gates to him, Clement absolved him, Mayenne abandoned the League's alliance with Spain, and, in alliance with England and the United Provinces, Henry IV rallied many of his subjects to him by declaring war on Philip.

Philip, therefore, discovered himself at war with enemies whose combined power seriously threatened his own, but the bullion continued to flow from America and from his bankers and he waged war with vigour. Support was sent to the Irish rebels in 1595, Calais was taken in 1596, and armadas were sent against England in both 1596 and 1597, only to be driven back by storms. If none of this led to very much, his enemies also achieved little. Henry IV was too busy negotiating with his own subjects, Maurice of Nassau could not break through into the southern provinces of the Netherlands, the Essex expedition of 1596 to Cadiz did nothing of permanent damage, and all the attempts of French, Dutch and English privateers to intercept the *flota* were prevented by the efficiency of the Spanish convoy system. In November 1596, however, Philip went bankrupt for the third time, and though the bankers were ready to renew the loan as the bullion began to arrive once more, Philip himself was worn out. In 1598, by the Treaty of Vervins (see page 341), he brought himself to recognise Henry IV as king of France, and in the same year he died, leaving his successors to settle the conflict with England and the Dutch republic.

God's blessing at Lepanto had been noticeably absent on the Armada campaign, and Philip's reign ended with a sense of moral disillusionment, underlined by the failure to defeat the English, the Dutch or the French, and heightened by the decline of the Spanish economy and the final bankruptcy of the government. But this is to misconceive the achievements of the reign as a whole. If Philip seemed to have failed against Elizabeth and Henry IV, it is worth remembering that he had helped to deny the English throne to a French puppet in the first half of the reign, and the French throne to a Huguenot in the second half; and if he lost eight provinces in the Netherlands, the remainder had at the last been welded together in an obedience to Spain which represented a triumph of the monarchy over the forces of particularism and independence. These, however, are mere debating points and conceal the true success of the king of the Golden Age of Spain. Philip II had inherited an empire in Italy and America which belonged to Spain as firmly on the day he died as on the day of his accession. To this he had added the rich territories of Portugal and her overseas empire, and at Lepanto he had won perhaps the greatest single victory of the sixteenth century. It was an achievement that few other sovereigns could equal.

The Austrian Habsburgs
and the Holy Roman Empire

The history of the Holy Roman Empire in the second half of the sixteenth century is often either ignored, or regarded merely as the prelude to the Thirty Years' War of the seventeenth century. Though the Empire seemed perennially to be on the brink of dissolution and the emperors themselves to be figures of no importance, the period is of importance for the fact that, remarkably, imperial institutions survived and the potentiality of imperial power was somehow preserved. The *Reichskammergericht* (see page 151) did indeed fall into disuse. It suffered from the main defects of other imperial institutions in that it enjoyed no regular income and had no means of enforcing its decisions. As a court of arbitration in disputes between members of the Empire, its verdict was acceptable only if it satisfied both parties, or a substantial majority of the German princes, or the very powerful few with whom, increasingly, real power resided. Its members, too often unpaid and frustrated by their work, drifted away into other employment, and, as the backlog of cases began to accumulate for lack of attention, fewer matters were referred to it unless both parties believed they had something to gain from endless procrastination. Ferdinand I in 1559 created a rival institution by making his own court council into an imperial law court, the *Reichshofrat*. Cases were dealt with rather more quickly, but there were many who suspected it because of its obvious dependence upon the emperor, and it suffered the same disadvantage as the *Reichskammergericht* in that its decisions could rarely be enforced against the will of the parties concerned.

The Diet on the other hand was extremely active in this period, settling disputes among its members or debating their grievances against the emperor. The electors, as senior members of the Diet, began to require from each new emperor not only that he reward them in the conventional way with gifts for their support in the election, but also that he agree to refer an increasing number of matters for their approval in the Diet, whose sessions became accordingly more important. Moreover, the continual threat of Osmanli attacks (see page 387) compelled the Diet to meet more frequently in order to raise funds for imperial defence. As a result of all this the Diet went so far as to appoint a committee to handle affairs when it was not in session, and to prepare the agenda for future meetings.

Greater activity did not result in greater effectiveness. The Diet, like the *Reichskammergericht*, lacked administrative and financial support, and was unable, without the backing of a strong emperor, to carry out its policies; on the other hand, as the assembly of the emperor's subjects, it was not prepared to remedy the emperor's weakness. In addition, its unity was impaired by the religious disputes which had been recognised but not resolved at Augsburg in 1555 (see page 245). The Catholics were in the majority, and the Protestant electors of Saxony and Brandenburg were so moderate in their views and so willing to co-operate with the majority that the minority of militant Protestants were driven, out of frustration, to disrupt the assembly's debates and to challenge its authority: for this reason, in 1597 for example, they even refused to contribute to the subsidy which had been voted to raise troops against the Osmanli Turks.

Within the framework of Imperial institutions, the German states were becoming more autonomous. Most of them, of course, were too small, their resources too limited for this to mean very much in terms of power, but in the larger states the princes self-consciously set out to model their governments on the monarchies of France and Spain. They introduced specialist councils to handle affairs of state, for example, and recruited professional civil servants to work them. Moreover, they attempted to undermine the authority of their own Estates, invoking the precepts of Roman Law to reinforce their jurisdiction over their subjects and, no matter whether Roman Catholic or Lutheran, establishing a firm control over their clergy. To a considerable extent, therefore, the rulers of Saxony and Bavaria and, to a lesser extent, of Brandenburg, were well on the way to creating miniature kingdoms of their own, and, in the absence of a powerful emperor, their influence proved to be decisive in resolving disputes within the Empire.

Wilhelm von Grumbach, a marauding knight who terrorised Franconia from 1559 to 1567, was outlawed by the emperor Ferdinand, but it was the elector of Saxony who finally captured and executed him. It was Saxony, too, who intervened where the emperor had failed to prevent a civil war between some of the Protestant princes and the Catholic duke of Bavaria over the abbot of Fulda. The former abbots had allowed things to go to rack and ruin, the monks had abandoned their duties, and Lutherans had settled on abbey land. A new abbot in 1570, impelled by the situation to choose one confession or the other, declared himself wholeheartedly for Catholicism, reformed the abbey and expelled the Lutherans. This last act was technically in breach of the Peace of Augsburg, and it was matters of this kind, involving territorial disputes between the rival confessions, which most threatened to disrupt the peace of the Empire.

A more serious occasion occurred in 1580 when the recently elected archbishop-elector of Cologne announced not only his conversion to Lutheranism but also his determination to retain the Electoral title, marry a nun, secularise his diocese and make it an hereditary possession. If he were allowed to succeed in this, the archbishop-electors of Trier and Mainz might eventually follow suit, and conclude the affair by voting for a Protestant emperor. It was an alarming prospect for the Catholic princes. In the event, they managed to forestall the archbishop's plan; but they could do nothing to prevent the less dramatic transfer of such wealthy bishoprics as Magdeburg, Bremen and Halberstadt to Lutheran control. By 1600 a strong Lutheran *bloc* had been created in north Germany, and it was not surprising that many Catholics welcomed the possibility of renewed warfare. Only in this way might the territories, and the subjects, of a Lutheran prince be restored to the Catholic Church.

The inability of the emperors to control affairs in Germany did not reflect any particular degree of personal inadequacy. Ferdinand who had acted on many occasions on behalf of his brother Charles V, was experienced, intelligent and well-balanced; his son Maximilian II (1564 – 76) was lively, likeable and a patron of the arts; Rudolf II (1576 – 1612) who withdrew in isolation to Bohemia, preferring astrology to government, was the only one to demonstrate ineptitude. In the last analysis, however, their failure to determine the course of events sprang from the fact that the territorial basis of their power had been reduced. Charles V had left the Netherlands to Philip II of Spain and thereby weakened the financial resources of the Austrian branch of the family. Ferdinand, it is true, had acquired Bohemia and Hungary, but the Bohemian nobility was far too independent to accept his direction, and most of Hungary had fallen under the Turks and the princes of Transylvania. Moreover, Ferdinand subdivided his territories at his death, leaving Styria, Carinthia and Carniola to the archduke Charles, the Tyrol, along with the scattered remnants of the ancient Habsburg patrimony in Swabia and the Upper Rhine, to the archduke Ferdinand, and Austria, with Bohemia and Hungary, to Maximilian II. Maximilian, therefore, had fewer resources at his disposal than any emperor since Frederick III (see page 150). Fortunately, he was wise enough not to subdivide what remained among his six sons, but it was a tragedy for the family that his eldest son, Rudolf, was ultimately to prove an incapable successor.

One other explanation of the relative weakness of the Habsburgs in Germany after 1559 was their constant preoccupation with the threat of an Osmanli invasion. Ferdinand had been compelled to purchase peace in 1562 by accepting humiliating terms as a tributary of the Turks (see page 230), but four years later Suleyman again launched an attack on Austria, which was only averted by the prolonged defence of Sziget (Szeged) and the death of the sultan himself. Thereafter, from the renewal of the truce in 1568, there was no major Osmanli invasion until 1593, but it would be wrong to suppose that the intervening decades were a period of peace. Frontier raids occurred each year, nor was there any way of telling in advance whether or not the raid presaged a major invasion. In addition, the Habsburgs became involved in an extensive and time-consuming effort to improve their defences. They strengthened their frontier fortresses at Kanizsa, Raab, Komorn and Erlau, constructed minor forts, known as *palankas*, at river crossings and at the approaches to the main cities, and established Hungarian refugees and Germans in a defence system of marcher lordships stretching from the Adriatic, via the river valleys of the Unna and the Kulpa, to the upper reaches of the Sava and the Drava. The Habsburgs' strategy, though expensive in that it absorbed almost entirely the revenues of Carniola, Carinthia and Styria, was well conceived. Since it took ninety days to supply an Osmanli army by camel trains from the Balkans, the season for campaigning was reduced by several months: the Austrians, therefore, relied on their new defence works to halt or at least to delay the invading army until the season was over.

In 1593 the Turks, who had been preoccupied for many years with campaigns in Persia, Southern Arabia and Russia, and distracted by a janissary revolt in 1589, launched a major attack up the Danube. Raab fell to them in 1594, and Austria was in danger until a Habsburg counter-attack succeeded in taking Gran in 1595. Coincidentally, Michael of Wallachia, who had risen in revolt against the Turks, defeated them in battle and threatened their supply routes along the Danube to Belgrade and Buda, while a new Transylvanian prince, Sigismund Bathory, Jesuit trained and inspired with the ideals of a crusade, declared his alliance with the Habsburgs and ultimately abdicated his throne to Rudolf. So serious was the situation for the Turks that in 1596 Mehmed III took the field in person, seized Erlau, thereby disrupting communications between Austria and Transylvania, and routed the relieving force which arrived too late to save the city.

Thereafter in the north-western Balkans the war became a matter of siege and counter-siege: Raab was recovered by the Habsburgs in 1598, Kanizsa was lost in 1600 but Pest was captured in 1602. In the north-east, Michael of Wallachia overran Transylvania in 1599, ostensibly in the name of the Emperor Rudolf, but in effect arousing popular feeling against both himself and the Habsburg alliance. After his murder in 1601, the Transylvanian nobles elected a new leader, Stephen Bocksai, and returned to their traditional alliance with the sultan. As a result the Turks surged back into northern Hungary as far as Gran, but with that they had to be content. The cost of siege warfare was proving to be too great, their lines of communication were stretched too far, and, as the Persian war had broken out afresh, the Turks agreed to peace in 1606. By the Treaty of Sitva-Torok, the emperor Rudolf paid a new indemnity – but was no longer tributary – and recognised the rule of Stephen Bocksai in Transylvania.

In addition to their other problems, the Habsburgs tried to cope with the problem of heresy. In Hungary and Bohemia, of course, there was little they could do. The nobility was too independent to be coerced in matters of this sort, and Bohemia in particular had been traditionally, since the days of Huss, the home of heterodoxy; thus when Rudolf finally retired there at the end of the century he was compelled to grant freedom of worship to Lutherans and Calvinists alike. Even in their German duchies Lutheranism was so well established, under the protection of many of the great families, that demands were made in the Estates for religious freedom.

Ferdinand moreover was too involved with campaigns against the Turks to be anything but conciliatory to his Lutheran subjects, and he urged the Council of Trent to permit clerical marriage and communion in both kinds in the hope that in this way they might be reunited to the Catholic church. Maximilian II was tolerant to the point of permissiveness, supporting the building of churches in Austria by either side and allowing North German theologians to advise the Austrian Lutherans on the formulation of their liturgy. Rudolf, however, who in other respects proved to be less able than his predecessors, nonetheless attacked the problem of heresy with greater vigour, and forbade Lutheran services within Vienna itself. There was little he could do in the country areas, where Protestantism was at its strongest, until a peasant revolt against taxes, from 1594 to 1597, brought Lutheran and Catholic nobleman together to reestablish Rudolf's authority; this in turn paved the way for the extension of Catholicism, at any rate among the lower classes. A significant success was also achieved in Styria, where the archduke Charles established a Jesuit university at Graz and where, after 1591, his successor Ferdinand annulled the freedom of worship granted to peasants and townsmen, and began to restore Catholicism with the force and vigour which, in the seventeenth century, were to make him the greatest protagonist of the Counter-reformation within the empire.

The second half of the sixteenth century was, therefore, a period of great difficulty and of little power for the Austrian Habsburgs. Nonetheless, the imperial institutions were still preserved and an emperor, strong enough to make them work by enforcing their decisions, could become a major force once again within the empire. Moreover, the emergence of such an emperor was possible if a respite were provided from Osmanli attacks, if the Habsburg territories could again be consolidated within the control of one man, and if such a man could show himself to be resolute in enforcing his policies against Protestantism. While Rudolf lived no such eventuality seemed likely, but in Styria Archduke Ferdinand was beginning to develop his talents in this direction to such good effect that the members of his family agreed to make him master of all the Habsburg territories in the empire. In 1619, when the Turks still kept the peace in the Balkans, Ferdinand was elected emperor, and his reign was to demonstrate again how powerful a Habsburg might be in German affairs.

11

Art, Music and the Sciences

Mannerism in Italian Art

THE self-confident humanism which underlay the serenity and the assurance of the High Renaissance evaporated very quickly in the first quarter of the sixteenth century as Italian artists began to flout the very principles of balance and restraint which they themselves had so successfully established. Even Raphael, who died in 1520 before the mood had changed entirely, could not remain unaffected, and his final major work, the *Transfiguration* (see page 63), indicated an entirely novel concern with the rendering of emotional tension by means of discordant gestures and dramatic chiaroscuro. Michelangelo, of course, survived him for nearly half a century, and in his subsequent development, whether as architect, sculptor, poet or painter, he revealed a personality wholly different from that of the young artist who had first caught the attention of Lorenzo de Medici. In his case the change was brought about by a prolonged and profound spiritual experience, strengthened ultimately by the close friendship of Ignatius Loyola, which led him to repudiate not only the platonic humanism of his youth, but even his own passion for art itself.

> Now well I know how that fond fantasy,
> Which made my soul the worshipper and thrall
> Of earthly art, is vain.

The sonnet concluded: 'Neither painting nor sculpture can now lull to rest my soul that turns to His great love on high, whose arms to clasp us on the cross were spread'.

This change was most immediately apparent in his *Last Judgement*, executed in the Sistine Chapel between 1535 and 1541. A fresco of the *Resurrection* by Ghirlandaio had been damaged beyond repair, and Michelangelo, commissioned to replace it, chose as his subject the resurrection of mankind at the Last Judgement. It provides a fascinating contrast to his former work on the ceiling: the lighter tones of the one (see page 61) give way to darker hues, bright clarity to smokey obscurity and ordered serenity to tension, fear and confusion. Michelangelo shared the view of many contemporaries that the Sack of Rome in 1527 had been an act of divine judgement, and the violence and terror engendered by that event are consequently reflected in his portrayal of the final judgement of mankind. Saints and sinners alike swirl across the wall in disorderly progression and, in the centre, Christ himself appears as an angry, menacing figure, whose arm is raised as though, like Jupiter, to hurl thunderbolts upon his creation.

Yet the figures of the *Last Judgement*, if not the informing spirit of its composition, still had much in common with the athletic giants of the ceiling. In contrast, no single work can better illustrate the changed mind of the artist than the *Rondanini Pietà* (see plate 13), sculpted and left unfinished in the last decade of Michelangelo's life. In this work, done solely for his own satisfaction, Michelangelo finally repudiated one of the fundamental principles of Renaissance art by rejecting the convention that physical beauty was a valid symbol of virtue. Indeed, he no longer sought to represent the human body at all. The figures of Christ and of His mother are virtually stripped of their physical attributes: scarcely identifiable, fused together in the unfinished marble, they express a mood of death and personal grief in a manner wholly alien to the High Renaissance.

It was characteristic of Michelangelo that the only commission he accepted in later life – and only then as an offering to God without payment – was the task of completing St Peter's. This had originally been entrusted to a rival architect, Bramante, who, following a pattern developed by several Renaissance architects, had designed the church on a central plan. After his death the plan was widely criticised but Michelangelo, once he had agreed to accept the commission remained loyal to Bramante's designs. The spirit of their execution was altogether different, however, foreshadowing the emergence of the Baroque. St Peter's was constructed not as a carefully balanced, ordered and articulated structure, but as a massive block of stone, a monumental podium in effect, to be crowned by an enormous dome. Impressive though it was, its very centrality made it impossible to accommodate the congregations to be expected at the heart of Latin Christendom, and Michelangelo's successors had to diminish the impact of his work by lengthening the nave.

Michelangelo's repudiation of the values of his youth sprang primarily from his own idiosyncratic experience of life, but it is significant that there were many other artists whose attitudes to life and art began to change as his had done in the years following the death of Raphael. Renaissance art, of course, had not been entirely a matter of beauty and serenity, nor was the Italy of the French invasions a particularly rational and well-ordered world, but the artists had believed in the value of these qualities and had worked strenuously to attain them. By 1530 the balance had shifted. The Sack of Rome had had the moral effect of a major earthquake in destroying the cult of optimism, and the creed of self-confident humanism lost its glamour once the Spanish armies throughout the peninsula had demonstrated the helplessness of the individual in the face of organised power.

The triumph of Spain moreover destroyed the multiplicity of minor states whose rivalry, interaction and mutual dependence had provided so exciting and challenging an environment for the patronage of the arts. It is true that the degree of freedom enjoyed by the artist in a Renaissance court has been exaggerated, but there was always the freedom to seek new patrons, and the variety of princely courts and city states encouraged experiment and innovation. Above all there was no overriding censor, no universal tendency towards conformity – not at least until the petty principalities and city-states fell under Spanish control and were compelled to accept Spanish etiquette and adopt Spanish fashions. Under the domination of Spain, in fact, the Italians suffered a fate similar to that endured by the Greeks many centuries before when:

> . . . free speech shivered on the pikes of Macedonia
>   And later on the pikes of Rome
> And Athens became a mere university city
>   And the goddess born of the foam
> Became the kept hetaera . . .

> *(Louis MacNeice)*

Then indeed, the Italians lost their vision. Their taste began to degenerate within the confines of their own coteries, their creative ideas were fossilised by theoreticians in petty academies and their culture, deprived of any new invigorating force, became increasingly provincial and complacent.

The new developments in Italian art of the sixteenth century reflected these important changes in the environment of the artists: in addition, they reflected something of the new problems which confronted the artists themselves in their professional life. In the first place they were faced with the consequences of their own improved status. Unlike the medieval artisan who knew exactly where he stood, enjoying the protection of his guild, maintaining the tradition of his craft, the Renaissance artist had won for himself a degree of social and professional independence which allowed him greater freedom to experiment as he wished. Unhappily, the problem of living as a self-directing artist in a competitive market, instead of working comfortably within the regulated companionship of the guild, led in many cases to a loss of professional confidence, and a sense of insecurity which in turn produced a nervous breakdown. Michelangelo himself ended his life in a condition of spiritual tension and despair, and if he were too unique an individual to epitomise a general trend, the trend is nonetheless illustrated by the suicide of Rosso, the melancholia of Parmigianino and the mental disturbances experienced by Tasso and El Greco.

A contributory factor was the problem of finding some acceptable way to follow the great artists of the High Renaissance. Raphael, Leonardo and Michelangelo had, in their various ways, provided solutions for all the technical problems which had hitherto been exercising the artists of Italy: for their successors, without the genius to surpass them, nor indeed the ability to understand them, there was nothing left but to imitate their mannerisms. This, however, was to enter a cultural cul-de-sac since the particular emphases, the idiosyncratic traits and the grand gestures which characterised and enhanced the work of genius, seemed ludicrous and out of place when imitated by more mediocre artists. Some of these minor artists devoted their lives to recapturing the composure of a Raphael madonna, the enigma of a Leonardo smile or the *terribilità* of a Michelangelo nude: they developed their techniques to the point of brilliance but they lacked the inspiration to produce great art. As a result, the more ambitious and the more talented deliberately set out to be different, and Mannerism, a term applied to their art, reflects not the imitation of the *mannerisms* of their predecessors, since this is what they purposely repudiated, but rather their own self-conscious *mannered* attempt to discover new horizons and to demonstrate novel approaches.

One of the greatest Mannerist painters was Francesco Parmigianino (1503–40). He was taken prisoner while working in Rome during the Sack of 1527, and eventually escaped to Parma. There he became eccentric if not insane, changing, as Vasari described him in his *Lives of the Painters*, 'from the delicate, amiable and elegant person that he was, to a bearded, long-haired, neglected and almost savage or wild man'. Before his experiences in the Sack, he had painted a self-portrait in 1523, in which the interest was centred less on the elegant young artist than on the remarkable fact that he chose to paint the self-portrait as seen in a convex mirror. What fascinated him was the new technique that had to be evolved – something that the giants of the High Renaissance had not attempted – and in the composition, which involved the distortion of features and the thrusting forward of a giant hand into the mirror, he deliberately repudiated the principles of Renaissance composition. His most famous painting, begun in 1532, was an attempt to create a madonna more graceful and more elegant than any by Raphael, not by emulating the techniques of the master, but by inventing his own. Consequently he elongated the limbs, exaggerated the delicacy of the fingers, and emphasised the flowing line to such an extent that his work has always been referred to as the *Madonna of the Swan Neck* (see plate 14). As in the self-portrait, too, there is not only the use of new techniques, but also the flouting of old conventions. The *Madonna* is not merely unnaturally constructed but her attendants are crammed into a pushing throng on the left of the picture, leaving the other side open save for a small figure and a puzzling pillar in the middle background.

Many of these particular points were generalised by Mannerist painters who declared a fascination with elegance and sinuosity, and especially with the *figura serpentinata*, the nude in convoluted poses. The *contrapposto* device, taken from Michelangelo, where one part of the body, the chest and shoulders for example, faces in an opposite direction to the hips and legs, was developed universally, with the placing of such a figure in the foreground of a scene so that it twisted round to face into the picture. Much of this was indeed elegant, novel and attractive; much, too, bordered on eccentricity. The more difficult the pose, the greater the virtuosity required to achieve it, and the end product was not always admired. 'It seems to them', wrote one critic of the Mannerists, 'that they have discharged their debt when they have made a saint, and have poured into it all their imagination and diligence in twisting the legs, or the arms, or the broken neck and made it distorted'.

Once the principle of the centrality of the composition had been abandoned, lines began to fly outwards to the frame. Indeed, they flew out of the frame altogether when the artist's virtuosity was challenged by the growing fashion for the *trompe l'oeil* in which the figures on a ceiling could be made to appear to break upwards through the roof. Correggio was a master of this. In the dome of one of the churches in Parma, he painted around the cornice a ring of apostles that owes much to the Sistine ceiling, but in the centre, breaking upwards through the clouds, he introduced the figure of the risen Christ floating into the heavens. In the cathedral nearby he was more ambitious, attempting to portray in similar fashion the Assumption of the Virgin, with hosts of angels and attendants, gliding and wheeling in concentric circles below her. For all that a Parma canon compared the result unkindly to 'a hash of frogs legs', Correggio's technique of *sotto in su* (seen from below) was an exciting novelty which posed many problems, and was to be developed a great deal in the following century.

Mannerist sculptors, like their colleagues, delighted in the solution of novel problems. No longer content to sculpt a figure to be seen from the front, they tried instead to create a multiplicity of views and silhouettes, so that the observer, to appreciate their work to the full, had to walk slowly round it. One of the foremost sculptors was Benvenuto Cellini whose *Autobiography* provides a vivid eye-witness account of the Sack of Rome, along with a delightfully immodest relation of his own acts of bravery. From Rome he fled to Florence, and subsequently went to France to work for Francis I. In his magnificent silver salt cellars for the French king, and, on a much larger scale altogether, in his *Perseus with the Head of Medusa*, he achieved silhouettes of such surpassing elegance and polished grace that the virtuosity of their creator can be admired independently of the works themselves. Even more talented an exponent of this kind of composition was Giambologna (Giovanni da Bologna). His *Mercury* poised for flight, standing on the toe of the left foot, successfully conveys by this brilliantly achieved balancing act the illusion of movement. More complex was the *Rape of the Sabines* with its three separate figures, bound together in a single upward spiral. In the hand of a lesser artist the effect could have been ludicrous, but so successful was Giambologna's control of balance and *contrapposto* that the whole group can be seen with equal fascination from all sides.

Mannerist architects, too, began to dispense with the accepted canons as they sought to achieve novel effects. Renaissance architects like Alberti and Bramante had defined and differentiated each part of their compositions, articulating the stories by the use of the appropriate orders, in order to establish a mood of serenity, balance, logic and control. With their successors the interest shifted from the basic composition to the decoration of its surfaces. Michelangelo himself revealed a Mannerist trait when he returned to Florence to design the Laurentian library for the Medici. Bored with the established motifs of Renaissance architecture, he handled them in a wholly novel manner, using them for decorative purposes regardless of function, and dispensing with conventions for the satisfaction of surprising the onlooker. The columns of the ante-room, for example, instead of projecting from the wall to carry the architraves, were deliberately recessed so that they appeared to be merely decorative, while the wall itself rather than the columns seems to assume the task of load bearing. By Renaissance standards the effect was disturbing. Equally so was Michelangelo's treatment of the Palazzo Massimo alle Colonne in Rome. In many respects the palace was conventional enough, but the windows of the upper storey were given wholly novel proportions relative to the other windows while, most original of all, the façade of the building was constructed on a curve.

As architects became obsessed with the decoration of surfaces, they covered their walls with pilasters, pediments and other classical features, executed in heavily rusticated stone work to give them special emphasis. Some indeed developed a kind of *horror vacui*, being unable to leave any part of the wall without some adornment, and where stone would not suffice ornaments were added in stucco. Within the buildings, too, they contrived the illusion of architectural features: walls, for example, were treated to look like marble, and the columns and balustrades of an entrance lobby were as likely to be the work of a painter as of a stone mason.

Not surprisingly, therefore, one of Raphael's most famous pupils, Giulio Romano, devised the Palazzo del Tè after this fashion for the Gonzaga of Mantua. The surface decoration, mainly in brick or stucco, bears no relation at all to the loadbearing wall, and in many respects comes nearer in spirit to stage scenery than to the façades of Alberti or Bramante. One disturbing example of the deliberate misuse of classical ornament is Romano's treatment of triglyphs – small projecting blocks with vertical grooves which had been a decorative device of classical architecture since the days when wooden beams had obtruded into the frieze. Romano placed them several inches below the frieze and, since they had no function in that position, their decorative effect is frustrated to some extent by the fact that their appearance there suggests that the frieze has begun to collapse. In part Romano was simply experimenting with new effects: in part too he was deliberately satisfying the taste of his patrons, the Gonzaga. Like several other princely families who had lost their political power to Spain, they had discovered a measure of solace and distraction by withdrawing into their own private world and making their courts the centres of a particularly esoteric culture. Sophisticated in the extreme and aware of all the conventions of the High Renaissance, they derived a special pleasure from the fact that since they alone knew all the rules, as it were, they too were the only ones with the intelligence and knowledge to recognise, and thus to enjoy, the occasions when the rules were self-consciously broken by the artist.

In the long run, however, the culture of these courtly coteries became sterile. Art could not develop merely as an intellectual pastime: it needed some new force to encourage the appeal to the emotions. This was eventually supplied in the second half of the sixteenth century by the Counter-reformation. Initially its tone was puritan, its effect restrictive. Castiglione's *Il Cortegiano* was consigned to the Index, the portrayal of biblical scenes was scrutinised to prevent the intrusion of secular incidents or pagan allegories, and undiscriminating eyes ordered the painting over of Michelangelo's nudes. Later, however, a new and different phase succeeded as the Roman Church became aware of the propaganda value of the arts to glorify the Church and its dignitaries, and to evoke the faith and piety of the masses. The first signs of a new emphasis are found appropriately enough in the Church of the Gesù, built for the Jesuits in Rome by Giacomo Vignola. To reassure the faithful and to silence the sceptics, he designed an interior of palatial splendour, which also reflected the special emphasis which the Jesuits placed on preaching. The wide barrel-vaulted nave ensured that none of the congregation was hidden away in side aisles or behind pillars, and the light streamed in above the crossing in order to illuminate the preacher. Externally the façade by della Porta made impressive use of double columns to flank the doorway, and of massive volutes to link the two storeys: the effect is one of dignity and power and the Roman Church was quick to exploit its value. Where the serenity of the High Renaissance was too detached to serve its missionary purpose, and the sophistication of Mannerism too trivial, the church of the Counter-reformation had thus discovered a bolder, more direct style which was to come to fruition in the seventeenth century as the Baroque.

The Art of Venice and Northern Europe

Venice, unlike the other Italian states, remained politically independent and commercially active. Spain could not extend her sway across the lagoons, and despite the problems of the Turks and the changing pattern of trade, the Venetians retained a considerable measure of their former prosperity (see page 174). Their self-confident mood made them unreceptive to the sophisticated Mannerism of the Italian courts, and their civic pride, as intense as that which had formerly inspired the art of Florence, found expression in the public employment of artists to advertise the glories of the republic. As Berenson has put it, the Venetians 'were not content to make their city the most beautiful in the world; they performed ceremonies in its honour partaking of all the solemnity of religious rites. Processions and pageants by land and by sea . . . formed no less a part of the functions of the Venetian State than the High Mass in the Catholic Church. Such a function, with Doge and Senators arrayed in gorgeous costumes no less prescribed than the raiments of ecclesiastics, in the midst of the fairy-like architecture of the Piazza or canals, was the event most eagerly looked forward to, and the one that gave most satisfaction to the Venetian's love of his State, and to his love of splendour, beauty and gaiety. He would have had them every day if it were possible, and, to make up for their rarity, he loved to have representations of them'.

In addition to their pageantry and civic pride Venetians enjoyed the clear open light of the Adriatic which flooded their canvasses and inspired their love of colour. Bellini (see page 57) had already discovered how to establish the form of an object by its colour, rather than by its outline, and his work was continued by his pupils. Giorgione, for example, specialised in the production of small oil paintings for private collectors, and for them he painted nudes of radiant beauty whose brilliant flesh tints still survive in his *Venus* and his *Concert Champêtre*. For them, too, he painted landscapes of a strangely moving quality like the *Tempest*, which tells no obvious story – though the imagination of art historians has been well put to it to create one around the figures of the foreground – but creates an emotive mood which takes possession of the onlooker and haunts his imagination. Sadly, Giorgione died of the plague in 1510 at the age of thirty-two, leaving his contemporary and pupil, Titian, without a major rival.

Titian lived on until 1576, one of the most professional painters of all time and the master of many genres. His first major work was the *Pesaro Madonna* (see plate 12), in which he retained the dignity and serenity of Raphael without forfeiting his own originality. The composition was novel without being mannered. Though the central place is occupied, surprisingly, by St Peter, it is the Madonna to whom all eyes are drawn as she sits to the right of St Peter but raised above him on a marble throne, her position accentuated by the steps which lead up to her and by a massive pillar rising immediately behind her.

The composure of Titian's work, combined with his acute observation, made him the finest portrait painter of the century, the favourite artist, and the friend, of Charles V; but it was above all his command of colour which won him universal admiration. A contemporary description recorded how 'he laid in his pictures with a mass of colour which served as a groundwork for what he wanted to express': on this he then built up his forms by further touches of colour. In his youth he was delighted by bright blues and reds, and his nudes glowed with warmth and charm. As he grew older he turned to rich sombre hues and his understanding of the play of light on colour made him almost unique. In *The Crowning with Thorns*, for example, a violent scene full of flames and torchlight, his treatment of the shimmering surfaces almost anticipated by two hundred years the style of the impressionists. Not only did his use of colour develop with age but also his personality. Without suffering the spiritual agony of a Michelangelo, nor the melancholia of a Parmigianino, he lost much of the self-confident serenity of his youth. The splendid optimism of his earlier portraits and religious studies and the sensual warmth of the *Poésie*, the mythological scenes which so delighted the cold Philip II, gave way to a more intense, more foreboding and indeed a more violent style. The lively myths were abandoned for the *Tragedy of Acteon*, the nudes in repose for the *Rape of Lucrece* and the calm splendour of the madonnas for the powerful emotion released in his *Martyrdom of Christ*.

Jacopo Sansovino who was born in Florence in 1486, worked in Rome until after the Sack and was finally appointed City Architect in Venice where he remained until his death in 1570. He introduced to the republic the new forms of Florentine and Roman architecture, endowing them with a greater degree of opulence and decoration which anticipated in part the splendours of seventeenth-century Baroque. The heavy rustication of the ground floor of his Palazzo Corner della Ca' Grande, the imposing double columns between each window on the first and second floors and the admirable proportions between all the parts appealed greatly to the Venetians, who discovered in his style an embodiment of the pride they felt in their city's achievements. Having designed the triumphal staircases in the Doge's Palace, and the Loggetta at the base of the Campanile, he was asked to build the civic library. This was a commission of the greatest importance since the new building was to face across the Piazzetta, which linked St Mark's Square with the Grand Canal, to the Doge's Palace, and Sansovino set out to achieve a monument of matching dignity and splendour. The façade is an impressive double arcade. Doric orders on the ground floor are surmounted by a frieze and balustrade: Ionic orders on the first floor bear a more delicate frieze and balustrade, and above them a row of statues. Between the orders, which give dignity to the building, a degree of splendid opulence is created by insetting the arches on smaller columns so that the whole façade creates the effect of interlocking tracery, and the illusion is heightened by the lavish use of garlands to decorate the balustrades.

Sansovino's superbly decorative buildings provided the architectural setting for much of the painting of Veronese, an artist who delighted in the Venetians' love of pageantry and who displayed it with brilliance, energy and warm colours. His style was essentially secular. As his mythological scenes were less the presentation of classical stories than the portrayal of opulent Venetian ladies in settings derived from Ovid, so in his religious work his preference was for Biblical scenes which could be transposed to a Venetian setting. His *Marriage Feast at Cana* and his *Feast in the House of Simon* were accordingly staged against a background which Sansovino might have created, and so Venetian was the character of the *Last Supper* that the Church regarded it as sacrilegious and compelled the artist to rename it *The Feast in the House of Levi.*

With Tintoretto, the last great artist of the Venetian Renaissance, the mood began to change. Born in Venice in 1518 he spent his whole life in the city, reluctant to leave it or his wife for any foreign commission, and his most important work was the *Narration of the Life of Christ* for the rooms of the Scuola di San Rocca. Yet, more than any other Venetian artist, he was influenced by developments elsewhere. Like Veronese he could paint optimistic, colourful and joyful scenes from mythology to decorate the Doge's palace, but he was increasingly affected by Mannerist influences and his work began to reveal a greater degree of tension. He reacted against the serenity of Titian's work, and allowed motifs of secondary importance – a massive winding staircase, for example, in his *Presentation of the Virgin* – to dominate his picture: he found it necessary to paint a Crucifixion from the side and in his *Last Supper* (see plate 15), though the figure of Christ is central, the table is set diagonally across the picture. Moreover, in this last work the bustle and activity around the room contrasts strangely with the traditional representations of the theme, and the whole scene is rendered more intense by the light from the smoky torches and an unearthly radiance surrounding the figure of Christ.

While Tintoretto's work became more turbulent, more mannered, the last of the great Venetian architects, Andrea Palladio, preserved to the end a calm and ordered classicism in the spirit of

Alberti and Brunelleschi. His *Treatise on Architecture*, derived from Vitruvius (see page 52) became not surprisingly a textbook for the architects of the Age of Reason in the eighteenth century, and his buildings in Venice and on the mainland proved to be models of their kind. The churches of the Redentore and of San Giorgo Maggiore in Venice were among the noblest, most impressive of the century: the Palazzo Chiericati in Vicenza, with its colonnaded façade, its inset loggias on the ground floor and on both wings of the first floor, established a style of town house to be found in many parts of Europe: above all his country houses, inspired by his studies of the classical villa, and enhanced by his unique feeling for setting a building in its landscape, won him universal admiration. The most famous of these was the Villa Rotunda (see plate 16). A cubic block around a central domed hall, relatively unadorned with ornament save for identical colonnaded porticos on each side of the cube, it stands superbly placed on a low eminence, with broad flights of steps leading down from each portico to the gardens. In the simplicity of its proportions is embodied the essence of Renaissance classicism.

Venice remained more or less independent of the stylistic developments of the rest of Italy, but the artists of northern Europe struggled to imitate what they observed there, with little or no understanding of the progression of styles from the classicism of the high Renaissance, through Mannerism, to the reestablishment of a new kind of classical order in the Baroque. As a result, each artist, and each patron, hit on whatever interested him as he travelled across Italy, so that his finished work was often an amalgam of various styles. The French, who spent so many years campaigning in Italy, were particularly anxious to introduce Italian fashions, and the leading patron of Italians was Francis I himself. At Blois he tried, rather unsuccessfully, to incorporate Italian features into an existing medieval chateau, but the new wing with its imposing staircase and arcaded galleries has a sense of balance and a degree of monumentality which is clearly Italian in inspiration. Similarly, the enlargement of his hunting lodge at Fontainebleau has none of the regularity and symmetry of a Florentine palazzo, but there is nonetheless the sense of an overall plan, and the storeys are clearly articulated by lines of well-placed pilasters. Even Chambord, under its Gothic complex of spires, towers and dormer windows, is remarkably restrained and balanced from the ground floor to the balustrades below the roof.

Much of the responsibility for introducing Italian ideas into France belongs to Sebastian Serlio, who had worked in Rome and Venice until the dedication of a series of architectural treatises to Francis I won him an appointment as *peintre et architect du roi*. He worked for Francis at Fontainebleau and at Ancy-le-Franc where he constructed one of the most perfectly ordered and graceful classical chateaux of the sixteenth century. His influence was at its greatest, however, through his publications which were widely studied across Europe and served as pattern books for local masons and builders.

Among the French-born architects who saw him work at Fontainebleau, and who also visited Italy to see things at first hand, was Philippe de l'Orme, who built the chateau and chapel at Anet for Diane de Poitiers, the mistress both of Francis I and Henry II. In all his work, as revealed in his designs published under the title *Architecture* in 1568, he found it relatively easy to handle Renaissance motifs, and their transposition to a late Gothic setting in France was achieved not merely without absurdity but with grace and self-confidence. This was true also of Pierre Lescot, who designed the south-west corner of what is now called the Square Court of the Louvre, an undertaking of great importance to Henry II who wanted to rival the plan of his wife, Catherine de Medici, to expand her palace nearby at the Tuileries. Lescot's handling of classical features of decoration indicated a remarkable understanding of the classical mood itself. The two simple blocks, at right angles to each other, are well proportioned and clearly articulated, and there is a pleasing variety achieved by bringing forward the whole wall by a foot or so at the first, fifth and ninth windows of each block: where the other six windows are marked by pilasters, these are framed by double columns which run up the façade to a rounded pediment, to create the idea of a series of triumphal arches across the three storeys.

By mid-century a shift of emphasis was apparent in French architecture. There was less striving after monumentality and an increasingly Mannerist tendency to emphasise the decoration of surfaces regardless of the structure. Indeed the element of fantasy in the decoration went beyond the general practice in Italy. Hughes Sambin, for example, designed a very charming town house in Dijon, the Maison Milsand, where the imagination has run riot in the matter of decoration, for the wall is encrusted with a medley of animal heads, long twisting chains of thick foliage and a general superabundance of vegetation. One of the most influential architects to encourage this trend was Jacques Androuet du Cerceau the Elder, first of a long line of distinguished French architects. Like Serlio his engravings were more influential than his own buildings; his *Premier Livre d'Architecture*, appeared in 1559, and two volumes of *Les Plus Excellents Bastiments de France* in 1576 and 1579. Throughout he emphasised the decoration of surfaces, using classical forms for visual effect without reference to any structural significance. In his designs for Charleval, for example, the ornament is crowded in a hotch-potch manner; tall, graceful arches alternate with short stubby square porticoes, and the eye is compelled restlessly to wander across what seems to be an exaggerated stage set for Hansel and Gretel. Yet du Cerceau was also a most practical builder, and his published designs for town houses, for nobles and prosperous merchants alike, were remarkable for their economy, both of ornament and space.

Of the Italian artists invited to France by Francis I, Michelangelo refused, Cellini stayed but a short time, and Leonardo arrived too late in life, but among the others Rosso Fiorentino and Primaticcio established what came to be termed the First School of Fontainebleau. Both of them were Mannerists, and Primaticcio in particular had worked for several years under Giulio Romano at the Palazzo del Tè (see page 396). Like Romano they combined the skills of painting, sculpture and architecture, and their task was to embellish Fontainebleau. There they introduced the elongated forms, the taste for allegory, the exaggerated elegance and the striving for effect which characterised Italian Mannerism: above all they showed themselves to be masters of decoration in the Long Gallery, where the life of Francis I was glorified in an astonishing amalgam of fresco, stucco and wood painting. After Primaticcio's death and Rosso's suicide, however, their style petered out as the Wars of Religion discouraged immigration from Italy, and France herself seemed unable to produce the painters to match her architects until the seventeenth century.

In Spain, Valencia became a centre for several artists who had spent some time in Italy and were influenced in particular by

Giulio Romano, but the Spanish suspicion of all things foreign which grew more intense during the second half of the sixteenth century (see page 353) discouraged the development of Mannerism. Philip II forbade his artists to study abroad, despite his own enthusiasm for the works of Titian, and the Inquisition subjected their work to excessive scrutiny in order to eliminate any trace of unorthodoxy. As a result, the most important artist was Luis de Morales, who eschewed fantasy and supplied works of unchallengeable piety in Toledo, the holy city of Spain, with its hundreds of religious houses and churches. His madonnas, a speciality, were tender to the point of swooning, and the exaggerated emotion of his Passion scenes exalted the faithful at the end of their pilgrimages.

The one artist of genius who settled in Spain in 1577 was the Cretan Domenikos Theotucopolis, El Greco, for whom Philip II showed no enthusiasm at all. His portraits, brilliantly observed, were executed in a conventional style, but his own intense religious belief led him to seek for extreme spiritual effects in his religious works. As a result of his Byzantine training, realism was as unimportant to him as to the painters of icons, and his period in Venice left his basic attitudes unaltered, though he had learnt there how to make his colours exciting, adding an almost acid quality to his shrill greens and blues. His apostles and saints are given flame-like figures – the impression of fire being reinforced by the colours he used – elongated limbs with relatively small, almost shrunken faces. The mood is one of mystic excitement. His object, like that of Loyola in devising his *Spiritual Exercises*, was to develop the capacity to perceive spiritual experiences, and to this end he pruned away ruthlessly all that was irrelevant to the essential, inner meaning of the scene. His work, owing little to past tradition, could not in turn be imitated by others and he remained a unique, indeed eccentric genius who finished his life in Spain without significantly affecting its art.

There was, of course, an independent tradition in Spanish and Portuguese architecture which owed its importance not only to the Gothic of the north, but also to the Moorish buildings of the south, whose surfaces were decorated with delicate filigree work; it is so like the filigree of silver work, *plateria*, that the style is known as Plateresque. In its most extreme forms it resembles a carpet of decoration hung over the building, as in the window of the Chapter House at Tomar: a more restrained example would be the façade of San Esteban at Salamanca, where the pilasters and roundels of Renaissance Italy mingle with the finials and heraldic devices of Gothic art, while the whole surface is delicately covered with the curvilinear rhythms of Moorish origin. Charles V, not surprisingly, preferred the Italian style, and his palace at Granada was a rectangular block around a circular courtyard, more or less classical in its mood and decoration, though the richly textured surface of the exterior was Mannerist-inspired. Philip II, rigorous as ever, would have nothing of decoration at all. His Escurial (see page 344) was built not in soft warm stone, but in granite with a high slate roof; it was constructed moreover on the plan of a massive gridiron, with its 4,000 rooms arranged with unyielding regularity around the sixteen inner courts of the palace.

If the exodus of artists from Rome after the Sack of 1527 had its effect on Italian art, the crippling effects of the religious conflict in Northern Europe were far more long-lasting. Commissions to produce religious art declined, reflecting a general fear that iconoclastic mobs would destroy sacred images. In Protestant Germany there were no more studies of the Virgin and saints, nor even of miracles, and the artists were limited to classical studies and, above all, to portraiture. Lucas Cranach the Elder, for example, had been fascinated to discover mystery and the presence of primeval forms in landscape, but as this was a limited field he set up his workshop in Wittenberg to produce solid prosaic portraits of a kind calculated to appeal to the solid prosaic Saxon burghers. He and his son became court painters to the elector of Saxony, and lived through the Reformation to found one of the wealthiest families in Wittenberg. Portraiture, too, was the field in which Hans Holbein the Younger was trained in Augsburg by his father, and ultimately settled in England under the patronage of Henry VIII.

In the Netherlands where the builders were extremely slow to adopt classical motifs, as can be seen from the predominantly Gothic town halls of Antwerp and Leyden which were constructed in the second half of the century, the painters were more susceptible to Italian influence. Peter Breughel the Elder, who died in 1569, had been brought up in the tradition of Flemish landscape painting with its detailed attention to the rendering of minor objects: to this he had added his own fascination for the mood of a landscape, as in his study of a *Stormy Day*. From his visit to Italy he then learnt how to create a coherent unity from the innumerable and accurately observed details which made up his pictures. His *Return of the Hunters*, for example, is a winter landscape with at first sight a mass of apparently unrelated observations, but is in effect a network of carefully composed diagonals and horizontals, all of which are directed to the ice-cold peaks in the distance.

There was a wealth of anecdote as well as natural observation in his scenes of peasant life, but the crowded canvases are skilfully organised to appeal directly to the sophisticated circle to which he belonged, and to Granvelle, his patron. His peasant studies are not so much an example of simple genre painting as sermons drawn from proverbs and biblical stories, and behind much of his work there is a discernible element, derived from Bosch (see page 71), of a surrealist, mystic symbolism. The moral of the parable of *The Blind Beggar* is self-evident, as is the theme of the *Triumph of Death*, and it is in keeping with his work that the famous *Wedding Feast* be seen less as a portrayal of peasant life than an indictment of gluttony.

Music and the Beginnings of Opera and Ballet

Charles V's Flemish choir, the most famous in Europe, was dissolved after his death, and the disruption to the economy caused by the revolt of the Netherlands dispersed the wealth which had formerly sustained the great age of music in the Netherlands (see page 74). Instead, the Netherlands furnished the rest of Europe with talented musicians. From 1543 they supplied seven successive musical directors at the Austrian court, and Orlando de Lassus, one of their greatest musicians, was employed by the dukes of Bavaria. Lassus began his career in the choir of Mons, but such was his fame that he was virtually carried off to sing in Milan and Naples. Subsequently he established his reputation as a composer, working for a time in Antwerp and then as *Kapelmeister* to Duke Albert in Munich. There he displayed considerable artistry in matching his music to the text, illustrating the prominent words or phrases by the emotive quality or expressiveness of his compositions.

It was fortunate for the development of German music that both Lutherans and Catholics alike had no theological or doctrinal bias against it, and that the more puritan Calvinists were in the minority. One of the best of the German school, Hans Leo Hassler, was, therefore, able to write motets for both churches, and was employed at various times by the Catholic Fuggers as well as the Lutheran electors of Saxony. Hassler owed much to the Netherlanders. He learned a great deal from those who were then directing the music of several German courts, but in addition he himself had been trained by other Netherlanders in Venice. Adrian Willaert had become *maestro di capella* at St Mark's in 1529, and with several of his fellow-countrymen had created a school of music which by mid-century had won for itself an international reputation. One of its most distinguished characteristics was the rich texture of its performance, assisted by trombone and organ accompaniments, and strengthened by the use of multiple choirs – a richness in fact which reflected the rich colouring of Venetian art.

There were many Netherlanders, of course, in Rome and it was one of their pupils, Palestrina, who became the greatest Italian composer of the century. Called after his village whose patron, the bishop of Pal, became Pope Julius III, he became a papal musician at the age of twenty-six. The next pope, Marcellus, set him a new task. Like many at the Council of Trent he was increasingly troubled by the polyphonic style; for all the expressive efforts of the composer to find the most suitable musical phases to accompany the words, the fact that the four voices followed their own separate lines often resulted in making the words incomprehensible. The Council of Trent, moreover, was alarmed by, 'sensual and impure elements, all secular forms and unedifying language'. As a result Palestrina was required to produce music, free of all secular taints, in which the words might be clearly heard and properly understood. The result of this commission, the *Missa Papae Marcelli* not only satisfied the pope by its brilliant clarity but also, through the richness of the accompaniment, established a new style of church music of great beauty and vigour. As a result, the succession of masses and motets which he composed earned him a reputation equal to that once enjoyed by Josquin des Près (see page 75).

Italian music was developed not only by the church but also by private families and courtly circles where madrigals were all the rage. In this genre, too, Palestrina excelled, developing a range of new techniques to embellish the polyphonic tradition derived from the Netherlands. Italian madrigals were generally of profound sadness, and the rich noble, Don Carlo Gesualdo, prince of Venosa, gave greater expression to these sentiments by the novel use of discords, of broken melodic lines and abrupt changes of rhythm. From this the Italians began to demand something even more exciting and, at the end of the century, Vincenzo Galilei, along with other Florentine musicians, created a more dramatic form, the opera, in which a single theme line is reinforced by orchestral harmony. The first opera to be publicly performed was *Dafne* in 1597, and so well was it received that within a decade the new art form had blossomed in the wealthy courts of Italy with the emergence of Monteverdi and the production of his first great opera, *Orfeo*.

The French court with its Italianate tastes initially looked to Italy not only for its musicians but also for its style of music. In the second half of the sixteenth century, however, the court poets, in particular the group known as the *Pléiade* led a vigorous attack on contemporary music in order that their own words when sung should be given greater importance and emphasis. Accompaniment was permitted for, as Ronsard put it, 'poetry without instruments or without the charm of one or several voices is not at all pleasing', but with poetry and drama temporarily ascendent at the French court, music was relegated to a subsidiary role.

One novel feature was the development of the *ballet de cour* which was ultimately to combine with opera to produce in the seventeenth century a spectacular form of entertainment in Paris and at Versailles. It was a peculiarly French genre which had originally been introduced as an attempt to revive classical tragedies with the aid of music and dance, but the declamation of words to music proved unpopular and was abandoned. In 1581 Catherine de Medici staged *Le Ballet Comique de la Reyne*, an impressive union of music, dance, poetry and spectacle, which also united performers and spectators, for everyone participated. Three points of *décor* were set up in the hall, with the dancers moving between them, and the audience joining in the set-pieces, such as the processions and the courtly dances. Performances could go on all night since there was no set pattern or form. Indeed, the *ballet de cour* became very much a *bonne à tout faire* with elements of pantomine, ballet, spectacle, masquerade and tournament; a performance of 1595, for example, made excellent use of a pair of camels which happened by chance to have been brought to Paris, and the *Carrousel* of 1612 in the Place Royale was essentially an outdoor *ballet de cour*.

The Prelude to the Scientific Revolution

In the Middle Ages scholars had been concerned less with the exact description of natural objects than with the construction of philosophical and logical systems. Yet this was not unreasonable. The classical scientists, Aristotle, Galen and Ptolemy, had already provided explanations of the material world which satisfied so fully the demands of common sense, and which were then so smoothly integrated into Christian theology by St Thomas Aquinas in the thirteenth century, that to question them was not only to question common sense but to venture into heresy. As a result scientific study in the Middle Ages was mainly the literary transmission of classical science, experiments being conducted only to demonstrate accepted truths. Albertus Magnus of Cologne, who is credited with the close study of natural history in the twelfth century wrote of the ostrich: 'It is said of this bird that it swallows and digests iron, but I have not found this myself because several ostriches refused to eat the iron which I threw them'. There were very few who wrote like this. The majority preferred their bestiaries stuffed with biblical exegesis and little natural history, following St Augustine's dictum that it mattered less whether an animal existed than what it symbolised.

Mathematicians at Oxford in the twelfth century and at Paris in the thirteenth began to query some of the principles of Aristotle's physics, the weakest element in the corpus of classical science, and when Duns Scotus and William of Occam, two English Franciscans of the fourteenth century, had exposed serious flaws in the philosophy of Aquinas, the way was prepared for further inquiry. Occam was particularly important for his belief that nature does everything in the simplest manner, and his famous Razor, 'entities must not be multiplied unnecessarily', was a plea for the rejection of unnecessary hypotheses. Under his influence Parisian scholars came close to the modern theory of impetus, and it might have been thought that a major breakthrough in science was to be expected by the time of the Renaissance. Curiously enough, though art and literature, politics and philosophy were immediately affected, the impact of the Renaissance on science was principally to reinforce the authority of the ancients, since it was they who were held up by the humanists as models of perfection. Nevertheless, the recovery of classical texts did lead to some discoveries in science: the full text of Aristotle on biology, his best subject, had never been accessible to medieval scholars, nor had the original text of Galen on medicine. Moreover, the revival of Platonic and Pythagorean concepts of the universe at variance with those of Aristotle, as well as the rediscovery of Archimedes, whose teaching did not fit into any of the accepted systems of thought, made it possible, as at the University of Padua, for Aristotle to be challenged; and it was no accident that there, in one of the few centres of relatively free thought, both Galileo and Vesalius were professors.

The great developments in Renaissance art did much to stimulate the study of anatomy, perspective and natural history, and Leonardo da Vinci, who combined the scientist's curiosity with the artist's eye, has been acclaimed the symbolic figure of the scientific revolution. This he was not; he experimented widely, he brought a freshness of observation to accepted doctrines, but he had neither the experimental method – the methodical collation of material and the systematic verification of hypotheses – the mathematics, nor the means of measurement which were to be among the great achievements of the seventeenth century.

In the light of what eventually took place in the seventeenth century it is clear that the foundations for the advance of scientific knowledge were laid not in academic circles but in places where the demands of practical problems compelled the formulation of new questions and answers. Artillery attacked the physics of Aristotle at its weakest point by compelling the study of ballistics. The sternpost rudder, which replaced what had virtually been an oar lashed to the stern, made ocean-going less hazardous in the sixteenth century and thus prompted a demand for better means of navigation. Mariners, therefore, became knowledgeable in the study of compasses and magnetism, of astronomy and tides. Men employed in land drainage also studied the tides, and it was Stevin, a Dutch engineer and mathematician, who produced in 1590 the first scientific tide-table: others, engaged in mining and metallurgy, studied the properties of metals, the mechanics of the pump, and the problems of hydrostatics and ventilation. So it was that away from the traditional centres of learning the scientific revolution was to owe its greatest impetus to the practical problems, solutions and equipment evolved by countless foundry-workers, instrument-makers, mariners, miners, smiths and engineers – some well versed in Euclid, others illiterate, but all alike driven by the profit motive and curiosity to experiment in their work.

One man who profited much from the experience gained by sailors, and also from his own extensive practical knowledge of mining and metallurgy, was William Gilbert, Fellow of St John's College, Cambridge, and physician to Queen Elizabeth I. Spending hours in the company of craftsmen, especially of Robert Norman, a retired mariner and compass-maker, he was prompted by them to examine the nature of magnetic variation, and the problem of the compass needle, which tilts at various angles according to its position on the earth's surface. Gilbert made a model of the earth, a *terella*, out of lodestone, a magnetic rock, and placed upon it a series of small iron needles. These behaved exactly like compass needles. Not only did they point to the *terella's* north pole, they also dipped at various angles in different places, horizontally at the equator, vertically at the pole. From this Gilbert demonstrated that the earth itself was a magnet with its magnetic poles near the geographic North and South Poles, and that between these poles there flowed lines of magnetic influence which governed the behaviour of the needles. In his *De Magnete* (1600), the first learned work to appear on experimental physics, Gilbert at one stroke transferred the whole subject of magnetism from the empirical to the scientific, though he did not fail in the dedication to acknowledge his initial debt to those, 'who look for knowledge not in books but in things themselves'.

Gilbert's advice had a particular relevance for the students of medicine, a science in which the importance of observation had always been paramount as doctors sought to establish connections between symptoms and diseases. But for all that, throughout the Middle Ages, men persisted in observing only what they had been taught to look for: over them. all fell the shadow of Galen, physician to the emperor Marcus Aurelius, whose teaching had since been integrated with Christian theology. Even a practical experiment was conducted under his dead hand: the purpose of dissection was not discovery but demonstration, and if the results contradicted Galen's teaching it was assumed that the demonstrator had bungled his job.

In the study of the circulation of the blood, Galen's influence was especially pernicious because it seemed to correspond so well to the facts. Since venous blood has a blue tinge while arterial blood is bright red, he assumed that there were therefore two distinct blood systems, the venous system which nourished the tissues of the body and the arterial system which gave the tissues life. Galen also assumed that all the blood was made in the liver, which was part of the venous system, and thus his chief problem was to trace the blood from the liver into the arterial system. This he did by finding a connection between the liver and the right auricle and ventricle of the heart, and since he also found a special passage between the right ventricle and the lungs, he believed that once the blood had arrived in the heart it was immediately cooled by air sent up from the lungs. It then passed into the left ventricle, there to be enriched, purified and strengthened by the addition of vital spirits, *pneuma psuchikon*, essential for life. Finally it surged into the body in a kind of tidal ebb and flow, the valves of the heart to some extent restraining the violence of the flow, while the rate of absorption of the blood into the tissues was balanced by the rate at which new blood was delivered from the liver to the heart. The greatest single difficulty about the theory was that the septum, the thick fleshy wall between the right and left ventricles, appeared impenetrable but Galen insisted that fine pores, invisible to the human eye allowed the blood to seep through: 'These indeed are seen with difficulty in the dead body, the parts being then cold, hard and rigid. Reason assures me, however, that such pores must exist.'

The discovery during the Renaissance of a Greek text of Galen's work revealed the hitherto unknown fact that all Galen's conclusions had been drawn from experiments on animals alone. Consequently, Vesalius, professor of anatomy at Padua, produced his own study of the body, *De Corporis Humani Fabrica* (1543), in which he exposed more than two hundred anatomical errors in Galen, among them the fact that the human thigh bone is straight, not curved as a dog's. The diehard Galenists immediately blamed this phenomenon on the narrow trousers of their day, and attacked Vesalius bitterly; but Vesalius himself was less of a deliberate rebel than a fervent Galenist with doubts. Above all, he was not satisfied by Galen's views on the septum, but as he could offer no alternative theory he enigmatically commented: 'We are driven to wonder at the handiwork of the Creator, by means of which blood sweats from the right into the left ventricle through passages which escape the human vision'. Four years later, in 1547, there was published a Latin translation of the theories and experiments of a thirteenth-century Arabian doctor who had not only denied the possibility of blood seeping through the septum, but postulated its movement from the right to left ventricles by way of the lungs. Another blow was struck by Leonardo da Vinci, who in his practical way tried in vain to pump air through the pipe which Galen had identified as bringing air from the lungs to the right ventricle. So great, however, was the authority of Galen that though his work was criticised in detail, no one presumed to challenge his general theories. Even when Fabricius of Padua discovered the existence of valves in the veins, a clear indication that the flow of the blood could only be in one direction back to the heart, he explained them away as barriers designed to prevent the rush of blood down to the legs.

One of the greatest difficulties in breaking the spell of time-honoured authorities was that science and religion had become indissolubly bound together. Medieval theories about the nature of matter, for example, represented a curious amalgam of two different approaches, physical and metaphysical. The physical analysis concentrated upon the four elements revealed by the process of combustion: a twig, for example, when it burns is resolved in flame, smoke, moisture and ash – four elements which Aristotle generalised as fire, air, water and earth. These elements were believed to possess properties which accounted for their action; earth and water had gravity, air and fire levity. Mixed up with this was the theory of the four primary qualities, heat, cold, dryness and humidity, so that fire was characterised as hot and dry, earth as cold and dry, air as hot and moist, water as cold and moist. The fusion of the elements thus produced different materials, and the mingling of the primary qualities resulted in secondary qualities like softness or acidity.

The alternative approach to matter was metaphysical, a distinction being made not between the separate elements but between Form and Matter. Form was believed to be the active agent, the principle which determined not merely the shape but the entire organisation of Matter: Matter was the passive agent, that which is organised by Form. Such a distinction was necessarily metaphysical since it was quite impossible to demonstrate it physically by combustion, by dissection or by any other experiment. In Christian theology there existed a hierarchy of Forms. God was Pure Form: from Him there descended the nine grades of angels down to man, and thence through the animal, vegetable and mineral grades to mere Matter, about which, since it had no Form, nothing could be said. Form determined the properties of material objects. Wood therefore floated in water because its Form dictated its activity: in other words it was its nature to float – an explanation which was both tautological and meaningless.

Whatever the method of inquiry, whether physical or metaphysical, whether things behaved according to the properties of their principal element or because of their Form, the tendency was to endow matter with attributes which explained its behaviour, as though matter was capable of self-direction. Usually these explanations were anthropomorphic, given in human terms such as horror of a vacuum. The falling stone accelerated because it was jubilant at returning home; things went where they belonged in the universe, and comets, earthquakes and other interferences with the natural order were ascribed to the power of supernatural forces. What could be demonstrated by experiment thus seemed reasonably satisfying, and what could not, and therefore required faith for its understanding, did not strain men's reason too greatly since men are essentially sympathetic to anthropomorphism.

The first to destroy the whole overburdened structure of tortuous verbosity and wishful thinking was Galileo. Son of the Florentine musician (see page 410) and appointed professor of mathematics at Padua, he was vitally interested in music and art and in practically every scientific subject under discussion in his day. His action with regard to the principles of matter was disarmingly simple, and performed with a ball of wax. First he placed the ball in a bowl of water, where it sank; then, by dissolving salt in the water, he caused the ball to rise. Thus were confounded all existing theories, for the action of the wax ball was interpreted no longer in terms of elements, properties or Form, but of specific gravity.

Galileo's introduction of quantitative experiment in place of qualitative analysis was to be of even greater importance in the study of physics and astronomy. From the earliest times the stars had aroused both interest and emotion in mankind, and their study had had practical results in the making of calendars and in navigation – and even in astrology which, if something of a bastard offspring, had at least kept its parent in business. As the Greeks had inherited the vast amount of data of the Babylonians and Egyptians and then rationalised it, so the medieval Church had adopted Greek astronomy and adapted it to its theology. By 1500, therefore, the study of astronomy rested upon three apparently incontrovertible authorities – scholastic theology, Aristotelian physics, and the observations recorded in Ptolemy's *Almagest*. More important still, perhaps, the *Almagest* tallied with common-sense observation. The earth, solid, spherical and immovable, lay at the centre of the universe. Around it the moon, the sun and the five planets were carried upon seven revolving concentric spheres, made of some translucent, crystalline substance. The eighth sphere held the fixed stars, the ninth, the *primum mobile*, imparted motion to the rest, and the tenth was believed to be heaven. The supralunary universe was deemed to be in a state of perfection, that state which the medieval mind wistfully regarded as one in which change and decay were impossible, owing to the addition of a divine quintessence to the existing four elements. Between the moon and the earth, however, there was no such preservative; the moon itself was obviously tainted by dark blotches, comets exploded across the sky in great exhalations of fire, and on earth the four elements existed in restless confusion.

Within this perfectly ordered universe the behaviour of the planets gave cause for concern since each was observed to follow an erratic course. It was for this very reason that Plato had christened them 'planets' (vagabonds), and many attempts were made to reconcile their apparent course with the theory of their uniform circular motion around the earth. Ptolemy suggested that they revolved in epicycles, the centres of which described a uniform circular path; this could be made to fit the observed facts provided that the construction of eighty such epicycles was accepted. Alfonso the Wise of Castile, a medieval patron of astronomy, complained: 'If the Almighty had consulted me before the Creation I should have recommended something simpler'. Such complexity was nonetheless effective since it accounted for every known irregularity of the planets, and tables composed on this system proved wholly reliable.

Less easy to solve was the problem of motion in the universe. The *primum mobile* was presumed to impart motion in some way to the other spheres, and Christian thought romanticised this by assigning the nine grades of angels to superintend the motion of the nine spheres. Celestial motion was circular because circular motion was deemed 'natural' to celestial bodies, a question-begging answer which went unquestioned in an age which endowed material objects with human aspirations. Terrestrial motion was more difficult to explain. Motion up or down was simple enough, since matter was endowed with the attributes of levity and gravity, but any other type of motion had to be assigned its due cause. This proved to be the weakest point of Aristotelian physics, which taught that since a state of rest was natural to all objects, nothing would move unless compelled to by some agent or force. This failed to satisfy the perplexity of those who pointed to the arrow which continued to fly through the air long after losing contact with its mover, the bowstring. Aristotle's own explanation of this was obscure and inaccurate, and was the target of learned criticism from the twelfth century onwards, with the result that by 1500 impetus was being considered as something like heat which gradually lost its potency.

The publication in 1543 of Copernicus's *De Revolutionibus Orbium Celestium* was an event of unusual importance. As befitted a canon of Cracow Cathedral, from whose tower he was permitted to observe the heavens, Copernicus was in most respects a medievalist: matter was endowed with aspirations and all bodies sought to assume the shape of the sphere since this was the perfect shape, and circular motion was perfect motion. But for many years Copernicus had also studied in Italy under de Novara, professor of mathematics and astronomy at Bologna, a fervent neo-Platonist whose mathematics was loaded with Pythagorean symbolism. Copernicus was inspired by him with a love for mathematical simplicity. He thus attacked the Ptolemaic universe as too cumbersome and claimed, purely as an hypothesis, that the whole problem might be simplified by assuming the sun to be at the centre.

What pleased him was not merely that the number of epicycles could be cut to thirty-four, nor even that, in Pythagorean terms, the light of the universe would now be in its most suitable place at the centre, but the elegant simplicity of his proposal: 'It is so bound together, both the order and magnitude of all the planets and all the spheres and the heaven itself, that in no single part could one thing be altered without confusion among the other parts and in all the Universe' (cf. Alberti's definition of beauty, page 55). His theory caused new problems. If the earth were to move around the sun, then its position in relation to the fixed stars would alter every month. Since no such parallactic shift was discernible, Copernicus had to save his theory by putting the fixed stars at so great a distance from the earth that no shift could be expected, but this, though correct, involved concepts of distance so immense that most men found them more difficult to accept than heliocentrism itself. Moreover, when Copernicus settled down to revise the *Almagest* in detail he found it impossible to put the sun exactly at the centre of the planets' orbits, which in turn compelled him to construct another twelve epicycles. Nor were his tables uniformly superior to those of Ptolemy and it was possible for men of the most open mind to choose equally between the two systems.

The most damning weakness of the Copernican system was that it could not be reconciled with Aristotelian physics, for to the mind brought up on this no force in the universe was capable of moving the sluggish earth. Hence the immediate importance of the publication, also in 1543, of a Latin edition of Archimedes, the greatest geometer of classical times, who had imagined how the earth might be moved with a lever. Archimedes had been known by name in the Middle Ages, but the texts were too inadequate and too corrupt to convey the originality of his thought. One of his greatest qualities was an ability to perform mental experiments in order to abstract essential from irrelevant factors, and to present them in mathematical terms. In dealing with fluids, for example, he ignored their taste, their colour and the attributes by which other scientists explained their activity, and considered only their motion. Similarly, having measured objects in air and in water he tried to imagine them unencumbered by either. If Aristotelian physics prevented the serious acceptance of the Copernican theory of heliocentrism then the revival of Archimedean teaching was a significant step towards its re-examination.

One other feature of the sixteenth century, vital to the subsequent revolution, was the work of Tycho Brahé, a Danish noble who studied at the royal observatory in Denmark until, after violent quarrels with his own countrymen, he went to Prague in 1596 at the invitation of emperor Rudolf II. His observations were unique both in their accuracy and their comprehension. Equipped with quadrants and direction finders, but without a telescope, he plotted the position of the planets and stars with unrivalled care. Though he accepted that the planets revolved around the sun he was not a Copernican, since he could discern no parallactic shift in the position of the fixed stars and believed that planets and sun together circled the earth. The first man to make a detailed study of the planets at every stage of their orbit, he was perplexed to find that the orbits were never circular. More disconcertingly, in 1572, he observed in the constellation of Cassiopeia a supernova – a star, previously faint, blowing up and gradually burning out – and in 1577 a comet which, far from moving in the sublunary sphere of change and imperfection, followed a track far beyond the moon, as trigonometrical observation confirmed. These observations ended the belief in uniform circular motion, in the immutability of the heavens, and in the crystalline spheres through which the comet must have crashed its way.

In 1600 Brahé appointed an assistant, Johannes Kepler, a poor but brilliant astronomer whose reputation had been made by his *Mysterium Cosmographicum*. A fervent Copernican, inspired by neo-Platonist and Pythagorean theories of the harmony of numbers and shapes, Kepler had been looking for one law to explain the distances between the planets. To his great delight he discovered a rough relationship between their orbits and the five regular solids: if the orbit of Mercury were imagined as a solid shell it would fit inside an octahedron whose points would touch the inner surface of the shell of Venus: Venus in turn lay within an icosahedron whose points touched the inner surface of the earth's shell, the earth lay within a dodecahedron, Mars within a tetrahedron, Jupiter within a cube. Around the cube fitted the orbit of Saturn. To Brahé this was mere romancing but he was struck by the observations Kepler had made, and he put him to observe the orbit of Mars. Within a year Brahé had died, leaving his collection of data to Kepler, who thus possessed more information on the behaviour of the planets than anyone had held before. He at once set out to postulate a theory to explain the motion of Mars in keeping with the recorded observations. This was soon done but, on comparing the positions computed from his system with the corresponding positions observed by Brahé, Kepler discovered a discrepancy of eight minutes of arc. This was negligible: even Ptolemy and Copernicus had been accurate only to ten minutes of arc, but so great was his respect for Brahé's records that Kepler refused to make the facts fit into the theory: 'And thus the edifice which we erected on the foundations of Tycho's observations we have now again destroyed . . . For if I had believed we could ignore these eight minutes I would have patched up my hypothesis accordingly.'

Kepler's scrupulous regard for eight minutes of arc caused him eight more years of intense labour, but at last he found an answer: the planets move in an elliptical path with the sun at one focus; as they near the sun they accelerate, as they veer away they slow down so that a line drawn from the planet to the sun sweeps out equal areas in equal times. Having published these laws in his *Astronomia Nova* in 1609, Kepler returned to his mystic preoccupation with the harmony of the spheres, preparing for publication his *Harmonica Mundi*. There among discussion as to whether Mars is a tenor and Mercury a falsetto, was included almost fortuitously the third of Kepler's laws, that the time taken by a planet to complete its orbit increases the further it is from the sun: indeed, the squares of the time of the planets' revolutions bear a constant ratio to the cubes of their mean distances from the sun. As for his explanation of the dynamics of the universe, he derived this from Gilbert's work on magnetism, and assumed that the sun maintained the planets in rotation by exerting an *effluvium magneticum*.

It was at this stage that Galileo's intervention proved invaluable. In the study of the universe his first great contribution was to convince most people that the Copernican system, operating by Kepler's laws, was fundamentally sound. This he did with the help of the telescope, the chance invention of a Dutch spectacle-maker between 1590 and 1600, which he copied and improved to a degree of magnification of thirty. Through this he studied the heavens more closely than ever before, and published the results in his *Siderius Nuncius* of 1610. Among many other novelties he recorded his observations of blemishes on the face of the sun, of eighty stars in the constellation of Orion and of forty in the

Pleiades where even Brahé had seen only nine and six respectively, of the four satellites of Jupiter, a Copernican system in miniature, of the Milky Way which he described as, 'nothing else but a mass of innumerable stars planted together in clusters', not, as believed, planted at a uniform distance from the earth in the sphere of the fixed stars. These observations compelled men to reconsider long-held beliefs, but the Church having successfully integrated Ptolemy into its theology, was reluctant to approve of change, and Galileo deliberately provoked a conflict.

He left Padua in the free territory of Venice for Florence, and then for Rome, the centre of the controversy, having published in 1613 his *Letters on the Solar Spots* and in 1615 a *Letter Concerning the Use of Biblical Quotations in Matters of Science*. The opposition to him however was more powerful than he had suspected. Indeed those who claimed that the moons of Jupiter existed only in the telescope had unknowingly some justification: the danger that so novel an invention might distort the truth was not illusory since spherical aberration, the failure of the lens to give a rectilinear image, was not identified and corrected until 1637, and the cause of chromatic aberration, the light from different colours coming to a different focus, was not analysed before Newton studied the problem in 1671. In 1616 the Church exacted from Galileo a promise to cease his public advocacy of the Copernican system but in 1632, after the accession of a pope whom he believed to be sympathetic, he published his major assault on the Ptolemaic universe, the *Dialogue concerning the Two Chief World Systems*. Though Galileo pretended to state both cases fairly, he portrayed the defendant of the old system as a thick-witted gull, aptly named Simplicio, who obligingly falls into each of his antagonists' logical traps. For this work Galileo was disgraced, since the pope mistakenly believed that the character of Simplicio represented himself.

Galileo realised that if his enemies denied the evidence of the telescope because it conflicted with their concepts of motion, then motion itself would have to be studied afresh. He began by observing the movement of the pendulum, discovering that a long swing took the same time to complete as a short one, and putting his discovery to practical use in the invention of a pendulum clock. Equally practical was his interest in gunnery. It had been proposed by another Italian, Tartaglia, that projection was most efficient at an elevation of forty-five degrees and that the trajectory was curved. Galileo identified the curve as a parabola, and wondered if the speed acquired by the falling cannon ball was in any way proportional to the time it took to fall. This led to his experiments with metal balls in which he rolled them down grooves lined with polished leather to reduce friction, and found that their final speed varied with the height at which they were released, not with the angle at which the plane was inclined. He also discovered the relationship he sought between the distance and the time, expressing it as $d = \frac{1}{2} at^2$ where a represents the constant acceleration caused by gravity. The formulation of the hypothesis was not new since medieval mathematicians at Oxford had arrived at the same truth in verbal terms: where Galileo broke new ground was first by conducting his experiments and then by expressing his findings in a mathematical equation.

Equally important was Galileo's attack on the problem of inertia. First he rolled a ball down one plane and observed it run up a second until halted by the force of gravity. Modelling himself on Archimedes from whose work he derived his greatest inspiration, he then tried to imagine what the ball might do if gravity and friction were dispensed with. He concluded that it would rise to the same vertical height from which it had started. Finally he realised that if the ball, instead of climbing the second plane, followed a horizontal course, it would continue to roll for ever, seeking to regain its original height. The problem of inertia was thus put in an entirely novel setting. For the first time in history, attention was thus directed not to the causes of motion, but to the forces which cause a body in motion to stop or alter course. As a result of this, and of Galileo's other achievements, the Aristotelian laws of motion were destroyed. With their destruction passed the last remnants of the medieval world picture: it remained for the seventeenth century to construct a new one.

Bibliography

1. ROACH, J., ed. *A bibliography of modern history* (1968)
   This book, produced in conjunction with the volumes of the *New Cambridge Modern History* is the most comprehensive bibliography available for most sixth-form students and undergraduates.

GENERAL HISTORIES

2. ALLEN, J.W. *Political thought in the sixteenth century* (1928)
3. BAKER, J.N.L. *A history of geographical discovery and exploration* (1937)
4. BRAUDEL, F. *The Mediterranean and the Mediterranean World in the age of Philip II* (2 vols, trans. 1972)
5. BRAUDEL, F. *Capitalism and material life, 1400–1800* (trans. 1967)
6. BUSH, M.L. *Renaissance, Reformation and the outer world* (1967)
7. *Cambridge Economic History of Europe* Volume IV (1967)
8. CIPOLLA, C.M. *Guns and sails in the early phase of European expansion* (1966)
9. CIPOLLA, C.M. *Before the industrial revolution: European society and the economy, 1000–1700* (1976)
10. CLOUGH, S.B. and COLE, C.W. *Economic history of Europe* (3rd ed., 1952)
11. DICKENS, A.G. *The age of humanism and Reformation* (1977)
12. DICKENS, A.G., ed. *The courts of Europe: politics, patronage and royalty, 1400–1800* (1977)
13. ELLIOTT, J.H. *Europe divided, 1559–1598* (1968)
14. ELTON, G.R. *Reformation Europe, 1517–1559* (1963)
15. GILMORE, M.P. *The world of humanism, 1453–1517* (1952)
16. KAMEN, H. *The iron century: social change in Europe 1550–1660* (1971)
17. KOENIGSBERGER, H.G. and MOSSE, G.L. *Europe in the sixteenth century* (1968)
18. LEACH, K., ed. *Sixteenth century Europe* (Documents and Debates series, 1980)
19. MATTINGLEY, G. *Renaissance diplomacy* (1955)
20. *New Cambridge Modern History* Volumes I–III (1957, 1958, 1968)
21. OMAN, C. *The art of war in the sixteenth century* (1937)
22. PARRY, J.H. *The age of reconnaissance* (1963)
23. PARRY, J.H. *Europe and a wider world* (1966)
24. PENROSE, B. *Travel and discovery in the Renaissance, 1420–1620* (1960)

25. ROBINSON, J.H., ed. *Readings in European history* Vol. I (1906)
26. ROSS, J.B. and McLAUGHLIN, M.M., eds. *The Portable Renaissance reader* (1977)
27. SHENNAN, J.H. *The origin of the modern European state, 1450–1725* (1974)

13, 14 and 15 are helpful for the beginner, and the volumes of the *New Cambridge Modern History*, 20, are excellent works of reference. 4 is one of the most exciting general studies to appear in recent years. 19 should not be overlooked by those who imagine it to be too specialised: it provides a useful analysis of international relations in sixteenth-century Europe.

There are, of course, many books of a general nature listed below, in particular 111, 119, 120 and 121 on economic affairs.

FRANCE AND BURGUNDY

28. BRIDGE, J.S.C. *A history of France* Volumes I–V (1924–9)
29. BRIGGS, R. *Early modern France, 1560–1715* (1977)
30. CALMETTE, J. *The golden age of Burgundy* (trans. 1962)
31. CHURCH, W.F. *Constitutional thought in sixteenth-century France* (1941)
32. HERITIER, J. *Catherine de Medici* (trans. 1963)
33. KINGDON, R.M. *Geneva and the consolidation of the French Protestant movement, 1564–72* (1967)
34. KNECHT, R.J. *Francis I and absolute monarchy* (Historical Association pamphlet 1969)
35. MANDROU, R. *Introduction to modern France, 1500–1640* (1976)
36. NEALE, J.E. *The age of Catherine de Medici* (1943)
37. SALMON, J.H.M. *The French wars of religion* (1967)
38. SALMON, J.H.M. *Society in crisis* (1975)
39. SHENNAN, J.H., ed. *Government and society in France, 1461–1661* (1969)
40. SUTHERLAND, N.M. *Catherine de Medici and the Ancien Regime* (Historical Association pamphlet, 1966)
41. SUTHERLAND, N.M. *The French secretaries of state in the age of Catherine de Medici* (1962)
42. SUTHERLAND, N.M. *The massacre of Saint Bartholomew and the European conflict, 1559–1572* (1973)

29 provides an excellent summary of recent research. 28 is valuable for its detailed account of French foreign affairs. 36 is helpful for those unable to read ROMIER, L. *Le royaume de Catherine de Médicis* (1922). Of the books listed below, 58 and 115 are relevant to French history.

SPAIN, PORTUGAL AND THEIR EMPIRES

43. ALVAREZ, M.F. *Charles V* (trans. 1975)
44. BOXER, C.R. *Four centuries of Portuguese expansion 1415–1825* (1961)
45. ELLIOTT, J.H. *Imperial Spain, 1469–1716* (1963)
46. ELLIOTT, J.H. *The old world and the new, 1492–1650* (1970)

47. DAVIES, R. TREVOR *The golden century of Spain* (1937)
48. GEYL, P. *The revolt of the Netherlands* (trans. 1958)
49. HARING, C.H. *The Spanish empire in America* (revised 1953)
50. HEMMING, J. *The conquest of the Incas* (1970)
51. KAMEN, H. *The Spanish Inquisition* (1965)
52. KIRKPATRICK, E.A. *The Spanish conquistadores* (1946)
53. KLEIN, J. *The Mesta* (1920)
54. KOENIGSBERGER, H.G. *The government of Sicily under Philip II of Spain* (1951)
55. LIVERMORE, H.V. *History of Portugal* (1947)
56. LIVERMORE, H.V. and ENTWISTLE, W.J., eds. *Portugal and Brazil, an introduction* (1953)
57. LYNCH, J. *Spain under the Habsburgs* Vol. I (1964)
58. MATTINGLEY, G. *The defeat of the Spanish Armada* (1959)
59. MARANON, G. *Antonio Perez* (trans. 1954)
60. MERRIMAN, R.B. *The rise of the Spanish empire in the old world and the new* Volumes I–IV (1918–1934)
61. MORISON, S.E. *Christopher Columbus, admiral of the ocean sea* (1942)
62. ORTIZ, A.D. *The golden age of Spain, 1516–1659* (1971)
63. PARKER, G. *The private world of Philip II* (1977)
64. PARKER, G. *The Dutch revolt* (1977)
65. PARKER, G. *Spain and the Netherlands* (1979)
66. PARKER, G. *The army of Flanders and the Spanish road, 1567–1659* (1972)
67. PARRY, J.H. *The Spanish seaborne empire* (1966)
68. PARRY, J.H. *The discovery of South America* (1979)
69. PIERSON, P. *Philip II of Spain* (1975)
70. PRESCOTT, W.H. *History of the conquest of Mexico* Volumes I–III (1842)
71. PRESTAGE, E. *The Portuguese pioneers* (1933)
72. WEDGWOOD, C.V. *William the Silent* (1944)
73. WILSON, C. *Queen Elizabeth and the revolt of the Netherlands* (1970)

45 is an excellent study, and 47, though dated, remains helpful for beginners. 4, referred to above, is particularly relevant to Spanish history, and 92 below is good on the war with the Turks. 43 is listed here because it is written from the Spanish standpoint but see also below, 59 and 62. The history of the Dutch revolt has been transformed by 64, 65 and 66. 54 has a broader significance than its title suggests. 58 provides a masterly survey of the international background to the Armada campaign.

THE EMPIRE, SWITZERLAND AND ITALY

74. ADY, C.M. *A history of Milan under the Sforza* (1957)
75. ADY, C.M. *Lorenzo dei Medici and Renaissance Italy* (1956)
76. ANGLO, S. *Machiavelli* (1969)
77. ARMSTRONG, E. *The emperor Charles V* (2 vols, 2nd ed. 1910)

428   BIBLIOGRAPHY

78. BEDOYERE, M. DE LA, *The Meddlesome friar. The story of the conflict between Savonarola and Alexander VI* (1957)
79. BONJOUR, E., OFFLER, H.S. and POTTER, G.R. *A short history of Switzerland* (1952)
80. BRANDI, K. *The emperor Charles V* (trans. 1939)
81. BROWN, H.F., Chapter entitled 'Venice' in *Cambridge Modern History* vol. I (1902)
82. CARSTEN, F.L. *Princes and parliaments in Germany from the fifteenth to the eighteenth century* (1959)
83. CARSTEN, F.L. *The origins of Prussia* (1954)
84. CHABOD, F. *Machiavelli and the Renaissance* (trans. 1958)
85. CLASEN, C.P. *The Palatinate in European history, 1555–1618* (1966)
86. DICKENS, A.G. *The German nation and Martin Luther* (1974)
87. HALE, J.R. *Machiavelli and Renaissance Italy* (1961)
88. KOENIGSBERGER, H.G. *The Habsburgs and Europe, 1516–1660* (1971)
89. SCHEVILL, F. *A history of Florence* (2nd ed. 1961)
90. SETON-WATSON, R.W. *Maximilian I* (1902)

Note that 81 refers to a chapter in the Old *Cambridge Modern History*. See above 28 for an excellent account of the Italian wars and 43 for an additional study of Charles V with some reference to German affairs. See below 123–56 for studies of religious affairs which closely affected the political life of the Empire and Switzerland.

THE OSMANLI EMPIRE

91. ALLEN, W.E.D. *Problems of Turkish power in the sixteenth century* (1963)
92. BRADFORD, E. *The great siege of Malta* (1965)
93. COLES, P. *The Ottoman impact on Europe* (1968)
94. COOK, M.A., ed. *A history of the Ottoman empire to 1730* (1976)
95. LYBYER, A. *The government of the Ottoman empire in the time of Suleiman the Magnificent* (1913)
96. McNEILL, W.H. *Europe's steppe frontier, 1500–1800* (1964)
97. MERRIMAN, R.B. *Suleiman the Magnificent* (1944)
98. SHAW, S.J. *History of the Ottoman empire and modern Turkey*, Vol. I (1976)
99. STAVRIANOS, L.S. *The Balkans since 1453* (1958)
100. VAUGHAN, D. *Europe and the Turk* (1954)

POLAND, RUSSIA AND THE BALTIC

101. ANDERSON, I. *A History of Sweden* (trans. 1956)
102. *Cambridge History of Poland* Vol. I (1950)
103. CLARKSON, J.D. *A History of Russia* (1960)
104. FENNELL, J.L.I. *Ivan the Great of Moscow* (1961)
105. HECKSHER, E. *An economic history of Sweden* (trans. 1954)
106. BERGENDOFF, C. *Olavus Petri and the ecclesiastical transformation in Sweden* (1928)

107. ROBERTS, M. *The early Vasas* (1968)
108. VERNADSKY, G. *Russia at the dawn of the modern age* (1959)
101 by a Swedish historian has been superseded to some extent by 107 which is written by the foremost English authority in Swedish affairs.

ECONOMIC AND SOCIAL HISTORY

109. CHAUNU, H. and P. *Seville et l'Atlantique* (12 vols, 1955–59)
110. EHRENBERG, R. *Capital and finance in the age of the Renaissance: a study of the Fuggers and their connections* (trans. 1928)
111. GREEN, R.W., ed. *Protestantism and capitalism* (1959)
112. HAMILTON, E.J. *American treasure and the price revolution in Spain, 1501–1650* (1934)
113. HARING, C.H. *Trade and navigation between Spain and the Indies in the time of the Hapsburgs* (1918)
114. LANE, F.C. *Venetian ships and shipbuilders of the Renaissance* (1934)
115. NEF, J.U. *Industry and government in France and England, 1540–1640* (1940)
116. PHELPS BROWN, E.H. and HOPKINS, S. 'Wages and prices; evidence for population pressure in the sixteenth century' *Economica*, new series, no. 24 (1957)
117. PULLAN, B.S., ed. *Crisis and change in the Venetian economy* (1968)
118. STRIEDER, J. *Jacob Fugger the Rich, 1459–1523* (trans. 1931)
119. TAWNEY, R.H. *Religion and the rise of capitalism* (1947)
120. TREVOR-ROPER, H.R. *Religion, the Reformation and social change* (1967)
121. WEBER, M. *The Protestant ethic and the spirit of capitalism* (trans. 1930)
122. WEE, H. VAN DER *The growth of the Antwerp market and the European economy* Volumes I–III (1963)
109 is unlikely to be read by most students but is one of the major works of recent scholarship. 111, 119, 120, 121 and 122 are on a famous topic, and 119 in particular remains a delight to read. Much economic and social material is to be found in books listed above, in particular 3, 4, 5, 6, 7, 8, 9, 10, 16, 22, 24 and 105.

RELIGIOUS HISTORY

123. ATKINSON, J. *Martin Luther* (1967)
124. BAINTON, R.H. *Here I stand: A life of Martin Luther* (1951)
125. BAINTON, R.H. *The Reformation of the sixteenth century* (2nd ed. 1957)
126. BRODRICK, J. *St Ignatius Loyola* (1934)
127. BRODRICK, J. *The origins of the Jesuits* (1940)
128. BROMILEY, G.W. *Zwingli and Bullinger* (1953)
129. BURNS, E.M. *The Counter-Reformation* (1964)
130. CHADWICK, O. *The Reformation* (1964)
131. DEMOLEN, R.L. *Erasmus: Documents of modern history* (1973)
132. DICKENS, A.G. *Martin Luther and the Reformation* (1967)

133. DICKENS, A.G. *Reformation and society in sixteenth-century Europe* (1966)
134. DICKENS, A.G. *The Counter-Reformation* (1968)
135. EVENNETT, H.O. *The spirit of the Counter-Reformation* (1968)
136. HALL, B. *Calvin* (Historical Association pamphlet, 1956)
137. HILLERBRAND, H.J. *The Protestant Reformation* (1968)
138. HILLERBRAND, H.J. *The world of the Reformation* (1975)
139. HUGHES, P. *A popular history of the Reformation* (1958)
140. HUGHES, P. *The Church in crisis* (1961)
141. HURSTFIELD, J., ed. *The Reformation crisis* (1965)
142. JACKSON, S.M. *Huldreich Zwingli* (1901)
143. JANELLE, P., ed. *Obedience in church and state* (1930)
144. JANELLE, P. *The Catholic Reformation* (1963)
145. JEDIN, H. *History of the Council of Trent* (2 vols, trans. 1957, 1961)
146, KIDD, B.J. *The Counter-Reformation* (1933)
147. McNEILL, J.T. *The history and character of Calvinism* (1954)
148. PARKER, T.H.L. *John Calvin* (1975)
149. PASTOR, L. VON *History of the Popes* Volumes XV–XXIV (trans. 1928–33)
150. POTTER, G.R., ed. *Huildrych Zwingli* (1976)
151. RANKE, LEOPOLD VON *History of the Popes* (3 vols, trans. 1907)
152. RUPP, E.G. *The righteousness of God* (1953)
153. RUPP, E.G. and DREWERY, B., eds. *Luther: documents of modern history* (1973)
154. SEARLE, G.W. *The Counter-Reformation* (1974)
155. WENDEL, F. *Calvin* (trans. 1963)
156. WILLIAMS, G.H. *The radical reformation* (1962)

The Reformation is well served with authors whose religious beliefs do not lead to partisan writing – cf. 139 and 125 by a Roman Catholic and a Protestant respectively. 124 is probably the best introduction to Luther, 152 describes his teaching and 155 is particularly good on Calvin. 133 and 134, by the same author (and in the same series), are both very attractively set out, extremely readable and reliable in their judgements. (Two other books by Dickens, 11 and 86, are also relevant.) 142 and 143 will seem old fashioned but they are classic studies.

CULTURAL HISTORY

157. BARON, H. *The Crisis of the early Italian Renaissance* (1955)
158. BENESCH, O. *The art of the Renaissance in northern Europe* (1945)
159. BLUNT, A. *Art and architecture in France, 1500–1700* (1953)
160. BOLGAR, F.J. *The classical heritage and its beneficiaries* (1954)
161. BUKOFZER, M. *Studies in medieval and Renaissance music* (1950)
162. BURCKHARDT, J. *The civilisation of the Renaissance in Italy* (trans. 1951)
163. BURKE, P. *Culture and society in Renaissance Italy* (1970)
164. BUTTERFIELD, H. *The origins of modern science* (1957)
165. CLARK, K. *Leonardo da Vinci* (1963)
166. COPLESTON, F.A. *A history of philosophy* Vol. III, part 2 (1963)

167. DIJKSTERHUIS, E.J. *The mechanization of the world picture* (trans. 1961)
168. FERGUSON, W.K. *The Renaissance in historical thought* (1948)
169. FISCHEL, O. *Raphael* (2 vols, 1948)
170. HALL, A.R. *The scientific revolution* (1962)
171. HAY, D. *The Italian Renaissance in its historical background* (1961)
172. HUIZINGA, J. *Erasmus of Rotterdam* (1924)
173. HUIZINGA, J. *The waning of the middle ages* (1924)
174. HYMA, A. *The brethren of the common life* (1950)
175. JACOB, E.F., ed. *Italian Renaissance studies* (1960)
176. JAYNE, S.R. *John Colet and Marcilio Ficino* (1963)
177. KOESTLER, A. *The sleep-walkers* (1959)
178. KOYRE, A. *From the closed world to the infinite universe* (1957)
179. KRISTELLER, P.O. *The classics and Renaissance thought* (1958)
180. KUBLER, G. and SORIA, M. *Art and architecture in Spain and Portugal 1500–1800* (1959)
181. LOGAN, O. *Culture and society in Venice, 1470–1790* (1972)
182. MURRAY, L. *The High Renaissance* (1967)
183. MURRAY, L. *The Late Renaissance and mannerism* (1967)
184. MURRAY, P. and L. *The art of the Renaissance* (1963)
185. MURRAY, P. *Architecture of the Italian Renaissance* (1963)
186. PANOFSKY, E. *Albrecht Durer* (3rd ed. 1948)
187. PEVSNER, N. *An outline of European architecture* (revised 1963)
188. PHILLIPS, H.M. *Erasmus and the northern Renaissance* (1949)
189. PLUMB, J.H., ed. *The Penguin book of the Renaissance* (1964)
190. POPE-HENNESSY, J. *Italian High Renaissance and Baroque sculpture* (2nd ed. 1970)
191. POPE-HENNESSY, J. *Italian Renaissance sculpture* (2nd ed. 1971)
192. PUYVELDE, L. VAN *Flemish painting from Van Eyck to Metsys* (trans. 1968)
193. RICE, W.F. *The Renaissance idea of wisdom* (1958)
194. SINGER, C., HOLMYARD, E.J., HALL, A.R. and WILLIAMS, T.I. *A history of technology* Volume III (1957)
195. SINGER, C. and UNDERWOOD, E.A. *A short history of medicine* (2nd ed. 1962)
196. SYMONDS, J.A. *The Renaissance in Italy* (7 vols, 1875–88)
197. TAYLER, H.O. *Thought and expression in the sixteenth century* (2 vols, 2nd ed. New York 1930)
198. TOLNAY, C. DE *Michelangelo* (5 vols, 1943–60)
199. VASARI, G. *Lives of the Painters* (trans. 1965)
200. WITTKOWER, R. *Architectural principles in the age of humanism* (3rd ed., 1962)
201. WOLF, A. *A history of science, technology and philosophy in the sixteenth and seventeenth centuries* (revised 1950)

162 is a classic work and 196 still merits attention. 163 and 181 provide detailed studies of the social and economic background to the arts, 193 is difficult but worth the effort and 160, though criticised by some reviewers, is extremely useful. 172 is a classic study of courtly society

and culture in France and Burgundy. 188 offers an easy introduction to Erasmus and in addition to 172, see also 131 above. 182, 183 and 184 do a simple and straightforward job of introducing the beginner to art history, and the relevant chapters of 187 are especially good. 164 was the pace-maker in the field of the history of science and 177 is very lively if rather idiosyncratic.

Index

The important references are given in bold type; those in italics refer to maps.